Sue + Wilt - Jason 6/10/77

THE GREAT GAME

LEOPOLD TREPPER

THE GREAT GAME

MEMOIRS OF THE SPY HITLER COULDN'T SILENCE

MCGRAW-HILL BOOK COMPANY
New York, St. Louis, San Francisco, Düsseldorf, Mexico, Toronto

Book design by Judith Michael.

English translation copyright © 1977 by McGraw-Hill, Inc.
All rights reserved. Printed in the United States of America.
No part of this publication may be reproduced, stored in a
retrieval system, or transmitted, in any form or by any means,
electronic, mechanical, photocopying, recording, or otherwise,
without the prior written permission of the publisher.

1 2 3 4 5 6 7 8 9 D O D O 7 9 8 7

Library of Congress Cataloging in Publication Data
Trepper, Léopold, 1904–
    The great game.

    Translation of Le grand jeu.
    Includes index.
    1. Trepper, Leopold, 1904–   2. World
War, 1939–1945—Secret service. I. Title.
D810.S8T65713   940.54'86'0924   76-7537
ISBN 0-07-065146-9

Originally published in French under the title Le Grand Jeu,
© Editions Albin Michel, 1975. Written by Leopold Trepper
in collaboration with Patrick Rotman.

To Luba, courageous companion of my life

Acknowledgments

I should like to express my gratitude to all those people, all over the world, who joined forces to enable me to leave Poland. Without the militants in the committees "for the liberation of Trepper," without the parties, labor unions, and organizations that took part in this struggle, and the private individuals, I would not have been able to write this book.

I should also like to express my appreciation to the following official and private organizations, which helped me with my research:

Mrs. Braem and her staff at the Division of Research, Documentation, and Death Records of the Belgian Ministry of Public Health and Family;

The directors of the Memorial at Breendonk, especially Professor Paul M. C. Lévy of the Department of Economic, Social, and Political Sciences at the Catholic University of Louvain;

Mr. J. Vanwelkenhyzen, director, and Messrs. Jean Dujardin and José Gotovitch of the Belgian Center for Research and Historical Studies on the Second World War;

Professor Jean-Léon Charles of the Belgian Royal Military Academy.

Thanks to them, this book is more complete and more accurate.

Finally, I want to extend to all the survivors of the Red Orchestra and their families my fraternal greetings and my continued gratitude for the help they gave me by their testimony.

L.T.

Contents

PART THREE: THE RETURN

The idea of writing my memoirs occurred to me while I was waiting for authorization to leave Poland, during the three years I spent in Warsaw in total solitude. As a "free prisoner," a condition which was very difficult to endure psychologically, my mind was occupied solely with remembering what had gone before.

For every man who is approaching the end of his life, there is always one period that leaves a more lasting impression than any other. When I look back over the seventy years I have lived, I feel that what happened to me between the ages of thirty and forty—the period of the Red Orchestra—is crucial. It is true that I lived then in a constant state of crisis, and that danger was my most faithful companion; but if I had to start all over again, I would do so with joy.

Today, at last, I no longer have anything to hide; I have no other ambition than to tell the truth about the fifty years of my life as a militant.

Here, then, is that truth.

PART ONE

APPRENTICESHIP

1

_J_ ust now two images came into my mind that show quite clearly the distance I have traveled. The first one takes me back to my early childhood, and to Novy-Targ, the little town in Poland where I was born. I can still hear a voice shouting:

"They've arrested a Russian spy!"

In minutes the rumor was all over town. Rumors were plentiful in those last days of July, 1914. From window to window, and in the street, people spread the news: "They've arrested a Russian spy in Poronin village, and they're bringing him here!"

Like all the children my age, I ran to the railroad station to watch the arrival of the prisoner. The train pulled into the station. A short, stocky man got out, flanked by two policemen. He had a little red beard and a big cap tilted over his forehead. Along with the other youngsters, I followed the strange trio across the central square, toward the town hall, which was equipped with a single cell for noisy drunks. The "spy" was locked up here. The next day the policemen took him to the jail, which was directly across from the synagogue.

It was Saturday. The Jews walked out of the temple in the midst of the service and stood around in front of the jail in little groups, discussing the war and the "Russian spy." A few days later, the prisoner was transferred to Cracow, and the inhabitants of Novy-Targ, especially the Jews, made jokes about a shopkeeper in Poronin who had extended credit to the spy and his wife for several months. The credulity of the Jewish shopkeeper remained a subject of amusement until one day in 1918, when he received a letter; soon the whole town knew what it said:

3

Please accept my apologies for leaving without paying you in 1914, owing to difficult circumstances. The money is enclosed.

Vladimir Ilyich Lenin

Lenin had not forgotten.

Such was my first encounter with "espionage" and communism—but I was only ten years old then and did not even know the meaning of those two words, words that would be with me all my life.

Years passed, filled with unforeseen battles; age came, and with it, solitude. Here is the second image. The date: February 23, 1972. It was my birthday. I was sixty-eight years old, and in my apartment. Images of birthday parties that brought my family together in the past came to mind and intensified my loneliness. Once there had been a dozen of us around the table: my wife, my sons, their wives, and the grandchildren.

In 1972 I was alone: for the past three years the Polish government had kept me a prisoner in my own home, refusing to allow me to join my family, who had been driven out by a campaign of anti-Semitism. For days on end the telephone had been silent; I was thoroughly isolated. Suddenly, that morning, the telephone rang, making me jump. It was my wife, calling to wish me a happy birthday; and all day long, from France, Denmark, Switzerland, Canada, Belgium, and the United States, my sons, friends, relatives—and strangers too, alerted by the campaign on my behalf that was being mounted all over Europe—called to let me know that they were with me. I was no longer alone.

On the 23rd and the days that followed, the postman brought me dozens of letters and telegrams every morning from the four corners of the world. Two packages mailed from the Netherlands contained hundreds of letters from schoolchildren; these childish drawings and words of friendship and comfort moved me to tears. No, I was not alone.

2

Novy-Targ

I was born on February 23, 1904, in Novy-Targ, a small town in Galicia that was hard to find on a map. The Trepper family lived at No. 5 Sobieski Street, in a modest dwelling my father had built himself, by piling up bricks and debts. The ground floor was a shop, a tiny general store that offered the peasants the few things they required. Big canvas sacks filled with seed lay right on the ground. The customers seldom paid for their purchases with money but exchanged them for some product of their land. The second story, above the shop, was divided into three simply furnished rooms, where we lived.

In the fragments of memories that I can recall, my childhood years seem to have been marked by quiet happiness, this in spite of my parents' extreme poverty. No doubt the dark images of the daily struggle fade more easily than the vision—still clear in my mind today—of the piece of candy my father used to slip under my pillow at dawn just before he started work.

My family was "typically" Jewish, very much like our neighbors. My name, Trepper, shows no trace of my origins. My friends—the Trauensteins, the Hamershlags, the Singers, and the Zolmans—also had Germanized names. One day, preoccupied by this question, I consulted the teacher who met with us once a week to give us an hour's lesson in the history of the Jewish people. At the end of the nineteenth century, he explained, the Jews of the Austro-Hungarian empire had been authorized to change their names. German surnames, it was thought, would enable the Jews to be more easily integrated into the Austrian population; even first names were changed. This is why my birth certificate bears the name of Leopold Trepper.

The Jewish community in Novy-Targ, which was about three thousand strong when I was a child, had been in existence since the founding of the town in the Middle Ages. The district was inhabited by very poor peasants, who had to struggle to extract a meager subsistence from unproductive land. In the villages the people ate bread only once a week. The daily fare was potato pancakes and cabbage. On Sunday, the peasants came to Novy-Targ by the hundreds to attend mass; they carried their shoes on their shoulders and did not put them on until they were just about to enter the church. The Jews who tilled the land were no better off—for them, too, a pair of shoes had to last a lifetime. In villages such as these, there were no rich farmers; directors of collectivization would certainly have had a hard time finding the kulaks. Even in the town itself, in Novy-Targ, prosperous middle class people were rare.

In the center of the town—the only part that has not changed to this day—lived a small number of well-to-do Jews and Poles: tradesmen, doctors, and lawyers. But as soon as you left this area and walked into the side streets, you were struck by the poverty of the craftsmen's stalls. In fact the number of people who left for the United States and Canada increased with every year. Hoping to find the new Eden, they prepared joyously for the long voyage. I can still see them, the collars of their shirts wide open over what passed for suits. They carried little wooden suitcases, and they looked proud in their magnificent bowler hats.

Anti-Semitism was unknown in Novy-Targ. The two communities, the Jewish and the Catholic, maintained very friendly relations. Perhaps this can be explained by the fact that in those days Novy-Targ belonged to the Austro-Hungarian empire, which had a rather liberal policy toward its national minorities. In this connection, a little story comes to mind. One day the archbishop of Cracow, Monsignor Sapieha, was expected in Novy-Targ. The Catholic congregation was getting ready to welcome him, as was to be expected. What was extraordinary was that the Jewish community also took part in this reception—with the result that on the day of the visit, in front of thousands of Catholics, the archbishop blessed the rabbi as he emerged in great state from the synagogue.

My parents were believers, but not fanatics. On Friday evening my mother lighted candles and served fish for dinner, even if the family had had to go without lunch to compensate for this luxury. On Saturday we went to synagogue. But for us children the most important part of our religion was observing the traditional holidays, when we sat down to the table with all our relatives to taste dishes that were so different from our everyday diet. Ordinarily we ate kosher, but there were exceptions. Sometimes my mother sent me to buy ham with the instruction, "Make sure nobody sees you go into the pork store!"

This peaceful, gentle family life was soon to be interrupted. In the first days of the war, the soldiers who made up Novy-Targ's small garrison left for the front. It was like a party. They left to the music of a brass band, with flowers in their guns, surrounded by excited throngs. I watched them go, these men who were being sent to fight for the Kaiser. Months went by, dreary and silent. Then I saw the disabled return and the hospitals fill up, and, child that I was, I understood that war was not a picnic.

One day a rumor—which had spread from town to town— broke like a wave over Novy-Targ: "The Cossacks are coming!" For a Jew, the word Cossack evoked the pogroms; thus, in great haste, an evacuation of the Jews to Vienna was organized. The Trepper family left with the others.

Most people believe that children are not concerned with politics. Usually, this is true; but we forget that politics is concerned with children. I myself began to read newspapers in Vienna. Through the papers, I followed carefully everything that was happening at the front. At the same time, I entered the Jewish highschool, and the religious question began to trouble me. For me, being Jewish was still a confusing idea.

I remember that on my way home from school I was in the habit of buying an ice cream from an Italian shopkeeper. In Vienna, the Italians had the reputation of making the best ice cream. But one afternoon my usual shopkeeper was not there. I went from shop to shop and found all the Italian shops closed. The reason, I discovered, was that Italy had entered the war against the two emperors. From that day, when the Viennese gave each other the traditional greeting, "May God punish England!" they added, "and destroy Italy!" What would God do? Would He listen to the Austrians? Would He make the French and British allies lose the war? Or would He do the opposite? How would He choose His side? All these questions puzzled me beyond explanation.

My confusion reached a climax on a day of rejoicing. The Austrian troops had occupied the fortress of Przemysl, and Vienna was celebrating this victory with large-scale patriotic demonstrations. The streets were decked with bunting, and joyous crowds were converging on the emperor's palace. Joy exploded all about me—people were embracing, laughing, screaming—everyone was running. Beside me, an old Jewish woman was trying to keep up with the rest. She was dragging along a little girl, and she shouted with all her strength, "Long live the Kaiser! Long live the Kaiser!" Soon she was out of breath, and she blurted out—in Yiddish—"Let him die, I'm worn out." Such a blasphemy was enough to upset a young boy on a day like that.

Life contained more uncertainties than certainties. Not only religion but war, too, belonged to this world of question. There were the flags, the bands, the reports of victory, the joy of the populace—but even as a child I could not fail to see the other side of the spectacle. The war had struck our own home. Both of my two brothers had been called up; one of them was missing in action on the Italian front, and the other was wounded there. As soon as we heard this news, my poor father set out, in the worst possible circumstances, in search of his wounded son. He went right to the front line, where he found him in a little field hospital. His son had been flung into a shell hole while under fire, and the explosion had left him deaf and mute. My father managed to have him moved to a hospital behind the lines, where he partly recovered his hearing, after prolonged treatment. It is not hard to imagine the sadness that reigned in our home during this period. In short, I saw in Vienna exactly the opposite of what I was taught in school. A bitter lesson indeed.

Two years after our arrival in Vienna, we returned to Novy-Targ, and it was around this time that my religious doubts changed into a feeling of rebellion. When, during his Yom Kippur address, the rabbi enumerated in detail the different kinds of death that awaited us, I saw the effect of his words on the congregation: when he finished, their faces were contorted in fear. I found this monstrous. I could no longer accept a submission that was maintained by ritual and had no other purpose but to make us forget our poverty.

Instead of being fed, the people were crammed full of opium. I found out this truth not by reading Marx, whom I had never heard of, but from life in rural Poland—a good book for anyone who wanted to learn.

In 1917, at the age of forty-seven, my father, old and worn out before his time, died of a heart attack. In accordance with the Jewish tradition, everything came to a standstill for seven days. In the house the shutters were closed, the mirrors were covered with cloths, and we lived for a week in semi-darkness, sitting in low chairs. A great many people came to the funeral; at the cemetery the rabbi, in his funeral message, accepted this death as the will of a kindly God. Once again, this submission to fate seemed to me intolerable, unjust. I was finished with religion. I broke away from this blind God and turned to my fellow men, my companions and brothers in misfortune. Having lost my faith in God, I began to believe in Humanity. Man would find his salvation in himself, I judged, not in some hypothetical beyond. This idea had become a self-evident truth. It was epitomized for me by the skill of the tightrope walker—my father had taken us to the Krone Circus in Vienna more than once, where the tightrope walker performed in space without a net.

That is how life seemed to me as I was leaving childhood: a dangerous exercise in equilibrium, a permanent risk.

I came of age at a time when the world was just emerging from years of barbarism. In the new Poland, reconstructed after the war, the minority groups that had once been under German, Austrian, or Russian domination constituted one-third of the population. Nothing had been prepared for the

assimilation of three million Polish Jews; the stage was
therefore set for a reappearance of anti-Semitism. Several
political parties openly declared themselves anti-Semitic, and
their influence was felt in the government. To cries of "Send
the Jews to Palestine!" the university established the *numerus clausus*, the quota system. The government issued de-
crees denying Jews access to government jobs, and a campaign was launched to persuade people to "buy Polish," not
from Jewish shops.

I was convinced that Judaism was not solely a religion, that
it was alive—kept alive by a national minority, which had
been forged by centuries of persecution and suffering and
possessed its own language, culture, and traditions. I joined a
Jewish youth movement, the Hashomer Hatzair. Zionist in
inspiration, founded in Vienna in 1916 by a small group of
young Jewish intellectuals, Hashomer Hatzair had expanded
rapidly. The organization proposed to find the definitive
solution to the destiny of the Jewish people in Palestine. Had
not the Balfour Declaration of November 2, 1917, stated that
the English were determined to create a national Jewish
center in Palestine?

The Hashomer Hatzair's ambition was to train a new breed
of men, who would break away from a lower middle class
lifestyle and establish—among themselves—the harmony of
brothers. The Marxist influence was strong in our organization, over which the October Revolution exerted a powerful
attraction. On July 22, 1918, in Tarnow, Galicia, the first
congress was held. The subject under discussion was the
fundamental issue: how was the national Jewish question to
be resolved? There were three conflicting schools of thought.
According to the first, the answer was to join the Polish
Communist Party, because only a social revolution modeled
on the Bolshevik pattern would provide a solution to the
problems of the national minorities. The second group
advocated leaving for Palestine and creating a state liberated
from capitalism; the militants would be obliged to leave the
universities and factories and return to the land and create a
new, egalitarian lifestyle. Finally, the third group, which I

belonged to, felt that, without severing our connection with
the Hashomer Hatzair, we should cooperate with the communist movement. No decision came out of this congress,
except that I became head of the organization for the town of
Novy-Targ. At the second meeting, in Lvov, in 1920, I was
elected to the national leadership. The same year, at the age
of sixteen, I left school and went to work as an apprentice to a
clockmaker. The most important part of my job was to wind
the church clock every day; I did not show any particular
aptitude, I confess, for this kind of work.

For me, 1921 was another turning point: my family left
Novy-Targ for Dombrova, in Silesia. This region was heavily
industrialized; the air was black with coal dust, and the
workers' living conditions were an atrocity. It was this place
that created, little by little, my consciousness of belonging to
the working class. After the Jewish question, I discovered the
class struggle. I was the head of the local Hashomer Hatzair
organization, but at the same time, secretly, I played a part in
the militant actions of communist youth groups. It was
during this period that I first adopted the pseudonym
"Domb," from the first four letters of Dombrova, for my
political work. It was a name I was to keep throughout my life
as a militant.

My family was—literally—dying of hunger, and I did not
succeed in finding a steady job. I worked in an ironworks,
then in a soap factory. It was to make some money that I did
my first illegal work. Under the local tax system, alcohol cost
less in Dombrova than it did in Cracow, so buying it in one
town and selling it in another turned out to be profitable.
Since the police made frequent spot-checks, I improvised a
special belt, into which I slipped the flat bottles. Under my
shirt, they were impossible to detect. Whenever I could, I
also profited from my trips to Cracow by attending courses at
the university. In those days my insatiable intellectual
curiosity—previously diffuse—began to focus on the social
sciences, psychology and sociology. I was reading Freud
avidly, trying to understand the secret impulses that motivate
our behavior; my friends in Hashomer Hatzair and I dreamed

of creating a new breed of men, free of prejudices, free of neuroses.

This did not mean that I neglected politics. On the contrary, my political activities were increasing every day. Meetings, demonstrations, and writing and distributing leaflets took up the greater part of my time. The working class movement was making rapid progress and fighting some important battles. In 1923 the workers in Cracow rebelled against poverty, declared a general strike, and took over the city. The government sent the lancers after them, and there were bloody confrontations for days. Since I took an active part, I had my first experience with police brutality. From then on I was blacklisted and no longer had any hope of finding work. I had to make a choice: either go underground, or leave for Palestine in the hope of building a socialist society where the "Jewish problem" would no longer exist.

3

Palestine

In April, 1924, with a group of about fifteen companions—all of us around twenty years old—I left for Palestine, equipped with a regular passport. We were penniless, and we carried our few belongings in bundles slung over our shoulders. Our first stop was Vienna. I remembered with emotion the trip I had made there with my family, and with my father, now dead. How long ago that was already! We stayed for free in an old barracks and we ran about, visiting monuments and museums with the enthusiasm of provincials discovering the big city. An organization that aided emigrants gave us enough money to continue our voyage; after a week in Vienna, we took the train for Trieste, and then Brindisi, where we boarded an old Turkish freighter that took ten days to reach Beirut.

Our freighter docked in Beirut alongside a ship that was being loaded with coal. Hundreds of Arabs, naked to the waist, black with dust, and bent beneath the weight of sacks, inched along single-file up the gangplank and onto the deck. This slow, methodical, swarming movement seemed to surge out of the mists of time. This was how I imagined the building of the pyramids in Egypt.

"How much are they paid for this slave labor?" I asked a sailor.

"You must realize, sir," he replied, "that you are entering a different world from the one you've known. Here men do the work of animals. What do they make? You'll see—they'll be eating it in a little while for lunch." A few moments later a whistle blast pierced the air. The column of workers dispersed. The men gathered in little groups and squatted on their heels; each one quickly swallowed a small piece of bread and some tomatoes. In Poland, I had known poverty; on my first contact with the Near East, I discovered starvation.

13

Our ship left shortly, and we finally got off at Jaffa.

After I had come down the gangplank, I stood motionless on the dock, my senses bombarded by the spectacle of this sundrenched port, so startling for a young European accustomed to low, grey skies. The harsh, dazzling light forced me to squint. Between half-shut eyelids I saw the extreme agitation of a multitude of people, people who seemed animated by some whirling, irrational frenzy.

The men, draped in their flowing multicolored robes, their heads wrapped in kaffiyehs, jostled each other with nervous, impatient gestures and shouted at each other with such violence they seemed to be quarrelling. The whole neighborhood seemed like one big row.

"They're just like us," I murmured to the friend who was standing next to me.

"Why?"

"They talk with their hands too!"

We walked into the city and we were in another world: narrow, winding streets, stalls humming with a varied population, but mostly Arab, veiled women walking with lowered eyes, incessant noise, shrill cries, the pungent odors of fruits ripening in the merciless sun—and stifling heat that was nearly unbearable for us young northerners with our pale faces. I was captivated immediately by this many-faceted life.

Our second stop was Tel Aviv. In those days it was still only a small town. The Center for Immigrants, where we had decided to stay for a few days, was outside the town proper; at night I awoke with a start to the howling of jackals that prowled outside.

I still had much to discover. The foreign food was a surprise that was also a treat: strange fruits tasted for the first time—olives, figs, and cacti, which an Arab taught me to open without pricking my fingers—were a welcome change from the potatoes and cabbage that were the staples of our diet in Poland.

We had to find work without delay. The organization in charge of finding employment for immigrants suggested that we go to the little village of Hedera, where a few rich Jews had some orange plantations. In those days, recently arrived immigrants were usually assigned to heavy work, road-building and excavation, and we were delighted at the prospect of starting immediately on the cultivation of fruit trees. When we arrived in Hedera, the view of the magnificent building that rose in the middle of the estate further heightened our boyish enthusiasm. The enthusiasm turned out to be premature. The owner led us to the edge of a vast marshy area:

"Find a place to pitch your tents," he said. With a sweeping gesture at the unhealthy swampland that stretched before us, he added, "All this will have to be drained!"

We had four tents among us. One served as our kitchen and dining room, and we lived in the other three. We were presented with a donkey so that we could get drinking water from a well several kilometers away, but the animal would have no part of it. No matter how much we shouted, begged, or pushed, he stubbornly refused to move a single step, until an Arab, amused by the spectacle, gave the animal's tail a sharp tug; he immediately took off.

We worked from dawn to dusk with our feet in the muck; at night we lay awake, devoured by thousands of mosquitoes. Each day three or four of us came down with malaria. But the deserted wastelands, the climate, the unhealthy conditions, could not discourage us—our youth and our enthusiasm overcame everything; we had our sleeves rolled up; we had come to build a country.

In the evening when our work was done, exhausted but happy, we gathered together to discuss this life which we had chosen and which we liked. In this new collectivist community, where absolute egalitarianism reigned—far from the restrictions of the bourgeois lifestyle—we were convinced that a new fraternal ethic was being born. That ethic could be the leaven of a more just society. Our preoccupations were primarily moral and idealistic, and curiously detached from social issues.

But social issues soon made their appearance. I saw that the rich Jewish landowners, who lived very comfortably, employed Arab agricultural workers almost exclusively to work on their plantations; and the Arabs were horribly exploited.

One evening after supper I mentioned this to my friends.

"If the landowners call themselves Zionists, why do they use only Arab labor?"

"Because it's cheaper."

"Why is that?"

"It's simple. The Histadrut—the General Federation of Jewish Workers—admits only Jews, and requires employers to pay a minimum wage. So the employers prefer to hire Arabs, who aren't protected by any union."

This discovery profoundly disturbed my serene idealism. As a young emigrant, I had come to Palestine to build a new world, and I was beginning to realize that the Zionist bourgeoisie, imbued with its privileges, was trying to perpetuate the very social relations we wanted to abolish. I was rediscovering the class struggle here, under the cloak of Jewish national unity.

In late 1924, a few months after my arrival, I decided to make a tour of the country on foot. At this time there were 500,000 Arabs and about 150,000 Jews living in Palestine. I visited Jerusalem, Haifa, already industrialized, and also Emek-Israel, Galilee, where some of my friends from the Hashomer Hatzair were working in kibbutzim.

Like myself, they had come to Palestine to create a new society, from which injustice would be banished. By a return to nature and to working on the land, they believed they could acquire the values of courage, self-sacrifice, and devotion to the community. Still, some of them were beginning to lose their illusions about the possibility of laying the foundations of socialism in a country still under the British mandate. To be convinced that they were right, one had only to look at the strapping English policemen who patrolled the streets in goodly numbers. It was futile, illusory, and even dangerous to try to build islands of socialism in this part of the world, where the British lion lay in wait with his claws extended, ready to pounce.

"Our action makes sense only if it is part of the antiimperialist struggle," said one of my comrades during one of our long conversations. "As long as the English are here, we can do nothing."

"But in this struggle," I retorted, "we need the support of the Arabs!"

"Precisely. The national question can be settled only by a social revolution."

"But the logical conclusion of your argument is to join the Communist Party."

"As a matter of fact, I just joined."

Almost all our friends did the same, and early in 1925, I joined the party myself.

Since 1917, I had been living with my eyes turned toward that vast and dazzling light in the east. The October Revolution had upset the course of history and ushered in a new era: the era of world revolution. Although I had been a Bolshevik at heart for a long time, I held back from joining the party because of the Jewish question. Convinced henceforth that only socialism could free the Jews from their centuries-old oppression, I threw myself into the fray. I felt great upheavals were imminent; it would be from these upheavals that this new egalitarian and fraternal society I longed for would be born. I had to help with this difficult but exciting birth. I abandoned an idealistic and naive morality and jumped right into history. What was the point of personal freedom unless we changed the world?

The Communist Party of Palestine, founded in 1920 by Joseph Berger, had been officially recognized by the executive committee of the Communist International in 1924. Most of the members of the new party had come to communism by way of Zionism. One of its best known leaders, Daniel Averbuch, had for a long time been the leader of the Left Poale-Zion party; as early as 1922, at the second congress of the Histadrut, he was defending communist theses before Ben Gurion. With considerable eloquence, he demonstrated the absurdity of trying to create a classless society while preserving the laws of the capitalist market. His speech, whose logic was relentless, impressed the congress, but convinced only part of the delegates that Zionism led inevitably to an impasse. As for me, in those days I did not believe that it was either possible or desirable to create a Jewish state.

I could not see why the five million American Jews, the three million Jews in the Soviet Union, and the millions of Jews scattered throughout the world should leave their homes and emigrate to Palestine in search of a hypothetical native land. In those days I felt that every Jew should be responsible for his own destiny. For those of us who wished to go to Palestine, it was unjustifiable to put barriers in the way. Those who were conscious of belonging to the Jewish race should be able to enjoy in each country the rights of a national minority. Finally, why should not those Jews who wished to be totally assimilated—a solution that I thought open only to part of the intelligentsia and to the rich bourgeoisie—be free to do so? I was convinced that the cultural traditions would be perpetuated for a long time, and, if permitted to develop freely, would enrich the collective heritage of the human race.

From its inception, the Communist Party faced the problem of how to wean the mass of workers away from the Zionist ideology; I was in favor of adopting a minimal program of immediate demands, realistic enough to arouse the Jewish workers. The party soon encountered another major difficulty: the English were not inclined to allow a Communist Party to develop. Zionist organizations and Arab reactionaries helped the police to hunt us down. We were a few hundred militants—a few thousand, counting sympathizers—devoted, generous, fearing neither clandestine life nor privations. Wherever we turned we faced opposition and hostility. It was at this time that the communist minority of the Histadrut, the "worker group," was thrown out of the union and associated itself with the Profintern, the Red International Trade Union. The party tried to win over the Arab population, but the efforts did nothing to weaken the influence of the Grand Mufti of Jerusalem, who was supported by the English.

I proposed to the leaders of the party, Averbuch, Berger, and Birman, the creation of a movement, the Ichud ("Unity")—Itachat in Arabic—to bring the Jews and Arabs together. Its program was simple:

1. to fight to have the Histadrut opened to Arab workers and to create a joint international union;

2. to provide opportunities for Jews and Arabs to get together, particularly through cultural events.

Right away the Ichud was a great success. By the end of 1925, there were clubs in Jerusalem, Haifa, Tel Aviv, and even in the agricultural villages where Arabs and Jews worked side by side. Meetings, to which admission was free, became more and more frequent. The influence the movement was beginning to have in the kibbutzim worried the leaders of the Histadrut; they could not seem to understand how Jews and Arabs could join forces. At the end of 1926 the first general meeting of the movement was held; more than one hundred delegates were there, including forty Arabs. On the evening of the first day, the delegates were amazed by the arrival of Ben Gurion, the national leader of the Histadrut, and Moshe Shertok, the specialist in Arab questions, who stared at the spectacle of Jews and Arabs sitting in the same room.

Our financial situation was precarious. Finding work when you were suspected of being a communist was not easy. Throughout 1925, ten of us lived in a shack in Tel Aviv, nine boys and a girl, for whom we fixed up a corner of her own. Those of us who had jobs pooled our wages, but the total was not enough to feed us all. We lived on the idea of revolution and a few tomatoes. Sometimes we went to little Yemenite restaurants, and to get credit we wore our work clothes, irrefutable proof that we were employed.

We had trouble adapting to the new climate, the sudden changes of temperature, the stifling heat of summer followed by the sharp cold of winter. I remember the way one of my friends, a native of Cracow, solved the problem of keeping warm during the cold season. He told me that he had found a job, which for an unemployed mason was a feat in itself.

Then he invited me to visit him "at home," a modest hovel.

"Look what I've done to beat the cold," he said. "I lie down on one table and put another one on top of me; it makes a wonderful blanket!"

This was Stokstil. He fought in the Spanish Civil War, where he was wounded, then lived in France under the occupation, where he took part in the resistance, and finally he died in Toulouse in 1943. Our little group included Sophie Poznanska, Hillel Katz, and myself; we were joined by Leo Grossvogel and Jescheskel Schreiber—we shall find them all again during the years of the war and the occupation. Most of the time we met at the Katzes' home, a makeshift garret slapped together with boards. Under the direction of Hillel, an experienced mason, we tore it down and built a solid house in its stead. We were very proud of the result, built with our own hands; it became our common meeting place. In 1926, finally, I rented a room in Tel Aviv over the local headquarters of the Ichud, so I could devote myself more fully to running the movement. It was there that I met—in a highly unusual manner—the woman who was to become my life's companion, Luba Brojde.

In the evening, after most of Tel Aviv was in bed, I heard a noise in the local. I went down to see what was going on, thinking I would find myself face to face with a thief, or a policeman overcome by curiosity. A beautiful girl was sitting there, comfortably reading our paper. I asked her, "But how did you get in?"

"Through the window, and this isn't the first time. When I come to the meetings, you see, your discussions make so much noise that I can't read."

Luba came from Lvov, in Poland, where she had worked in a factory and engaged in militant activities with communist youth groups. An *agent provocateur* was exposed—this man had betrayed a large number of militants to the police; the leaders of the party decided to have him shot, and a young Jewish communist, Waftali Botwin, organized the group in charge of the operation. Luba was a member of this group; the gun was hidden in her house. The informer was shot, but

Botwin was arrested and executed, and those who had taken part in the incident were hunted by the police. Luba had to leave Poland. She reached Palestine, where she worked first in a kibbutz, then as a house painter in Jerusalem. She had joined the Ichud and the worker group and also worked for an organization that aided political prisoners, but she refused to join the Palestinian Communist Party because they failed to understand the historic necessity of creating a Jewish state.

Luba paid for her devotion to our organization. In 1926 and 1927 she was arrested twice, in Haifa and in Jerusalem.

The English authorities were worried about the activities of the Ichud; a decree was issued prohibiting the meetings of the movement. The secretary of the worker group was arrested. I took his place. In 1927, the Jewish police, who were controlled by the English, made a raid during one of our meetings in Tel Aviv. I was arrested and put in a prison in Jaffa for several months, and there I discovered that prison bars are not always an impassable barrier. I arranged for Anna Kleinmann, a comrade who was devoted to our cause, to be hired as a housekeeper to the Jewish chief of police who had initiated the arrests. Later Kleinmann fought for the resistance in France, was arrested and deported, and she was murdered at Auschwitz. Here, in her position as housekeeper, she regularly searched the pockets of her employer; she found the list of our comrades under suspicion and warned them before they could be arrested. The chief of police was not forgotten. Later, he had a leg broken during a demonstration.

The Communist Party appointed me secretary of the Haifa section, which was one of the most powerful in Palestine; we were well established in the factories and among the railroad employees. By this appointment I became a regular member of the party. I fought with the energy of the neophyte; I was driven by the power of my vision. I was already living a clandestine existence: I could go out only after dark; even then I had to take a thousand precautions to elude the police. A good speaker, I appeared here and there addressing the workers. I organized political work, wrote tracts and manifestoes, and presided over the meetings—which we held in spite of the prohibitions. It was during one of these meetings, in the last days of 1928, that I was arrested once again, with twenty-three comrades, and incarcerated at Haifa. We had had time to destroy all compromising papers, so the police could produce no formal proof of our activities.

Subsequently we were transferred to the medieval fortress Saint-Jean d'Acre, where we endured extremely difficult conditions. The British authorities refused to regard us as political prisoners and treated us like ordinary criminals. All Palestine heard the story of the communist bakery worker who stayed naked in his cell for weeks rather than wear a convict's uniform. Time dragged on, with no trial in sight. We were unclassifiable; they did not know which jurisdiction should have us. The party's Central Committee warned us that the governor, Sir Herbert Samuel, was about to sign a decree authorizing the deportation to Cyprus of anyone suspected of pro-communist activities. We decided to go on a hunger strike to obtain either our release or a trial. After the fifth day, we refused to drink anything. Our obstinacy triumphed over injustice: the news of our hunger strike spread throughout Palestine; several Labor members of the English Parliament attacked the government on its Palestinian policy and denounced its excesses. On the thirteenth day we were told that our trial was about to begin. I was chosen to speak on behalf of my twenty-three comrades.

On the first day of the trial, several of us were so weak that they were taken in on stretchers; but there were to be no other days. No sooner had the hearing been opened than the judge, flanked by his two assistants, rose and stated in a tone that was meant to be sarcastic,

"Do you imagine that the British Government is afraid of you? There will be no trial. You are free."

With a wave of his hand, he ordered the policemen to eject us from the room. We had won.

In 1928, Palestine had an economic crisis that caused considerable unemployment. A great many Jewish workers were affected—about one-third of the total—and left the country in massive numbers. That year there were 5,000 departures, 2,700 arrivals. Then, also in 1928, anti-Jewish riots broke out, accompanied by lynchings. These riots were the occasion of a dramatic misunderstanding between the Palestinian Communist Party and the Comintern. In the eyes of the Comintern, pogroms of this sort signalled the beginning of the rise of the Arab proletariat, a movement it was absolutely necessary to encourage. The Palestinian Communist Party had not been able to establish itself among the native population; the Comintern announced the watchwords "Arabization and Bolshevization," as if the mechanical substitution of Arabs for Jews would ensure a greater implantation of the party among the Moslem population. This analysis met with strong opposition within the Palestinian party; a group of militants, myself among them, considered the Comintern's decision irresponsible. One of our militants was lynched near Haifa while trying to carry out the instructions to the letter, and it was necessary to take extraordinary measures to protect Smeral, the Czech representative of the Comintern, who was living in secrecy near Jerusalem.

This absurd policy undermined the influence of the party among the Jewish workers. For its part, the Palestinian Communist Party itself provided disastrous support for Soviet measures on the "Jewish question" in the USSR.

How had this situation developed?

After the October Revolution, the idea had been that the national life of the Jews in the Soviet Union would expand in those regions where they were already strongly implanted: the Crimea, the Ukraine, and Belorussia. In 1928, though, the Stalinist regime created an autonomous Jewish region in Birobidzhan, on the frontiers of Manchuria. This bureaucratic decision artificially produced a state in a Siberian country with a very harsh climate where there was not the slightest trace of a Jewish community. As a result, several thousand men and women were forced to leave their homes in the Ukraine or the Crimea, where they enjoyed the rights of a national minority. The Palestinian party was invited, along with those of the other countries, to seize this opportunity to demonstrate the fairness of communist policy with regard to minorities, and to encourage people to leave for Birobidzhan. One hundred and fifty members of the Gedud Ha-Avodah, Palestine's Work Brigade, went there and founded a community, Voja Nova—New Voice. Very few survived the Stalinist purges. As for the Palestinian leaders, they were very poorly rewarded for their loyalty. Moscow felt they needed to be "re-educated." The members of the Central Committee traveled to the Soviet Union to study at Kutv University (the communist university for the Near East). We can only assume that their re-education did not have the hoped-for results, since, beginning in 1935, they were all arrested.

For me, back in Palestine, the struggle went on. I was constantly hunted by the police. Neither Tel Aviv nor Jerusalem was safe; a clandestine life in such a small country was no longer possible for the best known militants. Deported by a decision of the English governor, I set sail for France with very few belongings, but with two documents more precious to me than gold: a recommendation from the Central Committee of the Palestinian Communist Party, which had approved of my departure, and a tourist's visa.

4

A t the end of 1929 I landed in Marseilles. The crossing had taken almost a week. Stretched out on the deck of a wheezy freighter, my head resting on a coil of rope, I had had a chance to think things over. Although I was barely a quarter of a century old, I was experiencing exile for the second time. I was not unhappy about it. For the born revolutionary, repression is no respecter of age. Being uprooted is painful only if one has roots, and the rocky soil of Palestine did not offer the most fertile terrain.

When I saw the French coast appear on the horizon, the joy of finally realizing an old dream swept away my last regrets.

France!

It would be difficult to imagine the emotional impact this name had on the young expatriate I was then. During the 1920s, eastern Europeans were always leaving home to try to become the American uncles of those who stayed behind in Warsaw or Bucharest; the Broadway shoeshine boy who became a businessman inspired many. But as for a young communist who was twenty-five years old in 1930, driven out of his native land by police persecution, propelled by the force of circumstance and the hazards of the class struggle, a traveling salesman for the revolution—his gaze turned toward Red Square, or toward the Place de la Bastille.

Entry to the Soviet Union, where the hope of centuries was being transformed into reality, had to be earned. You had to have proved yourself. Young Domb had taken only his first steps on this difficult journey, one you could travel only with tenacity, patience, and self-denial. The name France, moreover, for a political émigré, was almost synonymous with revolution. Of course the France of the Third Republic was not really a haven for new revolutionaries. The police were meddlesome, and when it came to work, the Republic generously offered only the most difficult jobs to foreigners. But a communist knows that in France he can count on his party comrades, and a Jew is aware that in the popular organizations of the Jewish community, he will find friends. So I would try being a militant communist in the milieu of Jewish workers, where I knew the party was growing and needed leaders.

I spent two weeks in Marseilles, since I did not have enough money to keep on traveling. The air on the boulevards of Marseilles was not unpleasant, but I was shut up all day in the kitchen of the little restaurant where I had found a job. I got my meals—and I could save my salary to buy myself a suit. At twenty-five, I had never worn a suit. In Palestine, shorts and a shirt constituted a whole wardrobe. Not for a moment, though, would I have dreamed of setting foot in Paris badly dressed. When I had my new clothes, I could not stop looking at the strange man I saw in the mirror, and I remembered the sartorial preparations of the Jews of Novy-Targ before they left for the United States.

It was with some pride that I got off the train and walked the streets of Paris. I was even holding a little suitcase—it was half empty, but what difference did that make! I knew where to go. My childhood friend, Alter Strom, had left Palestine a year before me and settled in the French capital. A specialist in laying floors, he had had no trouble finding work. The address he had given me—Hôtel de France, 9 rue d'Arras, Paris Vème—sounded impressive. The Fifth Arrondissement was the Latin Quarter, where the students lived. Hôtel de France! With a name like that, it could only be a palace. Had Alter Strom become a "capitalist"?

He had written that I could stay with him for the first few days. I arrived in a dark and narrow street. At No. 9, the elements had almost washed away the inscription on the grey facade of a small building: Hôtel de France. I asked for Monsieur Strom's room; it was on the top floor, under the roof. I pushed open the door and discovered all its opulence. An enormous bed occupied almost the whole room. In one corner was a little washbasin; by the window, a rickety table; in lieu of a closet, a few nails in the door. So much for the furniture.

I soon came to understand Alter Strom's choice. The Hôtel de France was one of the least expensive and the least watched by the police. Alter Strom's room was always open to his friends. The bed was so big that we could sleep across its width. It was not unusual to wake up in the morning and find there were four or five of us. Those who had no place to sleep slipped the night porter a few francs and came upstairs to take the places that were still empty.

There was one trouble: lice, which flourished everywhere. One day we bought two bottles of wine and renamed the Hôtel de France the Hôtel de Vance (in Yiddish *vance* means louse).

If I could prove to the authorities that I had a means of making a living, I would have no trouble obtaining the proper papers. My friends had long since solved this problem: they sent home the amount of money that the French police deemed necessary to live for a month. Their friends or relatives immediately sent back the same money, which was then used again for someone else. By showing the postal receipts at the police station, we could prove that we regularly received subsidies from Poland.

The first day, I had made contact with the Communist Party. Since Palestine, I had been carrying a little piece of cloth concealed in a lining; inside was the letter of recommendation from the Central Committee of the Palestinian party. I delivered it to the comrade in charge of immigrant labor. We agreed that I would start in as a militant as soon as I had a job. Not a steady job—steady employment belonged to the realm of fantasy; immigrant workers could hope for nothing but menial and intermittent positions. In those days the big department stores hired crews every evening to clean the floors. Along with a few dozen students, I "danced" all night on the floors of the Samaritaine or the Bon Marché, with a brush on one foot and a rag on the other. The work was hard, but it paid well. With what I made in one night I

could live for two or three days. Even more exhausting was
loading freight trains. All night long I loaded cars in the Gare
de la Chapelle. In the morning I would stagger back home to
bed with pains up and down my back.

In the construction business, they were hiring temporary
laborers. The construction foremen received a percentage of
your salary when they hired you; they looked your working
papers over less carefully than in some other industries. For
several weeks I worked at the construction site of the
Hachette building, then at Pantin, where I carried rails all day
until an enormous iron bar crushed my big toe. I have the
scar to this day.

These jobs did not add up to steady employment, but this
did not prevent me from resuming militant activity; all my
political activities were soon to be directed toward Jewish
immigrant circles, where the Communist Party was seeking
to extend its influence.

In speaking of the Jews of France—there were about
200,000 in Paris then—it would be much more accurate to talk
about "communities" than one community. There were
Alsatians, Lorrainians, Comtadins, and Bordelais who had
won their emancipation after a long, hard struggle but who
had gradually climbed the rungs of social success—these
were the oldest layers; then there were the successive waves
of recent immigrants. These Jews from Central Europe, who
had begun to move west at the beginning of the twentieth
century, and particularly after the big Czarist pogroms, were
essentially of proletarian origin. Some of them had already
been militants in leftist parties in their native countries, and
they had kept their convictions. Under the circumstances, it
was not surprising that after they arrived in France, they
resumed their militant activities. The political parties found
many recruits in these circles: the Communist Party, the
Bund, the coalition party, the Zionist groups, the Hashomer
Hatzair.

As for me, I was an active militant in the Jewish immigrant
labor section along with comrades who had been driven out
of their countries by repression. Every night we had meetings

that broke up very late. At that time the Trotskyite influence was very strong among Jewish communists; we others were ordered to "clean out the Jewish circle" of rival militants. Our discussions were often very animated. Gradually, the role of the Trotskyites among the Jewish immigrants was considerably reduced, but little nuclei of activists continued to reappear.

As Jews and communists, we participated not only in party activities but in the political battle in general. We were closely associated with the struggles of the working class. It was always a risk for us to participate in violent demonstrations, because in case of arrest, immigrants who were not naturalized were often deported. In spite of the risks, we took part in the popular demonstrations like the celebration of the anniversary of the Commune and of May Day. Our circle was also very active in cultural associations, such as the Culture Ligua, and in the labor unions, and there were numbers of Jewish militants in the fur and garment industries.

My personal life also became more stable. I had the joy of being reunited with Luba, who had come to live with me in 1930. Since she was wanted by the British police, she had to borrow her sister Sarah's identity to get out of Palestine—even today my wife is sometimes called by this borrowed name, Sarah Orschizer. She had to become married on paper to a friend who was a citizen of Palestine—then her marital status gave her the same rights as a British subject, and she could get a visa for France. As immigrants in Paris, though, we were once again to make the acquaintance of the police.

Very early one morning a few weeks after Luba arrived, there was a knock at the door of our room at the Hôtel de "Vance." I opened it to find a man whose appearance was not deceiving.

"I'm from the police. Your wife has been here a month and she still hasn't reported to the authorities."

"I'm sorry," I answered, and leaning forward, I whispered in his ear as if I didn't want to be overheard: "She's not my wife, she's my mistress. In forty-eight hours, she'll be gone."

"Oh, in that case," said the functionary, giving me a rakish look.

In France, love stories always work, especially with the police.

Already difficult, our financial situation became alarming with the approach of the birth of our first child. Quite by chance, and to return a favor, the Jewish owner of a small painting business hired me. But it takes more than a brush to make a painter; I did not have the touch, and remained only a very mediocre paint-splasher.

My wife did piecework at home for a furrier. Twice a week she went to pick up enormous packages of furs and worked ten to twelve hours a day. She was a militant in the ranks of the Communist Party and was even chosen to represent the Jewish section at the first anti-fascist congress, which was held in 1931, in Paris. Meanwhile, I had been named to represent Jewish immigrant labor at the Central Committee.

I was invited, with another comrade, to go to the headquarters of the Central Committee to meet Marcel Cachin. The editor of l'Humanité welcomed me cordially.

"Good morning," he said, "how's the work going among the Jews?" And he went on, without giving me time to answer: "The Nazi threat is growing greater; we must step up propaganda in Jewish circles. We need a newspaper in the Yiddish language for France and Belgium. That's what I wanted to see you about."

"Very good, but who will pay for it?"

"What," Cachin exclaimed, "haven't you read Lenin? Don't you know how a communist newspaper is financed? Organize a subscription drive among the workers . . ."

"We're prepared to launch a big subscription campaign, but will you take part in the meetings we organize to support it?"

"Of course, I'll be delighted to, whenever I'm free."

Not long after this conversation, a public meeting took place in Montreuil, where there was a large Jewish colony. The only space available was in the synagogue. I was sitting on the speaker's platform, next to Cachin. The old leader got up and began his speech in a strong and vigorous voice:

"Dear friends, it is a great honor for me to be here among the representatives of a race which has given the world some great revolutionaries. I am talking about Jesus Christ, Spinoza, and Marx!"

The speaker was interrupted by thunderous applause. Surprised and annoyed by these words, which had the ring of petit-bourgeois nationalism, I lowered my eyes, not daring to look around the room. But Marcel Cachin went on in the same tone.

"I'm sure you're aware, my friends, that Karl Marx's grandfather was a rabbi."

I could not care less about all this; but the audience was entranced by it. They seemed to find it much more important than the writing of *Capital* by the grandson of the rabbi in question.

The collection for the newspaper was taken at the door, and it went very well. Cachin was very pleased, and remarked as he left,

"You see, Domb, we did it. The paper will come out!"

A few weeks later the first issue of *Der Morgen* (*The Morning*) appeared. A four-page weekly, the newspaper quickly increased its circulation. I often wrote articles, and sometimes the editorial. Our financial status, though, was still precarious. A member of the editorial staff suggested we open a page to advertising, which until then had been banished from the communist press for moral reasons. Should we or should we not open our columns to capitalist advertisers? The question was submitted to the Central Committee, which agreed to try it as an experiment in our newspaper, on the condition that we take advertising only from small businesses, restaurants, and craftsmen. The comrade in charge of this page worked so hard and with such good results that he was offered the same job later on *l'Humanité*.

Our son was born on April 3, 1931. On that very day,

André Marty—a hero to all French communists—was released from prison. That evening, at La Grange-aux-Belles, Marty was to attend a meeting of Jewish workers. To commemorate this triple event, Luba and I decided to name our child "Anmarty." It must sound strange today, but this impulse shows the veneration in which the communist leaders were held, years before the famous cult of personality was denounced.

I can still see myself at the town hall of the XIXème Arrondissement, near the little apartment where we had moved. I presented myself to the government functionary to announce the birth of my son. When I told him the baby's first name, he started (although he was employed in a communist neighborhood).

"Anmarty, Anmarty? There's no such name!"

"But it's to celebrate the release of André Marty!"

"I realize that, but if you want to avoid trouble, take my advice and give him another name."

I went home to consult Luba. We decided, in memory of the first neighborhood in Paris that had welcomed us, to name him Michel.

Since Luba was as busy with militant activities as I was, we had to find someone to stay with Michel in the evenings. We enlisted the help of friends, who took turns babysitting. "Don't thank us," they said, "it's no trouble; and besides, it's as good a way as any of making ourselves useful to the party." There was only one drawback: soon certain comrades came to prefer staying with Michel and used it as an excuse not to attend meetings.

For better or for worse, we settled into our new life. We made enough money to survive, and we had enough political activity to occupy our minds. Revolutionaries, of course, cannot count on anything beyond the immediate. The road to revolution is full of pitfalls, and whoever wants to travel it must be ready for anything—above all, the unexpected. One morning in June, 1932, Alter Strom showed up, looking worried. He asked me whether I had received a letter for him.

"Is it a personal letter?" I asked.

"No, no, it's important."

I was amazed at this response. "It's not very wise," I said, "to have such letters sent to the home of someone involved in party business." Strom had been a militant with me in the Culture Ligua. In 1931, his parents sent him some money, and he enrolled in the Institut des Arts et Métiers, where he was studying to become a draftsman. Meanwhile, he had stopped appearing in public. I had not asked him for an explanation, but I suspected that he was participating in illegal activities for the Polish Communist Party.

Two days later Alter Strom came again, looking very preoccupied, and asked me whether I had received a letter for him yet.

He said as he left me, "Anyway, be careful!"

I had no idea where the danger might come from; but a few days later, the newspapers provided the answer. Alter Strom had been arrested for espionage on behalf of the Soviet Union. Evidently the head of the network, Isaiah Bir, possessed certain talents, for the police had nicknamed him "Fantômas," phantom-man, also the name of the hero in a series of popular thrillers. The incident became known as the "Fantômas Case."

Many Parisian newspapers gloated over this affair; they could not pass up the opportunity to launch a campaign of vilification against the Communist Party, which was accused of being "in the pay of foreigners." Inevitably, in a country where puns are a national pastime, they made a great to-do about the "Fanto-Marx" conspiracy. My only connection with the Fantômas group was my friendship with Strom, but as an active militant in the Communist Party, I felt it my duty to submit my case to my superiors. After examination, they decided there was a danger that the police might exploit my friendship with Strom to organize a campaign against the Jewish immigrants, and advised me to leave Paris. Their fears were not without foundation at a time when the reactionary press was already denouncing "illiterate immigration," and breathing on the still-hot coals of the most vulgar form of anti-Semitism. My own situation was perfectly legal and I could have gone to Brussels, for example, and waited for things to calm down. But I thought the opportunity to go to the Soviet Union, which I had been requesting since 1931, should be seized. Why? First, because since I had left Poland I had not had a moment's respite; and second, because although I had gained inestimably valuable experience in the field, I was lacking in theoretical knowledge. It was time to fill in the gap.

My application, submitted by the directors of the French Communist Party, was accepted in Moscow by the French section of the personnel department of the Comintern, under the direction of Mme. Lebiedewa, the wife of Manuilski. My wife would join me. So I left for the capital of the USSR in the early summer of 1932.

On my way to Moscow, I stopped for a few days in Berlin.

The leftist militants I met in the German capital underestimated the Nazi danger. Communists and socialists, reasoning solely in electoral and parliamentary terms, were sure that Hitler's party would never win a majority in the Reichstag. I objected that the Nazis might take power by force, and that the Nazis were much better prepared for such an eventuality than any of the workers' parties; but they did not see these points.

Yet every day the storm troopers' boots hammered louder on the pavement. Street fights were a daily occurrence; Hitler's shock troops did not hesitate to attack militants of the left.

Meanwhile, the Socialist and Communist parties, which between them numbered more than fourteen million voters, refused to form a common front. In the famous words of Thaelmann, secretary general of the German Communist Party, "The Nazi tree should not hide the Social Democrat forest." Six months later, the Nazi tree was casting its shadow over the whole of Germany.

It was not until 1935 that the Communist International, at its seventh congress, understood the lesson of this terrible defeat and advocated the united front that militant socialists and communists had been putting into practice for some time—behind the barbed wire of the concentration camps.

I left Berlin convinced that the catastrophe was imminent.

In the train that took me toward Moscow, travelers were few. As we approached the Russian border, I was the only passenger in my whole car. For the rest of the world, the Soviet Union was still an enigma. The nightmare of property owners on all continents, to me she represented the homeland of the working class.

The enormous sign that marked the entrance into Soviet territory came into sight, bearing Marx's famous appeal, "Workers of the world, unite." I had dreamed of the homeland of socialism. I was there.

At the frontier station, I changed to a car divided into compartments for two. After two or three hours, an officer of the Red Army came in. He was very happy to meet a foreign communist, and in a mixture of Russian, Polish, and German, we began to chat. As we approached Moscow, he began to reorganize his luggage. To my amazement, I saw that his two enormous suitcases were full of pieces of dry bread. He said as he closed his bags, "You see, I'm bringing some presents to my family, who live in the country."

In Moscow, an incredible sight greeted me. The station and the area around it were packed with thousands and thousands of peasant families, exhausted, clutching their belongings to them, waiting for their trains to arrive. I wondered where they were going. Later I learned they had been driven out of their villages and were going far away to the east, to Siberia, where there was virgin land to be cultivated.

As I was leaving the station, I spotted a policeman and walked over to ask for directions, leaving my suitcase where it was.

"Are you a foreigner?"

I nodded.

"Well, I'll give you some good advice. Always hold onto your suitcase, because there are thieves here!"

Thieves in Moscow, fifteen years after the October Revolution! I was dumbfounded.

I took a taxi to the home of my old friend Elenbogen, whom I had known in Palestine. He was very intelligent and a good organizer, and had been an active militant in the Unity group, but in 1927, ill and almost paralyzed, he had received authorization to return to the Soviet Union. I had notified him of my arrival from Berlin, and he was expecting me. On the table were bread, butter, sausage, and vodka. The Red Army officer's two suitcases filled with dry bread were still fresh in my memory. Elenbogen must have read the surprise on my face.

"You're probably amazed to find all these things in my home," he said. "They're black market goods. A man like me, who makes a good living"—he was an engineer and gave courses in two colleges—"can buy whatever he wants."

We talked all night. Elenbogen did not belong to the party, but he was far from being opposed to the Soviet regime; what he told me, though, about collectivization, life in Moscow, and the trials, was altogether different from what I had read and heard. From the first day, the gap between propaganda and reality appeared, and it was enormous.

The next day I went to Woronzowe-Pole, where the political emigrés were housed, and where I was given a room that I shared with two comrades. It was a big building, almost in the center of town, and it buzzed with excitement. Old militants, exiles from many countries, lived there—Poles, Hungarians, Lithuanians, Yugoslavs, and even Japanese. They waited weeks, and sometimes months, before receiving jobs, and they spent most of that time arguing. Some approved of collectivization, and others retorted that it had brought on the famine in the Ukraine; I learned, then, that people were starving in that region. The intensity and freedom of the discussions reminded me of those meetings in Paris when we had interminable and chaotic arguments with the socialist and Trotskyite militants.

I continued my discovery of Moscow. On Manezh Square, in the center of town, were the offices of the Comintern, an enormous and well-guarded building. Before you could go inside, you had to make telephone contact with the person you were coming to see. The various sections of the International shared the floors: the whole world was in that building. I was received by the secretary of the French section, who had been informed of my arrival. He had made the necessary arrangements for me to enter one of the communist universities—of which, at that time, there were four in Moscow. The first, the Lenin School, was designed for militants who had acquired considerable experience but had

had no opportunity to study. Through this university passed the future leaders of the communist parties. Tito was studying there at the time. Marchlevski University, where I was enrolled, was reserved for national minorities, and contained almost twenty sections: Polish, German, Hungarian, Bulgarian, and so on. Specialized groups of militants, belonging to the national minorities of the particular country, were attached to each section. For example, the Yugoslav section included a Serbian and a Croatian group. The Jewish section included both communist militants from all nations and Jewish militants from the Soviet Union—we knew what was going on in the country because some of the students in our section went home for the summer. The third university was Kutv University, for students from the Near East, and finally, Sun Yat-sen University was reserved for the Chinese. Between two and three thousand selected militants were enrolled in the four universities.

In 1932, the life of a student was not easy. Most of us lived a good distance away and had to travel for more than an hour. It was not until 1934 that construction began on a dormitory near our university for twelve hundred students. As for the food—it lacked variety, to say the least. Frequently, for a whole week we were on a diet of cabbage; the following week it would be rice. The university took charge of dressing the students. Whoever was responsible for clothing for our university bought seven hundred identical pairs of pants, so that when Moscovites passed us in the streets, they said,

"Look, there's a student from Marchlevski University!"

There were three cycles of study in the program. Under social sciences and economics were included the history of the peoples of the Soviet Union, the history of the Bolshevik Party and of the Comintern, and the study of Leninism. A second cycle was devoted to the study of the student's native country, the worker movement, the Communist Party, and national characteristics. An apprenticeship in languages formed the third cycle. In addition, those who had not studied them elsewhere could learn mathematics, physics, chemistry, and biology. The work was intense, an average of twelve to fourteen hours a day.

In our section, I was particularly interested in the study of the Jewish question. Our professor, Dimenstein, had been the first Jew to join the Bolshevik Party at the beginning of the century. Vice-Commissar for Nationalities under Stalin's direction after the revolution, he had known Lenin very well, and he often quoted his remark, "Anti-Semitism is the counterrevolution." From his numerous discussions with him, Dimenstein was convinced that Lenin advocated the creation of a Jewish nation within the Soviet Union that would enjoy the same rights as the other republics.

The students at the communist university were also given military training: the handling of weapons, exercises in shooting and in civil defense, the rudiments of chemical warfare. I had no taste for guns and I regularly missed the target.

Leaders from the Russian Communist Party and the Comintern frequently came to give lectures. Later, these visits became increasingly rare. We also took part in evenings organized by the Society of Old Bolsheviks, which was tolerated until May, 1935. Some distinguished militants—Radek, Zinoviev, Bukharin, and Kamenev—who already belonged to history, or who were still making it, led the discussions. Zinoviev made a bizarre impression on me, probably because of the incongruity between his words, always impassioned and violent, and the tone of his voice, which was shrill and slightly hysterical.

Bukharin, however, fascinated me. An excellent speaker, brilliant and cultivated, he had deserted politics to devote himself to literature. When he finished a lecture, he regularly received a veritable ovation—which he always greeted with a blank stare.

One day, looking sadly over a roomful of students acclaiming him, he muttered, "Each time they applaud it brings me closer to my death."

Radek, on the other hand, took refuge behind an abrasive and cynical irony. He always supported the political changes and wrote long articles—of which he did not believe a word—explaining the official line. Nobody, though, was taken in.

The world of foreign militants studying in Moscow was a very closed one—we seldom had the opportunity of traveling or making contact with the Russian people. But cut off from Russian social life, we were as a result still independent of the bureaucratic machine that was then extending its power over the country. Our political discussions often dealt with subjects that nobody dared raise any more in the party. Through the representative of our national section at the Comintern, we knew more than the Soviet citizens did about what was going on in their country, and when we disapproved of it, we did not hesitate to say so.

A few months after my arrival, we heard about the "suicide" of Stalin's wife. The students who took part in the funeral services whispered in each other's ears as they marched in the procession, "Did she really commit suicide, or was she put to death by Stalin?"

Luba arrived at the beginning of 1933 with our son; Michel was now eighteen months old. The French section of the Comintern enrolled her at Marchlevski University, where she studied until 1936. At the same time, she took part in militant activities in Moscow in the district of Bauman, whose secretary was Nikita Khrushchev. During the summers— until 1936, when foreign communists were removed from all important positions in the Russian party—Luba was sent into the collectives as political commissar to assume responsibility for the harvest and for economic planning.

The horizon that stretched before me in those days was not without clouds—far from it.

When I arrived in the Soviet Union, collectivization was a moot issue in the party; the old militants, though, were still talking about it, because the experience had been so traumatic for them. In the beginning, Stalin had decided to abolish the kulaks, the rich farmers who made their money at the expense of the poor. This notion went through some rapid changes. In March, 1930, when the campaign for collectivization was in full swing, an article by Stalin appeared called "The Vertigo of Success," in which he condemned the principle of voluntary integration in the collective farms. Henceforth the farmers would be integrated into the collectives at gunpoint, if necessary. We students had read Lenin, and we knew that collectivization had no chance of succeeding except through the education and persuasion of the peasant-farmers. Furthermore, it was not possible until after the achievement of a level of industrial development that could provide the rural areas with the necessary material infrastructure.

A rumor was going around the universities that collectivization had caused five million casualties. It was said that entire populations had been deported and decimated. On May 1, 1934, I headed a delegation of foreign communists to Kazakhstan. In Karaganda, we were received by the leader of the party, who showed us around the town. At the edge of town, he pointed to a huge camp, down below us.

"You see that? That's a camp for former kulaks," he said. "They were brought here with their families to work in the mines." With a cynicism that was completely unconscious, he went on: "The people in charge of setting up the camp thought of everything except running water. So an epidemic of typhus broke out, and there were several thousand victims. The ones you see today are the second wave."

41

That evening, we sat down to dinner with the secretary of the party and a colonel in the NKVD, the People's Commissariat for the Interior. The colonel pointed out four very well-dressed men who belonged to the generation before the revolution.

"Those are our engineers. They are in charge of mining the coal that will make Karaganda the second largest mining center in the Soviet Union."

The four engineers were introduced to us—and I jumped when I heard their names. In 1928, eleven engineers had been accused of sabotage and sentenced to death, after a trial that had caused a sensation in the Soviet Union. Now several of them were standing in front of me! I turned to the colonel in the NKVD and said,

"Look here, weren't these the principal defendants in the Chacty trial?"

"You're right, that's who they are."

"But they were sentenced to death, and we thought they'd been executed."

The NKVD colonel paused, and then said, "Shooting someone doesn't cost much, of course, but since they were particularly competent and we thought we could use them, we brought them here and told them, 'Beneath your feet lie enormous reserves of coal. After Donbass, this Karaganda region can and should become the second largest coal-producing center in the Soviet Union. It's up to you to take charge of the operation. You have two choices: either you succeed and your lives will be saved, or else. . . .' They have been here since the day after their conviction," he added. "They are free now, and they've sent for their families."

We were astounded. If the eleven engineers had committed the crimes they were accused of, they deserved to die a hundred times, and the bargaining that had gone on over them was inconceivable.

Former kulaks had been transformed into miners who were dying of typhus in camps without sanitation. Engineers sentenced to death for "sabotage" had been entrusted with the direction of the second largest mining operation in the

Soviet Union. For us, communists and students, an abyss was suddenly gaping between the theory disseminated at our university and reality.

In 1930, there had been another so-called trial involving an industrialist. Ramzin, the principal defendant, was accused of being in touch with French Intelligence and plotting to restore capitalism in Russia, and was sentenced to death. Five years later, he was released from prison and appointed director of a big institute for scientific research in Moscow. He received the Order of Lenin, and he died in his bed in 1948.

All these events began to disturb my fine certainties. I had arrived in the Soviet Union carrying in my baggage the dreams of a neophyte. I was young and an ardent communist, and I wanted to help change the face of the world, even though I knew from my years as a militant that direct contact with the concrete would inevitably lead me to revise certain enthusiasms.

It was during this period that I became acquainted with Lenin's "Testament," a typewritten copy of which was being circulated only among those students in whom the party leaders had particular confidence. Lenin's "Testament" is made up of the last articles Lenin wrote before his death. It was not until Khrushchev's report to the twentieth congress in 1956 that the authenticity of these texts was confirmed. Reading this manuscript in the 1930s was a revelation to me. "Stalin," wrote Vladimir Ilyich, "is excessively brutal, and this fault, which can be tolerated in private and among communists, becomes an intolerable defect in the person who occupies the position of secretary general. For this reason, I propose that the comrades study the possibility of dismissing Stalin from the post. . . ."

Profoundly affected and disturbed by this testament, I plunged into the recent history of the party, rereading all the Soviet newspapers for the last few years in the hope of understanding. I remember noticing that the first signs of the cult of Stalin had appeared in 1929, the year of his fiftieth birthday.

It was then that descriptions like "inspired," "great leader," "continuer of Lenin," and "infallible guide" began to appear in the newspapers—and the writers who constantly resorted to these epithets and signed the articles in *Pravda* or *Izvestia* were the former leaders of the opposition. Zinoviev, Kamenev, Radek, and Piatakov vied with each other in laudatory zeal, in an attempt to make people forget that they once had the audacity to oppose Stalin. By 1929, dissenting groups within the party no longer existed. They were defeated, and their leaders were being given positions of responsibility. Bukharin was editor in chief of *Izvestia;* Radek became one of the principal editors of *Pravda* and Stalin's adviser on foreign policy.

During Lenin's lifetime, political life among the Bolsheviks was always very animated. At the congresses, in the plenums, at the meetings of the Central Committee, militants said frankly what they thought. This democratic and often bitter clash of opinions gave the party its cohesion and vitality. From the moment Stalin extended his power over the party machine, however, even the old Bolsheviks no longer dared oppose his decisions or even discuss them. Some kept silent and suffered inwardly; others withdrew from active political life. Worse, many militants publicly supported Stalin's positions although they did not approve of them. This terrible hypocrisy accelerated the inner demoralization of the party.

Militants had to choose between their jobs, even their personal safety, and their revolutionary conscience. Many remained silent, bowed their heads, and submitted. To give your opinion on the issues of the day became an act of bravery. You spoke openly only to your trusted friends, and even then with trepidation. With everyone else, you recited the official litanies from *Pravda.*

After 1930, the party was run by people who were always unreservedly in agreement with Stalin on any question whatsoever. Exceptions were rare: a few leaders, some old communists who could not bear to see the party of Lenin being transformed into a religious order, sometimes had the courage to say no. For example, Lominadze and Lunacharski.

Lominadze committed suicide in 1935, as did Ordzhonikid-ze, an old friend of Stalin, who ended his life in 1937 after the NKVD made a search of his office. He had telephoned Stalin to protest, and Stalin had shouted at him,

"They have the right, they have every right, with you or anyone else!"

As late as 1930, Lunacharski intervened to defend intellectuals sentenced to death. In the army, in 1929, General Yakir did not hesitate to come to the defense of a group of innocent officers whom the NKVD had arrested. It was possible, to a certain extent, to oppose the machinery of the police state. I even had the experience myself.

One day in November, 1934, my wife was summoned to Lubianka Prison to give testimony. The next day it was my turn. The colonel who was conducting the inquiry informed us that a certain Kaniewski, whom we had known well in Palestine, had been arrested. He was a very fine militant—devoted and brave, always volunteering for the worst jobs. Imprisoned several times by the British, he had behaved courageously in prison.

"Kaniewski is suspected of working for British Intelligence," the colonel declared.

"No doubt," I said, "the British Intelligence Service is trying to recruit agents, but they would lose face if they wasted their time with someone like Kaniewski. He is absolutely incapable of doing that sort of work."

A few months later, my wife and I were told that a man was waiting to see us in the lobby of the university. We went downstairs and found Kaniewski, who had come to thank us, with tears in his eyes. He had been released from prison, he told us. The testimony against him had crushed him, but because of our statements, his life had been saved. Alas, testimony of this sort would become impossible in the years to come.

In 1937 I learned that my friend Alter Strom had been arrested. He had been working for the Tass Agency in the USSR since his release from a jail term in France, in connection with the Fantômas affair. Thinking there had been some misunderstanding, I asked if I could testify in his behalf. I had a very difficult time making contact with the colonel in charge of the investigation. I had to go through the political director of military intelligence, who thought I was crazy to come to the defense of a prisoner.

The investigating colonel, when I got to him, was not fully aware of the purpose of my visit. He received me very courteously, offered me coffee and cigarettes, and finally said,

"Well, comrade, you came to testify in the Strom case?"

"That's right."

"Well, I'm listening."

"I simply came to say that Alter Strom is innocent."

The pen fell from his fingers, his smile changed to a look of incredulity, and his face hardened.

"And you came here to tell me that?"

"That's right. I've known Alter Strom since he was a young man. I know he's not an enemy. It's natural that I should come and say so."

The colonel gave me a long look. "Let's speak frankly," he said. "The October Revolution is in danger. If we arrest a hundred people and only one turns out to be an enemy, that one justifies the arrest of all the others. The survival of the revolution is worth the price."

In one sentence, he had just summed up the political philosophy of repression.

"I don't see how the October Revolution is in danger," I answered, "and I'm amazed that after twenty years of experience a department like yours can't tell a friend from an enemy!"

7

A long with the cult of Stalin there developed the cult of the party. The party cannot be wrong, the party never makes a mistake; you cannot be right if you oppose the party. The party is sacred. Whatever the party says—through the mouth of its secretary general—is the gospel truth. To question it is sacrilege. There is no salvation outside the party: and if you are not with the party, you are against it. These were the unspoken truths that were beaten into the heads of skeptics; as for heretics, they were doomed to excommunication.

God-the-party and His prophet, Stalin, were the objects of immoderate worship. As in religious processions where, after Jesus, the saints' emblems are carried on crosses, in the official demonstrations, Stalin's portrait was followed by those of the principal leaders. To discover the exact hierarchical ranking of the leaders, all you had to do was watch the order in which the members of the Politburo entered the room at the big meetings.

In 1934, at the seventeenth congress of the party, was the first time no resolution came to a vote. By a show of hands, the delegates passed a motion resolving to let themselves "be guided by the ideas and objectives proposed in the speeches of Comrade Stalin." This sanctioned the total domination of the party by the secretary general. But every coin has another side. This absolute power, despotic and already tyrannical, which had slowly asserted itself over the past ten years, alarmed some of the delegates. The election of the members of the Central Committee by secret ballot was the occasion for a last flicker of life. The victory went to Stalin and Kirov. The official proclamation was that they had received the votes of all the delegates but three. What really happened was quite different: two hundred and sixty delegates, or over a quarter of the total, had crossed out Stalin's name. The organizer of the congress, Kaganovich, was terrified; he decided to burn the ballots and announce the same number of votes for Stalin that had actually been won by Kirov. Naturally, this behind-the-scenes transaction did not escape Stalin's notice; the vote triggered the bloody process that would lead to the great purges. The "rotation of officers" was beginning. Through the trapdoor that now yawned at our feet disappeared the vital forces of the revolution. At the head of the list were those who had taken part in the seventeenth congress. Out of the 139 members of the Central Committee who had been elected, 110 were arrested during the next few years. To unleash the purge, there had to be a pretext; since none existed, one had to be invented. On December 1, 1934, Kirov was assassinated.

Kirov had been secretary of the party for the Leningrad region for many years. Stalin had sent him to Leningrad in 1925 to combat Zinoviev's influence. Kirov was an uncompli-cated, easy-going man; he was popular; the opposition to Stalin had crystallized around his name, as the seventeenth congress made clear. There is no doubt that a democratic election would have carried Kirov to the head of the party; no one realized then, though, that this was the principal reason for his assassination. Stalin eliminated a rival and justified the purge at the same time: the martyrdom of Kirov served as a pretext for the elimination of his supporters. The repression—which was immediate, and led by Stalin himself—ended in a bloodbath. One hundred persons, ac-cused of conspiracy to arm the assassin Nikolaiev, were executed immediately. A trial was hastily arranged for the 15th and 16th of January; Zinoviev and Kamenev were dragged to the defendants' bench. They acknowledged that as the former leaders of the opposition, they bore the moral responsibility for the crime. They were sentenced to ten and five years, respectively, in prison.

At the university, we did not believe the assassination had been the work of an organized group, but the act of a fanatic. No one, in any case, had any idea of what lay ahead for us. The assassination of Kirov was Stalin's Reichstag fire.

On January 18, 1935, the central office of the Communist Party sent all local leaders the directive to "mobilize their forces to destroy hostile elements." This vague term, "hostile elements," gave the NKVD *carte blanche*. To uncover these "elements," the regime encouraged suspicion and informing. The press dutifully called for culprits. Hundreds of articles encouraged Soviet citizens to "speak the language of truth," which meant that their next-door neighbors, their fellow workers, the passenger on the bus, hurrying pedestrians—all became suspects. Observing, watching, and denouncing became a plague that swept the country. All levels of the population were affected. My son, Michel, then a student in a special boarding school for the children of Cominternians, told me a story that showed me how far the psychosis of spying had advanced.

One fine day, one of those missionaries of Bolshevism who had returned to Moscow came to school to see his son Misha. As was customary when a parent visited the school, there was a party. Before he left, the father told Misha, "I'll come back for you in two weeks." The next day, he was arrested.

Time passed. The child asked about his father. The school principal avoided the question at first, but finally he called all the children together and gave them this explanation:

"Remember the party we had a little while ago in honor of Misha's father? Well, that wasn't Misha's father you saw, but a spy who was pretending to be him. Misha's real father was killed by the capitalists. So, children, as our comrade Stalin says, we must redouble our vigilance to unmask the enemies of the people."

Next came the trials. Former Bolsheviks and friends of Lenin were accused of the impossible, turned into spies for the English, the French, the Polish—what difference did the country make? The evidence? Manufactured, trumped up, crude. At each trial, the prosecutor would name the members of the Politburo who had almost been assassinated by the defendants. The list varied. Sometimes at the next trial you found that those who had been "threatened" by some

conspiracy a few months earlier were now in the defendants'
box, accused of terrorism in their turn. This tragic spectacle,
whose obvious unreality should have opened the eyes of the
dullest, created terror in the hearts of Soviet citizens. An
incredible collective psychosis, maintained by the entire state
machinery, took hold of the country. The tide of excess and
unreason destroyed everything in its path. Why did communists like Kamenev, Zinoviev, and Bukharin confess? For
millions of people in the world, this question remained
unanswered for a very long time. Even in the Soviet Union,
the heavy veil of lies and falsification was not lifted until
much later and, even then, only in part.

The flagrant injustice, however, of the fates reserved for a
few dozen victims of the trials should not make us lose sight
of the fact that the repression affected millions of Soviet
citizens. For them, not even a confession was required—
because there was not even the pretense of a trial.

The Stalin regime failed to achieve any of its constructive
plans, whether for economic development, collectivization,
or industrialization. On the other hand, its plan for annihilat-
ing the leadership was carried out beyond anyone's expectations. The "rotation of officers" decreed by Stalin implied
that anyone who had occupied any sort of post within the
party was to be liquidated. The purge was organized scientifically: category by category, district by district, department by
department, discipline by discipline. Each victim brought his
companions, friends, and acquaintances down with him
when he fell.

The Piatnitski case is a perfect example of the way the
repression operated. Piatnitski was an old Bolshevik and a
close collaborator of Lenin's. After the creation of the Comintern, he became one of its principal leaders. A great organizer, he had been appointed head of the personnel section. He
selected and trained official representatives of the Comintern
and sent them into every country. Early in 1937, he was
arrested and convicted of being a German spy. I did not find
out the truth about this matter until 1942, when, as a prisoner
of the Gestapo, I was interrogated by the man who had

mounted the accusation against him. All the documents proving Piatnitski's guilt were forgeries manufactured by German counterespionage. The chiefs of Nazi counterespionage had decided to take advantage of the paranoia raging in the Soviet Union by inventing a German agent in the central leadership of the party. Why Piatnitski? Simply because the Germans knew that through him the whole of the personnel department of the Comintern would be liquidated.

Piatnitski was well known in Germany, where he had gone on a mission with Radek after the October Revolution. The Gestapo had arrested two militants of the German Communist Party who had been sent by the Comintern. Their arrest was kept secret—the two agents subsequently changed their allegiance and continued to work within the German Communist Party. One of them informed the NKVD that he had proof of the treachery of certain leaders of the Comintern. Then he sent Moscow a file on Piatnitski "proving" that after the First World War, he had made contact with German Intelligence. In the climate that reigned in Moscow at this time, this was enough to condemn an old militant. Once the machine was set in motion, the wheels turned by themselves. Along with Piatnitski, hundreds of leaders of the Comintern disappeared. It was one of the best favors Stalin ever did Hitler!

Foreign communists watched the tidal wave of repression build and break as privileged spectators. Far from resisting, the leaders of the communist parties, who presided at the head of the Comintern, overlooked and even encouraged practices that no longer had anything to do with socialism. I was in Paris when Marcel Cachin and Paul Vaillant-Couturier, who had attended the second of the Moscow trials at the head of a delegation from the French Communist Party, reported on the trial during a big meeting in the Salle Wagram. What did Marcel Cachin and Vaillant-Couturier do? They paid homage to the clearsightedness of Stalin, who had unmasked and dismantled the "terrorist group."

"We have heard Zinoviev and Kamenev accuse themselves of the worst crimes," exclaimed Vaillant-Couturier. "Do you

think those men would have confessed if they were innocent?"

Cachin and Vaillant-Couturier, like all the members of the
French Communist Party, relied exclusively on Soviet sources; but were they not aware that the three big trials were only
a vast spectacle that occupied the front of the stage and that
in the wings, without trials, without judgment, without
confession, thousands of communist militants simply disappeared? How could they have ignored it, when representatives of foreign communist parties who were in Moscow were
also disappearing? Several thousand communists from other
countries who were involved in militant activity in the
Comintern, the Profintern, the Peasants' International, the
Young People's International, and the Women's Organization were living in the Soviet capital at the time; 90 per cent
were liquidated. In addition, thousands of political refugees
from all over the world found in the Soviet Union the torture
and death that they had fled in their own countries. By what
right were all these persons, who did not belong to the
Communist Party of the Soviet Union, sentenced? The fact is
that the ruling group in the Soviet Union did not merely
aspire to be the ideological leaders of the international
communist movement. They also assumed the privilege of
giving directives to "brother parties," appointing their leaders, and sending them to death.

In the Comintern building, we had exclusive access to
rumors—alas, generally well founded—that kept us almost
completely informed about the situation in the country. It
was there that I learned about the Bela Kun case. The leader
of the short-lived Hungarian-Soviet Republic in 1919, a
much-beloved hero, Bela Kun was a member of the executive
committee of the Communist International and in charge of
the Balkan countries.

One day in the spring of 1937, Bela Kun arrived at a
meeting of the executive committee of the Comintern.
Around the table were Dimitrov, Manuilski, Varga, Pik,
Togliatti, and a leader of the French Communist Party.
Manuilski took the floor and said that he had an important

announcement to make. According to documents furnished by the NKVD, Bela Kun had been a Rumanian spy since 1921. Everyone there knew Bela Kun, everyone was aware of his devotion to the cause of socialism; only an hour before, they had been warmly shaking his hand. Yet not one of them protested or even asked for further information. The meeting was adjourned. Outside the building, a car from the NKVD was waiting for Bela Kun, who was never seen again.

A few months later: the scene had not changed, and the actors playing the prosecutors were the same. There were two empty places at the table now, those of the representatives of the Polish Communist Party. The inevitable Manuilski explained very seriously that all the leaders of the Polish party had been agents of the dictator Pilsudski since 1919. This outrageous lie was accepted without the slightest reservation.

The members of the Central Committee of the Polish Communist Party, who were on assignment in Paris or fighting in Spain, were summoned to Moscow. Ardent advocates of the formation of a united anti-fascist front to check the rise of Nazism, they assumed the summons had to do with this preoccupation—that they were going to be invited to discuss it with the Soviets. So they arrived suspecting nothing. The united anti-fascist front ended, for them, in the cellars of the NKVD, where old militants like Adolf Varsky or Lenski, who was known as the "Polish Lenin," disappeared forever. The liquidation of Bela Kun and the leaders of the Polish party was confirmed to me, with details I had not known, by survivors who shared my cell in Lubianka after the war.

In 1938 the Polish party was officially dissolved by the Communist International on the pretext that it was a favorite cover for the counterespionage activities of nationalists seeking revenge. This was an obvious subterfuge. Stalin, who was laying the groundwork for a rapprochement with Nazi Germany, knew very well that the communists of Poland would never accept this pact against nature, because it could not be carried out without strangling their country. At the same time and under similar circumstances, the Ukrainian party and the party of Belorussia in the west were also dissolved.

These decisions were made in official meetings of the International. How is it that no leader of the great parties of Europe raised his hand to call for the creation of a committee of investigation? How could they have looked on while their comrades in arms were sentenced without proof? After the twentieth congress in 1956, all these leaders feigned astonishment. To hear them, Khrushchev's report was a real revelation. In reality, they had been the knowing accomplices of the liquidations, including those of members of their own parties.

I still have memories from this dark period that time has not erased. At night in our university, where militants from all countries were living, we used to stay awake until three o'clock in the morning. At exactly that hour, headlights would pierce the darkness and sweep over the facades of the buildings.

"They're here! They're here!" When we heard that cry, a wave of anxiety would run through the dormitories. Standing at the windows, stomachs knotted with insane terror, we would watch for the cars of the NKVD to stop.

"It's not for us, they're going to the other end of the building."

Relieved for the night in this cowardly way, we could sink into restless sleep, which was haunted by high walls and iron bars. Other times, we listened panting, incapable of making the slightest gesture, hypnotized by danger, as steps came down the hall.

"They're coming." The noise got louder: dull thuds against the wall, shouts, doors slamming. They went by without stopping. But what about tomorrow?

The fear for tomorrow, the anguish that we might be living our last hours of freedom, dictated our actions. Fear, which had become our second skin, induced caution, guided us toward submission. I knew that my friends had been arrested and I said nothing. Why them? Why not me? I waited for my turn, and prepared myself for this end.

What could we do? Give up the fight? Was this conceivable, for militants who had invested their youth, their strength, and their hopes in socialism? Or on the other hand, protest, intervene? I want to cite the example of the Bulgarian representatives. They had asked to see Dimitrov, the Comintern president, and they used strong language: "If you don't do something to make the repression stop," they told him, "we'll murder that counterrevolutionary, Ejov." Ejov was the head of the NKVD.

The president of the Comintern left them no illusions. "I have no power to do anything; everything is in the hands of the NKVD."

The Bulgarians did not succeed in killing Ejov, but he killed them like rabbits.

Yugoslavs, Poles, Lithuanians, Czechs—all disappeared. By 1937, not one of the principal leaders of the German Communist Party was left, except for Wilhelm Pieck and Walter Ulbricht. The repressive madness had no limits. The Korean section was decimated; the delegates from India had disappeared; the representatives of the Chinese Communist Party had been arrested. The glow of October was being extinguished in the shadows of underground chambers. The revolution had degenerated into a system of terror and horror; the ideals of socialism were ridiculed in the name of a fossilized dogma which the executioners still had the effrontery to call Marxism.

And yet we went along, sick at heart, but passive, caught up in machinery we had set in motion with our own hands. Mere cogs in the apparatus, terrorized to the point of madness, we became the instruments of our own subjugation. All those who did not rise up against the Stalinist machine are responsible, collectively responsible. I am no exception to this verdict.

But who did protest at that time? Who rose up to voice his outrage?

The Trotskyites can lay claim to this honor. Following the example of their leader, who was rewarded for his obstinacy with the end of an ice-axe, they fought Stalinism to the death, and they were the only ones who did. By the time of the great purges, they could only shout their rebellion in the freezing wastelands where they had been dragged in order to be exterminated. In the camps, their conduct was admirable. But their voices were lost in the tundra.

Today, the Trotskyites have a right to accuse those who once howled along with the wolves. Let them not forget, however, that they had the enormous advantage over us of having a coherent political system capable of replacing Stalinism. They had something to cling to in the midst of their profound distress at seeing the revolution betrayed. They did not "confess," for they knew that their confession would serve neither the party nor socialism.

The former leaders of Palestine's Communist Party, all of whom I had known, also disappeared during the purges.

In 1929, the directors of the Comintern had given the Palestinian Communist Party the watchword "Bolshevization and Arabization." Since the party leaders were Jewish, they were all called back to Moscow. One after another my old friends Birman, Lechtsinski, Ben-Yehuda, and Meier-Kuperman were liquidated. I particularly want to talk about Daniel Averbuch. Born in Moscow, Averbuch was sent to the Near East to promote the communist movement and had become the dominant personality of the Communist Party in Palestine.

Called back like the others, Averbuch had then been sent to Rumania; later he was forbidden to leave Russia. The last time I saw him, in 1937, he was head of the political section in the Piatigorski state farm. This appointment was a mockery. Since he had never been interested in agricultural problems, he was totally incompetent in this area. Of course, in the eyes of leaders who wanted only to get him and his comrades out of the way, the problem of his abilities was secondary. The man I saw before me was unrecognizable. Broken, but fully conscious of what was going on, he lived like a condemned man whose execution has merely been postponed.

"One day," he told me, "I'll get a telephone call asking me to come to Moscow."

He was not mistaken. Some time later, the gates of the infamous Lubianka closed behind him.

Averbuch's son came to see me. He spoke to me out of anger and indignation, but at the same time he was perfectly lucid: "My father was accused of being a counterrevolutionary, but I say that it is the leaders of the country, starting with Stalin, who are the real counterrevolutionaries." He was arrested too, on the pretext that he had belonged to a group that had tried to assassinate Stalin. He was asked to admit that his father had been a spy. He refused and was sent to one of the worst camps, where he died. Averbuch's brother, who worked for the same newspaper I did, was arrested too. Maria, Averbuch's wife, went to live with her brother, who was Vice-Minister of Public Education. They thought they would be arrested at any moment—they stayed awake every night until two or three o'clock, waiting for the police to come and get them. Maria's brother could not endure it. His nerves gave way, he could no longer sleep at all; he ran around the apartment shouting, "My God, my God, will we ever know why they want to arrest us?" He never knew. They took him away one morning at dawn, and the darkness closed around him.

Many years later I saw Maria Averbuch again. She had become a very old lady, and with a protective gesture that must have stayed with her through all the ordeals she had suffered, she hugged a worn-out handbag to her breast. It contained treasures she had saved from the cataclysm, images of her past, photographs of her family.

"My husband, my sons, my brother, my husband's brother—they were all arrested and assassinated," she said, "I'm the only one still alive. But you know, in spite of what happened, I haven't stopped believing in communism."

Other information reached me about the calvary of the Palestinian communists: about Sonia Raginska, one of the best militants, very intelligent and active, who was thrown into prison and sank into madness; about Efraim Lechtsinski, a member of the Central Committee of the Palestinian Communist Party for years who, with great devotion and skill, had initiated young militants in Marxism. Every time he was about to be taken before the examining officer, they would throw into his cell a prisoner covered with blood and barely conscious who was returning from interrogation. This was one of the methods the men of the NKVD had perfected to impress militants whom they were about to question.

"You saw the other man," the examiner would then shout
at him. "You saw the state he was in; do you want the same
thing to happen to you?"

Efraim Lechtsinski could not hold out against this horrible
coercion. He went mad too. He ran back and forth in his cell,
beating his head against the wall, repeating over and over,
"What other name have I forgotten? What other name have I
forgotten?"

All the members of the Central Committee of the Palestinian party were purged except List and Knossov, who had not
gone to the Soviet Union. One survived, Joseph Berger
(Barsilai)—after a stay of twenty-one years in the Gulag. Of
two or three hundred militant party leaders, only about
twenty survived. It was not until 1968, more than ten years
after Khrushchev denounced Stalin and exposed his crimes at
the twentieth congress of the Soviet Communist Party, that
the Israeli Communist Party, the Maki, rendered homage to
the leaders assassinated during the Stalinist purges.

In the USSR, the repression struck the Jewish community,
which, like all the other national minorities, was decimated.
Nevertheless, the October Revolution had profoundly
changed the lives of the Jews. In our anti-Zionist propaganda, we communists of Jewish origin insisted proudly on the
respect shown the national and cultural rights of our community in the Soviet Union. When I arrived in Moscow in 1932,
the Jews and the other national minorities still enjoyed a
number of rights. Cultural life flourished in entire regions
where there was a Jewish minority; in the districts I visited in
the Ukraine and the Crimea, our language was the official
language. The Jewish press was prolific: five or six dailies and
several weeklies in the Soviet Union as a whole. Dozens of
Jewish writers published their works in editions of millions of
copies, and many universities offered courses in Jewish
literature.

I was also encouraged by what I saw in the economic
realm. In the Crimea, for example, the collective farms in the
predominantly Jewish regions were functioning very well.

They were taking advantage of the proximity of the health resorts and cultivating citrus fruits to sell to the population. The paths of assimilation were wide open to those Jews who desired to take them. No restrictions were placed on the lives, activities, or aspirations of Jews living in large cities like Moscow, Leningrad, and Minsk. Discrimination did not exist in social life; no quota system prevailed at the university. In comparison with the obscurantist policies of the czars, considerable progress had been made. It was only after 1935 that massive repression descended on the Jews. Beginning in regions with heavily Jewish populations, it soon spread to the whole country.

After I had finished my studies at Marchlevski University, where I had specialized in journalism, I was assigned, by decision of the Central Committee of the Russian Communist Party, to work on the daily newspaper *Der Emes* (*The Truth*), the Yiddish edition of *Pravda*. There were some very distinguished Jewish writers on the editorial staff, under the direction of an excellent journalist, Moshe Litvakov.

I was put in charge of a column on party activities. I often wrote articles and sometimes the editorial. One day the accountant came up to me in the hall and said, "When are you going to pick up your money?"

"What money? I've collected my salary regularly."

"I'm not talking about that, I mean the bonuses for your articles." The next day he handed me a sum of money larger than my salary. The whole editorial staff was on this system: we were far from the "worker's salary" advocated by Lenin. Lenin insisted that party officials should earn no more than a skilled worker.

Every week there was a meeting of the Central Committee, which was attended by representatives of all the Moscow papers. My editor in chief sent me to several of these meetings. At one of them, in 1935, Stetski—head of the press department of the Central Committee—announced that he had something important to tell us:

"I must inform you of a personal attitude on the part of

Comrade Stalin," be began. "Comrade Stalin is very unhappy about the cult that has sprung up around his personality. Every article begins and ends with a quotation from him. Comrade Stalin doesn't like this. Moreover, he has had an investigation made of those letters of praise signed by thousands of citizens that are sent to the editors of newspapers, and he has discovered that this correspondence has been solicited by the party, which sets a quota for each district. I have been asked to inform you," Stetski went on, "that Comrade Stalin does not approve of these methods and that he asks that they be discontinued."

I was very impressed by this speech, and when I got back I reported it to my editor in chief, Litvakov, who answered with a smile, "That will last for a few weeks."

"What, you don't believe it?"

"Just wait. You'll see."

Three weeks later, I represented the paper at another meeting, at which Stetski reported a decision made by the leaders of the party. "The Politburo understands very well the sincere desire of Comrade Stalin to do away with the cult that has sprung up around his personality, but the Politburo does not approve of these reservations. In the difficult times we are going through, Comrade Stalin has his hand firmly on the rudder; we must thank him and congratulate him for overcoming the difficulties of his task. The press must do everything it can to call attention to the role of Comrade Stalin."

When I reported these remarks to Litvakov, he was not at all surprised.

"I told you those instructions wouldn't last long. Stalin knew the Politburo would adopt that attitude, but he wanted to make sure the journalists knew just how modest he is."

Litvakov was quite aware of what was happening to the revolution. The work he had been entrusted with, which he performed thoroughly out of his professional conscience, did not prevent him from seeing things as they were, or from expressing his opinion in no uncertain terms when he so chose. In 1935, I remember, he had asked Radek, whose services were always available, to write an article for the anniversary issue in October.

Radek complied, of course, and sent in his article. Litvakov read it and said coldly, "We're not going to publish a piece of crap like this in our paper."

The article was nothing but a string of praises extolling the glory of Stalin. A few days later, I happened to be in Litvakov's office when Radek phoned to express his amazement that his bravura piece hadn't been published.

"Listen, Radek," the editor told him, "this is the last time I'll ask you for an article. If you think I'm going to publish it because you signed it, you're very sadly mistaken. It's worthless; the rankest amateur would have done better."

It was not with impunity that Litvakov affronted the vanity of a party leader and defied the omnipotence of the party. He was one of the first to be eliminated. From then on each month claimed its cartload of the condemned. Hachine, Averbuch's brother, disappeared; his crime was having lived in Germany. So did Sprach, who succeeded Litvakov as editor in chief and against whom there was no particular charge. The atmosphere at *Der Emes,* once so relaxed and open, now became charged with anxiety and suspicion. During 1937, fear became a permanent presence. Journalists arrived in the morning and shut themselves into their offices for exactly the length of time they were supposed to spend at the paper; then they went home again, not saying a word to anyone. At the start of 1938, the arrest of Strelitz, an old journalist who had fought in the Red Army during the civil war, shocked us all. Whenever one of ours disappeared, a hideous ritual resembling a funeral took place. The whole staff assembled for a self-criticism session. We each took a turn reciting the same refrain and pronouncing a public "Mea Culpa." The text did not vary by a word: "Comrade, our vigilance has slackened; a spy worked among us over the years and we did not unmask him."

In accordance with custom, we were summoned for Strelitz' "funeral," and the self-criticism began. Someone remembered a passing remark he had heard from the mouth of the "culprit" but had failed to report; another had noticed some odd behavior and admitted he had not raised it with the rest of us. We were indulging in this inglorious activity when in the midst of our litanies, we noticed our comrade Strelitz. He had been standing silently by the door for several minutes, listening as we recited our accusations, disowning him, denouncing him as a "spy." This unexpected confrontation, by all indications planned and organized by the NKVD, who had deliberately released him—this sudden apparition cast a glacial chill. Everyone fell silent. We did not know what to do.

Strelitz stood there silently. One by one, without a word, we left the room, with bowed heads, too ashamed to meet our comrade's eyes. At that moment I realized what depths we had sunk to, how much we had become the robots and accomplices of Stalinist repression. Fear had become a part of us, it had laid siege to our souls. We had ceased independent thinking. The NKVD had triumphed, it no longer needed to be physically present. It was there, master of our brains, our reflexes, and our behavior.

More than anyone else, the Jews paid their tribute to the repression, in the country at large as well as in our circle at the university. I have already described how the party had encouraged Jewish immigration into the district of Birobidzhan, primarily between 1931 and 1932. Above all they had encouraged the transfer of leaders and intellectuals. Many students who came out of our university left for this region, for which Professor Liberberg, a scholar very well known in the USSR, had been given responsibility. The repression was unleashed suddenly and was carried out by an NKVD team. Through two witnesses of this terrible, relentless purge, I learned how the arrests and executions were conducted. With the rudimentary logic of mechanized inquisitors, veritable robots of injustice elevated to dogma, the NKVD decreed that all Jews born in Poland were salaried spies of the Polish government, and that those who came from Palestine were in the pay of the English. On the basis of these criteria, they pronounced sentences without appeal that invariably ended in front of the firing squad. Our old comrade of the Polish party, Schwarzbart, one of the secretaries of the autonomous Jewish district of Birobidzhan, went before the public prosecutors. He was thrown into prison, where he became almost blind. One morning at dawn he was taken out into the yard and placed before the firing squad. Before he died, he shouted his faith in the revolution, and just as the bullets laid this old communist militant in the dust, from the cells rose the powerful strains of the *Internationale*.

There were thousands of communists who, like Schwarzbart, crossed the threshold of death with their heads held high. Esther Frumkina, an ardent militant, had been rector of our university for many years. Although she was very ill at the time, she was arrested in 1937 and imprisoned in Lubianka. During the preliminary examination, they tried to confront her with a witness who had testified against her. But Esther, braving the judges and the guards, threw herself at the accuser and spat in his face. She was sentenced without appeal and died inside the walls of Lubianka.

During this same year, 1937, Marchlevski University, the university for national minorities, was abolished and replaced by a pseudo institute for the study of foreign languages that was controlled with an iron hand. The gates of the university closed around the dead bodies of our comrades.

The Murder of the Red Army

It was in the summer of 1937 that the Moscow papers announced the arrest of Marshal Mikhail Nikolaievich Tukhachevski and seven generals. These leaders of the Red Army, heroes of the civil war and old communists, had been accused of deliberately working for the defeat of the Soviet Union and of paving the way for capitalism. The next day the whole world learned that Tukhachevski and Generals Iakir, Uborevich, Primakov, Eidemann, Feldmann, Kork, and Putna had been sentenced to death and executed. A ninth high-ranking officer, General Gamarnik, head of the political division of the army, had committed suicide. The Red Army was decapitated.

The truth was that for several years there had been a profound disagreement between Tukhachevski and his staff on one hand, and the directors of the party on the other. Stalin's official theory was that if another war should take place, it would be outside the territory of the Soviet Union. But Tukhachevski, who was observing the military preparations of the Third Reich with anxiety, believed that a worldwide conflict was inevitable, and that the Soviet Union should be prepared for it. At a meeting of the Soviet high command in 1936, he had expressed his conviction that it might very well be waged on Soviet soil.

History was to prove that Tukhachevski was right too soon. At the time when he was accused, all the opposition had been liquidated, and Stalin ruled the country with an iron hand. The Red Army was the last bastion to be removed; it alone still eluded his control. For the Stalin regime, liquidating the leaders of the army became an urgent objective. Since the leaders in question were old Bolsheviks who had distinguished themselves during the October Revolution, and since an accusation like "Trotskyite" or "Zinovievist" against a

Tukhachevski would not stick, it was necessary to strike hard and with great strength. Stalin used the complicity of Hitler to murder the army of the Russian people.

As in the case of Piatnitski, it was Giering of the Gestapo, head of the Sonderkommando and later in charge of combating the Red Orchestra during the Second World War, who told me in 1943 the details of the operation mounted against Tukhachevski.

The scene was Berlin, 1936. Heydrich, chief of Intelligence, received a visit from a former officer in the czarist army, General Skoblin. This general without an army was consoling himself for his inactivity by playing double agent on a grand scale. For many years he had been working for Soviet Intelligence in White Russian circles in Paris, while flirting with German Intelligence on the side. In short, an extremely suspicious character. The news he brought Heydrich was momentous: he had it on good authority that Marshal Tukhachevski was plotting an armed insurrection against Stalin. Heydrich passed this on to the Nazi high command, who discussed what course to follow. There were only two options: allow the head of the Soviet Army to go ahead with his plan, or warn Stalin and, as a bonus, give him proof of the marshal's collusion with the Wehrmacht. The second solution was chosen. It was not difficult to show that Tukhachevski had had contact with the chiefs of staff of the Wehrmacht, since before the Nazi rise to power regular encounters were organized between the two armies, and the Soviet government had even established military schools for the training of German officers. A dossier was prepared that revealed, with the aid of altered documents, that Tukhachevski was preparing a military coup in liaison with the German military leaders. The preparation of these revealing documents was not the work of a day. After the "proof" was assembled by Hitler's entourage, it was a spy's mission to get it into the hands of the leaders of the USSR. If we are to believe the memoirs of Schellenberg, then head of German counterespionage, the house the documents were in was burned and a Czech agent who had been alerted supposedly found the papers among the ashes. Another version has it that the Germans sold the documents to the Russians, using the Czechs as intermediaries.

By the end of May, 1937, the Tukhachevski file had found its way to Stalin's desk. The moustachioed Georgian had every reason to be satisfied. At his request, the Germans had provided him with all the material necessary for eliminating the man he had sworn to kill. In fact, Skoblin—I am still giving Giering's version—had not gone to see Heydrich on his own initiative. Stalin and Hitler had divided up the work. The first had had the idea for the plot, and the second had carried it out. Stalin wanted to break the last organized force opposed to his policies; Hitler was seizing an unexpected opportunity to decapitate the Red Army. The Piatnitski case had taught the Fuhrer that the purge would not be restricted to a few high-ranking officers. He was now convinced that the wave of repression would convulse the whole of the Red Army, and that it would take years to replace the murdered officers. This would free his hands in the east long enough to win the war in the west. As early as 1937, the rapprochement that would be confirmed by the German-Soviet pact was already taking shape.

In August, 1937, two months after the liquidation of Marshal Tukhachevski, Stalin called a conference of the political leaders of the Army to plan a purge of "enemies of the people" from military circles. It was the signal for a massacre. The blood of Red Army soldiers flowed: 13 out of 19 commanders of army corps, 110 out of 135 commanders of divisions and brigades, half the commanders of regiments, and most of the political commissars were executed. The Red Army, bled white, was hardly an army at all now, and it would not be again for years.

The Germans exploited this situation to the full, instructing their Intelligence Services to convey to Paris and London the alarming facts—and they really were alarming—on the state of the Red Army after the purge. I am inclined to think that the French and English chiefs of staff were less than impatient to seal a military alliance with the Soviet Union because the weakness of the Soviet Army had become clear to them. From then on, the way was clear for the signing of the pact between Stalin and Hitler.

10

I became a communist because I am a Jew.

In my contact with the workers of Dombrova, I had seen the extent of capitalist exploitation. In Marxism, I found the definitive answer to the Jewish question that had obsessed me since childhood. In my judgment, only a socialist society could put an end to racism and anti-Semitism, and allow the complete cultural development of the Jewish community. I studied anti-Semitism, its genesis and its mechanisms, from the pogroms of czarist Russia to the Dreyfus case. For me, Nazism was its most obvious twentieth-century manifestation. I saw the obscene beast growing—and I worried about the world's apathy. In Germany, the workers' parties were busy fighting each other instead of uniting against the common enemy. Many people felt that, once in power, Hitler would put away his uniform, forget *Mein Kampf* and turn his Storm Troopers into camp counselors. The German and the international bourgeoisie were inclined to think that a bit of housecleaning wouldn't hurt in a country where the Reds were so active.

Then, on January 30, 1933, Adolf Hitler was named Chancellor of the Reich. For a communist militant like me, the alarm bells rang. The door was open for barbarism, and the mask of the democrat that the little Austrian corporal had worn fell away. From now on, Germany—and soon all of Europe—would learn to live under the boot.

On February 27, 1933, the Reichstag burned. Within minutes after the fire started, Goebbels and Goering were on the scene. The next night, ten thousand communist and socialist militants were arrested. New elections were held on March 5th. Goering had warned, "In my future actions, I shall take no account of legal precedents. We need not be concerned with fictional justice. I shall give orders to destroy, as necessary." Consequently, all votes by communists were declared null and void. In spite of this atmosphere of terror, the communists and socialists received twelve million votes. The other parties got ten million, and the Nazis seventeen million. By Hitler's order, the communist mandates were invalidated. Ernst Thaelmann, secretary general of the German Communist Party, was arrested, and Dimitrov shortly thereafter.

The chain of events was ineluctable. By March 23rd, the Weimar Constitution was no more.

Germany had hesitated between the red and the brown. Now a torrent of mud submerged everything. Hitler, setting about to destroy the German workers' movement, sent his Storm Troops into action. On May 2, 1933, the headquarters of the labor unions—where it was believed that Hitler could still be stopped by a general strike—was occupied by Storm Troopers. Thousands of unionists were sent to join the communists and socialists behind barbed wire. But Hitler still lacked an arm to complete his reign of terror, and thus in April, 1934, the Gestapo was created.

Long before Hitler came to power, I had read *Mein Kampf,* much to the amusement of my friends. Later I realized that the development of Nazism had been described there in minute detail. Two themes recurred and recurred in Hitler's book: "crush international Jewry" and "destroy communism." As a Jew and a communist, I felt doubly menaced.

On the one hand, in January, 1935, the law on racial purity was issued; the persecutions of our German comrades were legalized. On the other, I was quite sure that Nazism would not long be confined inside the boundaries of the Third Reich, but would carry death and war into the rest of the world. The storm was approaching, and it was not hard to forecast. On January 13, 1935, the Nazi government made military service compulsory. Hitler threw the Treaty of Versailles in the wastebasket. The same year, 90 percent of the inhabitants of the Saar, which had been administered by the League of Nations, approved annexation of their province to the Reich.

The western democracies refused to look the danger in the

face. They temporized, waiting for a miracle, and did nothing, believing that public disapproval could turn the tide of Nazism. The more they hesitated, the more enterprising Hitler became. On March 7, 1936, German troops entered the Rhineland. There was no reaction. At the beginning of July, 1936, the Spanish Civil War began and, with it, World War II. The French and English governments, in the name of nonintervention, allowed the German and Italian legions to put down the Spanish revolution. Finally, in November, 1936, Germany signed the anti-Comintern pact, and Italy signed a year later.

The world had hesitated to check the brown plague in its early stages; it had allowed the disease to spread, and the contagion was gaining. On May 1, 1937, en route to an assignment in France, I stopped off again in Berlin. What a sight to discover! The spectacle of the streets was unbearable to me: thousands of workers in military helmets; thousands of young men carrying Nazi banners, singing—in full voice—Nazi hymns. Stupefied, standing on the sidewalk, I tried, and failed, to understand. What madness had possessed the German people? In that moment, hearing the loud songs all Europe would soon come to recognize, I was convinced that only a terrible explosion, a worldwide conflagration, could put an end to Nazism. In this pitiless struggle, on which the whole future of humanity would hang, I decided to take my own stand. In the front lines.

I found my opportunity through the Intelligence Service of the Soviet Army. Headquarters was not far from Moscow's Red Square, at No. 19 Znamenskaia Street. No. 19 was a small building called, because of its color, the chocolate house. In those days Soviet Intelligence did not operate like a western intelligence service. Created during the civil war, Russian Intelligence had not had time to train real agents, and so depended primarily on communist militants in all countries.

Soviet Intelligence was no exception to the basic rule that every secret service in search of information tries to recruit agents in the countries where it wants to work. Inevitably, the Red Army had at its disposal thousands of communists who regarded themselves not as spies but as fighters in the vanguard of world revolution. Soviet Military Intelligence preserved this international character until 1935, and the commitment of the men who worked in its ranks can be understood only in the context of world revolution. These militants—as I can testify, because I knew them well—were totally disinterested. They never talked about salary or money. They were civilians who were devoting themselves to a cause, just as they might have done in a labor union.

The Red Army Intelligence Service was under the direction of General Jan Berzin. An old Bolshevik, he had been sentenced to death twice before the revolution and had escaped both times. During the civil war, he had commanded a regiment of Latvians and Estonians in charge of guarding Lenin and the government. Internationalist, the Bolshevik leaders certainly were, to have entrusted their protection to foreigners!

The Comintern had its own parallel network, with an antenna in every country to gather political and economic information. The primary reason for this dual system was that, for a long time the USSR had no diplomatic relations with other countries. Information is usually transmitted through diplomatic channels; the Soviet Union made up for this deficiency through their local sections.

The third component of the Soviet intelligence system was the NKVD. In charge of internal security, its original function was to search for foreign agents in Soviet territory. In time, its powers expanded. It was entrusted with the security of Soviet citizens in foreign countries, then later with keeping an eye on the White Russians, who continued to conspire everywhere. In the end, the NKVD had as many external as internal activities; often it infiltrated agents into Military Intelligence—the two services competed with each other.

By the end of the revolution, the foreign embassies in Moscow had become centers of counterrevolutionary activity. At the British Embassy, for example, there was a certain Lockart, a megalomaniac from the British Intelligence Ser-

vice whose fantasy was nothing less than to overthrow the
Soviet government. He had made contact with extremist
elements who dreamed of crossing swords with the Bolsheviks, and Berzin had learned that he was trying to recruit
military personnel, soldiers and officers, to take part in the
plot. Berzin went to Lockart and told him he commanded a
regiment of men who asked only to go over to the other side.
He claimed his men were unhappy with the new regime; the
disillusionment of the masses who had been taken in by the
revolutionaries was complete; Russia was heading for a
catastrophe; something had to be done about public safety.
And Berzin wondered aloud, in front of Lockart, what could
be done to halt the disastrous course of events.

Lockart, who had been somewhat suspicious at the beginning of the conversation, fell into the trap. Little by little,
they worked out a plan designed to drive out the group in
power. An enterprise of this scope required substantial funds;
simply remunerating the soldiers who participated would
require a considerable investment. Accordingly, Berzin suggested an immediate "down payment" of ten million rubles.
Lockart arranged payment without batting an eye. After that
they went into the details. The plan was simple and radical:
surround the building where the government had its offices
and arrest the members. They even arranged what fate would
be reserved for Lenin—a well-known orthodox priest would
provide a church for the funeral service.

Berzin put the money in a safe place. On the appointed day
everything went off as planned. The rebel group marched on
the government building; a regiment of the Red Army
intercepted and surrounded it; Lockart was arrested and
deported to England.

This was Berzin's first great coup. After that he devoted
himself completely to organizing Soviet Intelligence. When I
met him, in December, 1936, he was already its undisputed
leader.

Berzin was universally respected. His personality in no way
corresponded to the stereotyped image of the professional
intelligence man. He used to say, "An agent in the Soviet

Intelligence Service must be endowed with three qualities: a cool head, a warm heart, and nerves of steel." He attached the greatest importance to human values in recruiting. Contrary to the custom in intelligence services, he never left his men in the lurch—never would he have sacrificed a single one. To him, the agents were human beings and, above all, communists.

Berzin always had personal relationships with his agents in foreign countries, so it was natural that he became very close friends with one of the great men of Soviet Intelligence, Richard Sorge. Sorge told me about his first interview with Berzin when I ran into him in Brussels in 1938. Sorge was an extremely intelligent and valuable man. He had once been a militant in the German Communist Party and was the author of several books on economics. He was carrying out a mission in China when he was called to Moscow in 1933. There Berzin had arranged for them to meet in a chess club that was popular among Germans. The meeting took place a few days after Hitler's takeover.

Right at the outset, Sorge told me, Berzin went to the heart of the matter: "What, in your opinion, is the greatest danger the Soviet Union faces at this time?"

"Even if we grant a confrontation with Japan," Sorge answered, "I think the real threat comes from Nazi Germany."

Berzin went on, "Well, that's why we sent for you. We want you to take up residence in Japan."

"Why?"

"Rapprochement between Germany and Japan is coming; in Tokyo, you will learn a great deal about military preparations."

Sorge, who was beginning to understand the nature of his assignment, interrupted Berzin: "What, go to Japan and become a spy? But I'm a journalist!"

"You say you don't want to be a spy, but what's your idea of a spy? What you call a 'spy' is a man who tries to get information about the weak points of the enemy so that his government can exploit them. We aren't looking for war, but

we want to know about the enemy's preparations and detect
the chinks in his armor so we won't be caught short if he
should attack." Berzin went on, "Our objective is for you to
create a group in Japan determined to fight for peace. Your
work will be to recruit important Japanese, and you will do
everything in your power to see that their country is not
dragged into the war against the Soviet Union."

"What name will I use?"

"Your own."

Sorge could not believe his ears. Berzin's assistants, present at the meeting, could not hide their amazement either:
"But he has a German police record for taking part in militant
activities for the party!" Sorge had, in fact, been a militant
with the German Communist Party in 1918–1919. "It wasn't
yesterday, but you can count on them not to have lost track of
him."

"I know," Berzin answered. "I'm aware that we're taking a
risk, but in my opinion, a man always walks better in his own
shoes. I'm also aware that the Nazis have just inherited the
police files. But a lot of water will flow under the bridges of
the Moskva before Sorge's file comes to light. Besides, even if
the Nazis find out sooner than we expect, what's to keep a
man who was a communist fifteen years ago from changing
his political opinions?"

Berzin then turned to his assistant in charge of Germany
and said, "Arrange to have him hired as a Tokyo correspondent of the *Frankfurter Zeitung*." To Sorge he said, "You see,
this way you'll feel at home and not as if you're playing spy."

Berzin had a golden rule: an agent's cover must not be
merely a façade. Sorge was duly hired as a correspondent; his
articles were very well received in official Japanese circles,
and threw open the doors that seemed most inaccessible.
First he met the Reich's ambassador to Tokyo, and then the
military attaché. Before long they thought of him as one of
them. The most confidential communications from Berlin to
its representatives in foreign countries passed through his
hands.

Two or three years before the war, the Gestapo sent a man

to Tokyo to keep an eye on the personnel at the embassy. In no time Sorge had made "friends" with him. Then, one day, what Berzin's colleagues had been afraid of happened—the Gestapo man received the "Sorge file" from Berlin, and it made reference to his communist past.

"Well," his Gestapo "friend" remarked, "you've had quite a colorful past!"

Sorge remembered his leader's advice. "Ah, well, an error of youth. All that is so far away."

A little later he went so far as to enroll in the National Socialist Party. His game turned out to be so effective that when he was finally discovered by the Japanese, the German ambassador in Tokyo officially protested the arrest of one of his "most valuable colleagues."

11

The Fantômas case had been the reason for my hasty departure from France; now it was one reason for Western Europe to become my home—this time for a long stay.

The French police had caught up with that "phantom," Isaiah Bir, in 1932, and with my friend Alter Strom too. They were sent to prison on charges of spying for the Soviet Union. At the end of 1936 they were released, and they went to Moscow. Until then the official French version of the Fantômas case, which was accepted by the heads of Soviet Intelligence, explained the fall of Isaiah Bir's group by the infiltration of an *agent provocateur*, Riquier, who was a journalist on *l'Humanité*. Strom and his friends were convinced of Riquier's innocence. They contested this serious accusation—which by implication smeared the entire French party—and proposed that a new investigation be made in Paris. The leaders of the Comintern, anxious to clear up this festering scandal, asked Strom whether he had anyone in mind for the job. He suggested me.

"Domb has all the qualifications," he declared. "He was in Paris at the time of the incident, but he wasn't involved in it. He speaks French, he's an old militant; he'll clear up the murk."

The Comintern gave their consent and passed along the proposition to General Berzin, who made no objection. This was the occasion of my first contact with Soviet Intelligence, in order to make arrangements for my mission in France. I had two or three meetings with the man in charge of Western Europe, Colonel Stiga—"Oscar"—to finish up the details of the investigation. "It's simply a matter of getting together with the lawyers, Ferrucci and André Philip," Stiga told me. "You'll have to go over all the trial records and try to find out the truth."

At the end of our last conversation, Stiga handed me the passport of a businessman from Luxemburg and asked, "And do you have the right clothes?"

"No."

"Clothes are very important. Several of our agents were exposed because of the pleat that a Warsaw tailor used to put in the middle of the jacket collar!"

"I have friends in Antwerp. I'll stop there for a couple of days and go to a good tailor; I'll have a suit made in the French style."

"Excellent; and now the boss would like to see you."

I was shown into an enormous office with a long desk in one corner. A map of the world ran the entire length of one wall. Berzin asked me to sit down and we began by talking about Paris. Then he came to the point. "You're going to find a ton of documents in the archives of the Palais de Justice," he said. "I won't give you any advice on how to find out the truth because, actually, it's a very easy case. There's only one thing you should know about: don't be surprised if you see some familiar faces in the Paris hotels. There are a lot of people going to Spain, you know."

Thinking that our conversation was over, I started to get up, but he gestured to stop me. "If you have a moment, I'd like to talk to you." And he went on in a very direct manner: "How much time do you think we have left before the war?"

I was overwhelmed by the confidence he showed in me—and that he introduced a problem that was close to my own heart. I answered him, also freely: "Our fate is in the hands of the diplomats, and the question is whether they will continue to give in to Hitler."

I understood from the face Berzin made that he had no doubt about what the diplomats would do, and that war would inevitably follow.

"Where do you think the theater of the coming war will be?" he asked.

Berzin was certainly giving me proof of his confidence. I was amazed: the frankness that was developing between us was not usual in Moscow in 1936. After some hesitation, I took the plunge.

"Comrade Berzin, I don't think the most important question is whether the war will begin in the west or the east. The conflict will be worldwide, and even assuming that it starts in the west, that will change nothing. All nations will be involved, for nothing will be able to stop the German army. No obstacle will make Hitler retreat from his two objectives. I mean aggression against the Soviet Union and annexation of the Ukraine, and the extermination of the Jews."

"I wish all our political personnel reasoned the way you do," Berzin said. There was great intensity and regret in his voice. "Here people talk and talk about the Nazi threat—but it is talked about as a remote problem, far away. This blindness threatens to cost us a great deal."

I observed, "But, after all, you have an intelligence service, and I can't believe that your agents don't keep you informed of Germany's preparations. One doesn't have to be clairvoyant to see where all this will lead."

"Our agents, you say. Do you know how they proceed? They start by reading *Pravda*; they leave out of their dispatches anything that might displease their superiors. We are terribly handicapped by the party's decision not to send agents into Germany. You're going to pass through Germany; take advantage of the opportunity and observe what's going on there as well as you can. When you've completed your mission come and see me again, and we'll talk about it some more. By the way, what are you doing right now?"

"I'm a journalist for *Der Emes*."

"I see. Well, don't worry—if necessary, we'll find you a replacement."

Our meeting was over. As I walked out of Berzin's office, considerably impressed by his cool lucidity, I did not fully realize that I had taken the first step toward a great commitment.

The date of my departure was approaching when an event—by no means unexpected—caused a delay. Edgar, our second son, came into the world.

Then on December 26, 1936, I took the train for Finland. By way of Sweden, I went to Antwerp, where I bought a new suit. At last I arrived in Paris, on January 1, 1937. The next day, I went to see the lawyer, Mr. Ferrucci.

He received me very cordially, and played a record of the Red Army Chorus in my honor.

"I have come to investigate the Fantômas case," I said.

"The whole thing was fishy, you know, but there's one thing I'm sure of: Riquier is innocent. It's a classic case of diversion—accuse an innocent man in order to clear the real villain."

"Will I be given access to the trial documents?"

"Yes, but not for a month. I'll be able to take the file out for a day."

Totally free, I took a little trip to Switzerland, happy to be able to visit the Alps as a tourist and to consume some delicious pastries. In a militant's life, such opportunities are too rare to let pass. When I returned to Paris, in excellent spirits, Ferrucci and Philip turned the Fantômas file over to me. I plunged into the documents and discovered twenty-three letters that, by chance, had not been mentioned at the trial, letters between a Dutchman named Svitz and the American military attaché. The Dutchman had obviously denounced the group to the French police, and he had been released after the intervention of his influential protector. The letters I read provided indisputable proof of his guilt for the arrests of Bir and Strom.

Svitz's past life shed some light on his behavior. He had worked for Soviet Intelligence and been sent on a mission to the United States; there he was quickly discovered. In Panama, American counterespionage noticed that his passport was false. It did not take him long to decide to work for the Americans, without severing his connection with the Soviet services. Two years later, Moscow, very satisfied with the performance of this paragon of the double game, decided to send him to Paris to become the leader of the Soviet Intelligence group there. That was when he made contact with Bir.

When the Fantômas case broke, Svitz informed Moscow that he had succeeded in clearing himself but would have to disappear for a while. He hid so well that he was never seen again.

The French police, who were looking for a culprit, were only too happy to kill two birds with one stone and compromise the Communist Party through one of its members. The choice fell on Riquier for the sole reason that he edited the column on the Rabcors. (The Rabcors were workers in hundreds of business enterprises who sent reports on working conditions, strikes, and so on to *l'Humanité*. In companies where the work related to national defense, the reports were more confidential and were sent to another address.)

When I went back to Moscow, in the spring of 1937, Berzin's service was not convinced by my explanation, which lacked formal proofs of Riquier's innocence. We agreed that I should return to Paris. During this second trip, I persuaded the keeper of the archives at the Palais de Justice to let me have the documents photographed.

Since there was no question of my crossing the border with the documents on my person, it was agreed that I would turn them over to a member of the Soviet Embassy, who would have them forwarded via the diplomatic pouch. A meeting was arranged with the emissary of the embassy, in a café near the Parc Monceau.

On the appointed day, I walked in and saw a man sitting at a table whose appearance corresponded to the description I had been given. He was about forty years old, wore glasses, and was reading *Le Temps*. I walked over—but just as I was about to speak to him, I saw he was not wearing a bandage on his finger; the bandage had been agreed on so I could identify him without risking an error. I stammered out a few words and left, very confused. Eight days later, I went to the emergency rendezvous. This time there was a man there wearing a bandage. I gave him the documents, folded inside a newspaper. We struck up a conversation, and he asked me whether I would be in Paris a few more days. I answered that that was the plan.

"Then give me your telephone number," he said, "so I can call you in case I need you."

I told him the number, which was only to be used in case of danger, and saw my "diplomatic" spy write the figures in his notebook without taking the elementary precaution of putting them in code.

This incident gave me a singular insight into the efficiency of Soviet Intelligence. How was it conceivable that agents delegated by the embassy could act with such naïveté?

I returned to Moscow in June, 1937. Berzin was in Spain, where he was acting as military adviser to the Republican government. Colonel Stiga received me, and I gave him a report on my mission. He assured me that in his eyes the Fantômas case was closed for good.

Riquier was completely exonerated. After this, the heads of the Comintern decided that Soviet Intelligence would no longer use communist militants. There would be a total separation between the secret service and the party—a decision that was overdue but justified. The effectiveness of the Rabcors was actually very limited; instead of trying to coordinate bits of information from various sources, it is preferable to have one man placed at a central observation point.

I saw Stiga rather frequently, back in Moscow now, working on *Der Emes* again, and the result was that I agreed, in principle, to join the Red Army Intelligence Service. By neither taste nor vocation was I drawn to espionage. Nor was I a soldier; my only ambition was to fight fascism. But I let myself be won over by his arguments. The Soviet Army needed militants who were convinced that war was inevitable, not robots and bootlickers.

The die was cast.

12

Like any myth, the one that I was working for Soviet Intelligence as early as 1930 and even before has roots in fact—facts that were distorted and exaggerated and then, in their misshapen form, repeatedly presented as proofs. In the archives of the French Sûreté and the Gestapo, one actually finds documents that are "evidence" of my participation in the Fantômas network.

When I was arrested by the Gestapo in 1942, the Germans knew only my *nom de guerre*, Jean Gilbert, but in the course of an investigation conducted in Belgium, they found my real passport, made out in the name of Leopold Trepper. Now, since the beginning of my life as a militant, I had called myself Domb. It was under this pseudonym that I was known to the French police. I wanted to do everything I could to prevent the Gestapo from making the connection between Domb and Trepper, for several dozen militants known in the '30s as contacts of Domb's would have been in immediate danger.

In 1932, the French police had fallen down on the job. In their files they too had failed to make the connection between Trepper and Domb. On the one hand, they were watching a communist agitator named Domb, who was active in Jewish circles; on the other hand, they had got their hands on letters that Alter Strom was waiting for, addressed to a man named Trepper.

The Gestapo, making use of the French police files, saw only that Leopold Trepper, whom they had arrested as the head of the "Red Orchestra," had already been involved in a case of Soviet Intelligence, the Fantômas affair, in 1932. Better yet, the passport discovered in their investigation established the fact that this Trepper had been in Palestine from 1924 to 1929. The Germans needed to glorify their prisoner in the eyes of their superiors in Berlin; thus they invented an

83

amazing pedigree for me: I had been a Soviet agent since my youth—first in Palestine, then in France. During the interrogations, I agreed to play the part of this character, for the more important the Gestapo made me, the wider my margin of operation. For example, the Gestapo was convinced that I had been trained as a spy in Moscow. I contributed to the ambiguity by telling them that I had been a student at Podrowski University.

Even today you can read in certain books that I was a student at Podrowski military academy, in the espionage department—though in fact there never was any such place.

Because it served my needs in my struggle against the Gestapo, I allowed the myth to develop that I had been active as a Soviet agent since childhood. It now has a life of its own.

PART TWO

THE RED ORCHESTRA

1

The Birth of the Orchestra

I saw General Berzin again after his return from Spain, and he seemed a different man. He had learned there that Tukhachevski and his staff had been liquidated. He knew that the "evidence" gathered against them was false, and he had been stunned. Further, he was too lucid to nourish any illusion about his own fate: the wave of repression that had swept away his comrades would drown him also. In spite of the danger, he had come back, on his own initiative, to protest to Stalin against the massacres of communists that had been perpetrated by the OGPU* in Spain.

General Berzin knew he was signing his own death warrant. But as a confirmed communist conscious of his responsibilities, he could not bear to see his best officers, men he had personally selected and trained, disappear. Time was against him. The little he had left he intended to put to good use.

He granted me an interview, and our conversation is still vivid in my memory. How could it be otherwise, when that day was decisive for my future as a man and a communist?

"I propose that you come and work with us, because we need you," he told me. "Not here in the central organization; this is not your place. I want you to lay the basis of our activity in Western Europe."

Since my first conversation with Berzin, I had thought constantly about the prospect of joining the Intelligence Service and fighting at his side. The time was approaching, I was convinced, when Hitler's hordes would descend on Europe. In that struggle, the weight of the Soviet Union would be decisive.

With a sick heart, I watched the degeneration of the revolution to which I, like millions of other communists, had

*Later to become the NKVD and ultimately the KGB.

given my all. We were ready to sacrifice our youth so that some day the world might have the face of youth again. The revolution was our life; the party was our family, in which brotherhood transcended every private action.

We wanted to belong to a new race of men. In order that the proletariat could be freed of its chains, we were prepared to wear chains ourselves. What did we care about our little share of personal happiness? We had offered our lives to history so that it might at last cease to be one long tale of oppression. The road to heaven is not strewn with roses—who could know that better than we, who had come to communism from childhoods in a world dominated by imperialist barbarism?

But if the road was strewn with the bodies of workers, it did not, it could not, lead to socialism. Our comrades were disappearing. The best of us were dying in the cellars of the NKVD; Stalin's regime was distorting socialism to the point where it was unrecognizable. Stalin, the great gravedigger, was liquidating ten times, a hundred times, more communists than Hitler.

Between the hammer of Hitler and the anvil of Stalin, the path was a narrow one for those of us who still believed in the revolution. Over and above our confusion and our anguish was the necessity of defending the Soviet Union, even though it had ceased to be the homeland of the socialism we had hoped for. This obvious fact forced my decision, and General Berzin's proposition allowed me to save my conscience. As a Polish citizen, as a Jew who had lived in Palestine, as an expatriate, and as a journalist on a Jewish daily paper, I was ten times suspect in the eyes of the NKVD.

My path was decided. It might end in a prison cell, a concentration camp, or against a wall. Yet by fighting far from Moscow, in the forefront of the anti-Nazi struggle, I could continue to be what I had always been: a militant revolutionary.

Having arrived at this conclusion—not without inner struggles—I began during my travels in Europe to sketch plans for an intelligence network that would encompass all of

Europe. I presented these to General Berzin. We would establish ourselves in Germany itself and in the neighboring countries: this core group of anti-fascist fighters would not go into action until Germany triggered the war in Europe, and the struggle against Nazism would be their only mission. Our immediate task would be to create bases with intelligence work in mind—the bases would have to afford us contacts, cover, and financing. Then, during a transitional period, we would be largely concerned with protecting our liaison with the Center. When war did break out and we went into action, the networks would be composed exclusively of enemies of fascism—although they might have varying political and religious backgrounds—whose ideological convictions were proof against any test. There was no question of using paid agents. We needed men and women who had, or were capable of developing, contacts in circles that were vitally involved in military operations—among the German high command, and in governmental, political, and economic institutions. Our principal objective would be to provide the military, in time to make use of it, with accurate and verified information collected from various sources on the plans and activities of Nazi Germany.

I explained to General Berzin that I would need three top associates in each country. The first—who would not necessarily have to be Russian—would have the requisite qualities to lead the group. The second would be a technician capable of setting up a network of radio transmitters and training operators. Finally, I would need the services of a military specialist, who would carry out on-the-spot preliminary screenings of the information we collected.*

Overall, the general approved; but he noted two problems: "We already have an exceptionally good group in Germany, but we're operating under tight restrictions. The party leaders are afraid of provocative incidents, so they don't want us shaping an active network on the territory of the Third Reich.

---

*We did not, of course, call ourselves the Red Orchestra then. The name was supplied later, by German counterintelligence.

Second, you believe that a commercial cover is going to provide material and financial means for the groups. I'm skeptical. Judging by our experience over the past twenty years, that system provides nothing, and the money that we invest is always lost."

"Look here," I replied, "the problem is not to save the Soviet government money. During the war it will be very hard for money from Moscow to get through to us, and it's possible, you know, that the people who set up your companies in the past weren't very good at business. I believe that in a capitalist country shrewd professionals can make money. My plan is to start an import-export house based in Belgium, with branches in several other countries."

"How much will you need to launch this venture?"

"Oh, we'll begin modestly. I'll enter as a partner in a business, and invest $10,000."

"What? You think you'll make enough with $10,000 to cover your expenses for the duration of the war?"

"I hope so."

"In any case, if you ask for more money a few months from now, we'll grant it. So far the most difficult problem hasn't been gathering military information but maintaining stable liaisons with our people."

The conversation was drawing to a close. General Berzin seemed relaxed, almost happy.

"You have approximately two years before the war breaks out," he told me. "Take every precaution to see that your network remains dormant until the beginning of the war. Don't jeopardize it by engaging in other activities. The defeat of Nazism is our sole objective. Don't concern yourself with anything else—your job is to combat the Third Reich, and only the Third Reich. I have agents in all these countries, but your group will be completely independent. We'll try to send you radio operators and equipment from here, but don't expect too much, even along these lines. You must rely primarily on yourself. Try to recruit and train personnel.

"As for the group leaders in each country, I warn you in advance: they will have to be recruited on the spot." His tone betrayed an emotion, the significance of which I would not understand until much later. A large percentage of the qualified leaders who could have performed this work had already been arrested and interrogated by the NKVD.

Finally, we agreed that my family should join me as soon as possible; a man who lives alone is always suspect. I wanted to enter completely into the role of the easygoing and successful industrialist.

"I have confidence in you," Berzin went on. "I am sure you'll succeed. When you're sending information, never ask yourself how the Center is going to react to it. Never concern yourself with pleasing them, or you won't be doing your job." And he added, giving me definite proof of the confidence he placed in me, "Tukhachevski was right. War is inevitable, and it will be fought on Russian soil." Never before had I heard anyone in Moscow, in the grip of the Stalinist terror, praise a man who had been executed for "treason."

He accompanied me to the door of his office. "Listen only to your conscience," he told me. "For a revolutionary, that is the final judge."

I believe that his political testament was contained in those few words. All his life his conscience had guided his actions.

At that time, General Berzin already knew that he was doomed, but he had no regrets. To be convicted by Stalin's courts was to win one's case before the tribunal of history. For a communist, that was all that mattered.

It was the fall of 1937 and it had been agreed that I would leave as soon as the preparations were complete. One month, then two months, passed, and I heard nothing. I had no idea what had happened to our plans. I had gone back to work on the paper. In the last days of the year, I heard from various sources that terrific upheavals were taking place in the Intelligence Service. Their meaning and consequences seemed clear: our project had miscarried. The creation of bases for intelligence activities directed against Germany, an idea that had the enthusiastic support of a Berzin or a Stiga, was contrary to the ideas and ambitions of the party leaders.

I had given up hope when in March, 1938, I received a telephone call from a captain, an assistant of Stiga's and consequently a subordinate in the Intelligence Service, asking me to stop by.

I had been to the "chocolate house" four times, and I had a clear enough memory of the faces I had seen there to realize immediately that some very substantial changes had taken place—changes that could not have occurred by chance. Much later, when I was in Belgium, I learned from an unimpeachable source that General Berzin and his high command had been executed in December, 1938.

In March, 1938, I was shown into the captain's office, and as soon as I sat down he said, "We must start to work at once. We have lost six months, and now there's not a minute to waste; we must make up for lost time."

"For a meeting of this importance," I remarked, "I expected to see Colonel Stiga himself."

The sideways glance he threw me, and his embarrassment, were more eloquent than words. Nevertheless, he decided to provide me with an explanation: "The fact is, you see, we have had to reorganize the service. Some of us have been transferred to other departments and have been given other jobs. Now we must prepare your passport and the itinerary of your trip, and schedule a half-day's work to familiarize you with the codes."

"I am still ready," I answered. I had no other choice.

I went home very depressed. Why had I been spared? Why was I being called on? The dismissal of Berzin, which I no longer doubted, and which came as a profound shock to me, had not prevented me from saying yes. This was because I was convinced that General Berzin would not have advised me otherwise. The mission entrusted to me was the same one that Berzin himself had approved and prepared—so I was following in his footsteps, being faithful to our agreement. That was all that mattered. More than ever, the struggle against Nazism had to be the dominant, exclusive objective. At least I was going to fight, and this combat was essential. The groups that I was going to create, the machine whose parts I was going to assemble, would be my responsibility; and once that machine was set in motion, nothing would be able to stop it.

When I saw the captain again, my conviction was stronger than ever. I made only one condition: "It must be clear that I am devoting myself to this work as a communist militant. I am not a soldier, and I have no desire to become an officer in the army."

"Just as you like," he replied. "Whether you're in the army or not, though, you'll have the rank of colonel."

"You can give me any rank you like, it makes no difference to me."

The captain introduced me to a specialist in coding. Ours was based on a novel by Balzac, *La Femme de trente ans.* He spent several hours teaching me to encode a dispatch.

There were still a few loose ends to take care of: I was to be given the passport of a Canadian from Quebec—which meant I would not have to speak English—and my contact in Brussels would be an employee of the Soviet commercial delegation.

I had been told that before my departure I would have to meet with the new director of the Intelligence Service. He received me in Berzin's office, which otherwise had not changed at all. He, too, was a general—but how could he take the place of Berzin, in my affections or in my respect? He was about forty-five years old. He received me warmly and tried to reassure me: "We will be following the previous plan in every detail."

He got up and walked over to the big map of the world that was still on the wall. "I am aware that for the moment we are not doing very much in Germany"—I remembered Berzin's telling me that this was on Stalin's orders, on the pretext that it was necessary to avoid provocations—"but we might consider forming a group in a German town very close to the border."

As he spoke, he tried to locate a point on the map with his finger. Years later this detail would flash back into my mind, when I read in Khrushchev's report to the twentieth congress that Stalin habitually pointed to a map of the world with his index finger while talking strategy to his generals.

He went on, "Yes, a German town—it might be Strasbourg——"

Good Lord! I said to myself, I'm in good hands if the head of Soviet Intelligence thinks Strasbourg is in Germany. I had just realized for the first time—and on what a level!—the result of the "transfers" brought about by Stalin. The NKVD had simply pushed one of its own men to the top of the secret service, I thought, and if he had as much talent for intelligence as for geography, I could certainly look forward to difficult times in the days ahead. Unfortunately, the future would confirm my suspicions.

There was a brief moment of silence among us—the general, the captain (who was also present at our meeting), and me. From the captain's expression, the general realized that he had blundered. I had no choice but to throw him a line to help him out of the hole: "You're quite right," I exclaimed, walking over to the map. "Strasbourg really has all the characteristics of a German town, in spite of its position inside the French border. We'll try to set up a new group there."

"That's right," he went on, completely reassured, "that's what I meant: a French town very close to the German border."

"You handled that very well," murmured the captain when we had left that office. "What a *gaffe!*"

"Oh, you know," I answered with a straight face, "anyone can make a mistake." But I was convinced that with expertise of this sort, my troubles were not over.

Before leaving Soviet territory, I went to say goodbye to my son Michel. It broke my heart to leave him in his boarding school, which looked to me so much like an orphanage.

"Michel," I told him, "I'm going to do a job for the party. I will be away for a while."

He did not answer. I had the painful feeling that I was abandoning him. I hugged him, and left. When I arrived at the railway station some two kilometers from the boarding school, I heard screams behind me. I turned around—on the road, I saw a little figure running toward me. It was Michel, my son, shouting these words that I will never forget: "Don't leave me, don't leave me, I don't want to be alone!" I was not to see him again for sixteen years.

I left for Belgium by way of Leningrad and Stockholm. In Antwerp, at a prearranged meeting, I was handed my new passport in the name of Adam Mikler, a Canadian industrialist about to set up a business in Belgium.

2 The Foreign Excellent Trenchcoat Company

It was no accident that Adam Mikler, the "Canadian indus-trialist," decided to begin his activities in Belgium. Since this little country was theoretically neutral, her laws offered unique possibilities for intelligence activities, provided the activities were not directed against her. Her geographical situation was favorable too: it permitted rapid communication with Germany and France as well as the Scandinavian countries. Besides, and this was a very important point, Adam Mikler could count on certain established connections that would help him launch his business schemes.

When I proposed the idea of creating a group of commercial enterprises to General Berzin, I had a precise plan. In 1937, before starting back to Moscow after my second trip to Paris, I had stopped in Brussels long enough to say hello to my old friend Leo Grossvogel. Now I rushed to see him as soon as I arrived.

Since our days in Palestine, I had seen Leo several times, when I came to Brussels to give lectures while I was living in Paris, between 1929 and 1932.

The Grossvogels were a Jewish family from Strasbourg. Leo had started studying in Berlin, but in 1925 he had given up everything to go to Palestine, where he had shown ability and ardor in the ranks of the Communist Party. In 1928 he went to Belgium and there joined two members of his family who were the proprietors of a business called Au Roi du Caoutchouc. He soon became its commercial director.

This did not mean that Leo Grossvogel had repudiated his old convictions. A respectable manufacturer, known in industrial and commercial circles all over Brussels, he continued to act as a liaison between the Comintern and the communist parties of the Near East. Now he was to give up this very important function in order to devote himself to intelligence.

But first, the "cover."

Since Au Roi du Caoutchouc made raincoats, Leo's plan was to create an import-export company that would market the products through numerous branches in foreign countries. So it was that in the fall of 1938 the Foreign Excellent Trenchcoat Company began its legal existence. Thanks to Leo's savoir-faire, it grew rapidly. One of the directors was Jules Jaspar, a long-time acquaintance of Leo's. Jaspar's family was very well known in the political world; his brother had been President of the National Assembly, and he himself had been Belgian consul in several countries. He established branches quickly in Sweden, Denmark, and Norway. In his own country, Belgium, he was assured of the support of official organizations, which at that time were eager to develop a languishing export trade. Another long-time acquaintance of Grossvogel's was head of the accounting department: Nazarin Drailly, an energetic and competent man, and a confirmed anti-Nazi. He was not unaware that the firm's profits went toward financing organizations that were fighting fascism.

Leo Grossvogel was the director of the Foreign Excellent Trenchcoat Company and Adam Mikler became his investor. The business grew rapidly. In May, 1940, branches were prospering in the Scandinavian countries, and relations had been established with Italy, Germany, France, Holland, and even Japan, where we bought artificial silk. All these branch offices were run by respectable businessmen who were far from imagining the objectives of the parent firm.

In the beginning of the summer of 1938, Luba, my wife, arrived in Belgium with our second son, Edgar, who was then a year and a half old. Michel did not join us—it was a habit in the Soviet Union to keep one, at least, of a family there; one of the children was to remain in Russia and receive education in the Soviet spirit.

I was the very image of the well-to-do industrialist, serious and reassuring, with my wife and child in my home. Luba was a very efficient housewife who, when she had finished with her domestic and social duties, acted as liaison with the representative of the Center, a member of the Soviet commercial delegation in Brussels. We had moved into a modest building on the Avenue Richard-Neuberg. The Grossvogels were our neighbors, at 117 Avenue Prudent-Bols. As was perfectly natural for business associates and friends, the Grossvogels, Draillys, and Miklers saw each other frequently.

It was inevitable that we would stumble from time to time on the path we had chosen. Luba had one such experience on her trip from the Soviet Union to Brussels. To avoid complications, she was using the passport of a French schoolteacher; however, it had been impossible to anticipate every detail. In Helsinki, a cab driver, a White Russian émigré, said to my wife in astonishment, "You say you are French—how is it that the little boy speaks Russian?"

Luba hadn't noticed the slip, but it was true; Edgar had just said a few words in Russian.

"That's true," she answered, "the child has a real gift for languages. He learned a lot of new words during our visit to the USSR."

One can never take too many precautions; I was to realize this myself a little while later. My new life as a Brussels industrialist had been proceeding according to schedule. I had opened an account in a large bank in the city. Some time passed and I still had not received my checkbook, so I went with Leo to inquire about the delay.

The answer we were given was disconcerting: the management had recently decided that foreigners who opened accounts should be investigated in their country of origin. It was easy to imagine the result of such an investigation for the aforesaid Adam Mikler, "citizen of Quebec." Leo and I put our heads together and decided to invite the president of the bank to dinner.

Right in the middle of the meal, I told him a little story. "I am Jewish," I told him, "and in addition to my activities as an industrialist, I am trying to assist my compatriots who wish to withdraw their funds from German banks. All these operations require absolute secrecy, and I have asked your colleague in Quebec to reply to any inquiries that I am 'unknown.' "

The Brussels banker believed me, and after saying that he was sorry he hadn't been told sooner, he sent a telegram to Canada canceling the formalities.

I received my checkbook a few days later, and to prove to the president that I had not lied, I deposited in my account a large sum of money "collected from German Jewish families."

As soon as our commercial cover was deemed sufficiently reliable, the Center began sending additional personnel. The spring of 1939 saw the arrival of Carlos Alamo, "Uruguayan citizen," better known in Russia as Mikael Makarov, Soviet officer. He came to us from Spain, where he had fought with a unit of the Republican air force, inspired by that rash courage born of youth and idealism. This incident will give the measure of the man and the soldier: one day when Franco's troops made a sudden and dangerous advance the air force was asked to intervene. The planes were there, ready to take off, but for some reason there were no pilots. So Alamo stepped forward, leapt into a plane, dashed off, completed his mission, came back, and landed. There was only one small detail: Alamo was not a pilot, but a mechanic.

Our first meeting was set for 8:30 in the morning in the Antwerp zoological garden. At the appointed hour Alamo arrived, walked toward me, and passed by, pretending not to see me. Three days later we had another rendezvous in the same place. Alamo was there, but instead of approaching me he quickly walked away. Through Bolchakov, my contact at the Soviet commercial delegation, I learned that Alamo had not spoken to me because he was being followed. Intrigued, since I had noticed nothing myself, I asked for him to tell me more.

"Both times, there were men running all over the place," Bolchakov told me.

"The guy is a fool! They've been running there for ten years! They're athletes who come to the zoological garden every morning to work out."

I began to think that Alamo had been overrated, and lacked experience in the sort of work that would be entrusted to him. A battlefield hero does not necessarily make a good intelligence agent. At the Center, he had had only three months' training as a radio operator, which was hardly enough to make him a virtuoso. But his qualities as a human being made up for everything else; before long I was favorably impressed with him.

Naturally, Alamo was given the protection of the commercial cover, and was appointed manager of a branch of Au Roi du Caoutchouc in Ostend. He showed little interest in selling trenchcoats. I understood him—from the skies of Asturias to a shop in Belgium is a long way to fall. We solved the problem by hiring an excellent manager, Madame Hoorickx, to take over the practical side of the job.

During the summer of 1939, Victor Sukulov, also a Soviet officer but likewise a "Uruguayan citizen," arrived to be second in command, under the name of Vincent Sierra. We will encounter him often in the following chapters under the pseudonym Kent. It had been agreed that he would remain only a year in Belgium before taking over a branch in Denmark. With equal energy, Alamo pursued his dilenttantism and Kent set to work enthusiastically studying accounting and commercial law, at the university in Brussels. Luba, who was enrolled in the literature department at the university, maintained our contact with him.

Kent, who had also acquired a service record in Spain and carried out secret missions, did not seem so credible to me as his comrade. I suspected him of having worked for the NKVD and Military Intelligence at the same time. This was not unheard of, since the NKVD had the bad habit of infiltrating its agents into the Red Army's Intelligence Service.

The Red Orchestra was no exception to this infiltration, as I was to discover on several occasions. Early in 1940, our contact at the commercial delegation, who was our liaison with the Center, informed me that he could not continue his work. He said NKVD men were following him constantly. I immediately informed the Director at the Center; after that the shadowing stopped.

Similarly, in 1941, I noticed that one of the couriers in liaison with the Soviet military attaché in Vichy was a little too interested in matters that did not concern him.

Such liaisons, in fact, had no reason for existing. It was dangerous for communications between the networks and the Center to go through the intermediary of the official Soviet services, for the simple reason that employees of these organizations are closely watched by counterespionage, which can also intercept dispatches from embassies. It was a terrible mistake not to take advantage of the few months of peace that remained to us to establish direct contact by means of radio operators, trusted couriers, and post office boxes in the neutral countries. We were to pay very dearly for this error.

From the summer of 1938 until the war broke out, we laid aside all intelligence work, properly speaking. Our objectives were to consolidate our commercial cover and to lay the necessary groundwork so we would be ready when the first shots were fired.

We did not have a minute to lose.

3

The Great Illusion

PEACE!

In bold letters running the width of its front page, *Paris-Soir* announced the good news on October 1, 1938. The night before, in Munich, Daladier and Chamberlain had given in to Hitler's demands on the Sudetenland. They went home to heroes' welcomes: we had avoided war. The better to preserve the "peace," the French and English governments, blinded by cowardice, had signed nonaggression pacts with Nazi Germany.

Hitler signed with both hands, and entered Czechoslovakia. The "democracies" were indignant, but they soon dried their tears in the white folds of the flag of capitulation, and resumed their pursuit of compromise.

Stalin was no better. In the early hours of August 24, 1939, the nonaggression pact between Hitler's Germany and the Soviet Union was signed in the Kremlin. My future "guardian angel," Gestapo officer Berg—then Von Ribbentrop's bodyguard—would later describe to me the jubilant atmosphere of that ceremony. Everyone was guzzling champagne in celebration, and Stalin had raised his glass and made an unforgettable toast: "I know how much the German people love their Führer, and that is why I have the pleasure of drinking to his health"—a pleasure that was certainly not shared by the thousands of German communists crouching in concentration camps by the grace of their beloved Führer.

At the end of 1939, I received several communications that showed me the new directors of the Center were no longer interested in the forming of the Red Orchestra. Not only had the Center stopped sending the promised emissaries to the branches of Au Roi du Caoutchouc, but several dispatches urgently requested me to send Alamo and Kent back to

102

Moscow, and Leo Grossvogel to the United States. I too was asked to return to Moscow. These were all requests, not orders—very carefully worded.

My answer was clear and concise: war between Germany and the Soviet Union was inevitable. If the Center required it, Alamo and Kent would return to Moscow, but they should not expect me, or Leo Grossvogel, to destroy what we had constructed.

This attempt was not an isolated case. The Center decided to bring Richard Sorge back to Moscow from Japan, and to replace him with an obscure colonel. They realized, though, after a time, that Sorge could not be replaced, and in the end, they left him in Tokyo. From then on Sorge was suspected at the Center of being a double agent and—crime of crimes—a Trotskyite. His dispatches would go for weeks without being decoded.

Manuilski sent directives to all sections of the Comintern ordering the approval and application of Stalin's policy. This policy could be summed up as follows: the war between Nazi Germany and the French and English allies is a war between imperialisms, and is therefore of no concern to the workers. For years, the leaders of the Comintern had explained that the struggle against Hitler was the struggle of democracy against barbarism. Now, by virtue of the pact, the war became imperialist. The communists would now campaign against the war and denounce the imperialist goals of England.

"We must destroy the myth of the justice' of this so-called anti-fascist war," as Dimitrov put it.

I could see how profoundly this policy had disoriented the Belgian communist militants. Some were torn, but resigned themselves; others, in despair, left the party.

On September 1, 1939, at 4:45 in the morning, the Wehrmacht entered Poland. We were kept informed through our liaisons of the German advance and the crimes committed by Hitler's hordes along the way: special groups of SS assassinated thousands of Jews and Poles. On October 8, according to the information that reached us, while Goebbels was staying in Lodz, Nazi gangsters organized a pogrom, and Jewish children were thrown out of windows.

Meanwhile, the Red Army, for which I was supposedly working, occupied the other part of a divided Poland, and Molotov sent a telegram to Von Ribbentrop congratulating him on the "splendid successes of the German army" that had made it possible to "throw away the bastard Treaty of Versailles."

How obvious it now appeared why Stalin had liquidated the Polish Communist Party the year before. Never would the communists of that country have tolerated such a crime.

They proved this during the first days of the war when the imprisoned militants demanded their release in order to go and fight at the front against the Wehrmacht.

One month after the signing of the pact, Stalin's intention became even clearer. The Soviet Union and Germany signed a treaty of friendship, on September 28, 1939. The negotiations continued throughout the last three months of 1939, and culminated in a plan for the division of spheres of influence between the Third Reich and the Soviet Union once the Wehrmacht had triumphed over England.

During this great upheaval, in which long-established beliefs and ideals were being contradicted by actions, we who formed the initial nucleus of the Red Orchestra clung to a single idea. In spite of all Stalin's contortions, war with Germany was inevitable. This compass in the storm saved us from foundering. We had to keep going, no matter what happened. We might have inner conflicts, but we had set a mission for ourselves, and we did not have the right to abandon it. Besides—wouldn't our desertion be exactly what Moscow wanted?

The Center's attempt to make me give up my work thus had no effect, even though at the end of 1940, the Center informed my wife, then back in Moscow, of my imminent arrival! From that time on, some of the directives I received had nothing to do with the formation of the Red Orchestra, and even jeopardized its existence and objectives.

One of the first jobs I was asked to do was to forward money to Tokyo for Richard Sorge. Making use of our connections with Dutch bankers, I carried out the assignment with pleasure. I knew Sorge, and I appreciated his intelligence and foresight. Then, at the end of 1939, four agents arrived, sent by the Center and provided with Uruguayan passports. I was asked to send them to America. South American nationals who wanted to go to the United States, however, had to ask permission from the consulates of their countries. The Center had overlooked this little detail. Of the four "Uruguayan citizens," only one spoke Spanish and knew something about Uruguay. He took the risk of asking for his visa—but what was I supposed to do about the other three? The Center decided to repatriate them.

Such blunders confirmed my opinion that the directors of the Intelligence Service were not equal to their task. The young people they were sending out on missions were intelligent, capable, and courageous, but in no way prepared for intelligence work.

Then one day I received a directive that left me speechless. The Center was asking me to create a "shoe factory." In the jargon of intelligence, "shoes" refers to false identity papers and, logically enough, a forger of such papers is known as a "shoemaker." Such an undertaking is dangerous by its very nature. It leaves clues; sooner or later, a "re-soled" passport falls into the hands of the police. Above all, I was afraid that shoemaking would draw attention to my Belgian counterespionage group. But an order is an order, in the secret service as in the army, and we had no choice but to carry it out.

Grossvogel, who had connections absolutely everywhere (don't forget, he had been in Belgium since 1928) put his hand on a rare pearl, a certain Abraham Raichmann, who was undoubtedly the most talented "shoemaker" in Belgium. I believe he had learned his trade under the tutelage of the Comintern, in Berlin, where the manufacture of false papers was a veritable industry. Since then, on the strength of his experience, he had gone into business for himself, supplying the needs of Jewish immigrants driven out of Germany.

Although he promised to stop his "private" activities, I decided as a precaution to keep him apart from the group. In fact, we had proof that he had bribed employees of various Latin American consulates who were providing him not only with real passports, but also with certificates of naturalization. He augmented his stock by recovering passports sent back by Europeans who had emigrated to the United States. Unquestionably his greatest coup was procuring a package of blank passports direct from the printer who made them in Luxembourg.

In the end, Raichmann was done in by his own perfectionism. The police raided another shoemaker and arrested him; this competitor denounced Raichmann—he was jealous of Raichmann's success. Raichmann was tried, and he told the judges, with every sign of innocence, that he collected passports the way some people chase butterflies or collect postage stamps. He was acquitted for lack of proof. During the time he spent in prison awaiting trial, we helped him find the best lawyers, and we looked after his family, who were without resources. He was touched by our solicitude and did not forget it. Although we carefully avoided integrating him directly into our group, we had sufficient appreciation for his intelligence and his stubborn refusal to talk to regard him as a useful element.

All the same, this was the end of the shoemaking, about which I had always had my doubts. The Center had received such an enormous number that it could get along comfortably for years.

France and England were ostensibly at war with Germany as of September, 1939—but it was a "Phony War," in which hostilities were confined to isolated skirmishes. By the spring of 1940, it was blindingly clear that this situation would change soon—and dramatically.

Various elements of the German plan of attack had been communicated to us and had convinced us of the effectiveness of their imminent offensive. The Belgians knew what dangers they faced; the neutrality of their country was only a thin smokescreen between them and the tanks of the Wehrmacht. After the abandonment of Poland, nobody had any illusions about French or British military aid. Not for a moment, as the German troops launched their attack on Poland, had the French army even considered attacking the Siegfried Line, then depleted of troops. There is no point in rewriting history; yet it is not inconceivable that if Hitler had been obliged then to fight on two fronts, he might have been forced to withdraw.

After Munich, the French government was preparing for a new capitulation. Protected behind the Maginot Line—a line of defense that stopped at the Belgian border, owing to Belgium's neutrality—the chiefs of staff felt invulnerable. There was no dearth of reports revealing the German preparations, but the French government refused to take them into consideration.

On May 10, 1940, at dawn, the Wehrmacht moved on Western Europe. German planes bombed Brussels. I had gone to see Kent to write my first coded dispatch on the military operations. During my absence, three Belgian police officers presented themselves at the Rue Richard-Neuberg, where Luba and I had been living as Adam and Anna Mikler since 1938, both of us very busy with the first phases of organizing our network. They told her they had orders to arrest us and send us to a concentration camp. We were to take a change of linen and a couple of days' food. The reason? Although we were naturalized Canadians, in their opinion we were of German descent, and Belgium had decided to lock up all nationals of the Third Reich and their relatives residing on her territory. The moment was critical, to say the least.

Not losing her head, Luba asked the three policemen to come in and sit down, and explained to them that the town we came from, Sambor, was in Polish territory. She got out the Larousse Encyclopedia so the inspectors could see for themselves. Uncertain what to do, they decided to go back to their superiors for further instructions.

A good thing they did. I arrived home a few minutes later. When my wife told me what had happened, I congratulated her on her initiative and decided to break camp without delay. The police would certainly be back, and this time they would not pass us by. We hastily packed our bags and left the premises.

The first thing to do was to put Luba and our son in a safe place. After consulting with Leo Grossvogel, we decided on the commercial delegation of the Soviet Union. I got in touch with our liaison there, who arranged for the transfer. Since the Soviet Embassy and the commercial delegation had been surrounded by the Belgian police since morning, Luba and the child crossed the barricade in a diplomatic corps car. They stayed in the embassy for two weeks before finding lodgings in a clandestine apartment.

Later, Luba and little Edgar returned to the Soviet Union, where our eldest son still was. The headquarters' opinion was that the situation in Belgium was getting risky for Soviet diplomatic and trade representatives and their families. It was suggested that my wife and son should return with them to the Soviet Union to avoid any danger. The Soviet authorities also made it a principle that the family of a person working in intelligence during wartime should be separated from him and live in Russia. The purpose was to facilitate control of the intelligence agent.

As for me, I went to see Leo, who lived very close by, and walked out of his house equipped with new identity papers in the name of Jean Gilbert, industrialist, born in Antwerp. Leo became Henri Piper, a tradesman, likewise a native of Antwerp. Our underground life was beginning.

The next day, as we had foreseen, the Belgian police appeared at our house again with formal orders to take us away. They were too late—but my career as a secret agent had come very close to ending on the first day of the war.

The police continued to look for me for several days. They knocked at the door of an American friend, Georgie de Winter, whom I had met not long before and saw frequently.

"You haven't seen Monsieur Mikler lately, have you?" they asked her. "He's a German."

"You're mistaken, he's Canadian."

"Canadian! He's as Canadian as you are Belgian."

Meanwhile, the military situation was deteriorating. Even the most pessimistic observers had not expected the German advance to be so swift. On May 13, the Wehrmacht's advance troops crossed the Meuse in Belgium and in France, and the tanks of General Guderian swept into the breach of Sedan. German agents, parachuted from mysterious airplanes, dropped from the sky like autumn leaves. The demoralized population was seized by a veritable epidemic of "espionitis." By I know not what association of ideas, Hitler's spies were suspected of disguising themselves as priests. On May 11, in Place de Brouckere in Brussels, I witnessed an incredible spectacle. A hysterical mob attacked a young clergyman and pulled up his cassock to see whether he was wearing a German uniform underneath. I did not witness any scenes of this sort involving nuns, but I know that Fifth Columnists were suspected of hiding under nuns' robes, too.

Panic spread; tens of thousands of Belgians left everything behind and fled toward France. The official communiqués were regularly one battle behind, and occupied towns were reported as still being free. The English soldiers had the brilliant idea of blowing up the bridges on the little canals of Brussels, in order to delay the advance of the Wehrmacht—

but the surrounding buildings blew up along with the bridges, adding further to the demoralization of the people, who realized that the allied armies could no longer do anything to help them.

Careful observation of this *Blitzkrieg* provided valuable information, and I promised myself I would send an accurate report to the Center. But before we did anything else, we had to get our radio station into operation.

Our transmitter was concealed in Knokke, on the coast, in a villa we had rented. Transporting it to Brussels in the middle of the war was obviously a delicate problem; but since Knokke was not yet occupied, there was still a reasonable possibility of recovering the set, provided we lost no time. I entrusted Alamo with this mission—but Alamo thought that two days more or less would make no difference, and took a side trip to Ostend to see his friend, Madame Hoorickx, who was in charge of our branch there. By the time he was ready to start for Knokke, it was too late.

Leo and I had to start from scratch. Once again we put our heads together, to try to make the best of a bad situation. We decided to appeal to the good will of a man in the Bulgarian consulate in Brussels with whom we were on excellent terms, but who obviously was not in on our secret activities. He had a car and Bulgaria was an ally of Germany, which meant that he could come and go freely. We asked his help in getting some objects of value from the villa, which we were afraid would be plundered. Soon we were on our way to Knokke.

The town was deserted; the houses had been "inspected." Ours had been stripped of furniture, literally ransacked from top to bottom. The only thing that had been left, no doubt because of its size, was a huge wardrobe—in which we had made a hiding place for the radio transmitter, by putting in a false ceiling. The wardrobe proper was empty, but the hiding place had not been discovered, and the precious transmitter in its suitcase was still there.

We loaded our suitcase into the diplomat's car. On the road back, they were not letting through any cars but German ones—and ours. Barricades here, inspectors there, but we came through beautifully with our diplomatic registration, the sight of which brought the soldiers of the Wehrmacht to respectful attention.

Halfway to Brussels, however, we ran out of gas. The car refused to budge. We got out and, with our suitcase beside us, tried our luck at hitchhiking. What a scene! Two Soviet agents with no baggage but a radio transmitter, accompanied by a Bulgarian diplomat, hailing German vehicles as they went by. A luxurious car—filled with high-ranking SS officers—stopped. They listened to our explanations and we got in, after one of the officers had instructed the chauffeur to put our suitcase in the trunk. We spent the rest of the trip in friendly conversation—how could one refuse anything to a Bulgarian ally?—and after dissuading the Germans from seeing us to our homes, we wound up in a café, where we toasted our meeting (and our separation) with plenty of cognac.

Alone at last, we took a taxi to the apartment where we were to hide out. Alas, when Alamo went to work, it was only to discover that neither the transmitter nor the receiver was in working order. Once again we had to make use of the military attaché to send our report on the military situation.

Our expedition to Knokke was fruitful at least in one respect: it gave me another idea. Since we had traveled so easily in our Bulgarian friend's car, why not make an auto tour of the theater of military operations? I mentioned this possibility to our diplomat, explaining that it would be very useful to us to visit the branch offices of Au Roi du Caoutchouc in several towns in the north of France. He was fond of auto trips, even when they were a little risky; he had time on his hands; and he was cooperative by nature. He placed himself at our disposal, adding that he would take the opportunity to visit his compatriots in the region. We left Brussels on May 18, equipped with diplomatic passes that paved the way for us.

The trip lasted ten days. We took advantage of the breakthrough made by the Wehrmacht at Sedan; we witnessed the fighting around Abbeville and the attack on Dunkirk. Back in the Belgian capital, I wrote an eighty-page report in which I summed up everything I had learned of the "lightning war": the very deep penetration of armored tanks behind enemy lines, the aerial bombardments of strategic points, the mechanisms of communication between the rear and the front, and all the rest I had seen.

These ten days spent with the Teutonic warriors convinced me that it was simple to make contact with them. Both officers and enlisted men drank heavily and talked freely. The psychology of the victor drove them to boasting. They hoped that by the end of the year the war against France and Great Britain would be over, after which they would settle with the Soviet Union. A whole program, in short.

The opinion of the SS officers we met a little later was different. They were beginning to think, they explained to us, that the war with the USSR would not take place. This view was obviously the result of Nazi propaganda—which was echoed in the Soviet press. In Russia at that time it was fashionable to celebrate friendship with Germany. (A directive was sent to Russia's concentration camps forbidding the guards to call the political prisoners "fascists.") On the German side, even Goebbels was erasing from his delirious speeches all traces of anti-Sovietism. During these painful months we frequently heard German officers make the unbearable comparison between Hitler's regime and Stalin's. To hear them talk, there was not much difference between National Socialism and socialism; they argued that both had the same goal, though they were pursuing it by different paths. We preferred not to recognize the miserable, watered-down product they designated by the term socialism. I can still see that German officer slapping the hood of his car with the palm of his hand, exclaiming:

"If we have succeeded in our offensive beyond all hope, it is thanks to the help of the Soviet Union, which has provided us with gas for our tanks, leather for our shoes, and wheat for our granaries!"

5

s the war was moving south, we had to follow with a view to a new "tour of inspection." This time we set our sights on Paris. Petrov, our Bulgarian friend, who had taken us to Knokke and Abbeville and Dunkirk, was at the wheel again. We arrived in the French capital a few days after the Germans. It was a heartbreaking spectacle: flags bearing swastikas floated over the city, and men in grey-green uniforms filled the streets. The Parisians themselves seemed to have "deserted" to avoid witnessing the arrival of the enemy hordes.

For the whole summer of 1940 I concentrated my efforts on the formation of the Parisian group. I should like to introduce, here, a few of the principals. Hillel Katz helped me a great deal. I had known him in Palestine, like Leo Grossvogel, and then met him often again during my first time in France, 1929 to 1932, but after that we had lost sight of each other.

Katz was of medium height, with keen, intelligent eyes behind thick lenses, and a high forehead crowned by an abundant head of hair. Others were easily infected by Katz's enthusiasm and *joie de vivre*. A musician, like his father, he also knew how to handle a trowel and build a house. He had committed himself to communism at a very early age, and his faith in the ultimate victory of his ideas never faltered, even at the height of the storm. He was very fond of children, and active in several communist youth organizations. His direct, open attitude was endearing and he had friends everywhere; later, such contacts helped him in his work. A foreigner, he had enlisted as a volunteer in the French Army in 1940. After France's capitulation, he was demobilized and received a military identity card in the name of André Dubois.

Hillel Katz started work at my side immediately. True to our habits, we created commercial enterprises to serve as cover for our activities. On January 13, 1941, "Simexco" was born in Brussels and "Simex" in Paris.

Katz and a man named Alfred Corbin had met and become friends during the brief war; as prisoners, they had escaped together by swimming across the Somme. A shared experience of this kind is not easily forgotten.

After his discharge, Corbin had started a poultry-feed factory in a mill he had acquired in Giverny. Our first contact was very promising. Realizing immediately that we could count on him, I asked "Do you think we should continue the struggle?"

He answered, with a little smile, "Of course we should. The only question is, how?"

"The forms and methods must change," I told him. "From now on the battle will be fought underground. Are you ready?"

Was he ready? The next thing I knew, he was volunteering to install our first radio transmitter on his property in Giverny. Corbin was appointed manager of Simex in Paris— then we moved the "music box" out of his house, for our commercial cover had to be absolutely flawless.

Grossvogel, Katz, and Corbin will appear many times in the course of the story of the Red Orchestra.

I personally had no official position at Simex, but the Germans knew that a "Monsieur Gilbert" was financing the operations. Many of our associates, of course, were completely in the dark about our real purposes. Robert Breyer, a dental surgeon and a friend of Corbin's, was our chief stockholder, but he knew nothing about our underground work. Then there was Vladimir Keller, whom I met while I was looking for good interpreters to translate correspondence with German firms. He was born in Russia, but had lived for many years in Switzerland, where he had acquired sound habits of seriousness and discipline. Convinced that he was working for a very respectable company, he would pick up our telephone and shout, "Heil Hitler!"

Suzanne Cointe became office manager. Suzanne was a communist militant of long standing. She knew Katz from the days when she was a piano teacher and involved in a chorus of young communists, the *Chorale musicale de Paris*.

Katz recruited Emmanuel Mignon, a worker in a printing plant. We were not aware that Mignon was a member of a resistance group called La Famille Martin, whose objective was to keep an eye on businesses working for the Germans. Mignon, we learned later, informed a certain Charbonnier—who posed as a member of the resistance, but was exposed and executed after the war as an agent of the Gestapo—that Simex was collaborating with the occupying forces. In this way—as luck had it—we were placed above all suspicion.

Simex moved into offices on the Champs-Elysées. We did business principally with the Todt Organization, whose offices were directly across from ours, and which supervised all works of construction and fortification for the Wehrmacht. They were real profiteers in uniform. Simex was of interest to the people of Todt insofar as we could furnish the materials they needed on the black market.

Madame Likhonin made contact with Simex as soon as she learned of its existence. Madame Likhonin was quite a character. At the time we started dealing with her, she was prospecting for the Todt Organization. A little later, in fact, she represented Simex's interests before them. She was the wife of the last Russian military attaché in France during the First World War, and a violent anti-communist; after the October Revolution, she did not return to the Soviet Union. An intelligent woman, who was not afraid to take initiative, she immediately understood the profit she could derive from the occupation and devoted herself to it gladly.

Although Simex and Simexco had been designed primarily to serve as a cover and to finance the network, we very soon realized that they would allow us to penetrate the official German services in an unhoped-for manner. Soon, because of their business relations with the Todt Organization, the principals in Simex and Simexco received *Ausweis*, or passes, which opened every door for them. Business relations with the German officers multiplied.

In the course of good meals washed down with plenty of

wine, the Nazi leaders talked readily—and too much. We sat with glasses in hand, smiles on our lips, and an approving air, drinking in their words and remembering the revelations they contained. The information we accumulated this way was considerable. For example, it was one of the engineers of the Todt Organization—Ludwig Kainz, who had taken a liking to Leo—who first gave us information on the preparations for the war in the east. He had worked on the construction of fortifications at the German-Russian border in Poland. Then, in the spring of 1941, during another trip, he observed that the Wehrmacht was preparing an offensive against the Soviet Union. He told us about it when he returned. Kainz, in fact, had broken away from Nazism. Later, after Germany invaded Russia, he was to witness a horrible event: the Babi Yar massacre, in the region of Kiev, where tens of thousands of Jews lost their lives.

We set up a branch in Marseilles, on the Rue du Dragon, in the fall of 1941; in Brussels, Kent was the manager of Simexco. Leo Grossvogel supervised operations in the two companies in Paris and in Brussels.

Jules Jaspar, officially the director of the Marseilles branch of Simex, was already organizing an escape network through Algeria and Portugal, which would be used by a hundred-odd members of the resistance. In Vichy, Jaspar made a number of fruitful contacts. Vichy was a seething hotbed of intrigue, a frenzied menagerie where collaborators, resisters, and spies rubbed elbows; in Vichy, a pair of sharp ears in the right place at the right time could pick up all sorts of rumors, even secrets of state. There was nothing about the seamy side of the politics of Vichy, the behind-the-scenes maneuvering, the diplomatic games with Italy, Spain, and the Vatican, that the Center did not know. For example, since Vichy had taken on the expense of maintaining the German army, as a result of the stipulations of the armistice agreement, we were informed every month of the state of their bookkeeping. It took no great genius to deduce from this the movements of the troops.

I established liaisons with the resistance organizations through Michel, the representative from Communist Party headquarters, with whom I met regularly. Thanks to the organization of railway employees, we had complete information on the movements of the German troops in France. Immigrant workers in the great industrial centers, with whom I had maintained close contact, sent us valuable information about production. Some remarkably well-placed agents had sources of information that were inexhaustible.

There was Baron Vasily de Maximovich, whom Michel introduced to me at the end of 1940 as a White Russian emigré who wanted to work for the Red Army!

Maximovich was a curious product of the period between the two world wars. His father, a general in the czarist army, was one of the glories of the imperial court. At the time of the October Revolution, Vasily and his sister Anna left Russia and settled in France. Vasily entered the Ecole Centrale and became an engineer. When war was declared, he was declared suspect by the authorities, like so many other foreigners living in France, and was interned in a camp in Vernet.

Fate held out a hand to Vasily one day, after the armistice, when a German delegation led by Dr. Hans Kuprian went to the camp at Vernet to recruit workers for the Third Reich. Kuprian took an interest in Vasily. Shocked to find a Russian baron in such "bad company," he had him released and introduced him to some officers who worked at staff headquarters in the Hotel Majestic.

Kuprian assumed that, being a baron and a White Russian, Maximovich must be a confirmed anti-communist. At the Hotel Majestic, Vasily came and went freely, and observed. Fiercely anti-Nazi, a fox in the farmyard, he made contact with us. No doubt the Germans had released him in the hope that he would be able to "make himself useful," and in this they were not mistaken. He was extremely useful—but to us.

And then, very conveniently, love entered the picture. Kuprian's secretary, Anna-Margaret Hoffman-Scholz, fell in love with the baron. Before long she was working for the Third Reich's "ambassador" to Paris, Otto Abetz. The trickle became an unending flow, and confidential documents made their way to Moscow in the form of dispatches.

Anna Maximovich, Vasily's sister, a psychiatrist who ran a

clinic in Billeron, also became involved in our work. Her chateau was frequented by the personnel of the German organizations. This cheerful woman doctor, six feet tall and built like a lumberjack, practiced an unusual type of therapy with her patients. She was matchless in the art of confessing the secretaries and employees of the Wehrmacht.

Among Anna's patients was a young German woman of thirty-five, Kaethe Voelkner, secretary to the president of the Sauckel Organization—which was in charge of manpower for the Third Reich. Vasily Maximovich had noticed her first. After a few preliminary tests, he turned her over to Anna for the final examination. The results were conclusive. We began receiving first-hand information on the manpower needs of German industry and the economic problems of the Third Reich. In addition, Kaethe procured blank forms and certificates of employment for the network; in the event of an inspection, these would certify that their owner, a worker in Germany and consequently an "excellent European," was currently on vacation.

We also delegated a special group of technicians to set up a monitoring board on the telephone lines of the Hotel Lutetia, headquarters of the Paris Abwehr. In this way the director in Moscow could read transcriptions of the conversations between the German counterespionage group in Paris and the central office in Berlin.

Another method of investigation, less technical but also very effective, was the use of prostitutes in Paris nightclubs frequented by the Nazi army. Every day hundreds of German soldiers arrived in Paris to forget the hell of combat. One of our men worked in the office that organized their leaves and, by keeping track of their original divisions, could reconstruct the marching orders of the Wehrmacht. One of the guides who had the job of showing them around Montmartre and the Eiffel Tower—an itinerary calculated to relax the weary soldier—was also working for us. He steered them toward certain bars where several of our correspondents, with the aid of liquor, took a real interest in the lives and troubles of the German soldier. A classic method, to be sure, but from these

smokefilled dives many interesting facts reached us: about
the strength of the divisions, casualties, supply problems, the
morale of the troops, and other items.

In Belgium, the director of Simexco, Kent, socialized with
high-ranking German military personnel and local manufac-
turers, and in this way picked up a large quantity of military
and economic information. The home of his mistress, Margarete Barcza, became a very popular salon with Nazi officials.

The Belgian group made a choice recruit in Isidore Springer. I had known him personally since the thirties, when, as a
militant in Hashomer Hatzair, he used to argue with me in
the lectures I came to give in Brussels. Later he joined the
Belgian Communist Party and enlisted in the International
Brigade.

The signing of the pact between Germany and the Soviet
Union was traumatic for this anti-fascist fighter. As soon as
we made contact with him, he agreed to work for us, and with
the help of his wife, Flore Velaerts, he outdid himself. He had
his own little personal network of technicians and informers,
army men (he had been an officer in the Belgian army in
1940) whose expertise was essential in weighing the value of
the information we collected, and a great many specialists in
industry. He himself was a chemical engineer.

Hermann Izbutski ("Bob") was part of the Belgian group.
His parents were Polish Jews, but Hermann was born in
Antwerp; he had been working with us since 1939. An ardent
communist, he gave freely of his time. We made him a
traveling salesman for the Red Orchestra: he rode his bicycle
to all the surrounding communities, no matter how small,
making contacts, spotting isolated houses, and enlisting
liaison agents.

Izbutski recommended a young man to me, one of his new
recruits, assuring me that he would make an excellent agent.
I met the boy, and as his first assignment gave him a very
heavy locked suitcase—I did not tell him what was in
it—which he was to take from Antwerp to Ghent. Izbutski
was to go with him.

A few days later I received a report that aroused my suspicion. Our young candidate had told a friend of his, swearing him to secrecy, that he was transporting weapons. It was the old story: I'll tell you, but don't tell anyone else; in this way, the most confidential information becomes an open secret. A talker and a braggart—a bad combination.

Tests of this kind helped us to find out whom we could count on.

I turned the keys to the suitcase over to the boy and to Izbutski, telling them that detailed instructions were inside. The boy rushed over and opened the suitcase, only to find that it was full of rocks.

In 1933, shortly after Hitler came to power, a twenty-four-year-old German aristocrat by the name of Harro Schulze-Boysen and his friend Henry Erlanger were arrested by the SS. Since March, 1932, Schulze-Boysen had been publishing a review of which Erlanger was one of the editors, which was open to all political opinions. Its title indicated at least one exception: *Der Gegner* (*The Enemy*). The enemy was Nazism.

Now that Nazism had triumphed in Germany, the SS, the front-line troops of the "master race," wanted to make the Schulze-Boysens and Erlangers pay for months and months of impassioned campaigning against the future dictator and his movement. In this specialty the SS had predecessors and teachers: the Italian fascists and their "punitive expeditions."

The men who arrested Schulze-Boysen and Erlanger went to work. The two prisoners were stripped to the waist and made to run the gauntlet between two rows of fanatics who beat them with riding crops; when they reached the end they had to begin again. Their bodies were covered with wounds, but Schulze-Boysen, when he reached the end the second time, turned to his tormentors and shouted, "You can do it again, if you like!" Whereupon he saluted the SS commandant and said, "I've completed my tour of inspection."

The Nazis were astonished, and approached Schulze-Boysen. "Join us," they said. "Men of your caliber should be on our side." At the same time, they fell on Erlanger and murdered him before his friend's eyes. Erlanger was a Jew.

Schulze-Boysen confided to his friends some time later, "Erlanger's death helped me to take the decisive step." From that day Schulze-Boysen's commitment was irrevocable.

The seizure of power by the Nazis made some courageous men and women decide to join the resistance. The first group that formed around Schulze-Boysen included the writer Günther Weissenborn, Dr. Elvira Paul, Giselle von Pernitz, Walter Kuchenmeister, and Kurt and Elisabeth Schumacher. Later their little group was reinforced by other members.

In 1936 Schulze-Boysen married Libertas Haas-Heye, granddaughter of Prince Philippe von Eulenburg. One of the friends of the family was a man named Hermann Goering. The marshal took a keen interest in Harro and sent him to the institute that bore his name, where, under the regime of the Third Reich, the most advanced military research was being carried out. Schulze-Boysen made rapid progress. By the time the war broke out, he occupied a key position in the Luftwaffe. More than ever, he devoted himself to his resistance activities. In 1939, he and his followers joined forces with Arvid Harnack's group.

Schulze-Boysen was as passionate and hot-headed as Arvid Harnack was calm and reflective. Harnack was older than Harro; he came from an academic family, had a degree in philosophy, and had studied economics in the United States. While there he had met and married Mildred Fish, a professor of literature. On his return to Germany he went to work for the Ministry of Finance, and he already occupied a very important position when Soviet Intelligence approached him in 1936. He had little chance to use his talents in those years, though, since Stalin had forbidden intelligence agents to operate on German territory—on the pretext that agents would be exposed to provocation and could thus endanger the Russian-German peace.

The Schulze-Boysen and Harnack group was joined by some new members: the writer Dr. Adam Kuckhoff and his wife Greta; Dr. Adolf Grimme, the socialist ex-minister of Prussia; Johann Sieg, an old militant and editor of the *Rote Fahne*, the newspaper of the German Communist Party; and Hans Coppi, Heinrich Scheel, Hans Lautenschläger, and Ina Ender, former members of communist youth organizations. When the war broke out, the best members of the group were assigned to intelligence work, but in practice there was no rigid separation between the Red Orchestra network and their resistance activities; Schulze-Boysen ran both of these—and this confusion of tasks was an unpardonable error, which would be paid for very dearly.

The activities of the resistance group did not go unnoticed in the capital of the Reich: the leaflets that were put in mailboxes; the posters that appeared on walls; the publication of a newspaper, *The Home Front*, in five languages, which circulated among prisoners of war. Nor was the work limited to propaganda: escape routes were set up for Jews and prisoners, contacts were made with foreign workers, secret groups in numerous enterprises sabotaged war production.

One of the most spectacular efforts was directed against an exhibit, organized by Goebbels' services, called "The Soviet Paradise." A group of young Jewish militants led by Herbert Baum had tried to burn the exhibit. They were denounced by a provocateur, and twenty-eight were arrested and beheaded. Schulze-Boysen's group took a different tack: in one night, the walls of Berlin were covered with posters that proclaimed, NAZI PARADISE = WAR, FAMINE, LIES, GESTAPO. HOW MUCH LONGER?

Can anyone realize what this action meant in the capital of the Third Reich in 1942? On that occasion, Schulze-Boysen's group was more fortunate than the twenty-eight young Jewish militants.

Schulze-Boysen himself did not enter into full contact with Soviet Intelligence until 1941. He had tipped his hand, though, as early as 1936, when he sent the Soviet Embassy a list of Nazi agents who had infiltrated the International Brigade in Spain. A few days before the invasion of Poland, Schulze-Boysen transmitted the Wehrmacht's plans for the offensive to a Polish liaison in Berlin.

After the declaration of hostilities, Harro Schulze-Boysen took advantage of his position with the Luftwaffe to collect a large amount of information. He was helped by Colonel Erwin Gehrts, head of the third group of officers' training of the army air force; Johann Graudenz of the Messerschmitt factories; Horst Heilmann, a former member of the Hitler youth movement who worked in the group that decoded dispatches for Dr. Vauck; and Herbert Gollnow, who was chief of the section of parachutists operating behind the Soviet front.

As for Arvid Harnack, he had access to the most confidential industrial plans, including military production.

This gives some idea of the decisive position the Berlin group occupied in the Red Orchestra.

It is undeniable that German resisters working on the inside played a very special role in the struggle against Nazism. Obviously, for a Frenchman, a Belgian, a Pole, or a Czech, commitment to the struggle raised no problem of conscience; indeed, it had the force of duty. But for a German, did it not amount to betraying his own country?

The Schulze-Boysens and the Harnacks did not hesitate over the answer. They had close experience with the monstrousness of Nazism, they had weighed the consequences of a Nazi military victory, and they knew it would mean darkness covering the earth. They knew that only the allied armies could crush the beast—but they also realized how much help people like themselves, in the heart of the German machine, could provide to the chiefs of staff of the countries united against Hitlerism. So they made their choice.

I am aware that often today this choice is held against them, and that in West Germany they are frequently regarded as traitors, while agents who worked for the English are celebrated as heroes. As if, because they collaborated with the USSR, these men and women had not contributed to the same victory.

7

"*Wir gehen nach England . . .*" We're going to
England . . .

After the defeat of the French army, the favorite
song of the German soldiers left no doubt about the Nazi
chiefs' next objective. Under the code name Sea Lion, Hitler's
generals were feverishly preparing to invade the British Isles.
In August, the high command of the Wehrmacht gave the
order to launch the offensive against Great Britain on land,
on sea, and in the air. On September 7, the first bombs fell on
London. For sixty-five consecutive nights the English slept in
bomb shelters. Everyone felt that a German landing was
imminent.

Then on the 12th of October, there was a dramatic reversal.
On Hitler's orders, preparations for Operation Sea Lion were
suspended with no date set for their reactivation. I learned of
this decision immediately through our agents—they had
succeeded, thanks to their *Ausweis*, in getting to the Atlantic
Coast; there it was easy to see that the excitement had died
down. Old cargo vessels had replaced the warships. Even
more important, the divisions that were to have taken part in
the invasion had been withdrawn. I sent a dispatch to the
Center stating that the Germans would not attempt a landing
in England in the foreseeable future. Soon we had confirmation that the troops had been sent east: three German
divisions (the Fourth, the Twelfth, and the Eighteenth) that
had been stationed on the Atlantic were now billeted in
Poland, near Poznan.

On December 18, 1940, Hitler signed Directive Number 21,
better known as Operation Barbarossa. The first sentence of
this plan was explicit: "The German armed forces must be
ready before the end of the war against Great Britain to defeat
the Soviet Union by means of a *Blitzkrieg*."

Richard Sorge warned the Center immediately; he forwarded them a copy of the directive. Week after week, the heads of Red Army Intelligence received updates on the Wehrmacht's preparations. At the beginning of 1941, Schulze-Boysen sent the Center precise information on the operation being planned: massive bombardments of Leningrad, Kiev, and Vyborg; the number of divisions involved— In February, I sent a detailed dispatch giving the exact number of divisions withdrawn from France and Belgium, and sent to the east. In May, through the Soviet military attaché in Vichy, General Susloparov, I sent the proposed plan of attack, and indicated the original date, May 15, then the revised date, and the final date. On May 12, Sorge warned Moscow that 150 German divisions were massed along the frontier. On the 15th, he cited June 21st for the beginning of the operations, a date that was confirmed by Schulze-Boysen in Berlin.

The Soviet services were not the only ones in possession of this information. On March 11, 1941, Roosevelt gave the Russian ambassador the plans gathered by American agents for Operation Barbarossa. On the 10th of June the English released similar information. Soviet agents working in the frontier zone in Poland and Rumania gave detailed reports on the concentrations of troops.

He who closes his eyes sees nothing, even in the full light of day. This was the case with Stalin and his entourage. The generalissimo preferred to trust his political instinct rather than the secret reports piled up on his desk. Convinced that he had signed an eternal pact of friendship with Germany, he sucked on the pipe of peace. He had buried his tomahawk and he was not ready to dig it up yet.

Thirty years after the war was over, Marshal Golikov, writing in a Soviet historical review, officially confirmed the value of the information received:

"The Soviet Intelligence Services had learned in good time the dates of the attack against the USSR and had given the alarm before it was too late. . . . The intelligence services provided accurate information regarding the military potential of Hitler's Germany, the exact number of armed forces, the quantities of arms, and the strategic plans of the commanders of the Wehrmacht. . . ."

Marshal Golikov was in a good position to make such a statement. From June, 1940, to July, 1941, he was the Director of Red Army Intelligence. If the Russian chiefs of staff were so well informed, what was the reason for the débacle after the German attack? The answer is no doubt contained in a note Golikov himself addressed to his services on March 20, 1941:

"All the documents claiming that war is imminent must be regarded as forgeries emanating from British or even German sources."

On the most important dispatches sent to him by Sorge, Schulze-Boysen, and me, Golikov noted in the margin "Double agent" or "British source."

Marshal Golikov was not the only man to rewrite history. In 1972, there was a conference in Moscow at which Susloparov took the floor and told how he, the military attaché in Vichy, had warned Moscow that the German attack was imminent. It is a pity that I was unable to add my testimony, which might have obliged Susloparov to be more modest. Every time I had handed him information on the preparations for war against the Soviet Union, he had patted me on the shoulder condescendingly and said, "My poor fellow, I will send your dispatches, but only to make you happy."

On June 21, 1941, we had confirmation from Vasily Maximovich and Schulze-Boysen that the invasion was set for the next day. There was still time to put the Red Army in a state of alert. I rushed to Vichy with Leo Grossvogel. As incredulous as ever, Susloparov tried to convince us:

"You're completely mistaken. Only today I met with the Japanese military attaché, who just arrived from Berlin. He assures me that Germany is not preparing for war. We can depend on him."

I preferred to depend on my own informants, and I insisted that Susloparov send the dispatch. Late that evening I went back to my hotel. At four in the morning the manager woke me up, shouting in my ear,

"It's happened, Monsieur Gilbert! Germany is at war with the Soviet Union!"

On the 23rd, Wolosiuk, the attaché for the army air force under Susloparov, arrived in Vichy, having left Moscow a few hours before the outbreak of the war. He told me that before his departure, he had been called in to see the Director, who had given him a message for me:

"You can tell Otto"—my code name—"that I have passed on the information on the imminence of the German attack to the big boss. The big boss is amazed that a man like Otto, an old militant and an intelligence man, has allowed himself to be intoxicated by English propaganda. You can tell him again that the big boss is completely convinced that the war with Germany will not start before 1944———"

The "complete conviction" of the big boss, Stalin, was to be expensive. Having decapitated the Red Army in 1937—which was responsible for the first defeats—the inspired strategist then turned over what was left of the army to Hitler's hordes. During the first hours of the German offensive—in defiance of all the evidence, and because he had the idea of a planted rumor so firmly in mind—he refused to allow a counterattack. A rumor planted by whom, and for what reason? No one knew. He was the only one who was so convinced, but he forced everyone else to share his conviction.

The results: the airfields pounded by German bombers; the airplanes smashed to pieces on the ground; the German fighter planes masters of the sky, transforming the Russian plains into graveyards strewn with demolished tanks. On the evening of the 22nd, the leaders of the army, whom Stalin had forbidden to put their troops on alert, received the order to drive the enemy outside their borders. By this time the armored divisions of the Wehrmacht had already penetrated several hundred kilometers into Soviet territory.

It would take the sacrifices of a whole nation rising up against its invader to reverse the military situation. But meanwhile, Stalin's error would cost Russia millions of lives and prolong the war.

My comrades and I lived through these first days of the war between Germany and Russia with mixed feelings.

The defeats of the Red Army worried us, but above and beyond the courage of the people, we were counting on the vast reserves of the Soviet Union in manpower and material. Psychologically, though, we felt relieved of a great burden. As communists, we had never accepted the non-aggression pact of 1939. As intelligence men, we had not believed that it would last. From now on, things were clear: the USSR was engaged in the struggle against fascism. For us this meant an increase in effort and determination. We had to be ready to collect a greater amount of military, economic, and military information. In this way we would be contributing our share to the victory.

8

W ho was it who defeated the Axis? It was the Russian footsoldier with his feet frozen in the snows of Stalingrad; the American marine with his nose in the red sands of Omaha Beach; the Yugoslavian or Greek partisan fighting in his mountains. No intelligence service determined the outcome of the conflict. Neither Sorge, in Japan, nor Rado, the head of the network in Switzerland, nor I had a decisive influence on that outcome. As partisans stationed in the front lines, we did, within the limits of our resources and thanks to the devotion of our comrades, contribute to the ultimate success of the armed forces. The Red Orchestra was one of the essential elements of Soviet Intelligence, but it was not the only one: there were networks in Poland, Czechoslovakia, Rumania, Bulgaria, Switzerland, Scandinavia, and the Balkan countries.

I think it is necessary to put things in their proper perspective. The Red Orchestra was a fine idea, but what was its purpose? A group of courageous men existing right under the enemy's nose and stealing information and documents is all very well, but just how important and valuable was this material?

Between 1940 and 1943, the musicians of the Red Orchestra—that is, the radio operators, also known as "pianists"—sent the Center about 1500 dispatches. The first category of dispatches had to do with the material resources of the enemy: war industries, raw materials, means of transport, new types of armaments. In this area, the Red Orchestra scored some dramatic victories. The top-secret plans for a new German tank, the T6-Tiger, were sent to Moscow in time for Soviet industry to prepare the KV tank, superior from every point of view to the German machine. The appearance of the KV on the battlefield was an unhappy surprise for the German High Command.

In the fall of 1941, the Center received Dispatch Number 37: "The daily production of Messerschmitt Airplane ME-110 is from nine to ten aircraft per day. Their losses on the eastern front are reaching forty planes per day." The implications of the arithmetic were not difficult to grasp.

At the end of 1941, we warned the Director that "The Messerschmitt Company has been working for three months on the construction of a new fighter plane equipped with new motors that will enable it to reach 900 kilometers per hour," and the plans for this new plane went to Moscow on microfilm. A few months later a new fighter plane, superior to the Messerschmitt, emerged from the Soviet factories.

A second category of dispatches provided information on the military situation: the number and placement of divisions; available armaments; plans of attack.

For example, here is Dispatch Number 42, dated 10 December 1941:

"The Luftwaffe in its first and second echelons possesses 21,500 machines of which 6,258 are for transport; 9,000 planes are presently on the eastern front."

Or again:

"November '41—Source Suzanne: the chiefs of staff of the German army have proposed to hold all winter the line running through Rostov—Izyum—Kursk—Orel—Briansk—Novgorod—Leningrad."

And the follow-up, a few days later:

"Hitler has rejected this proposal, and given the order for the offensive to be launched against Moscow for the sixth time, using all the forces available on that part of the front."

At the end of 1942:

"In Italy, various sectors of the army leadership are beginning to sabotage directives from above. We must not rule out the possibility that Mussolini will be overthrown," a forecast that came true six months later. "The Germans are concentrating their forces between Munich and Innsbruck with a view to possible intervention."

Finally, the chief agents regularly sent syntheses and analyses of current and future trends. Here is an example:

"The leading circles of the Wehrmacht feel that the *Blitz-*

krieg has failed in the east and that Germany is no longer assured of a military victory. Tendencies to push Hitler into making a separate peace with England. In the high command of the Wehrmacht, some generals think that the war will last another thirty months and will end with a compromise."

It would be a mistake to imagine that the reports sent by Sorge, by Schulze-Boysen, or by me were received in Moscow as the gospel truth. All the material that arrived at the Center passed through the decoding department first, then it was screened and checked by military and political specialists. The information was collated with other data arriving from different sources. Thus, in the fall of 1940, when I warned the Center that three German divisions had been withdrawn from the Atlantic coast and sent to Poland, the Center received confirmation of this through a network of conductors of the trains that had convoyed these troops, and then through the Polish network.

In the fall of 1941, the Red Army was in a critical position. In five months, the Wehrmacht had advanced 1,200 kilometers. The fall of Kiev had given the Germans access to the wheat granaries of the Ukraine. To the extreme south, General Manstein occupied the shore of the Black Sea. To the north, Leningrad was threatened; and in the center of the German-occupied area, the fall of Smolensk had opened the way to Moscow.

Hitler was able to announce triumphantly: "The Russian army has been destroyed. We will enter Moscow in a matter of days."

The German High Command was preparing a plan for occupying the capital and replacing the government—Hitler was convinced that the fall of Moscow would so demoralize the army and the people that Stalin would be brought to his knees. He summoned his generals to his headquarters at Rastenburg, in eastern Prussia, to plan the offensive. The Führer was in favor of a frontal attack on Moscow, but his chiefs of staff recommended surrounding the city. According to their plan, the Fourth and Third Armies would join forces behind Moscow after a vast movement of encirclement. It was this latter solution that prevailed.

Today I can reveal that a member of the Red Orchestra was present at this summit meeting. The stenographer who carefully took down the remarks of Hitler and his generals was a member of Schulze-Boysen's group. The Soviet chiefs of staff were informed of every detail of the attack, in time to prepare the counteroffensive that succeeded in driving off the Wehrmacht.

This same stenographer also warned the Center, nine months in advance, about the offensive against the Caucasus. On November 12, 1941, the Center received the following dispatch:

"Plan III, Objective Caucasus, originally scheduled for November, to be carried out spring 1942. Placement of troops to be completed by 1 May. Total logistic effort toward this end effective 1 February. Bases of deployment for offensive on Caucasus: Losowaia—Balakleya—Chuguyev—Belgorod —Achtynka—Krasnograd. Headquarters: Kharkhov. Details follow."

I must emphasize the remarkable value of the information sent by Sorge, who stated positively that Japan would not make a move against Russia. Consequently, the fresh divisions freed in the east were able to play a decisive role in the Red Army victory around Moscow.

On May 12, 1942, a special courier arrived in Moscow, bringing the microfilm in which I gave all the information on the major elements of the offensive. In August, the whole of the Caucasus was to be occupied, in order to hold Baku and the oil wells. Stalingrad was a major objective of the attack.

On July 12, an army high command for the Stalingrad front was therefore organized under the direction of General Timoshenko. The trap was set—the Wehrmacht would fall into it.

9

Fernand Pauriol

One of our most important activities was broadcasting. Obviously, there would not have been much point in accumulating information if we had no way of getting it to its destination. Liaisons in an intelligence network are like oxygen to the deep sea diver. If the mouthpiece is obstructed, paralysis is inevitable.

It must be admitted that when the war broke out we were cut off. We were not ready to broadcast for the good reason that the Center had not been willing to grant the necessary attention to communications. We lacked transmitters and pianists. Little by little, the Orchestra assembled the instruments and the performers. Ultimately there were three transmitters operating in Berlin, three in Belgium, and three in the Netherlands. For the time being, however, France was silent, and we waited impatiently for her to join the concert of the airwaves.

Radio broadcasting was not the only means of transmitting messages at our disposal. In the first place, not all information can be communicated in the form of a radio dispatch: one cannot broadcast diagrams of ports and fortifications, for example, or military maps, or charts of the chain of command of organizations and services. In the case of such documents, we worked with invisible ink and, even more, with microfilm. Until June, 1941, most of the material collected in France was sent through the Soviet military attaché in Vichy, Suslo-parov. Above all, we avoided carrying documents across borders or the lines of demarcation of military control. We had devised an alternative system that Leo and I preferred to all others: the first step was to reserve a berth in a sleeping car. Another member of the network would independently reserve a compartment, which would remain empty—preferably it would be one that communicated with the first. After the ticket-taker had passed through, the agent would leave his sleeping car, go into the compartment, unscrew an electric light fixture, place the fountain pen in which the microfilm was concealed inside the fixture, and return to his own place.

At Moulins, for instance—the station at the line of demarcation between Occupied and Unoccupied France—our courier and his baggage would naturally be searched. Then the German police would open the compartment, see that it was empty, and go on without stopping. After that the agent had only to retrieve the pen with its storehouse of information.

For the management and staff of Simex and Simexco, mobility was greatly facilitated by the documents that came from our commerce with the Todt Organization. Certain other couriers were no less improbable. One of our liaisons between Berlin and Brussels was the very beautiful Ina Ender, a fashion model in the *salon de couture* where Hitler's mistress, Eva Braun, and the wives of Nazi dignitaries bought their clothes. Simone Pheter, an employee of the Paris bureau of the Belgian Chamber of Commerce, took charge of transmitting messages between Paris and Brussels. All she had to do was send her material to her correspondent at the Stock Exchange in Brussels, who passed it on. We also used train conductors who crossed the line of demarcation, and sailors on ships that made the crossing to Scandinavia.

But with the beginning of the war in the east the expansion of our activities obliged us to become more professional. However ingenious and effective these devices were, however appealing to the imagination and enlivening to the pages of spy novels, they did not adequately answer the needs of a secret service that had to send large numbers of dispatches at maximum speed. After the Soviet Union entered the war, the military attaché, Susloparov, left Vichy. The only channel we had left was the transmitting station in Brussels, but this was inadequate in both security and efficiency.

Consequently, we needed—urgently—sending stations in France. I asked the Director to put me in touch with one of the head radio men of the Communist Party, who could certainly help us in this undertaking. He agreed. And so a rendezvous was arranged with Fernand Pauriol, "Duval."

Our first meeting was encouraging from the start. I rea-

lized that he was the right man for the job, and besides, there
was a vitality about him that won me over. In spite of his very
heavy party responsibilities, he agreed to train pianists and
look for sets.

A southern Frenchman, a man of verve and gaiety, Pauriol
had the knack of approaching the most difficult projects with
a smile full of the light of the land of sunshine. Born into
one of those families that teach the children to read from
l'Humanité, he had become a militant at a very early age, first
in communist youth groups and then in the party. Tempted
by a life of adventure, he had studied at the naval training
school in Marseilles and earned a degree as a ship's radio
operator in the merchant marine. He had served for three
years, but after his military service he could not find work, as
he was already known to the police.

Pauriol went into journalism, then, with a vengeance. He
devoted all his time to it, writing in *La Défense,* the official
newspaper of the international *Secours Rouge,* and giving
frequent lectures for the party. In 1936, the Communist Party
started a bi-weekly newspaper, *Rouge-Midi,* in Marseilles.
There was not a penny in the till, but Pauriol became its
editor-in-chief. He was a born newspaperman: he wrote, he
went everywhere, looked for printers, played errand boy.
Thanks to him, the readership of the newspaper grew.

When the war broke out, Pauriol was assigned to the
"gonio," the service for detecting radio broadcasts. The irony
of fate: the future radio chief of the Communist Party and the
Red Orchestra was working on the detection of underground
broadcasts! After France's capitulation and his own demobili-
zation, Fernand immediately involved himself in the resistance, and he began setting up radio stations and training
operators.

We appreciated the value of this gift from the Communist
Party. Fernand very quickly assembled a radio set. As for
prospective pianists, the military attaché Susloparov put me
in contact with the Sokols.

The Sokols, who came from a region that had been
reannexed to the USSR after the division of Poland and the
signing of the German-Soviet pact, had asked to be repatriat-

ed to Russian territory. Hersch was a doctor and Mira was a professor of social sciences, but in going through the formalities, they had presented themselves as radio repairmen. The USSR needed technicians, and they knew they would stand a better chance of getting admitted that way than by reporting their real professions. Their application passed through the Soviet Embassy in Vichy, and landed on Susloparov's desk. Knowing that I needed radio operators, he sent them to me.

The Sokols were old communist militants; they did not hesitate to accept my proposition. Fernand Pauriol took them on and, in record time, made them operational. By the end of 1941, Fernand had seven new students: five Spaniards and the Girauds, a couple. In a few months—which was a record—the French Orchestra was ready to start playing. For dispatches of major importance, Pauriol set up a special line of communication that passed through the underground center of the French Communist Party; more about that later.

Meanwhile, the Center put me in touch with Harry Robinson, a former member of the Spartacus group, headed by Rosa Luxemburg, and a distinguished veteran of underground activities who had been living in Western Europe for many years. Robinson had broken contact with the Center. The Director left it up to me to decide whether relations should be resumed.

"Since the purging of the Soviet intelligence services, I broke contact with them. I was in Moscow in 1938, I saw the best men liquidated, and I couldn't go along with it"— Robinson explained to me. "At the moment, I'm in touch with representatives of De Gaulle, and I know the Center doesn't allow such contacts——"

"Look here, Harry," I told him, "I don't approve of what's going on in Moscow either. I, too, was sickened by the liquidation of Berzin and his assistants. But this is no time to cling to the past—right now, we're at war. Let's forget about what happened before and fight together. You've been a communist all your life, and you're not going to stop being one just because you're in disagreement with the Center." My arguments moved him, and I was glad they did.

He had a radio set and an operator, but he would not allow

their use—he refused to subject the operator to any risks. But he made me a proposition: "Let's agree on a regular rendez-vous, and I'll give your agents the information I have—which I will encode myself—and you'll see that it reaches the Center."

The Director accepted his proposition. Robinson's information reached me regularly. I helped him financially, for he was having trouble making a living, but he never belonged to the Red Orchestra.

One day in the fall of 1942 he sent me word that he wanted to see me without delay. A rendezvous was arranged. What he had to tell me was indeed important:

"You know I'm in contact with London," he told me. "A representative from De Gaulle is here and wants to meet with the Communist Party leaders."

"For what purpose? Do you know?"

"Because De Gaulle would like the party to send him an emissary. The leadership of the Communist Party is so well camouflaged that for three weeks our man hasn't been able to make the slightest contact."

I promised Harry I would take care of it. I had an opportunity of meeting with Michel in two days, and I passed the message along. Michel set the rendezvous for a short time later.

That is how the French government-in-exile first made contact with the underground leaders of the French Communist Party. The result was that a few months later Fernand Grenier was sent to London as secretary to General De Gaulle's government.

My Double Life

Myths about espionage die hard. People imagine that a secret agent takes courses in some school where he is initiated into the arcana of the occult science of intelligence. On the benches of these special universities, the future agent studies espionage the way other people study mathematics. When he leaves he is handed a diploma, and the new graduate goes out into the world to put theory to the test of experience. People forget that the laws of intelligence are neither theorems nor axioms, and that generally speaking, they do not appear in books. These schools exist, but I have doubts about their usefulness.

I have never taken a course in espionage. In this field, I am merely a humble self-taught man. My school was my life as a militant. Nothing could have better prepared me to lead a network like the Red Orchestra than the twenty tumultuous years of activity—often clandestine—before I entered Soviet Intelligence. I learned about the underground in Poland and Palestine, and this irreplaceable experience was worth all the courses in the world. My old friends Leo Grossvogel and Hillel Katz, who played such a decisive role in the formation and development of the network, had attended the same school. As communist militants, we had learned to be like fish in the water everywhere; intelligence work requires the same ease, the same imagination. When Kent, fresh out of his "academy of espionage," went into a working-class bar in the Paris suburbs and ordered tea, he aroused ridicule but, above all, he attracted attention. For an intelligence man, this is against the rules. At school they forgot to teach Kent to be inconspicuous.

To pass unnoticed, not by pretending to be invisible, but by living normally, was the golden rule. In this, the cover is decisive. The agent must not "act," he must "be." In Brussels I not only assumed the identity of Adam Mikler, I became Adam Mikler. The most attentive and persistent observer would not have noticed any difference between my life and the life of any of the other businessmen I met at the Stock Exchange or in a restaurant.

To fit into the mold meant that you had to have an intimate knowledge of the country you supposedly came from, the social circle you moved in there, and the profession you practiced. So Adam Mikler was from Quebec? I could talk for hours about the charms of Montreal and baffle any curious mind. In Brussels, the presence of Luba and one of our sons facilitated my acceptance into the life of the community. Then, during the war and the occupation, I had to redouble my precautions.

On the surface, my life in Paris had not changed. Jean Gilbert, stockholder in Simex, lived under that name on the Rue Fortuny, or later on the Rue de Prony; his neighbors and landladies knew him as a Belgian industrialist. I lived alone, and in those two "official" apartments I received few visitors. My friend Georgie de Winter never came there. She had left Belgium in the fall of 1941, and since the United States had entered the war she had been living under the name of Thevenet in Pigalle. Later she rented a little house in Vésinet. She was discreet and intelligent, and all she knew was that I was fighting Nazism. Sometimes Leo came to see me in the Rue de Prony. One evening when he was caught by the curfew he slept over. From that day the landlady, who until then had always been pleasant and obliging, was obviously put out with me. Two or three weeks later a woman came to see me. The next day the landlady was all smiles. Intrigued, I asked the reasons for her metamorphosis.

"Monsieur Gilbert," she said, "I always thought you were a respectable man. And then, the first person who spent the night with you was a man. Yesterday when I saw the lady, I was relieved; I was afraid you were a homosexual."

Jean Gilbert went several times a week to the Simex offices. Except for Leo Grossvogel, Alfred Corbin, Hillel Katz, and Suzanne Cointe, the employees were unaware of my role. Everyone thought I was an industrialist who handled a

lot of business. Of course, it was against the rules to bring
compromising material to Simex and, above all, to talk about
network matters while there. The cover had to remain
flawless. To close the very important deals we made with the
Germans, Leo Grossvogel organized intimate dinner parties.
The black market dealers of the Todt Organization were
particularly fond of a Russian restaurant, Chez Kornilov, and
even a Jewish restaurant that had been spared by the
occupying troops and reserved for their exclusive use. Before
going to these suppers, which demanded a great deal of
attention and caused considerable tension, we took certain
precautions. We would swallow a mouthful of olive oil or a
spoonful of butter so that we would stay sober. Fatty sub-
stances prevent alcohol from acting on the system, and this
enabled us to remain dignified and lucid right to the end,
which—need I say?—was not the case with our partners. My
tailor, my barber, and the owners of the bars and restaurants
I frequented were happy to see Monsieur Gilbert, who
smoked cigars and handed out big tips.

Behind this mask was the other personality, always present, of the head of the Red Orchestra. Between Jean Gilbert
and Otto the separation was total. It was in the transition
from one to the other that danger lay. No one must be able to
follow Gilbert when he moved into the shadows.

Twice a week, I went to one of the twenty to twenty-five
hideouts Leo had selected—usually a villa in the suburbs.
Katz or Grossvogel, who had picked up in a series of
rendezvous the intelligence gathered during recent days,
would bring me this material. I sorted it and classified it; from
this mass of information I wrote a brief, condensed report,
which I divided into four or five dispatches. This job required
at least a day's work. A liaison agent then took charge of the
material and passed it on to a coder, usually Vera
Ackermann, who would in turn pass it on to the Sokols for
radio transmission. Each stage of this process was carefully
separated from the others. The members of the network
knew only what was absolutely indispensable. In this organization, liaisons were the lifeblood; and from the beginning,

we paid particular attention to the technique of the rendez-vous.

The greatest degree of security was achieved when two people met in their natural environment, such as the contacts that took place in 1939 between Luba and Kent when they were both students at the university in Brussels. This school setting was exceptional, however. More often, two agents who were to meet would leave their homes well before the hour set for the rendezvous. They would not loiter in the streets, but go about their normal occupations, being careful to stay as far away from the meeting place as possible. As a rule, they would take the Metro, always riding in the last car and getting off among the last to leave so that they could watch the other passengers. Then they would transfer to another line and repeat the same procedure until they were absolutely certain they were not being followed. Each of the two liaison agents would then go into a telephone booth agreed on in advance and look in the phone book to see whether the code word had been underlined—for example, the tenth name in the second column of a particular page—which would indicate that the coast was clear.

The meeting itself, which had to look accidental, never lasted longer than a few seconds and usually took place in the corridors of the Metro. I also had occasion to arrange rendezvous in a swimming pool. The two agents simply went into two adjacent dressing booths. Since the partition did not extend the full height of the room, it was a simple matter to pass on the message. A simple variation on this technique was to meet in the lavatories of out-of-the-way bars or restaurants. Two members of the Orchestra could also meet at the theater. Naturally, they did not know each other, but fate—in the form of a third person who bought the seats—decreed that they find themselves side by side.

The dispatches discreetly passed from hand to hand in this way were written on very thin paper. In the case of very important information, we used invisible ink and wrote between the lines of a perfectly innocuous letter. Sometimes the transfer of the material took place without the agents' seeing each other. One would leave his "package" in a specified place, at the foot of a tree or statue, and the other would come and pick it up shortly afterwards.

We made it a rule never to say anything over the telephone. In Brussels, I had given my telephone number to Kent—with instructions to use it only in case of exceptional danger. One day as I walked in my front door, I heard Luba talking on the telephone. It was Kent, who had called her about some trifling matter. This incident provoked one of my rare fits of anger. The telephone was used by us primarily as a means of verification. After a broadcasting session, I would often call the apartment or villa where it had taken place. As soon as I heard the familiar voice answer, I would hang up, which meant that everything was all right. I also used a code system: "Hello, does Monsieur X live there?" "No, you have the wrong number." In "clear"—that is, decoded—this meant that everything was going normally. If it was absolutely necessary for us to talk over the telephone, we always used inverted language: "I'm leaving Paris" meant "I'm staying in Paris"; "I'll be back Monday" meant "I'll be there Saturday." We never gave the correct day or time of day.

Month by month we made progress in the technique of liaisons, and by 1941 we had the system operating almost like clockwork. The machine was functioning from top to bottom without incidents. Nevertheless, intelligence agents have their weaknesses just like anyone else, and it is sometimes difficult or delicate to correct them. For example, Alamo adored cars. Because of the necessity of registration and the risk of accidents and attention, we did not, as a rule, have automobiles. But I was fond of Alamo, and I agreed to make an exception for him. He drove his sports car like an airplane. One day when he was driving me to Knokke, we left the ground completely. I got out of the car, of which there was not much left, without making any comment. Alamo looked at me and burst out,

"Well, go ahead and chew me out, Otto—I could have killed you!"

"What do you want me to say, you idiot, you're not even capable of driving a car!"

Drinking, except when on "special duty," was prohibited.

So was gambling. There was nothing more dangerous than an agent who spent his nights playing cards. But the most delicate question was the matter of women. One day Alamo brought up the subject.

"Listen, Otto, I've got a problem. I want to follow orders, but after all, I'm not a monk."

"What did they tell you in Moscow?"

"They said it was against the rules to have relations with women."

"And I suppose they castrated you before you left! Do what you want, but let me give you a few words of advice: avoid whorehouses, don't lose your head, and steer clear of the wives of friends."

Alamo kept his word—in his own way.

Having a mistress is a source of unforeseeable problems for a member of the underground. During the day, we can control our reactions and our language, but at night, how can we be sure we won't talk in our sleep in our native language? For me, language was not a handicap. In French, I have a strong accent and I don't have command of all the fine points of syntax, but for a Belgian born in Antwerp, what could be more natural? Nevertheless, we all ran the risk of attracting the attention of a sharp ear. One day in Brussels, Kent showed up at a rendezvous in a state of panic.

"I've been discovered," he said. "I telephoned to rent an apartment and the landlord asked me if I was Russian."

"Repeat exactly what you said to him."

"*Bonjour, Mossieur . . .*"

"That's enough," I cut him off.

The landlord, who must have known some Russians, was no doubt familiar with the peculiar difficulty Slavs have in pronouncing *monsieur* correctly.

Little incidents of this sort were not disturbing in themselves, but I could not overlook the fact that sooner or later one of these clues might put the Gestapo on our trail.

11

t was 3:58 A.M. on June 26, 1941, in Eastern Prussia when
the operator on duty at the German listening post at Cranz
picked up the following message:
KLH DE PTX 2602 0330 32 WES N 14 K BV . . .
Then, thirty-two groups of five characters:
AR 503 85 KLK DE PTX . . .
The operator recorded the material, but the origin, destina-
tion, and meaning of the message were a complete unknown.

Since the beginning of the war, innumerable voices had
been babbling through the ether, transmitting in cryptic
symbols the conversations of secret services, orders,
counter-orders, information from the opposing camps in the
shadow war. German listening posts like the one in Cranz
were accustomed to hearing little evening concerts, generally
intended for English ears. But this time? This time the
harmonies did not belong to a score that would have suited
the listeners in Albion.

In the three months until the end of September, 1941, two
hundred and fifty such "concerts" were intercepted. Not until
then were the Germans absolutely sure that these mysterious
and untranslatable dispatches were being sent to Moscow.

In fact, they were being broadcast by the Red Orchestra.

When the German High Command received the report,
their stupefaction was total. They were ready for anything
except "concerts" being broadcast to the Russians. Had not
the Abwehr (military counterespionage) and the SD (security
service) repeatedly told them that in Germany and the
occupied territories no Soviet intelligence network existed?
They were certain of this because they knew of Stalin's
orders forbidding his agents to operate in Reich territory.
Besides, when the dispatches were intercepted for the first
time during that night in June, 1941, it had been only five
days since the union between Germany and the Soviet Union
had blown up.

145

Five days—was that enough time for new orders from Stalin to go into effect? At the time Operation Barbarossa was launched, had not Heydrich himself personally guaranteeing the convictions of his specialists, handed the Führer a report assuring him that all German territory had been "purged of the Soviet vermin"?

After revelations of this magnitude, a special meeting was called in Hitler's presence. For the first time, the various clans of the Nazi cabal overcame their rivalries. Heydrich, whose imprudent statements had not damaged his authority, took the situation in hand. Under his direction, Admiral Canaris of the Abwehr; General Fritz Thiele of the Funkabwehr; Schellenberg, the head of the Secret Service; and Müller, the big boss of the Gestapo, decided to coordinate their activities. The combined forces of German intelligence and police declared war on Soviet espionage. As Schellenberg later wrote in his memoirs:

> Himmler was put in charge of supervising the close collaboration of my intelligence service with Müller's services [Gestapo] and with Canaris' counterespionage. These operations, which were given the name of *Rote Kapelle* [Red Orchestra], were coordinated by Heydrich. After Heydrich's assassination in May, 1942, Himmler took over the supervision and coordination of the *Rote Kapelle*.

The term "Red Orchestra" hence comes directly from the German.

Over all the territory under Wehrmacht control, radio-direction-finding teams were put on the alert and intensified their efforts. The Germans had discovered a clue to our existence; sooner or later, depending on their skill and the whims of fate, it would lead them somewhere. In fact, in November, 1941, Captain Harry Piepe of the Belgian branch of the Abwehr located a radio transmitter in Brussels.

Before that, on our side, toward the end of 1940, I encountered some difficulty in getting broadcasting stations in Belgium into operation. To this end, I had asked the Center to put me in touch with a specialist capable of repairing sets and training operators. This was how I met Johann Wenzel. Wenzel had been living in Belgium since

1936 and was the head of a small group that specialized in collecting information on military industry.

Wenzel's past was the logical antecedent of his present. He had been a militant at a very early age in the German Communist Party. A native of Danzig, he had started a group in the Ruhr that specialized in industrial espionage before coming to Belgium. Finally, this veteran of underground activities was also an extremely competent radio technician.

For everyone in the Brussels group, Wenzel was "the Professor," a professor who practiced what he taught, for besides training "pianists," he himself transmitted. His first student was Alamo; since in the middle of 1941 the French group lacked soloists, I decided to send him two "graduate assistants," David Kamy and Sophie Poznanska. Kamy was the archetype of the revolutionary, the fighter who knew no national boundaries. He was introduced to me by Hillel Katz; they had known each other in the Communist Party, in the section for the Fifth Arrondissement in Paris. As a young man, Kamy had lived in Palestine; then he had gone to fight in Spain, like so many other members of the Red Orchestra. Before joining us, he had worked in the technical department of the French Communist Party. Crazy about radios, a good chemist, he had set up a little underground laboratory where he made gadgets: invisible ink, documents that destroyed themselves, and other such experiments. He was above all our specialist in microfilm, a field in which he achieved perfection.

In Professor Wenzel's school, Sophie Poznanska was Kamy's classmate. I had known her in Palestine, where she had already shown rare qualities of courage and intelligence.

Naturally, I was very concerned about my two prize students. I asked Kent to find each of them a very safe hideout, but he did nothing of the sort. Sophie was staying at 101 Rue des Atrébates, in a rented house we used for broadcasting, and Kamy was living with Alamo. The most elementary requirements for security had not been respected. If we had deliberately set out to bring on a catastrophe, we would not have acted otherwise.

In the beginning of December, 1941, Sophie sent an

anxious message asking me to come and restore some discipline. Wenzel had suspended broadcasts from the Rue des Atrébates temporarily; the previous month they had been going on several hours a day—and he was quite right to suspend them, I found. On the 11th, when I arrived in Brussels, I saw that what was going on was not, in fact, very orthodox, and it was potentially very dangerous. The incorrigible Alamo was coming to work in the villa and bringing with him friends of both sexes who were strangers to the group!

On the 12th of December at noon, I met with Sophie Poznanska, who reported on the disastrous working conditions at the Rue des Atrébates house. I decided right then that I would send her back to Paris with Kamy and leave the task of replacing them to Kent. I made an appointment to meet all of them at noon the next day, at 101 Rue des Atrébates. I wanted to inform them, then, of the new arrangements.

On the other side, Captain Piepe of the Abwehr had begun a race against time. He had been able to zero in on the transmitter to some extent, but he was still hesitating between numbers 99, 101, and 103. During the night he made up his mind, went into action, and surrounded number 101. Starting at the ground floor, he and his men first encountered Rita Arnould, an anti-Nazi Dutchwoman who had been responsible for renting us the house but who knew almost nothing about our activities. On the second floor, Sophie was in the process of decoding dispatches. She heard the sound of boots on the staircase and threw everything she could into the fireplace. Most of the material was burned, but the Germans retrieved one piece of paper that was only half consumed.

Kamy was working in another room, listening on the radio to a transmitter that was operating elsewhere (in accordance with the procedure we had established of always checking our own broadcasts at another post). He heard the Germans and ran down the stairs. In the street, there was a wild chase—and he was caught. Rita Arnould, Sophie, and Kamy were taken away, and the Germans set a trap.

The next day at 11:30 Alamo, unsuspecting, arrived for our appointment. Before he had crossed the threshold of the house, the German police pounced on him: "Your papers!"

Alamo had not shaved in several days, and he was carrying a basket of rabbits for dinner. Without losing his poise, he rummaged in his pocket and brought out his Uruguayan passport in the name of Carlos Alamo.

The Germans started firing questions: "What are you doing here?" "Where are you coming from?" "What is your occupation?"

He told him his little story. His shop in Ostend had been destroyed—which was, in fact, the truth; since then, he said, he had been forced to sell on the black market for a living. "I had just rung the doorbell, to try and sell my rabbits." An altogether plausible explanation: with his shabby appearance and his rabbits, he looked the part of a street vendor. The police conferred together and ordered him to remain with them.

It was noon when I rang the doorbell. A German policeman opened the door. We were face to face. I had the definite sensation that my heart stopped beating. An effort, and I pulled myself together. With an instinctive reflex, I drew back and threw out a remark.

"Oh, excuse me, I didn't realize this house was occupied by the Wehrmacht. I must have the wrong address."

I did not convince him. He grabbed my arm hard enough to break it and pulled me inside.

The house had been searched from top to bottom, and the disorder was indescribable—the classic image of a police raid. This would be a tight one. I was in a large room; through the glass partition that separated me from the stairway, I saw Alamo. I got out my papers without waiting to be asked, in a deliberate way, with an air of confidence, and handed them to the German.

His jaw dropped in astonishment. The document I handed him, which was covered with official stamps and signatures, said the bearer, Monsieur Gilbert, had been commissioned by the president of the Todt Organization in Paris to look for strategic material destined for the Wehrmacht. The president requested the different branches of the army of occupation to facilitate Monsieur Gilbert's search in any way they could.

To break the silence, and by way of further explanation, I said: "There's a garage across the street where I thought I might find some old cars for scrap iron. It's closed, and I rang this bell to find out what time it opens."

A little more pleasantly, he said: "I believe you, but you'll have to wait until the chief gets back."

"That's impossible, utterly impossible. I have to catch a train. The president of the Todt Organization is expecting my report this afternoon. You're going to create an incident, you know! Take me to your superior officer, or telephone him!"

The German policeman hesitated for a few moments, then decided to call Captain Piepe; he told him about my arrival. I can still hear the thunder of abuse that crackled in the receiver: "Imbecile! Why are you holding this man? Release him immediately!" The German soldier grew pale and looked as if the sky had fallen on his head.

Alamo, who had come closer to us, had heard everything too and threw me a conspiratorial look. I walked downstairs again with my policeman and when we had reached the door I asked him,

"What's going on here, something to do with the Jews, perhaps?"

"Oh, no, it's much more important than that."

"More important! But what could it be?"

"A matter of espionage."

I put on a very serious expression to show him that I understood the gravity of the situation. We parted good friends, and I told him, "Next time you get to Paris, you must come and visit me. I'd be delighted!"

Out on the street, I realized the gravity of the situation. We had suffered a very serious blow. Several of our people had fallen into the nets of the Abwehr. Where would it stop? I looked at my watch: it was 12:15. Everything had happened so quickly—— A moment later I remembered that I had a rendezvous with Springer nearby. I did not have a minute to lose. When I did not show up, he might come to the Rue des Atrébates and fall into the trap too. As luck would have it, he waited for me. Quickly, I explained what had happened, and I asked him whether he had any compromising documents on him.

"My pockets are full of them," he replied.

"Exactly what do you have with you?"

"The plans of the port of Antwerp."

"Oh God, is that all!" I remembered that a few weeks before, the Director had expressed a desire to have a detailed plan of the port showing where submarines might have access to it. Springer had managed to procure one. "Let's get out of here. All we need is to get stopped and questioned."

An hour later, I met Kent. I had no trouble impressing him with the danger that surrounded us. Three of our people had been arrested, and although I had the utmost confidence in them, we had everything to fear if they should be turned over to the Gestapo. The arrest of Rita Arnould bothered me particularly, since she was not one of us and did not have the same reasons as the others for remaining silent. I was almost sure she would talk—and she had seen Kent twice, knew Springer very well, and had heard of Wenzel.

With what they had got their hands on by way of dispatches, the Germans would certainly try to break our code. Of course I did not know then that Sophie had been so quick, that she had destroyed almost all of them, and the Germans would have only a fragment to work with.

Emergency measures had to be taken to protect the network. Kent and Springer would leave Belgium as soon as possible, and the others would go into complete hiding. The Belgian group would be silent. There was no other solution.

We had to act very fast. I drove to Lille, and from there I caught a train to Paris. The next day, I met with Leo Grossvogel and Fernand Pauriol. We decided to form a special group, made up of a few reliable men and headed by my two friends, which would be responsible for following the course of events in Belgium and France and warding off the enemy's blows. It was obvious that with the fall of the Atrébates house, the time when we were secure was over. From now on the Germans would hunt us relentlessly.

Leo and Fernand left for Brussels and took matters in hand.

Arrangements had to be made for Kent to leave for Paris and for Springer to leave for Lyon, and instructions had to be given to Izbutski, Raichmann, and Wenzel. The latter immediately moved to another apartment, covered his tracks as well as he could by changing his habits, and suspended communication with the Center for a period of two months.

The first priority, though, was to keep abreast of what was happening to our comrades incarcerated in Saint-Gilles Prison, in Brussels. Leo and Fernand made contact with some guards who were members of the resistance, and the guards kept them informed of the prisoners' fate. We learned that the Germans had not discovered their real identities. Alamo had been registered on the prison log by that name, Kamy under his pseudonym of Desmets, and Sophie Poznanska as Verlinden.

That was the situation at the time of their arrest in December. By the beginning of April, 1942, our informants reported that the Germans had discovered Sophie's identity and that Kamy-Desmets had become Danilov.

We understood easily enough why Sophie Poznanska revealed her true identity. Besieged with questions by the Germans, she had chosen a convincing way of demonstrating her good will. Throughout her career as a militant, she had in fact been known by a borrowed name, so there was no risk of tracing other people through her. There was something else, too, which we had no way of knowing at the time: she took the precaution of concealing the fact that she was born in the little town of Kalisz, in Poland, in order to spare her family possible reprisals.

Kamy became "Danilov" for the same reasons: in his twenty years of underground work he had come in contact with a great many people, and he wanted to avoid the possibility that numerous militants would be betrayed. So, during an interrogation more prolonged than the others, this expatriate Jew "confessed" that his name was Anton Danilov and that he was a lieutenant in the Soviet Army. He knew enough Russian to make his story stick. Employed in 1941 at the Soviet Embassy in Vichy, where he told them he had

stayed until the beginning of the German-Russian war, he
had been sent to Brussels to work with Alamo. He said he
knew no one outside of the people who had been arrested
along with him. The Germans swallowed this story. Several
months after his arrest they were still talking respectfully
about that Soviet officer by the name of Danilov (passing
himself off as an officer was the height of cunning) who
behaved so courageously and who refused to say anything.

After the Rue des Atrébates, Springer was in grave danger.
Rita Arnould had given Piepe two addresses, either of which
might have led to Springer.

One was the address of a man named Dow, a friend of
Springer's and an active member of the resistance. On
December 16th, three days after the raid, a strange-looking
man walked into Dow's fur shop in the Rue Royale and,
claiming to have been sent by the "Big Chief," said he
wanted to meet Springer. Dow smelled something fishy; he
asked his visitor to return in forty-eight hours. Then he
mentioned the matter to Springer, who advised him to be
careful, suspecting that the man was a German agent.

The man returned as arranged. Dow showed him into the
back room of the shop. A friend of his was waiting nearby,
ready to step in if necessary. At this point the agent took out
a gun and placed it within reach. Dow did not panic and
explained to the man that he had not seen Springer. A few
days later, he saw the man again, sitting in a parked car, and
he looked for all the world like a Gestapo officer. Dow had
just enough time to disappear.

Rita Arnould had given a second address that might also
have led to Springer, and through him, to the very heart of
our network—that of Yvonne Kuenstlunger, her cousin, who
was our liaison between the Rue des Atrébates and Springer.
This time the men of the Gestapo were a little cleverer. After
sending Yvonne several very obvious agents, they shadowed
her rather than trying to intimidate and arrest her, in the
hope that she would lead them to Springer himself; but
without success.

Disturbing news about Alamo reached us from Saint-Gilles

Prison. The guards told us that he had been transferred to Berlin, which was extraordinary enough in itself, and then brought back, and that on his return he had been registered under the name of Mikael Makarov.

For me, this new name for Alamo was a surprise, though not an unexpected one, for the rule was that for reasons of security, none of us knew the other's real identity. Nevertheless, I checked with the Center whether this was Alamo's real name; the reply was "affirmative." I immediately sent another dispatch to the Director to warn him of the danger to us all.

The Abwehr were after us now, but they had got off to a bad start. In the case of Alamo in particular, they came close to missing the truth altogether. At about the same time that Piepe made his raid on the Rue des Atrébates, several members of the resistance, including one who had been secretary to André Marty during the Spanish Civil War, were arrested in the north of France. The Abwehr became convinced that this group and the militants of the Red Orchestra belonged to a single network of veterans of the International Brigades. Piepe sent Berlin a report to this effect and proposed that the persons arrested be sent to a concentration camp. Here Giering, a man who was to enter my own life very shortly, came into the picture.

Giering was a Kriminalrat, a high police official, and thus Piepe's report reached his desk. Giering did not believe that former membership in the International Brigades indicated a continuing connection between the two groups, but he did remember that at the time of the break-up of a network in Czechoslovakia that had come under his jurisdiction, the Soviet agents who had been arrested had referred in their depositions to a Soviet aviation officer who had belonged to the International Brigades.

The description reminded Giering very much of this Alamo whom Piepe was talking about, and to put his mind at rest, he decided to come to Brussels and get the prisoner. He took a plane and brought our agent back to Berlin. There, instead of putting him in prison, he kept him in his home for two weeks. A policeman with some experience in the anti-communist struggle, Giering was not devoid of psychological awareness. His son, who had lost an arm fighting in the Luftwaffe, found plenty to talk about with Alamo. While they were exchanging their impressions, Giering went to see the imprisoned agents from the Czechoslovakian network and interrogated them. Had they known Alamo? Had he fought with them in the International Brigades? To support his questions, he showed them a photograph. The men were positive: it was indeed he, their former classmate at the intelligence training center in Moscow. The game was over.

Giering had scored an important victory. He sent Alamo back to Saint-Gilles Prison where, thanks to the guards, we learned for the first time that his name was Mikael Makarov. Then the torturers, with proof of Alamo's role in the underground struggle, deduced that Sophie Poznanska and David Kamy worked with him. They wanted to know more about it. They suspected there was much to learn. The torture sessions began.

Sophie Poznanska, in Saint-Gilles, committed suicide.

At the beginning of the summer, Alamo and Kamy were transferred to the fort of Breendonk, where they were subjected to constant brutality. With courage that nothing could defeat, they obstinately refused to talk. They did not reveal a single name. Not one arrest would be made because of them. The trail leading to the Red Orchestra stopped short there, for the men of the Abwehr.

12

The Mistakes of the Center

So our Belgian group had evaporated.

Kent stopped off in Paris on his way to Marseilles. His companion, Margarete Barcza, whom he had married in June, was to have followed him a few days later, but he did not want to be without her and had brought her with him. It was essential to get Kent to a safe place. After his numerous trips to Germany, Czechoslovakia, and Switzerland, he knew much too much to be exposed for a single minute to the possibility of arrest.

The Kent I saw in Paris seemed to have been very much affected psychologically. After his year of intensive work with the Belgian group, for which he was responsible, its decimation had broken his spirit. With tears in his eyes he told me, "Your decision to send me to Marseilles is fair, but I'm sure they won't understand it in Moscow. I'm a former Soviet officer, and on my return to the USSR, I'll have to answer for what happened at Atrébates!"

Since Springer and his wife planned to set up their own network in Lyon, I proposed to the Center that the rest of the Belgian group be dispersed. The most capable members—Izbutski, Sésée, and Raichmann—would be provided with their own transmitter and would maintain their own contact with the Center. Nazarin Drailly would replace Kent as the manager of Simexco.

The Director's response to my proposals amazed and upset me. I was ordered to meet with Soviet Army Captain Efremov and to place the former members of Kent's Belgian group, in addition to Wenzel and his network, under his direction.

I had never heard of Efremov. When I met him in the spring of '42 in Brussels, my impression was unfavorable. He had been living in Belgium since 1939. A chemist, he had been posing as a Finnish student enrolled at the Polytechnic

Institute. His record of achievements in intelligence was unimpressive. The value of the information he had been transmitting was nil. It was an amateurish performance bordering on caricature, a collection of gossip and misinformation picked up in nightclubs frequented by the Wehrmacht. Information gained in nightclubs could be useful, but only when it was carefully checked out. Efremov, however, with the help of snatches of unconfirmed information, would compose long "syntheses" based largely on his own imagination. That did not matter; the bureaucrats at the Center preferred a captain who had taken a three-month course at the intelligence school to an old veteran of underground intelligence like Wenzel.

Stifling my anxiety and anger, I turned my information over to Efremov. The Veterans—Wenzel, Izbutski, and Raichmann—were very upset over this decision. "What! Obey that idiot? He'll get us all killed!" exclaimed Raichmann when he heard the news. I had to persuade each of them to go along with it in a spirit of discipline. To leave no doubt about my own position, in April, 1942, I sent the Center a report in which I criticized the arrangements that had been made in no uncertain terms. Two months later, the Director replied that after reconsidering the whole matter, he agreed with me and asked me to disperse the Belgian group.

Too late! In July, 1942, Efremov was arrested. Through lack of experience, he had rushed headlong into a trap that had been set for him.

In April, when I had come to Brussels to meet Efremov, Raichmann told me he had run into the Belgian police inspector, Mathieu, who had handled his case in 1940, the one concerned with false identity papers. Mathieu had confided to Raichmann that he belonged—or so he said—to the resistance, and had offered to help him, for he suspected that he was working for an underground network. For instance, he could be useful to him by providing him with authentic identity cards.

I did not trust this Mathieu for a minute, and I ordered Raichmann to sever all contact with him. Efremov, however, finding it perfectly natural that he should be brought brand-new identity papers on a silver platter, went even further in my absence: when Mathieu proposed that Efremov hide a transmitter in Mathieu's home, he agreed eagerly and then set a new record for stupidity by turning over his photograph so he could be provided with an identity card. A rendezvous was arranged near the Observatory, but Mathieu did not come alone: the men in gabardine were there in their black cars.

Izbutski rushed to Paris to inform us of Efremov's arrest. Immediately, Leo Grossvogel left for Brussels, to follow the events there. Three days later, Efremov reappeared, free as a bird, in the company of a "friend." He told his landlady that he had had to have his papers checked by the Belgian police, but that everything had been taken care of.

Everything had been taken care of, all right. In the days that followed, Sésée, Izbutski, and Maurice Pepper (Pepper had been the liaison with the Netherlands) were arrested. On the 17th of August, under torture, Pepper revealed the contact with the head of the Dutch group, Anton Winterinck, who was thereupon captured.

Nine members of the group, and two transmitters, escaped the Germans.

Efremov also turned over the first information on Simex and Simexco, without specifying their exact role, which indeed was unknown to him. From that day forward, the activities of both organizations were discreetly watched.

When Piepe was told the address of Simexco, he thought it was some kind of practical joke; he had rented an office in the same building! When he heard Efremov's description of the Big Chief, he slapped his brow and exclaimed,

"My God, I've met him on the stairs, and I've even tipped my hat to him!"

Efremov talked without being tortured. The men of the Gestapo skillfully flattered his nationalist sentiments and played on the old chord of anti-Semitism: "You, a Ukrainian—you work under a Jew?" First they threatened him with reprisals against his family; then they took him on a little tour of Germany and showed him the achievements of the Great Reich—— In short, Efremov talked. All in all, because of him, more than thirty people were arrested, including whole families. Several were members of the Belgian group—it was destroyed now—and several of those arrested were unconnected with the group.

We first learned that Efremov had been "turned" at the end of August. None of the arrests had yet been made. Efremov ran into Germaine Schneider, who belonged to Wenzel's network, and revealed his game to her. He had been arrested, he told her. The Germans knew everything, and he had decided to save his skin. He proposed to Germaine that she work with him, and told her,

"You know how it is. Otto will always get out of it; we're the ones who'll have to pay. So our best bet is to go over to the German side, to save our property."

Germaine told him she would think it over, and she rushed to Paris to warn me. I immediately sent her to Lyon.

The Schneiders, who were of Swiss nationality, had been working within the organization of the Comintern for over twenty years. As liaisons, couriers, and "mailboxes," Franz and Germaine Schneider had met and known a great many European militants. Until the war, their house in Brussels had served as a hideout and stopping-off place for eminent leaders, Thorez and Duclos among them. They had very close connections with the "oldtimers" of the Comintern, especially Robinson and his ex-wife Clara Schabbel, who served as a liaison between Berlin and Wenzel.

Franz Schneider was not an active member of the Red Orchestra, but through his previous contacts, he was aware of a great deal. Having noticed the disappearance of his wife, the Germans made contact with him, with help from Efremov. Schneider did not believe that Efremov was playing a double game—and without realizing it, he worked for the Germans for almost three months. Among other things, he gave them the name of Robinson's friend Griotto, a radio operator. By order of the special kommando, Raichmann made contact with Griotto and in this way the Germans got as far as Robinson himself. After that day, Harry Robinson was under close surveillance. It was not until October, 1942—when the Sonderkommando realized they could get no more information out of Franz Schneider—that he was arrested, along with Germaine's two sisters.

When I informed the Center of what was happening, however, I only received a bewildering reply from the Director: "Otto, you are completely mistaken. We know that Efremov was arrested by the Belgian police and that they checked his identification, but everything has been taken care of. Furthermore, Efremov continues to send us some very important material which, after very careful verification, has turned out to be of the highest quality."

The Center did not even bother to wonder why Efremov had suddenly become so much more active. The truth was that an insidious counter-plan had already begun to operate.

At the beginning of September, the Director, apparently feeling that the list of arrests was not complete, asked me to go to Brussels and meet Efremov. Our surveillance group, sent to the scene of the rendezvous, saw customers lingering in the surrounding cafes who were more interested in watching the street than in the contents of their glasses. And not far from there, the black cars were performing a disturbing ballet.

All this time, Wenzel, with great courage, continued to broadcast, his revolver within reach, along with chemicals that could destroy his dispatches within a few seconds. His house was spotted by the direction-finding equipment and surrounded in the middle of the night. He ran up to the roof, firing at his pursuers. Hundreds of people, awakened by the shots, saw his fleeing figure. He disappeared into an adjacent building. The Germans found him in a cellar.

I know that in the German archives, Wenzel was described as a traitor who agreed to collaborate with the enemy after his arrest. This was a crude maneuver—designed to discredit an old militant, a friend of Ernst Thaelmann. The reality was quite different, as we shall see.

In the last days of January, our surveillance group reported that the house in the Rue des Atrébates was no longer watched. Immediately, I sent two men, equipped with papers that showed they belonged to the Gestapo, to retrieve the books I hoped were still in Sophie Poznanska's room. The books had a very special value—the code system for our dispatches was based on one of them.

Dr. Vauck, the head of the code-breaking team, knew this and he put in a request at Gestapo headquarters in Brussels for the books that, he assumed, had been confiscated at the time of the raid. The Gestapo replied that they knew nothing about the books and that in any case no books were in the room now. Vauck then realized what had happened. He did not give up: he had Rita Arnould interrogated once again. Rita Arnould remembered the titles of five books that used to sit on Sophie's desk.

To help him find the book containing the key to the code, Dr. Vauck had only one word, "proctor," which his elaborate calculations had decoded from the little fragment of a dispatch found half-burned in the fireplace. The word "proctor" did not appear in the four books. The fifth, *Le miracle du professeur Wolman*, was nowhere to be found. On May 17, 1942, after a long search among second-hand booksellers, Captain Karl von Wedel got his hands on a copy of this book. Now Dr. Vauck went to work on the dispatches that had been sent in this code, 120 of them, all the ones that the German listening stations had intercepted since June, 1941.

On July 15, 1942, Vauck's code breakers succeeded in decoding a dispatch from the October 10, 1941, dispatch:

KL 3 DE RTX 1010-1725 WDS GBT FROM DIRECTOR TO KENT/PERSONAL:

Proceed immediately Berlin three addresses indicated and determine causes failure radio connections. If interruptions recur, take over broadcasts. Work three Berlin groups and transmission information top priority. Addresses: Neuwestend, Altenburger allee 19, third right; Coro Charlottenburg, Frederiastrasse 26a, second left; Volf-Friedenau, Kaiserstrasse 18, fourth left . . . Bauer. Call name here 'Eulenspiegel.' Password: 'director.' Report before 20 October. New plan, repeat new, in force for three stations gbt ar KLS RTX.

Incredibly, the Director had sent over the air the addresses of the three leaders of the Berlin group, Schulze-Boysen, Arvid Harnack, and Kuckhoff. At the time we received it, I had been appalled. If the Germans should ever succeed in cracking the code—for I was well aware that no code, however clever, is unbreakable—they would be able to read the addresses in black and white. I did not protest this breach of security to the Center, who had done it—one cannot always protest; and the mistake was so elementary. Then, on July 15, 1942, the code had been broken.

The Gestapo took their time in exploiting this wonderful gift. Slowly they set their traps, started their shadowings, hooked up their telephonic listening posts.

One of the members of the Berlin network, Horst Heilmann, worked for Dr. Vauck—the German in charge of code breaking. Heilmann had no knowledge of the famous and decisive dispatch until August 29. Without losing a minute, Heilmann telephoned Schulze-Boysen—but unfortunately Schulze-Boysen was away. Heilmann left a message, asking him to call him back immediately at his desk. Early the next morning, the 30th, Schulze-Boysen called back, but it was Dr. Vauck who picked up the receiver:

"Schulze-Boysen here . . ."

Vauck, astounded—suspecting some sort of trick, hardly believing that it was really Schulze-Boysen calling—nevertheless warned the Gestapo. Schulze-Boysen was arrested the same day. Starting August 30, in less than three or four weeks, sixty members of the Berlin group were arrested. By the end of October the number of arrests had exceeded one hundred and thirty. By the beginning of 1943, a hundred and fifty people had been imprisoned, many of whom had nothing to do with the Red Orchestra.

The list of people arrested since the raid on the Rue des Atrébates was long.

13

The Sonderkommando on Our Trail

The operations against the group at 101 Rue des Atrébates had been led by the Abwehr. To make the struggle against the Red Orchestra in France and Belgium more effective, a new organization—the Sonderkommando Rote Kapelle—was created in July, 1942. At its head was Karl Giering, who had demonstrated so much detective ability in identifying Alamo. Under him was a carefully selected team of SS who had been specially trained in underground warfare, including Obersturmbannführer Heinrich Reiser, who led the Paris branch as of December, 1942. The head of the Gestapo, Müller, supervised the operations, for which Himmler and Bormann themselves had assumed responsibility.

At the beginning of October, 1942, the Sonderkommando arrived in Paris and moved into the fifth floor of a building in the Rue des Saussaies, the former headquarters of the Sûreté, the French department of criminal investigation.

The struggle against the French group began.

In fact, we had already suffered a setback Giering did not know about. Two radio operators, Hersch and Mira Sokol, had been caught on June 9, 1942, in a villa in Maisons-Laffitte, as they were finishing a broadcast. This arrest was the result of chance: one of the direction-finder cars happened to be patroling the suburbs west of Paris at the exact moment that the Sokols were working; the Germans quickly located their house and made a raid.

At the time, the Gestapo did not connect them with the Red Orchestra, since the Sokols' set, which Fernand Pauriol had built, was too weak to broadcast all the way to Moscow. The dispatches had been sent to London, then rebroadcast to the Soviet Union, which led the Germans to conclude that the Sokols were working for the English.

We knew about the arrest of Mira and Hersch Sokol as

163

soon as it occurred. Fernand Pauriol, who had been following their broadcasts on another set, noticed the sudden interruption of radio signals. I sent a messenger to Maisons-Laffitte, and he confirmed the arrest. Our "housecleaners" immediately went to work on the Sokols' Paris apartment and did such a thorough job that when the Sonderkommando's men arrived, they did not discover any important clues. On the same day, I sent the coder, Vera Ackermann, to Marseilles and went to warn the Spaaks, who were friends of Mira and Hersch. The Sokols were horribly tortured, and they were heroes. Not one name was extracted from them, nor did they reveal the code, right up to their deaths.

Giering was unaware of the role the Sokols played in the Red Orchestra, but the decoding of the dispatches in Berlin through the offices of Dr. Vauck and the "confessions" of several militants arrested in Belgium had given him a great deal of information. Raichmann had also been terribly tortured and had cracked when he learned of Efremov's treason. He and his mistress, Malvina Gruber, agreed to work for the Sonderkommando. Thanks to them, Giering had quite a clear picture of the French group. His first move was to try to draw me into a trap. Madame Likhonin, the White Russian who handled many of the commercial transactions between Simex and the Todt Organization, was offered a fantastic deal involving industrial diamonds, on the condition that she do business with Monsieur Gilbert in person.

Our first rendezvous was arranged in Brussels. The agents of the Sonderkommando stupidly revealed to Madame Likhonin that I was a "Soviet agent." They underestimated Russian patriotism.

"I am an anti-communist," she told me immediately, "but first of all, I am a Russian—and I don't want to turn you over to the Gestapo!"

I calmed her down and suggested she inform the Germans that I had suddenly become ill and was therefore unable to come to the next rendezvous.

After the failure of this plan to use Madame Likhonin, Giering sent Raichmann after me. Raichmann made the rounds of the addresses and mailboxes he had known during a brief stay in Paris after the Atrébates episode, but the word was out and the doors closed in his face. The Sonderkommando was getting nowhere. Giering knew that the nerve center of the Red Orchestra was in Paris. He had tracked down several active members of the network, but he could go no further.

Giering had learned through Malvina Gruber, who had accompanied Margarete Barcza to Marseilles, that Margarete was there with Kent. He unleashed his men in that city. On November 12, 1942—the Wehrmacht having occupied the Free Zone of France—the couple fell into his hands.

The truth is that Kent could very easily have escaped the Germans. He had not followed the instructions to leave for Algeria that I had given him in August. Nothing could have been easier, but Kent was too demoralized to act. In October, I had gone to Marseilles to see him. He felt threatened; the occupation of the Free Zone was only a matter of weeks away.

"I can't go to Algeria," he told me. "I'll be called back to Moscow, and I'll have to answer for the debacle of the Belgian group."

"So what do you plan to do?"

"If I'm arrested, I'll play along with the Germans to find out their objectives."

"That's impossible. To play that game, you must have a way of warning the Center. You won't be able to do that; on the contrary, you'll be forced to give them your code, and it will be the Germans who will manipulate you."

I was well aware that I had not convinced him. I suggested that he hide out in Switzerland, but he replied that his companion, from whom he did not wish to be separated at any cost, was still waiting for her passport. The Germans closed in on them the very next day after the occupation of the southern zone. The Sonderkommando did not waste any time.

And Kent talked, without the Gestapo's having to use force. The prospect of being separated from Margarete was enough. Kent knew the role of Simex and Simexco in the network and knew the importance of Alfred Corbin.

On November 17, I met with Corbin.

"You're in danger, Alfred," I told him. "You must leave."

"Why me? The only man who can implicate me is Kent. Kent's a Soviet officer—a Soviet officer doesn't betray anyone, does he?"

"Alfred, you're a great realist when it comes to business, but otherwise you're a hopeless dreamer. You have no idea of what the Gestapo is capable of. You must leave for Switzerland immediately, with your family."

"It's impossible. My wife knows nothing about my activities, and she'd never agree to give up her apartment."

On November 19, the Sonderkommando made a raid on Simex* and arrested the main leaders: Alfred Corbin, Suzanne Cointe, Vladimir Keller, and Madame Mignon.

Leo Grossvogel, Hillel Katz, and I retreated to Antony, a suburb of Paris, to a villa that only we three knew. We quickly took stock of the situation. It was far from brilliant: after Brussels, Amsterdam, Berlin, and Marseilles, now Paris. We agreed to give first priority to security: those of the fifty-odd members of the French group who were still at liberty received their orders. With Michel, the representative of the Communist Party, a new code for our meetings was established; Leo Grossvogel did the same with Fernand Pauriol.

But there was something that had even more serious implications for the future of our activities: the Center had obviously lost confidence in us. We realized this when, in answer to our dispatches announcing the arrests, they replied, "You are mistaken. The broadcasts continue, and the material sent is excellent."

---

*Certain "specialists" in the Red Orchestra (with the notable exception of Gilles Perrault) have referred to a secret room at Simex where the Big Chief is supposed to have stored top secret documents.

The last thing you'd do when you were creating a cover for a network would be to endanger it in any way. It would have been absurd to store, even in a secret room—and how long would it have been secret, in the event of a raid!—obvious proof of the activities of the network.

The Center was not wrong; it was true that the broadcasts were continuing. Had not Fernand Pauriol picked up dispatches sent on Efremov's set, as well as broadcasts originating in the Netherlands and Berlin? Clearly this meant that the Sonderkommando wanted to prevent the Center from finding out about the arrests, and that in order to conceal them, they were conducting the Orchestra themselves. For what reason, we could not yet discern. For a radio operator to have been arrested and "turned" in order to send false information and confound the enemy was altogether likely and belonged to the logic of underground warfare. But for transmitters that had fallen into the hands of the Germans to send "excellent material" seemed incredible.

Such an unprecedented tactic, we thought, probably concealed a far-reaching operation whose purpose escaped us at the moment. Our duty, therefore, was to try to discover its motives and thwart it, whatever the circumstances. In the event of our arrest, we were therefore prepared to make a show of collaboration, the better to infiltrate the enemy's ranks.

Once again, it was necessary to try to warn the Director of the way things were developing. On November 22nd, I sent him a dispatch containing a detailed report, and at the same time I wrote Jacques Duclos telling him what had happened. After that, we agreed to disappear for a while. Disappear was the word: in Royat, a little town near Clermont-Ferrand, I had prepared my own funeral service. The death certificate and the memorial plaque were all ready. Jean Gilbert was going to die in a few days.

I was to leave Paris on the 27th, and Katz was to follow me shortly after. Leo was to disappear into the south of France as soon as he received his new identification papers.

Before leaving, I telephoned the dentist, who was to put caps on two of my teeth; I asked him whether he could see me sooner than we had arranged. He happened to have some time on the 24th and gave me an appointment for two o'clock in the afternoon.

14

November 24: I got up rather early. I dressed slowly, going over the recent events in my mind and weighing the difficulties that were piling up around us. We had to be very cautious. The more I thought about it, the more I was convinced that our decision to disperse, at least for a time, was wise and necessary.

I had lunch with Katz. We talked little. It was no time for long conversations or emotional scenes. We agreed to meet again at about four o'clock, after my visit to the dentist. After that I would go and say goodbye to Georgie de Winter. Then that evening we would have a final rendezvous with Leo. That night I would take the train to Royat, having decided to advance my departure by three days.

Accompanied by Katz, I left for the dentist's office in the Rue de Rivoli, but Katz and I separated quickly. Katz walked a few dozen yards behind me. We had perfected this technique because of the risk of arrest. At exactly two o'clock, I arrived in front of the building and glanced quickly to right and left. The coast was clear, no suspicious-looking figures or parked cars. I walked up the stairs and rang the bell. The dentist answered it himself. I was surprised: ordinarily his assistant came to the door for the patients. I was also puzzled to find that the waiting room was empty. As a rule, it was full. Furthermore, the dentist took me into his office immediately. I looked at him. He seemed anxious; he was pale and his hands were shaking. I asked him,

"What's the matter? Aren't you feeling well?--

He stammered a few inaudible words and then pushed me toward the chair. I sat down and propped my head back as he asked me to do. He picked up his instruments. No sooner had I opened my mouth than I heard a noise behind me. I should have suspected something from all those unusual circumstances and made my escape—but now it was too late.

There was a shout: *"Hände hoch!"*

Hardly more than a minute had elapsed since I had entered the office. Two muscular men aimed revolvers at me. Their faces were as pale as the dentist's; they were trembling, too, from sheer nervousness. What a scene!

After this sudden moment of emotion—and I am not sure that I was the most upset—I very quickly recovered my poise. The blood flowed back into my face. I slowly raised my hands and said calmly, "I'm not armed." This undoubtedly reassured them.

A third man slipped quickly in front of the window—to keep me from jumping out, I suppose.

They handcuffed and searched me. They seemed stunned that everything had come off so quickly and easily. If they had spoken, they would have said, "But you've been walking around unarmed! You don't even have a bodyguard!"

The dentist walked over to me; he seemed to be the only one present who had not recovered. His voice was shaking: "Monsieur Gilbert," he said, "I had nothing to do with this, I promise you." He was not lying, as I found out later.

Meanwhile, I was in the hands of the Gestapo. I had to face that. It was very hard, but I had to maintain my confidence. I knew instinctively that the game was not yet over for them or for me.

After the arrest of the employees of Simex, the Gestapo had conducted interrogations around the clock, making use of torture in the first and second degrees. Only one question was asked of the prisoners: "Where is Gilbert?" Corbin was the only one who knew, and Corbin did not talk. In the meantime, though, unknown to us, Madame Corbin and her daughter were in their apartment under the surveillance of Lafont's gang, the French auxiliaries of the Gestapo. Believing that I was unaware of Corbin's arrest, they were waiting for me at his home and holding his wife and daughter as hostages.

On the 23rd, Giering and Captain Piepe of the Abwehr arrived from Brussels. They were very angry with Eric Jung, one of the members of the Sonderkommando, who had been responsible for making the raid on Simex. Giering would have preferred, understandably enough, to put the personnel of Simex under surveillance and have them shadowed, because this was his best chance of finding me.

On the evening of the same day, Giering had Corbin's wife, daughter, and brother imprisoned at Fresnes. On the morning of November 24, 1942, Giering conducted the interrogation of Madame Corbin in person. He informed her very coolly that if she did not tell him where I was, within the next few hours, Alfred Corbin would be shot before her eyes and the rest of her family sent to a concentration camp. The pressure was too much. The poor woman was desperate. She remembered that one day, at the beginning of the summer, I had had a toothache and had asked her to give me the address of a dentist. She had said, "Why don't you go to our dentist?"

It was about eleven o'clock on the morning of that 24th of November when Madame Corbin gave Giering the dentist's address. I do not consider that she betrayed me in doing so. She was sure she was not subjecting me to any danger since a few weeks before that she had asked me how my teeth were, and I had answered, "My troubles are over. I won't have to go back to the dentist." She behaved like any intelligence agent who knows his job: she turned over a piece of useless information in order to protect what was essential.

During this interrogation, Corbin was in the next room and heard everything through a half-open door. I imagine he was very happy to hear that his wife had invented something to satisfy the Gestapo.

Giering and Piepe rushed off in pursuit of me. At 11:30, they arrived at the dentist's office; the dentist, Dr. Maleplate, was not there, according to his assistant, but at the hospital. They ordered the assistant to telephone and ask him to return to his office at once. Dr. Maleplate, worried about the health of his sick father who lived on the floor above, came back immediately—to be greeted by the men of the Gestapo. They ordered him to read them the names out of his appointment calendar, one by one. Gilbert's name did not appear on the list. Giering checked for himself. At the last minute, Dr. Maleplate remembered that the patient who had been scheduled for two o'clock that same day had cancelled his appointment and that Monsieur Gilbert was to come in his place.

Giering and Piepe realized they had never had such a good chance of catching me, but they had to move quickly. They had the dentist describe this patient: he was a Belgian industrialist, he told them, who had originally had an appointment for the 27th but had changed it at the last minute. They said nothing, merely telling him, as they left, "Don't leave your office."

It was about twelve-thirty. Giering and Piepe estimated how much time they had left. It was too late to mount a vast operation, so they would carry out the arrest themselves. At one-thirty they went back to Dr. Maleplate's office and warned him, "We are going to arrest Gilbert here. Do whatever you usually do. Put him in the chair and prop up his head."

The rest you know. My freedom hinged on this little twist of fate. Life is made up of unforeseen events, and an intelligence agent has to anticipate the unexpected. This is what I was thinking as Giering and Piepe led me toward a car. We drove away, and after a moment of silence I said to Giering, "You're in luck. If you hadn't arrested me today, you might have been looking for me until the end of the war."

"I'm delighted," he replied happily. "It's been two years since we started looking for you in all the countries Germany occupies."

I was taken into German headquarters on the Rue des Saussaies. They took me up to the fifth floor where the Sonderkommando had its offices. After a brief lull, the parade began. The news spread through all the offices, and everybody and his brother came to get a look at the strange creature.

A fat, greasy fellow with the face of a drinker appeared and exclaimed when he saw me, "At last we have him, the Russian bear!" That was Boemelburg, head of the Gestapo in Paris.

Giering had disappeared. He returned an hour later, beaming, having personally telephoned Hitler and Himmler, he said, to inform them that "the Big Chief has been arrested." Giering went on, "Himmler is very happy, and he told me 'Now, be careful. The best course would be to tie his hands and feet and bury him alive. With him, you never know what will happen.'"

After it got dark they took me down the street, taking precautions to be sure we met no one. Some cars were waiting. My hands were manacled. Three agents of the Gestapo accompanied me. We set off, one car driving ahead of us and another behind. As we turned into the Avenue du Maine, I realized we were going to Fresnes. When we arrived in front of the prison, we waited half an hour, long enough to empty the premises. Clearly, they wanted to keep my arrest a secret. When we walked to the special section where the members of the Red Orchestra were imprisoned, all the halls were deserted.

I was pushed into a cell. The door slammed. Around me was the décor I knew so well from my previous experiences in Palestine: the small table, the straw mattress, the high window.

I began to assess the situation. I was worried about what had happened to my friends: first of all, Katz, with whom I had had a rendezvous for four o'clock. He must have waited for me, but we had agreed that if I did not come he was to telephone the dentist's office. Later I learned that an officer of the Gestapo who spoke French had answered the phone and told him that "Monsieur Gilbert did not show up for his appointment"—a poor move, since Katz had seen me walk into Dr. Maleplate's building. While Katz was waiting for me in the vicinity of the Rue de Rivoli, the Gestapo had made a raid on his home.

As for Georgie, it was only by a miracle that she escaped Giering's men. Around six o'clock, since I had not appeared as arranged, she decided to go to Katz' house, thus rushing headlong into the trap. When she entered the building, the concierge warned her that the Gestapo were upstairs. She had just enough time to get away.

Meanwhile, I was in my cell. Hours went by without anyone's appearing—I could not help observing how strange this was. I had already been initiated into prison rituals. Ordinarily one goes through various formalities: forms, searches, undressing.

And then I was assailed by dark thoughts. I said to myself, "Suppose Giering has already obtained the confidence of the Center to the point where he no longer needs you. Worse, suppose a 'turned' Orchestra—a Brown Orchestra—is functioning well; then your arrest would risk upsetting the game. They're going to liquidate you, and until the end of the war the Gestapo will dupe Moscow."

The thought that these might be the last moments of my life did not prevent me from sinking into sleep. But not for long. The door opened suddenly, a light flashed, someone shouted,

"Aufstehen! We're leaving."

Once again, the deserted halls. We returned to the three cars used that afternoon and off we went again. After we had been on the road a few minutes, our car stopped. The night was very black. It was impossible to tell where we were. My guards got out; moving shadows conferred in whispers. At that moment I did not doubt that I had reached the end of my journey. The door of the car was still open. It was dark and I had an opportunity to escape. The chances of carrying it off were minimal, but at least I would force them to chase me, to fire at me. I would die fighting. Flight was the last reflex, the only way I had left of saying "no." I hesitated a few seconds. Too late! The gentlemen got back into the car, cursing.

"That idiot of a driver in the first car has lost his way!"

Twenty minutes later we were back at the Rue des Saussaies. Up to the fifth floor again. An unexpected consideration: they removed my handcuffs, and like a headwaiter apologizing for the slowness of the service, a member of the Sonderkommando walked over to me and said ceremoniously: "Excuse us for not giving you any dinner at Fresnes, Monsieur Gilbert, but we did not want the administration of the prison to learn of your presence."

I had suspected as much.

I was shown into a big room where seven men were sitting behind a table. I recognized three of them. Among the other four, who, I was told, had just arrived from Berlin for the occasion, I identified Gestapo-Müller. Giering was in the middle and seemed to be presiding. I was given a chair behind a small table. All that was missing was the traditional glass of water to complete the impression of being in a lecture hall.

"Perhaps after a day like this you would like a cup of coffee," Giering suggested.

I accepted it very gladly; the hot liquid fortified me.

Then Giering got up and addressed me in German, deliberately amplifying his voice.

"So, Herr Otto, as head of Soviet espionage in the countries occupied by Germany, you have been of great service to your Director. That is agreed. But now we must turn the page. You have lost, and I imagine that you know what fate awaits you. But let me remind you that it is possible to die twice. The first time you will be shot as an enemy of the Third Reich. But in addition, we can also have you shot in Moscow as a traitor."

I looked into his eyes and replied,

"Herr Giering . . ."

"Why do you call me Herr Giering?" he interrupted. "Do you know my name?"

"What do you take us for? Do you suppose that we don't know the names of all the members of the Sonderkommando, that we don't know everything that goes on here? You have been willing to admit that I have had a certain amount of experience in intelligence; there's proof of it."

I waited for this to sink in and then went on, "Well, Herr Giering, this threat of two deaths—how many times have you used it before?"

Loud laughter from the men behind the table. I went on.

"As for myself, I can answer you. I do know, indeed, the fate that is ahead for me, and I am prepared to meet it. As for the symbolic execution you refer to, I will tell you frankly—I don't give a damn. Sooner or later, the truth will be known, no matter what you do. All that matters to me is my conscience."

Giering changed the subject: "Do you know where Kent is?"

Now it was my turn to laugh.

"You know as well as I do that he was arrested in Marseilles on the 12th of November. I don't know what prison you put him in, but that operation Boemelburg carried on with the French police is an open secret."

They were aghast, and besieged me with questions: how did I know about that?

"It's too bad you don't read the French press. On the 14th of November, a Marseilles paper made a big to-do over the arrest of a group of Soviet agents. Besides, you carried out the operation with French policemen. Are you so sure of their loyalty and that they won't talk?"

This last observation was carefully planned to cast suspicion on the French auxiliaries. The fact was, their collaboration with the German police was very dangerous: many times the Gestapo would not have been so effective without the aid of the French police who advised them. The card files set up before the war on leftist militants—particularly stateless persons—were not lost in every case. From the first day of the occupation of Paris, June 14, 1940, the Paris police had been ordered to turn over any "interesting" files, especially those of political refugees.

Still, I had not realized that I had hit so close to home; forgetting all about me, the highest leaders were demanding explanations from Giering. How was it possible that French or Belgian auxiliaries could have taken part in an operation that had been classified in Berlin as a "state secret"? Giering defended himself by arguing that their participation had not been his decision. In any case, I achieved my objective. From that day on, as I learned later, the Sonderkommando were forbidden to use Frenchmen for this type of assignment.

After this interlude, Giering tried to regain the upper hand: "Since December, 1941, Moscow has lost confidence in the information you send them." He showed me three voluminous files. On the first was written, in big letters, "Red Orchestra—Paris"; on the second, "Red Orchestra—Brussels," and on the third, "The Big Chief." I learned that this flattering designation referred to me. "In this first file," Giering went on, "are the dispatches decoded in Berlin at the beginning of '42, which show that the Center was dissatisfied with the measures that you took after the 13th of December, when we captured your Brussels station. They considered them too severe."

I remembered this exchange with the Center perfectly well, but since then I had justified my decisions with the Director by showing him that the danger was real and far from having been averted.

The head of the Sonderkommando wanted to exploit his argument to the maximum:

"Here is a dispatch from summer, 1942, which you sent the Center informing them of Efremov's arrest, and here is the Center's reply: 'Otto, you are mistaken. We know that Efremov was arrested by the Belgian police and that they checked his papers, but everything has been taken care of.' So you see," Giering went on, "the Director has lost confidence in you. Actually, you were right, for I will not conceal from you the fact that Efremov is working for us—and he is not the only one. We," he boasted, "are stronger than you are."

"Herr Giering, let us imagine that I have not been arrested, and let us talk together like two professionals. I say this to you: don't be too sure of yourselves. That is the greatest temptation that threatens those of us in intelligence. You are convinced that you have the Director's confidence. Well, since you have started reading the dispatches, look for the one in which the Director asks me to go to Brussels to meet Efremov. He specifies the date, the time of day, and the place. You intercepted that dispatch. And now, Giering, tell these gentlemen: did I go to that rendezvous?"

"No, you did not."

"But how is that possible, in view of the strict discipline that is observed in intelligence work? I will tell you myself.

The reason is that I received another dispatch, through another channel, ordering me not to go to the rendezvous. The meeting was a trap set by the Director, who wanted to make sure that Efremov had really been arrested."

The men behind the table exchanged looks. I went on, "You see, one can't be sure of anything. How do you know that the Center isn't aware of your plans?"

"We know that Moscow believes Kent to be at large," Giering replied.

"Has Kent gone over to your side?"

"Yes."

"Are you sure?"

"Absolutely. He encodes the dispatches we send to the Center."

"That's no proof."

Once again Giering shifted ground.

"Say, Otto, what is this special liaison with Moscow that passes through the leadership of the Communist Party?"

"So you know about that channel. It was Kent who told you about that, wasn't it? But did he tell you how to make use of it?"

I was very intrigued to hear Giering's answer.

"Not yet, but that is not important. By the way, are you familiar with Schulze-Boysen's group?"

"No, I've never heard of it."

"It's a communist intelligence group in Berlin. It has been completely liquidated, and yet communication with Moscow goes on as if nothing had happened."

"Exactly what do you want with me?" I replied. "I am a prisoner, and I want to tell you at the outset that nothing you say has any effect on me. I already know it, and what I also know is that you do not have the confidence of Moscow. Besides, every day that I spend here will help Moscow to see through your game."

This time Giering did not answer. It was two o'clock in the morning. My listeners were visibly fatigued. The discussion, which I have only summarized, had been long and tense. I was beginning to understand the enemy's plan. It was clear that I was dealing with an attempt at deception on a vast scale and not some little *Funkspiel*, or radio game, that would be over in a few weeks. In a radio game, the Germans would continue broadcasting over a transmitter they had captured, imitating the pianist's style and giving out false information—such a game did not last long. But I could not make out the ultimate objective of this "great game" that was taking shape before my eyes. This, neither Giering nor the others had confided.

Giering adjourned the meeting: "That's enough for today," he said. "We'll continue tomorrow."

I spent the rest of the night in a small room, stretched out on a sofa. Two SS underlings kept an eye on me. No one came to see me in the morning.

In the afternoon, Giering appeared and announced, "Our most immediate concern is keeping your arrest secret. I am sure that you find it bizarre that we are so frank with you. All the important members of the Red Orchestra have been arrested. Some of them are collaborating with us; some refuse to do so. I repeat: you have lost. But one question certainly interests you: what we hope to achieve. Well, Herr Otto, we will talk about that this evening."

15

I must diverge from the chronology of events to make an accusation. The responsibility for the end of that vital group, the Berlin branch of the Red Orchestra, lay squarely with the leaders of the Military Intelligence Service in Moscow and the Central Committee of the German Communist Party.

Between 1930 and 1941, by Stalin's orders, the Military Intelligence Service had refrained from carrying out operations inside Germany—I have already explained this in detail. After 1933, several resistance groups formed in Germany: Harro Schulze-Boysen's group, Arvid Harnack's group, another with marked communist leanings run by John Sieg, an equally communistic group run by Wilhelm Guddorf, Dr. John Rittmeister's group, the Jewish youth group under the direction of Herbert Baumann, the Rotholz group, and others. Beginning in 1938–1939, the German resistance groups carried on their activities within the Schulze-Boysen and Harnack organizations.

The leaders of the Communist Party approved the activities and efforts of these resistance groups in Germany. In 1937, in my last conversation with General Berzin, I asked him about the prospects in Germany for the creation of a military intelligence group along the lines of the Red Orchestra. He answered that the leaders of the Military Intelligence Service had high hopes invested in certain people—who had been warned not to engage in any potentially compromising activities until the war broke out. Berzin must have been thinking primarily of the group run by Harro Schulze-Boysen and Arvid Harnack.

How could the heads of Military Intelligence in Moscow and the Communist Party in Germany have allowed Schulze-Boysen and Harnack to become the leaders of a vast resistance network—and consequently, to be in constant danger of falling into the hands of the Gestapo?

There are two answers. The first is that after the execution of General Berzin, the new leaders of Soviet Military Intelligence followed Stalin's policy, as did the illegal German Communist Party. They expected a compromise with the Third Reich to eliminate any danger of war in the years to follow. This situation lasted until 1941—and it was in 1941 that Schulze-Boysen and Arvid Harnack founded the group that was devoted exclusively to military intelligence. Only twenty to twenty-five of the persons who were arrested belonged to this inner circle.

The second answer has to do with the ground rules for a conspiracy: this military intelligence group, in its work as well as its leadership, ought to have been rigorously isolated from all groups involved in resistance. If General Berzin had been alive and in charge, it is certain that he would have insisted on this. But lesser people had the power—and what happened was absolutely incredible. Known communist militants became leaders of the Schulze-Boysen and Harnack groups—Wilhelm Guddorf and John Sieg, as the official representatives of the German Communist Party. Further, in spite of their new responsibilities, Harro Schulze-Boysen and Arvid Harnack continued, along with John Sieg, Wilhelm Guddorf, Walter Husemann, Herbert Grasse, and other communist leaders, to run action groups involved in internal resistance.

The discovery of the Schulze-Boysen and Harnack group, in 1942, by no means came as a surprise.

For one thing, there was the abysmally dull-minded—and highly dangerous—radio message sent by the Center on October 10, 1941. It contained three addresses, and asked Kent to leave for Berlin and make contact with five people: Schulze-Boysen, Harnack, and Adam Kuckhoff, all in the Red Orchestra, and also Ilse Stöbe, an agent who had been working for Moscow since 1932, and Kurt Schulze, a radio operator who had been working with the heads of military intelligence since 1929. Neither of the latter had any connection with the Red Orchestra. As soon as the message was decoded it would immediately put the Gestapo on their trail.

It had been received at the Rue des Atrébates, and two
months afterward the Rue des Atrébates operation was
captured. The likelihood was enormous that the message
would eventually be decoded, but the Center paid absolutely
no attention to my warning.

In April, 1942, I sent the Center another warning: the
Germans had discovered that Alamo's real name was Mikael
Makarov, and that he was an officer in the Military Intelligence Service. Unfortunately, this news also produced no
reaction from Moscow. It was Makarov and Sophie Poznanska who coded and sent the telegrams to Moscow from the
house in the Rue des Atrébates until the day the house was
captured, December 13, 1941. As we now know, neither
Sophie Poznanska nor Makarov betrayed the code they used
to the Gestapo. Rita Arnould remembered what books had
been on Sophie's desk, and the Gestapo got copies of them.
Copies of all but the right one—but on May 17, 1942, Captain
Karl von Wedel found the book, *Le miracle du professeur
Wolman*, on which the code was based, in a second-hand
store in Paris.

The Gestapo had long suspected Schulze-Boysen. We
know this from what Elsa Schulze-Boysen wrote in her book,
Harro Schulze-Boysen, Portrait of a Freedom-Fighter:

> Meanwhile, Hitler's henchmen had their eyes on him for a
> long time. His apartment was searched twice in the first half of
> 1942, but nothing was found, and he was not worried. He had
> removed his papers and documents and was storing them with
> friends.

The Gestapo had him under surveillance even before the
radio message was decoded. Elsa Schulze-Boysen has the
benefit of hindsight; if the Center had not piled error upon
error, perhaps there would be more of us now to use
hindsight.

What happened next is clear. Official German sources have
informed us that the fatal dispatch addressed to Kent on
October 10 was decoded the following July 15. From that date

it took only a few weeks of intensive research: on August 30, the Gestapo had assembled sufficient material to arrest sixty persons, a majority of whom belonged to the Military Intelligence Service. Naturally, not one of the fifty to seventy messages decoded mentioned any names, but the content of the telegrams provided the Gestapo with obvious information on the senders, who all belonged to the circle of friends and acquaintances of Schulze-Boysen and Harnack.

Immediately after the arrest of Schulze-Boysen, his wife, Libertas, and Horst Heilmann gave the alarm. In a very short time Arvid Harnack, Johann Graudenz, Günther Weissenborn, Hans Coppi, Adam Kuckhoff, Anna Kraus, Erika von Brockdorff, Hans Helmut Himpel, "pianist" Helmut Rolof, and many others had been alerted. Unfortunately, they did not know the Gestapo had been watching them night and day for a long time; they thought if they simply destroyed their radio sets, they would not be arrested. They did not: they were caught in the Gestapo's horrible nets.

If the central Red Orchestra nucleus had been rigorously isolated from the other resistance groups, there is no doubt that more than thirty persons would have escaped falling into the hands of the Gestapo.

The first result of this appalling error was the arrest of Ilse Stöbe and Kurt Schulze, who did not belong to the Red Orchestra and who did not get caught up in the wave of arrests until the information was given by the Center in Moscow. These two arrests encouraged the Gestapo to intensify their search for members of the Military Intelligence Service whose activities paralleled those of the Red Orchestra.

Although several members of the resistance groups were seized with panic after the arrests of Schulze-Boysen and Harnack, few of them realized the full extent of the danger that threatened them, or that it was necessary to disappear. They stayed where they were or took refuge in the homes of friends, where the Gestapo had no trouble finding them.

By the end of October, 1943, the Gestapo had got their hands on more than one hundred and thirty persons. About twenty-five of them had belonged directly or indirectly to the Schulze-Boysen–Harnack group. There were eight parachutists, as well as ten persons who had been working for Soviet Military Intelligence since 1930 and who had nothing to do with the Red Orchestra. In 1937, they had lost contact with the Center in Moscow, but after the outbreak of the war between Germany and Russia, the Center had resumed relations with them, making the Red Orchestra group their intermediary, and thus creating an additional danger for the members of the Red Orchestra. The rest of the men and women arrested belonged to various anti-Nazi resistance groups; they had never worked for the Intelligence Service.

When did the Center in Moscow learn of these arrests?

Back before the Berlin arrests, by the beginning of August, 1942, I had warned the Center and informed them of the arrest of Efremov, who had turned traitor. The Center knew perfectly well that Efremov had contacts within the Schulze-Boysen and Harnack group. But once again, alas, my warning fell on deaf ears. In September, 1942, the Center gave Otto Pinter, who was working in Switzerland, the assignment of collecting accurate information on the Berlin group. At the end of September, Pinter warned Moscow that many parts of the network had been discovered, that numerous arrests had already been made, and that others would certainly follow. Those arrested to date had been leaders and radio operators. The Director answered Pinter that this information was not sufficient, and that he would have to find out exactly when the group had been discovered, when the arrests had started, and who had been arrested.

Albert Hossler was not arrested until the end of September. I am sure that after the arrests at the beginning of September he must have had the opportunity to send at least one message to the Center to inform them of the situation of the Berlin group, and if he had that opportunity, he would have taken it. But the Center did not take any of these communications seriously. For instance: in October the Gestapo used a captured radio set to send the Directors a message asking them to send a parachutist to Berlin with money for Ilse Stöbe; in fact, she had been arrested. Ilse was to renew contact with Rudolf von Scheliha, an adviser in the Foreign Ministry. The Directors complied—they behaved as if they had no knowledge of the mass arrests that had taken place! On October 23, Heinrich Koenen landed in Eastern Prussia; on October 28, in Berlin, he met with a Gestapo agent who posed as Ilse Stöbe; on the 29th, Heinrich Koenen was arrested; on the 30th Rudolf von Scheliha was arrested.

It is obvious, then, that the Center in Moscow bears the major responsibility for the liquidation of the Berlin group, as well as the Belgian and French groups. Moscow would never have gambled so casually with the lives of these wonderful people, so full of the spirit of self-sacrifice, if General Berzin and his staff had not been executed in 1938 and replaced by men with no experience in intelligence work.

After the war, Gestapo officers spread the myth of the treason of the leaders of the German group of the Red Orchestra, just as they did in the case of the leaders of the Belgian and French groups. According to the Gestapo, these men and women gave the names of their comrades, making it possible for them to be arrested in large numbers.

I shall not deny that among the hundred and thirty persons arrested, there were a few cases in which persons subjected to torture and brainwashing did inform on their comrades. But there could be no more shameful lie than to accuse men like Schulze-Boysen, Harnack, Kuckhoff, and other leaders of the Red Orchestra of treason. I give my word here that, up to the last moments of their lives, these men were able to bar the Gestapo's way to many highly placed persons, both military and civilian, who were working for the Red Orchestra. Moreover, the Schulze-Boysen and Harnack group was in contact, through couriers, with Soviet Intelligence Services in various countries, and not one of those liaisons was discovered by the Gestapo.

After horrible torture sessions, John Sieg and Herbert Grasse, militants of the German Communist Party, committed suicide to block the path that might have led to numerous groups of the resistance movement.

These monumental errors, which cost blood and lives, were haunting me in my captivity. I did not then know all the details that I have recounted here, but I knew that the Center had stumbled, badly, with deadly results. Now the Sonderkommando had some "great game" in mind; would there be any way to safeguard our people against the Sonderkommando's schemes?

16

t about nine o'clock on the evening of the 25th of
November, I appeared again before the "tribunal."
After all the maneuvering of the previous day and the
attempts at demoralizing me on the theme "you have lost"
(but if I had lost, why did the Sonderkommando need my
"services"?), I wondered what they had in store for me.

More surprises, it turned out: Giering did not address me
as the defeated prisoner as he had the day before; instead he
shifted his tactics slightly and, in a different tone, launched
into a solemn, almost ceremonious, speech on high-level
politics—which would have delighted an audience of diplomats.

His opening statement was: "The sole objective of the
Third Reich is to arrive at peace with the Soviet Union."

That was news to me. He must have noticed my puzzled
expression, but, ignoring it, he went on with his "truths."

"The bloodbath that is spreading between the Wehrmacht
and the Red Army can please no one but capitalist plutocrats.
The Führer himself has called Churchill an alcoholic and
Roosevelt a miserable paralytic. But although it is easy to
establish contacts with representatives of the western powers
in the neutral countries, it is almost impossible to meet with
emissaries of the Soviet government. This problem was
insoluble for us—until the day we hit upon the idea of
utilizing the Red Orchestra. The broadcasting stations of the
network, once they are working for us, will be the instruments of this advance toward peace."

Here Giering, sure of his success, interrupted his speech to
read some dispatches that had been sent through captured
transmitters, to illustrate his point. He was pleased with
himself; triumphantly, he added that Moscow had noticed
nothing.

He pursued this: for the Center, there was "nothing new in   **186** the west''; everything went on as usual, and this was perfectly comprehensible, since the material sent continued to be of the highest quality, from the political as well as the military point of view. He, Giering, was not attempting to give false news, but to maintain Moscow's confidence. For the moment, nothing could persuade him to alter this tactic: "For several months we shall continue to make these little sacrifices for the greater cause. But when the time comes that we are convinced that not a shred of suspicion remains on the Russian side regarding the networks in the west, then the second phase will begin. On that day your Director will begin receiving reports of capital importance originating in the highest circles in Berlin, all confirming the fact that we are seeking a separate peace with the Soviet Union."

Giering had reached the end of his speech. He turned to me and put his trump card on the table.

"I have revealed our program to you because you are no longer an obstacle to its realization. You have your choice: either you will collaborate with us, or you will disappear."

So this was what he had been driving at. This was the meaning of the stage-setting, and the conclusion of all the long speeches. The Nazis were offering me two alternatives: either work with them to achieve a "reversal of alliances," in which case I would become a major pawn on the new chessboard, or simply be removed.

It was an enormous blackmail. As the head of the Sonder-kommando spoke, I quickly and feverishly assessed the scope of the maneuver and perceived very clearly the trap that had been set for me. My first thought was that this was not a complete surprise: no, it had already occurred to me that the Germans were not so much trying to destroy the broadcast-ing stations and physically liquidate the militants as trying to get them to change sides. This tactic became quite common during the Second World War, and I would not be the only object of an attempt at manipulation. But Giering and his friends—this was my second thought, and it was no less important—were lying brazenly when they claimed the Third Reich wanted a separate peace with the Soviet Union.

In this month of November, 1942, I knew for a fact, and had known since the fall of 1939, that in certain leading Nazi political and military circles, hope was being cherished for a compromise with the west. If there was to be a separate peace, it was intended to be with the "capitalist plutocrats," however "alcoholic" or "paralytic," and behind the back of the USSR.

Coming from the Abwehr or from Admiral Canaris (whose game would be clearly revealed after the war), such a conciliatory attitude would, of course, have been conceivable; but from the Schellenbergs, Heydrichs, Müllers, and Himmlers—from the masters of the Gestapo—it was a bit much. I felt like shouting at Giering, "How do you expect us to believe that you are ready to negotiate with the foremost socialist country?" For those fanatics, there could be no question of a separate peace; their only purpose was to undermine and destroy the anti-Hitler alliance. That was the function of this crude, infernal plot they intended to associate me with, and that was its principal danger: they would arouse suspicion and then hostility among the allies, and then simply reap the benefits.

For fighters in the Red Orchestra, the war between Hitler's Germany and the Soviet Union had always seemed inevitable; even the German-Soviet pact had not changed our point of view. Frenchmen, Belgians, Poles, Italians, Spaniards, Jews, we were all guided by one fixed idea: the annihilation of Nazism, the total elimination of the brown plague. We had judged the risks of a separate peace and a rupture among the allies, and found it insupportable: it would achieve only a remission of a disease that had to be eradicated altogether.

At the beginning of the war the Nazis had profited from the lack of communication between the Soviet Union and the western democracies, for which the populations of Europe had paid a high price. In this year of 1942, the alliance was showing signs of weakness. The Red Army had been forced to withdraw over hundreds of kilometers, and it had suffered considerable losses in men and materiel. This retreat had aroused suspicions and fears in the west. How much longer

would the Red Army withstand the onslaught of the Wehrmacht?

From another point of view, the English and Americans
seemed reluctant to open a second front; it was constantly
being postponed. This kept suspicion alive in Moscow. The
Soviets wondered whether the westerners were waiting,
arms at the ready and reserves intact, until the Red Army and
the Wehrmacht had bled each other white, to see what they
could salvage from the slaughter.

We have since realized that our apprehensions were exaggerated. We know now that those elements in the German
High Command, and even in Hitler's entourage, that were
working toward a separate peace with the west behind the
back of the Soviet Union "with or without Hitler" did not
enjoy a great deal of influence. Furthermore, although we
were aware that a number of politicians in Great Britain and
the United States looked favorably on the idea of an arrange-
ment with a "Germany delivered from Hitler," we were sure
that Roosevelt and Churchill would never consider this
solution but adhere to their requirement of unconditional
surrender.

But getting back to my appearance before the "tribunal"
. . .

Giering and the others had not lost their illusions, and
continued to describe their plans complacently. However, in
revealing their game to me, their prisoner, they showed they
were not absolutely sure they had succeeded in deceiving the
Director. They were testing my reactions, and the possibility
of my own collaboration.

For me, only one thing was clear: in the weeks and months
to come, the Center was going to be duped—and on a vast
scale. Military, political, and diplomatic information that had
been completely fabricated by the German services would
eventually be taken for sound currency in Moscow. For the
moment, they were still at the stage of preparing the bait;
once the fish had been hooked, it would be easy for Giering
to bring him in with some skillful manipulation.

Although my mind was very agitated, I forced myself to

appear completely calm. My first intention was to shake their fine assurance. I made up a story that was sufficiently coherent to convince Germans, who are particularly susceptible to logic:

"Your reasoning is based on the hypothesis that by using pianists who have turned traitor, you are playing the game well enough that the Director is maintaining contact as before. However, it is possible to consider another hypothesis, which is no less plausible: the Director is not blind, or rather, not deaf, and he is aware that there have been false notes in the orchestra. However, he is pretending to have noticed nothing. In this case, who is pulling the strings, you or he?"

Giering looked flustered for a moment, but retorted, with an ironic smile: "Your exploit of December 13, 1941, did not solve all your problems. Now Moscow no longer has confidence in you, and you have not succeeded in convincing the Director that you managed to escape on that day, thanks to the Todt Organization."

They all burst out laughing, except for Captain Piepe, who had given the order to release me when I was at the Rue des Atrébates.

Giering added, "You are quite aware that in Moscow they do not believe people who have been in the hands of the Gestapo, if only for a minute."

At that point I decided to drop a bombshell:

"Gentlemen, I am afraid that you are unaware of one very important fact: there exists a counterespionage group completely independent of the Red Orchestra, whose function is to look after the security of its members. This group informs Moscow directly, through a special channel, of what is happening in the field."

If I had revealed that Hitler was a Soviet agent, their astonishment could not have been greater. To espionage specialists, such a group sounded altogether likely. Such an organization could have been able to function unknown not only to the Germans, but to most of the agents of the Red Orchestra itself.

The phantom counterespionage group reversed the situation. Doubt crept into the minds of my enemies and gradually turned into certainty. I went on:

"You will understand that under the circumstances I must view the possibility of collaborating with you with very profound reservations. I am in complete agreement with Bismarck that Germany must at all costs avoid a war on two fronts, especially with Russia, but I feel that I cannot take part in building a castle on the sand. It would be ridiculous for me, as a prisoner, to enter into a game of which the Center already knows all the rules——"

Giering's answer provoked laughter: "But the logical conclusion of what you have just said is that I must release you!"

I retorted in the same forceful tone, "That would be your best course, if you really wanted to arrive at a separate peace with the Soviet Union!"

Our second conversation finished here, but I was satisfied that I had practically achieved my objective, to undermine their assurance. On the 26th and 27th of November, I had private interviews with Giering, in which the weak points of the Great Game became clear. In the first place, the operation was only in its preliminary stages; for the time being, the Germans would be obliged to send valuable material in order to reassure Moscow that no transmitter had fallen into the hands of the enemy. This allowed a certain respite. But above all, Giering realized that the special liaison through the Communist Party, which Kent had told him about, was capable of wrecking the Great Game completely. He was afraid that the Center had been informed through this channel of the partial destruction of the Red Orchestra in France, and he knew that to reassure the Director once and for all, he would have to send him a message by the same route. Since Kent had told him that I was the only person who could use it, Giering therefore needed me. I repeated with assurance that his operation was doomed to failure and that he would realize this himself before long—every day that passed without my making contact with the French Communist Party would only increase the Center's suspicions.

My argument was by no means all bluster. I was hoping that at one point or another, Giering would be obliged to take me into the Great Game, not as a pawn to be manipulated, but as an indispensable partner. Then, from the inside, I would be able to throw the machine out of gear.

"What guarantees of your loyalty can you give me if you take part in the game?" Giering had asked.

"The question of confidence does not arise," I had replied. "You must take your risks. If you ask for my help, it is because you need me, isn't it? Without my participation, your structure will collapse."

But Giering was not yet ready to take the risk. For six weeks, he attempted to make contact with the French Communist Party without my help.

17

Six Defeats for Karl Giering

Giering met with six defeats in a row, which encouraged me to persevere in the struggle.

The first was one he was unaware of. Giering asked me to behave in such a way that the Director would not know I had been arrested. I immediately suggested that I telephone the owner of a café on the Place de la Madeleine and leave the following message for an "André" (who was Hillel Katz): "Everything is going well, I'll be back in a few days." As far as Giering could tell, the text was logical. He had no way of knowing that in the Red Orchestra we used the telephone only under exceptional circumstances, and that when we did, we made use of an inverted language in which "everything is going well" meant "everything is going badly." Katz would read the message as: "Everything is going badly, and I won't be back," and would thus have new confirmation of my arrest.

Second defeat: Giering had Kent send a dispatch to the Director asking for direct contact with the leaders of the French Communist Party, parallel to my contact with them. He justified his request by stating that I was not "reliable," and that it was preferable to divide the contacts in this way. The Director replied categorically in the negative. He stated emphatically that if insecurity reigned within the groups, he saw no reason to share the risks with the comrades of the Communist Party. Not every move of the Director's lacked elemental sense.

Third defeat: through Kent's transmitter, the Sonderkommando asked the Director—in my name—to alert the leaders of the French Communist Party and to set the place, date, and hour of a meeting with their representative, Michel. The Director replied in the affirmative and gave the coordinates of the meeting in every detail.

The men of the Sonderkommando were beside themselves with delight. They immediately held a war council and decided not to arrest Michel; on the contrary, the agent who met him would ask him to advise the Director that in spite of the arrests the Gestapo had made at Simex, Otto and the members of the Red Orchestra had not been disturbed.

The loud rejoicing of the Sonderkommando was premature: Michel did not come to the rendezvous. Giering and his men were not privy to the special arrangements I had made with the representative of the Communist Party before my arrest. We did not go to meetings as arranged by the Center, but to a place we had agreed on between us, and two days and two hours before the appointed time.

Giering was utterly at sea: how was it conceivable that anyone could fail to come to a rendezvous arranged by the Center? I explained that since Michel was on the spot, he must have sensed much better than the Center, three thousand kilometers away, that something had happened to me.

Fourth defeat: Giering sent another dispatch through Kent, and told the Center I was having trouble communicating with them through Marseilles; further, the broadcasting channel of the Communist Party had not functioned for some time, for unknown reasons. He therefore requested permission to arrange a meeting with "Duval"—Fernand Pauriol—who was in charge of this liaison. As in the case of Michel, the Director arranged the date, place, and hour of the rendezvous. Once again the Sonderkommando thought they were close to their quarry, but once again their hopes were disappointed. Since November, we had been using the same system with Fernand that we had with Michel. Besides, only Grossvogel was authorized to meet with Fernand Pauriol. Pauriol came to the appointed place at the time that corresponded to our system, but found no one, since by this time Grossvogel had already been arrested. This incident confirmed his suspicions that the Center's communications were compromised.

Giering was becoming more and more perplexed. He had

succeeded in gulling the Center—but what good had it done? The Director's orders were no longer being carried out in the field.

Fifth defeat for Giering: since 1941 a Parisian confectioner's shop had served as a mailbox for dispatches forwarded through the Communist Party. A very delightful old lady worked there, Madame Juliette Moussier, who was very highly regarded by the management and the other employees. She had been a militant with the French Communist Party for many years. Dozens of customers went in and out of this shop all day long, and Fernand Pauriol and I had had the idea that it would be easy to exchange the little tubes that held the dispatches while making some minor purchase. Contact was made with Madame Juliette, and she agreed to act as a liaison agent. This channel was chosen for the transmission of the most important messages, and functioned without a hitch for a year and a half. Outside of Hillel Katz, who was a friend of Madame Juliette's, only two or three comrades, including Raichmann, who had been in Paris since the Atrébates arrests, had worked with her as transmitting agents.

After he was arrested and subjected to terrible tortures, Raichmann agreed to work for the other side, and he revealed Madame Juliette's role to the Sonderkommando. So, Giering decided to take his chances. One day in December, Giering had Raichmann go to the confectioner's shop and ask Madame Juliette to take a message for the "old man," that is, for me. Madame Juliette told him very coldly that there must be some misunderstanding: she did not know to whom she had the honor of speaking, nor was she acquainted with the "old man" to whom he had referred.

Again Giering was at an impasse: why did Madame Juliette refuse to recognize a man she had been in contact with before? What he did not know was that we had been suspicious of Raichmann ever since Efremov's arrest, and we had given the order to sever all contact with him. From then on it had been agreed that, aside from Hillel Katz and myself, anyone who presented himself to Madame Juliette would hand her a red button. Raichmann was unaware of these new security arrangements.

Giering then wondered what to do about Madame Juliette. Should he arrest her? It would not be the best solution, because that would permanently cut off the road that might lead him to the leaders of the Communist Party. Moreover, her arrest would be tantamount to an admission that the "old man" had been arrested and that Raichmann was working for the Germans. So he refrained, and here again he was "muzzled."

The sixth defeat, the sixth severe blow for Giering, was the escape of "professor" Wenzel.

The Germans had put their hands on six broadcasting stations, but they did not know the relative importance of each of them. Furthermore, in this false orchestra, Wenzel's transmitter was missing.

Immediately after his arrest, Wenzel was imprisoned in the Belgian fort of Breendonk, where he was tortured. In November, the Sonderkommando realized that he could not be dispensed with: the absence of this soloist would be noticed in Moscow. It was out of the question to replace Wenzel with a pianist of the Sonderkommando, because the "professor" was a great virtuoso whose very personal style of broadcasting was familiar to the Center. So the Germans were extremely pleased when, in November, Wenzel agreed to start sending messages for them.

He was very closely watched—nevertheless, in his first broadcast, Wenzel succeeded in giving the alarm signal that had been agreed on in advance. Thus the Center was warned that the music had been arranged by the enemy.

Wenzel, in "collaboration" with the Germans, took part in the writing and sending of two messages sent over the name "German," his *nom de guerre*. We know these two dispatches from Soviet sources:

To the Director, urgent. The usual liaisons with the Big Chief are under surveillance. Give directives for new meeting with

the Big Chief. Very important I meet with the Big Chief.
German.

And the second dispatch:

To the Director, very urgent. According to what we have
learned from German sources, the code book has been discovered. I have not yet been advised of a meeting with the Big
Chief. My contact with you functions regularly. There is no
sign of surveillance. How am I to arrange my liaisons with the
Center? Request immediate reply. German.

These two dispatches left no doubts at the Center, for we
never made use of the term "Big Chief."

Gradually, Wenzel succeeded in gaining the confidence of
the Sonderkommando, who installed him with his equipment in a room in the Rue Aurore in Brussels. During the
early days of January, 1943, the "professor" knocked his
guard unconscious while the latter had his back turned to
light the stove. He locked the guard in the room and fled
without leaving an address.

For Giering, this escape was a catastrophe. There was a
risk that Wenzel would inform Moscow of everything that
had happened in the Red Orchestra in Belgium since December, 1941. In fact, he did just that, crossing over to the
Netherlands, and using one of the transmitters that the
Germans had not found to send the Center a full report.

Nevertheless, the Sonderkommando had scored some very
important points since the Rue des Atrébates incident. Half a
dozen transmitters in five countries were sending the Center
dozens of dispatches. Judging by his answers, the Director
suspected nothing. But later the directives of the Center had
not been carried out; therefore, the machine must be jammed
somewhere. Giering had met with six serious setbacks in the
space of a few weeks, and his castle on the sand threatened to
collapse.

It was clear that the Sonderkommando head had only one
trump card left: to obtain the collaboration of the "Big Chief"

so that he could reassure the Center by making use of the French Communist Party channel. The risk was great for Giering, but he had no choice.

By the end of December, my conversations with him and his assistant Willy Berg were taking a different turn. The atmosphere had changed. I had been waiting for my moment; now it had come.

18

The tense battle of wits I was engaged in with Giering had not made me lose sight of the fact that several of our comrades who were still at liberty had to protect themselves from the Sonderkommando. I was thinking primarily of Leo Grossvogel and Hillel Katz; but I saw no immediate reason for concern in either case. I was convinced that they had escaped the most recent round of arrests, and I imagined them to be in safety. In Hillel's case, I had been positive. For the first few days, he had had a very safe hideout in Antony, and after that it had been agreed that he would leave Paris for Marseilles, where he would lie low for a few months.

It was Berg, Giering's assistant, who told me the bad news: "We have arrested your friend Katz, you know."

"Ah? When?"

"About three weeks ago."

So Hillel Katz had fallen, too. I did not understand, nor did I learn until later how, in spite of all his precautions, my good friend had been taken.

Upset by my arrest, Katz had spent several days preparing his departure. His wife, Cecile, had given birth on the 19th of November, and he did not want to disappear until mother and child had been taken to a safe place. His eldest son, Jean-Claude, was already with Maximovich's psychologist sister at the Chateau du Billeron.

After I left Poland in 1973, I learned from Cecile Katz that on November 29, 1942, her husband had come with Grossvogel to see her at the hospital. They both knew about my arrest, she told me, and were extremely worried. Katz returned to the hospital on December 1st; the next day he was to take his wife and baby daughter away. There was no next day. That evening he lingered too long in Paris and the curfew trapped him. Not wishing to take the risk of returning to Antony, he went to the home of one of our friends,

Modeste Ehrlich, a French schoolteacher who had married a Jewish engineer and former member of the International Brigade.

Since the beginning of the war, the Ehrlich apartment had been used as a meeting place and mailbox. It was there that Raichmann had met Hillel Katz early in 1942. After Raichmann's arrest and confessions, the Gestapo had placed the apartment under surveillance. In spite of my strict orders to stop using this apartment, Hillel decided that evening that he might spend a few hours there, provided he left very early the next morning. Gestapo agents, who were keeping a constant watch on the place, immediately alerted Reiser, head of the Sonderkommando in Paris, who organized a raid and had Hillel Katz and Modeste Ehrlich arrested the same night (December 1–2, 1942). I managed to convince Giering that Modeste Ehrlich did not belong to the Red Orchestra, and that we were using her apartment without telling her anything about our activities. Nonetheless, she was subsequently sent to a concentration camp, where she died.

Leo Grossvogel was arrested in his turn by the men of the Sonderkommando. They caught up with him only by using the basest form of coercion.

Through a rather extraordinary coincidence, Leo's wife had also just given birth to a child. Being in prison, I was naturally unaware of this detail—which had its importance, from every point of view!—and I was not unduly worried about our friend, knowing that everything had been set up for his trip to Switzerland. Leo's wife, Jeanne Pesant, did not suspect the seriousness of the situation and refused to go to a safe hiding place. As a result, agents of the Sonderkommando found her on November 25 in an apartment she had rented in a suburb of Brussels. Employing a method that was by no means uncommon with them, they threatened to kill the baby before her eyes unless she wrote a letter to Leo arranging to meet him. Leo suspected a trap, but, impelled by a desire to see his family one last time before disappearing into the shadows of underground life, he went to see them at Uccle, on the Avenue Brunard, where he was arrested on December 16, 1942.

Four days before that, Berg had announced to me casually, "Today we are going to arrest Robinson."

Quite expansive, as usual, Berg told me about the Sonder-kommando's plans. This half-friendly attitude toward me would be very useful to me later on.

"We spotted him several months ago," Berg went on, "and we've decided to intercept him at the moment of one of his rendezvous, which we know about. Reiser has organized a regular military expedition. Dozens of agents are scattered all around the meeting place with copies of his photograph to help them identify him. I'm warning you, Reiser will suggest that you come along, but it's just to test your reactions, because he doesn't have authorization to let you be seen there—that would be the end of the Great Game. If you refuse, his conclusion will be that you refuse to collaborate, and he'll tell anybody who'll listen."

"If I understand correctly, Reiser wants to feel me out and also to set up a trap for me."

"You can interpret his behavior as you like."

Good; I had been warned. At noon, I was taken to Reiser. He took up Berg's refrain:

"Well, Otto, today we arrest Robinson!"

"You're making a mistake, Reiser. He's just a nuisance. He doesn't know a thing." The classic tactic: always minimize the role of your comrades.

"Perhaps," he replied, not taken in. "But if it's all the same to you, we will judge his value for ourselves. In any case, you will come with us."

"As you like."

I said this in such a cheerful and conciliatory tone that Reiser sat there dumbfounded with astonishment.

In any case, Berg had not lied.

In the car that took us toward the scene of Robinson's rendezvous, I wondered how I should behave. I decided that the only way I could be useful to Robinson was to attract his attention by making a noise of some kind. If the Germans planned to exhibit me with handcuffs on my wrists, it meant they had decided to put an end to the Great Game, for the men of Harry's protection group would not fail to see me, and my arrest would instantly be known. But the car stopped two hundred yards from the scene of the rendezvous. I watched Harry's arrest without being able to do anything.

At Raichmann's trial, which took place after the war before a Belgian tribunal, one of the points against the accused was that he had collaborated in the arrest of Robinson. Actually the Gestapo had been on Robinson's trail since the arrest of Franz Schneider in August. Robinson's ex-wife, a member of the Berlin group, had been arrested along with his son, a soldier in the Wehrmacht. The Gestapo had not struck sooner because they believed that Harry was running a group of important militants from the Comintern, including the former secretary of the organization, Jules Humbert-Droz, and the former leader of the German Communist Party, Willy Münzenberg. (This was reported in the German weekly *Der Spiegel* in a 1968 series of articles.)

This powerful secret group was a figment of the imagination of Müller and his men, who invented conspiracies where none existed. Humbert-Droz had by that time been excluded from the Communist Party. Willy Münzenberg had been removed from the staff of the German Communist Party and the Communist International in 1937. In 1940, he had been imprisoned by the Daladier government in the camp for foreigners at Gurs. It was there that two agents of Beria, fellow prisoners of his, were given the job of executing him. The two men proposed that he escape with them. Only too happy to take advantage of the opportunity, he agreed. He was found hanged two hundred yards from the camp.

The Germans wanted to get their hands on all the members of this mythical secret group, and to this end they had put Robinson under close surveillance. Their intention was to stage a sensational trial in which Harry would play the starring role. Their objective was to denounce "international Bolshevism" before the eyes and ears of the peoples of the "new Europe."

In December, the Gestapo finally realized that Robinson's trail led no further than Robinson himself, and decided to arrest him. Our last conversation had taken place on the 21st of November, two days after the arrests at Simex. I had explained the perilous situation of our group, and by common agreement we had decided to break contact with each other. Robinson was arrested on the 21st of December.

Anna and Vasily Maximovich had also been spotted as of June, 1942. At that time, Anna Maximovich had been summoned by the Kommandatur of Paris, who had questioned her about her past. On the occasion of Maximovich's "engagement" to Miss Hoffman-Scholz, secretary to the German Consulate in Paris, the Gestapo had carried out a routine investigation at police headquarters, where foreigners were required to register. When we found out about this, we tried to ward off the blow by asking our contacts at police headquarters to hide his file, but it was too late. The Gestapo already knew of it and learned of Maximovich's pro-Soviet sympathies. They took away the permit that had given him access to the Hotel Majestic, where the Wehrmacht had their staff headquarters. Already more than suspect, Vasily was completely unmasked by the dispatches deciphered in Berlin by Dr. Vauck, which left no doubt about the source of the reports. His "fiancée" had gone to be with her family in Germany and, on her return, had told us of the destruction suffered by the towns. We sent this information to Moscow. By cross-checking, the Gestapo identified her.

They had been following Maximovich since October. Far from concealing themselves, the agents of the Sonderkommando did not hesitate to go to the Chateau de Billeron, where they explained to Anna that they had collected ample proof that she and her brother were members of an espionage network working against the Third Reich.

"You can be useful to us," they told Anna, "by arranging a meeting between your leader and a certain German. This meeting could take place in the unoccupied zone. We would give you every assurance that you would not be bothered, for it involves a matter of great political importance."

Anna immediately informed me of Giering's proposition. At that time, I could only interpret his request for a meeting as a crude maneuver for the purpose of kidnapping us; with hindsight it seems likely he was trying to lay the groundwork for our future "collaboration."

These converging indications showed how seriously Vasily and Anna were threatened. I offered to help them disappear.

"We can't do that," he answered, "because of my old mother and my other sister. What would become of them without us? Have you thought about reprisals?"

And he added, "If I'm caught, I'll commit suicide."

"No, Vasily, we have to get as many of these bastards as we can!"

Vasily did not alter his habits, but continued his work as in the past. On the 12th of December, he was arrested in the office of his "fiancée."

Kaethe Voelkner was also on the Gestapo's wanted list after the dispatches were decoded. She knew the fate in store for her. The Gestapo has made a statement to the effect that Maximovich helped the Gestapo arrest Kaethe Voelkner— that is a flagrant lie. In December she left for Germany to visit her family; twenty-five years later her uncle told me that she had indeed been aware of the danger stalking her. Her companion, Podsialdo, was apprehended by the Gestapo and horribly mistreated. Kaethe returned at the end of January. As she had foreseen, she was also arrested, on January 31, 1943.

As for Springer, in December, 1941, as I have mentioned before, he had escaped to Lyon with his wife, Flore. There he had continued to be extremely active. He had made contact with Balthazar, a former Belgian government official, and the American consul, and had found new sources of information. He was an inexhaustible fighter, and he would die a hero's death after fighting the men of the Gestapo with gun in hand.

I had met with Springer in April and had advised him to be cautious. He would not hear of it. He asked me for the code, which I gave him.

"And what will you do for a radio set?" I asked him.

"I have everything I need. My American friends have provided me with a little jewel."

In October—by which time we knew that the southern

zone would be invaded in a matter of weeks—I returned to Lyon. Once again I recommended to Springer that he be careful. He flew into a rage: "I'm quite aware that Flore and I could leave for the United States, but I refuse to do that, and so does she! Does a soldier at the front retreat when the going gets tough? No? Well, we're like them! Me, I'm a fighter in the front lines. I'll work right up to the end, and if they come for me, I'll be ready for them!"

Springer had installed his transmitter in a little village seventeen kilometers from Lyon. He had hooked it up to some high tension cables that passed near the house.

"If they come," he told me, "I'll blow up the whole works!"

He did not have time.

On the evening of December 19, 1942, Springer returned to the room he and his wife had rented in Lyon. They had a window signal, which was supposed to tell them whether it was safe to come upstairs or not. It was dark, all the lights were out, and he should have suspected something. Instead, he walked up the stairs, gun in hand. Perhaps the Gestapo were waiting for him up there—so what, he would take his chances. He opened the door and there they were, sitting, standing, thick as vermin. He fired into the thick of them, wounded two, and tried to swallow the capsule of cyanide that was always with him.

Springer was imprisoned in Lyon, then transferred to Fresnes the next day. He was tortured for four days. To avoid the possibility of talking, he climbed over the guardrail of a fourth-story balcony and threw himself into the void. It was Christmas Day.

His wife, Flore Velaerts, was arrested the same night he was. She was incarcerated at Fresnes, and decapitated in Berlin in July, 1943.

Springer's brother and his cousin, Yvonne, did not learn the circumstances of his death until after the war, when they read Colonel Rémy's book, *Livre du courage et de peur.* In Volume II, page 27, Remy writes: "Christmas Day began with a suicide. A desperate man climbed over the railing of the upper balcony. Many prisoners heard the dull thud his body made as it hit the ground. . . ." Everything is accurate except the description of Springer as a desperate man. He did not act from desperation, but deliberately, in order to avoid at any price the possibility that he might talk under torture. I knew him well enough to be able to testify that he was capable of such courage. He had greeted the men of the Gestapo with gunfire, he had tried to poison himself. His last gesture at Fresnes was exactly in the tradition of those exemplary militants who die fighting. His body was exhumed, identified, and buried in the family vault. My friend Springer was decorated posthumously by the Belgian government.

Also in Lyon, the Gestapo, whose head man was the infamous Barbie, arrested Joseph Katz, Hillel's brother, and my old comrade Schreiber. Neither of these men was a member of the Red Orchestra. Joseph had asked me if he could work with us, but I had refused because I did not want two members of the same family—and a family that was so close to me—risking their lives at the same time.

As was the case with so many of my brothers in clandestine struggle, I had known Schreiber in Palestine. An ardent communist militant with a mind of his own, he did not hesitate to express criticisms, which alienated the doctrinaire. He was refused permission to go to fight in Spain when he volunteered, on the pretext that his views deviated too greatly from the party line.

One of the first things I did when I arrived in Paris in the summer of '40 was try to find him—Schreiber was too active and committed to have given up the fight. I learned from his wife that in 1939 he had started a used car business, which could serve him as a cover in case of war. The Center was interested in him, and sent him a young Soviet officer who, curiously enough, answered to the name "Fritz" and was appointed manager of the business as a facade.

Fritz, alas, was even less talented than other representatives of the Center. One day in the fall of 1939, two policemen made a routine visit to the garage; Fritz, the officer on special assignment, was in the back room. He jumped out the window and went, with great perspicacity, to take asylum in the Soviet Embassy. There he told all about how he had just barely escaped a police raid.

Fritz's contact at the embassy was an intelligence virtuoso of the same caliber, and he very cleverly wrote the address and telephone number of Schreiber's business in his appointment book. Since he was being watched by French counterespionage, along with all the other employees of the embassy, he was arrested for a few hours on some pretext and searched.

The inevitable result of all this amateurish bungling was that Schreiber was arrested by the French authorities and sent to the camp at Vernet, after the signing of the German-Soviet pact. Then the Germans arrived in France, and Schreiber was still a prisoner. I decided to have him escape. I mentioned my plan to Susloparov, the Soviet military attaché at Vichy; he preferred, though, to make a show of legality, and said it would be easy for him to add Schreiber's name to the list of imprisoned Soviet citizens he was going to submit to the Germans, to obtain their release. Schreiber was in fact released; but then Germany's entry into the war against the Soviet Union caught him in Marseilles before he had time to leave for Moscow, where his wife, Regina, and his daughter had taken up residence. Schreiber went underground, but the Gestapo found him and arrested him. Either he was shot for "attempted escape," or else he was sent to a concentration camp. One thing is certain: he did not reappear after the war.

As for Joseph Katz, he disappeared during deportation.

I have mentioned these two cases together because I believe that the same person, Otto Schumacher, was the informer in both instances. Schumacher belonged to the ranks of those dubious individuals whom the enemy infiltrates into a network to undermine it from within. I have every reason to believe that he was in the pay of the Gestapo, who had introduced him like a termite into the Red Orchestra. It was he who rented the apartment where Wenzel was arrested. Contrary to all expectations, he was not bothered himself.

After the liquidation of the Belgian group, Schumacher

arrived in Paris. There he lived at the home of Arlette Humbert-Laroche, who acted as a liaison agent between Harry Robinson and myself. In November, 1942, despite my strict orders to the contrary, he went down to Lyon, where he made contact with Springer (whose heroic end I have described) and Germaine Schneider. In December he went back to Arlette's house and asked her if he might meet Robinson (who was to be arrested by the Germans, it will be recalled, with a great deployment of police). Arlette hesitated, but finally agreed to introduce him to our friend; she never came back.

Arlette Humbert-Laroche, a member of the Red Orchestra, had fallen in love with a secret informer of Giering and his men. She was a charming, delicate girl, who left some lovely poems behind her.

In 1946, Editions Realités published a collection of Arlette's poems, with a preface by Charles Vildrac. "It was in the summer of 1941 that Arlette Humbert-Laroche began bringing me her poems," writes Vildrac, "asking for my criticism and advice. Toward the end of 1942, she left a big envelope with my concierge. It contained all her poems, which she entrusted to me, leaving me to divine the reason. I never saw her again . . ."

Arlette wrote, in the spring of 1939:

I, too,
would leave my perfume
on the earth

. . .

and live in such a way
that men, my brothers,
would remember me . . .

On November 25, 1942, after the night of my first interrogation, Giering had to face the problem of my detention. It had two aspects: where, and how? He had to find a place sufficiently isolated that the secret of my arrest would be safe and I could neither escape, which was elementary, nor communicate with the outside world.

This last point had its importance in the case of an organization like the Red Orchestra. In this area, the Sonderkommando suffered some serious setbacks. Never did it succeed in completely isolating agents who had been taken prisoner. It should not be forgotten that during the occupation some of the guards from the prewar period maintained their jobs. Not infrequently, they would give information to members of the resistance, or transmit messages for them, even when they were not actually affiliated with a network. As I have already described, the guards at Saint-Gilles Prison in Brussels informed us of the fate of the prisoners who had been arrested at the Rue des Atrébates.

The prisoners of the Red Orchestra in France were kept in a special section in Fresnes. When they were transferred from one place to another, they had to wear hoods over their heads. It was strictly forbidden for them to be moved around within the confines of the prison. Their identity was known neither to the penal administration nor even to the other German services. Each member of the Sonderkommando was in charge of one or more precisely designated prisoners, and it was against the rules for him to pay attention to any others. All these precautionary measures were intensified after my arrest.

Since the Sonderkommando had arrived in Paris, at the beginning of October, 1942, they had made their headquarters, as I have said, on the Rue des Saissaies, in a building which before the war had contained the offices of the Sûreté

Française. The Sonderkommando headquarters was on the fifth floor. On the 26th of November, I was taken down to the ground floor, where the offices of the police treasury had formerly been located. Giering intended to keep me there incognito, in a large room that had been fitted out as a cell for a "special prisoner." It was divided in two sections by a grill with a door in it. On one side a table and two chairs were set up for two SS noncommissioned officers, who were to guard me night and day. On the other side was my corner: a bed, a table, and two chairs. A window with bars on it looked onto a garden. The front door was reinforced with a metal lining.

After two or three days a set of regulations was worked out in Berlin for the regime I had to follow and the duties of my guards. It was a veritable masterpiece of German bureaucracy. For instance, my guards were forbidden to speak to me or to answer any questions that I might ask them.

Shortly after I moved in, Giering introduced me to the man who was to have special responsibility for taking care of me, Willy Berg. He could come and see me at any time and talk to me whenever he wanted to, and he was in charge of my food, which was brought three times a day from the nearest military mess hall. Every day he accompanied me on my walk in the inner garden.

Willy Berg will play an important role in this story. Short, squat, with a plump face and strong hands that could hit hard, he carried his fifty years heavily. Of average intelligence, he was cut out for supporting roles, which he played diligently under Giering. He was Giering's friend and confidant, and the only man who was thoroughly familiar with the details of the special group and the preparations for the Great Game. Willy Berg was a professional policeman; he had begun his career under the Kaiser and kept going under the Weimar Republic, before ending up in the service of Adolf. He had often been assigned missions that were delicate and shady. For example, he had been Von Ribbentrop's bodyguard when the latter had gone to Moscow to sign the German-Soviet pact.

In the literature that has been devoted to the Red Orchestra, it has sometimes been maintained that Berg was a double agent who kept me informed of all Sonderkommando decisions. Nothing could be further from the truth—it is a fantastic hypothesis.

What is true is that I sensed from the very beginning of my association with Berg that I would be able to make use of him. I realized, quickly, that he was vulnerable; that the assistant to the head of the Sonderkommando was a very unhappy man whose personal life had been a long series of disappointments. Two of his children had died of diphtheria during the war, and the third had died in an air raid. His wife, unable to endure this series of blows, tried to commit suicide and was confined to a mental hospital. Psychologically, Berg was in a very weakened state.

At the end of 1942, he had his doubts—as did his friend Giering, for that matter—about the final victory of the Third Reich. He had decided upon a line of conduct within the framework of the Sonderkommando that left room for two possibilities. Either the conflict would end in favor of the Soviet Union and her allies, in which case he could prove that he had treated me with humanity, that he had facilitated my task in the Great Game; or the Third Reich would win, and he would pose as a hero in the struggle against "communist subversion." Willy Berg was a recent member of the Nazi Party, and although, by necessity, he used Hitler's phrases, he showed great skepticism with regard to the Führer's politics. Among the ideological confessions that he made to me, I particularly remember this one: "I was a policeman in the time of the Kaiser," he told me one day. "I was a policeman under the Weimar Republic, and now I'm a cop under Hitler. Tomorrow, I could just as easily serve Thaelmann's regime."

In the first days of my captivity, on the pretext of perfecting my knowledge of German, I asked Willy Berg to convey my request for a dictionary, paper, a pencil, and the daily newspapers. The permission was granted. At that time I had a hope—slightly mad, I will admit—that I would be able to send my report to the Center. I had not the slightest idea when or how. For the immediate present, I found a strength against despair in these few elements prisoners dream about: to have within reach the means of writing, to know that one may, perhaps, be able to renew contact with the outside world.

But it was clear that I would be able to write nothing at all until my guards relaxed their vigilance. The guard changed twice a day, at seven in the morning and seven in the evening. Each time new faces appeared. The SS noncommissioned officers on duty had been informed of the regulations, and were so impressed that for hours on end they did not take their eyes off me. For my purposes it was necessary that my guards be always the same. That was my only hope of establishing a relationship with them. I decided to talk to Giering about it.

"You must admit," I told him, "that you have increased the risk that my arrest will not remain a secret for long. In the past two weeks more than fifty guards have taken turns watching my cell. If there's a single talker in the lot—and I'd bet on the probability—everyone will know that there's a 'special prisoner' in the Rue des Saussaies."

From that day on, only six men were assigned to guarding me.

My relations with Berg became more and more cordial. Bit by bit, during the daily walks—which provided an opportunity for developing our relationship—he dropped snatches of information. When they were put together like the pieces of a puzzle, these tidbits gave me a very accurate picture of the Sonderkommando, and flashes of insight into its plans. Obscure points were clarified. Berg even went so far as to talk about what went on in the upper echelons of the Berlin Police Department.

Berg was a virtuoso of unconscious humor. One day he told me, without a trace of irony in his voice, "You know, Otto, I hope we will have good results and that the war will be over soon. But if it should happen that a squad of German soldiers marches you to the stake, I'll come and shake your hand and say a last goodbye."

1 Leopold Trepper (in the center) with some friends from the
 Hashomer Hatzair, in Novy-Targ, 1920.
2 Trepper (seated, center) with militants from the Hashomer
 Hatzair in Dombrova-Gornicza, 1922.

3 The Ichud (Unity) group in Tel Aviv in 1925: Leopold Trepper (standing, second from left), Jeschekel Schreiber (standing, fourth from left), Leo Grossvogel (standing, last at right), and Hillel Katz (seated, third from right).
4 Luba Brojde and Leopold Trepper in 1925, the year they met.

„Перед вами
строительства,
можете решить
овладев всем
ным знанием".

Мособлит М.—875—14

5 General Jan Berzin, chief of Red Army Intelligence Services; executed December, 1938, by Stalin's Order.

6 Certificate of Comrade Trepper's graduation from the communist university, 1935. The quotations under the photographs of Lenin and Stalin read:
"You must resolve the problem of construction, but you are able to do so only if you possess all contemporary knowledge."
—Lenin
'Theory can be a great force in the workers movement if theory stays continually in close rapport with revolutionary practice."
—Stalin

7   8

7 Leopold Trepper (at the time he called himself Adam Mikler)
8 "Anna Mikler" (Luba Brojde, his wife)
9 Their son Eddy, photographed in front of the door of their building on the Rue Richard Neyberg in Brussels, 1938.

The first fighters in the Red Orchestra
10 Leo Grossvogel and his wife Jeanne Pesant
11 Jules Jaspard and his wife
12 Alfred Corbin and his wife

10

11

12

13

13 Hillel Katz.
14 Simexco associates, January 13, 1941, the day Simexco was created: Nazarin Drailly and his brother Charles Drailly, Maurice Beublet, Jean Passelec, Robert Christen, Henri Seghers and Henri Deryck. In the foreground, Kent.

14

Arrested on the Rue des Atrebates

15 David Kamy
16 Sophie Poznanska
17 Carlos Alamo, or Mikael Makarov; after a Gestapo interrogation (Gestapo document)

15

16

17

Other members of the network
18 Herman ''Bob'' Izbutski
19 Isidore Springer
20 Springer's wife, Flore Velaers
21 Johann Wenzel, ''the Professor''
   (Gestapo document)
22 Vera Ackermann
23 Hersch and Mira Sokol
24 Georgie de Winter
   (Photo Verhassel)

18

20

19

21

22

23

24

25
26

25 Suzanne Spaak
26 Fernand Pauriol

Directors of the Berlin group
27 Harro Schulze-Boysen at his
work at the Air ministry
28 Adam Kuckhoff
29 Mildred and Arvid Harnack

27

29

28

30

30 Lubianka: in a building that housed the Ministry of the Interior, a small prison was set up; it was there Trepper spent most of his ten years' prison time. Inset: Trepper at the time of his release from prison.

31 The shack in the Moscow suburbs where Luba and the children lived during Trepper's detention.

Форма № 30

С П Р А В К А

Военная Коллегия
Верховного Суда
Союза ССР

8 июня 1955 г.
№ 4н-04094/54

Москва, ул. Воровского, д. 13.

Дело по обвинению ТРЕППЕРА Леопольда Заха-
ровича пересмотрено Военной Коллегией Верховного
Суда СССР 26 мая 1954 года.

— Постановления Особого Совещания от 18 января 1947 года и 9 января 1952 года в отношении
ТРЕППЕРА Л.З. отменены и дело за отсутствием
состава преступления прекращено.

ВРИО ПРЕДСЕДАТЕЛЯ ВОЕННОЙ КОЛЛЕГИИ
ВЕРХОВНОГО СУДА СОЮЗА ССР
ПОЛКОВНИК ЮСТИЦИИ

/БОРИСОГЛЕБСКИЙ/

32 The document from the Military Chamber of the Supreme Court
of the U.S.S.R., June 8, 1955, reads: "The accusation against
Trepper Leopold Zakharovich has been re-examined by the
Military Chamber of the Supreme Court of the U.S.S.R., on May
26 1954. The decisions of the Special Commission of January 18
1947 and January 9 1952 concerning Trepper L.Z. have been
annulled and the case has been dismissed for absence of basic
elements of crime."

33 The Trepper family in Varsovie, 1960

33 Leopold Trepper addressing the last meeting of the Cultural
Association of Polish Jews, 1966

33

34

35 Michel Trepper, on a
hunger strike to obtain
his father's release from
Poland; Copenhagen, 1972.
On the right is Bent
Melchior, Chief Rabbi of
Copenhagen. *(Photo
Busser)*

36 Copenhagen, 1974. *(Photo
John R. Johnsen)*

35

36

I answered him in the same vein: "And if it should happen that a squad of Russian soldiers marches you to the stake, I too will come, I promise you, and shake your hand and say a last goodbye."

During the latter half of December, several prisoners of the Red Orchestra tried to commit suicide at Fresnes. The order came from Berlin to tie the captives' hands behind their backs. I was granted a special dispensation and allowed to have them tied in front.

Under the circumstances, it was impossible to write a word. I complained about the decision to Berg. He sympathized, declaring that he knew how difficult it was to sleep with your hands tied. Then he showed me how to manipulate the bonds to free my right hand. Meanwhile, the guards, who believed me to be hobbled like an old animal, were sleeping peacefully. Every night between two and three o'clock, the time I had judged to be most favorable, I drafted my report, scribbling on little scraps of paper.

I pointed out to Berg that my bed was too short and too hard, and he helped me once again. I was given a new bed, with a good mattress. The frame was made of steel, and I noticed that the four legs were hollow tubes. This was quite a bonus—they made an excellent strongbox for a prisoner!

A few days after I had moved to these quarters, I received a visit from three SS medical officers, who examined me from head to toe. I immediately asked Berg the reasons for this procedure.

"They want a comparative picture of your physical condition," he replied. "Let's say that it's to test your capacity to endure an intensified interrogation."

It must have been illuminating, I thought, with my high blood pressure, my bad heart, and the after-effects of my hunger strike in Palestine. I wanted to know more about it.

"They concluded, on the basis of anthropological criteria," Berg added, "that you aren't Jewish. Giering was delighted."

I almost doubled up laughing. I learned, later on, what Giering had had in mind. He felt that proving I was a "good Aryan" would facilitate Berlin's consent to the Great Game.

In the high circles that were interested in my case, who would have trusted a Jew, who would have considered the possibility of collaborating with a representative of the "accursed race"? Giering needed an Aryan.

Giering's explanations were not lacking in humor. During one of our conversations, I told him I had been born into a Jewish family, and I had been circumcised immediately after my birth. His answer was amazing: "Frankly, you amuse me. That only goes to show that Soviet Intelligence knows what they are doing. At the beginning of the war, you know, agents the Abwehr sent to the United States had been circumcised in order to facilitate their work. When they were arrested by American counterespionage, the hoax was quickly discovered, because the operations were too recent." Giering's mind was so steeped in tales of intrigue involving secret services that he could explain away my genuine circumcision by the superior skill of the technicians and specialists of the Russian secret service.

I had told him several times that I was Jewish—hence the deduction that a man who falls into the hands of the Gestapo and claims to be Jewish can only be lying.

In the end, Giering conducted an investigation. In Grossvogel's wife's home in Brussels, the Germans had found an old passport I had used in Palestine in 1924, which showed my real identity, Leopold Trepper, and my date of birth, February 23, 1904, in Novy-Targ. In December, 1942, a team of sleuths from the Sonderkommando left for Novy-Targ to try to trace me there. In the report they sent back, they explained they had found nothing because, and I quote their own language, the town had been "cleansed of the Jewish vermin, and the cemetery plowed under."

Now Giering's certainty was confirmed. I was not Jewish. When the Soviet secret service sent me to Palestine, they had deliberately invented a Jewish identity for me, and Trepper was an assumed name.

Even so, Giering was not really deceiving himself—he "believed" whatever was expedient, and changed his beliefs to fit changing circumstances. As soon as it no longer suited him to have me Gentile—and that time would come—he would reinstate my rightful heritage.

What mattered to me was that the Gestapo did not discover the name I used as a militant, Leiba Domb.

The Sonderkommando had a very peculiar way of keeping secrets. On the door of my cell—which dozens and dozens of people passed every day—they had placed a large sign: "Attention! Special Prisoner—Entry is Forbidden!" I learned later, and it did not surprise me, that rumors were being circulated in collaborationist circles all over Paris about an "exceptional Soviet prisoner."

Curiosity often got the better of discipline—even German discipline—among my guards. They had been subjected to a Draconian regime in their assignment regarding this "special prisoner" (and of course they had been told nothing of importance)—naturally, then, after a certain point, they could not restrain themselves from engaging in conversation with me. They waited until the middle of the night, and when they were sure they were not going to be caught, they tried, first in round-about ways, and then more and more openly, to find out more about me. So we would chat for an hour or two, and these rambling conversations were very valuable to me. Two of the men were stupid automatons and thorough-going bullies. The others—I recall that they were Waffen SS—had been trained in this service, but showed no blind loyalty to Nazism. If they had been given the order, of course, they would not have hesitated to commit any crime whatever, such as to kill me on the spot; but I succeeded in establishing a certain rapport with two of them. I especially remember the one who belonged to some religious sect, and who announced to me that while he guarded me all night, he prayed for the salvation of my soul. He even offered to convey a message to my family.

20

Giering had failed in all his attempts to establish contact with the leaders of the Communist Party without my collaboration. Since he still could not make up his mind to risk using me, he resorted to the last card in his hand: forcing Leo Grossvogel and Hillel Katz to talk.

Throughout the month of December, the men of the Sonderkommando worked Grossvogel over. They believed that since he had been my assistant, he must know how to make contact with the French Communist Party. He invariably answered them, as we had agreed, that in our organization he was concerned only with commercial matters, and referred them to me. The Sonderkommando decided then to apply the most powerful pressure at their disposal. He would furnish the information, or else his wife and child would be executed before his eyes. He did not flinch; with a serene composure, which Berg admitted impressed the Germans very much, he replied,

"You can start with me, my wife, or the child, it makes no difference—you won't find out anything."

Giering and his henchmen realized that they would get nothing out of Leo. I believe that in the face of such strength of character, they abandoned the idea of torturing him. And I had warned Giering that if they mistreated him, I would consider myself released from any obligation toward the Great Game, that Leo was absolutely indispensable to our plans, and that sooner or later the Center would find out what had become of him.

Having failed with Leo Grossvogel, the Sonderkommando fell back on Hillel Katz, whom they hoped to use as a liaison with Juliette, the woman in the confectioner's shop who was our go-between with the Communist Party. Later, in April, 1943, when I saw Hillel at the prison in Neuilly, he told me everything he had been forced to endure: a veritable hell.

216

The relentlessness of the torturers made it clear that Raichmann had informed them of the role our friend Juliette had played in the Red Orchestra. First they tried to persuade him by proposing that he go to see Juliette and say I had sent him. He would give her dispatches I had supposedly written, so that she could pass them on to the leaders of the Communist Party.

"Otto is my superior," Hillel replied, "and I will obey no orders but his."

The men of the Sonderkommando revised their tactics and resorted to the familiar scenario of the threat against his wife and two children, who were under Raichmann's surveillance at the Château de Billeron. A wasted effort: once again, Hillel Katz rejected Giering's offers.

So the torture began, in hideous, uninterrupted sessions. The instigator was Reiser, head of the Sonderkommando in Paris. The Germans were demanding that Katz tell them everything he knew about the Red Orchestra, which they suspected was a great deal. The truth was that there was nothing he did not know; he was in on all the important secrets. He was subjected to horrible treatment for some ten days; then Eric Jung, the famous sadist of the Sonderkommando, went to work on him. Since Katz did not give in, they sent to Berlin for reinforcements: a group that specialized in forced interrogations, licensed professionals in the field of torture, gangsters whose hands were stained with blood. Hillel told them over and over, as we had arranged before our arrests:

"Talk to Otto, he'll tell you. I was only an unimportant employee in Simex, I wasn't in on the secrets."

Then, near the end of his strength, he tried to commit suicide by slashing the arteries in his arm, but Giering's men did not permit him to finish the job.

Meanwhile, Giering, who had gone to Berlin, returned to find Katz in a pitiful condition and tried to repair the ravages of his subordinates. Giering knew that Hillel could be useful to him in the Great Game and that without my authorization he would not talk, that he would do nothing without me. He was shrewd enough to foresee that a man who endures the worst brutalities and who is prepared to end his own life is not a potential collaborator. He sent Willy Berg to inform me that the decision to torture my friend had been made behind his back. Then he asked me to tell Hillel Katz that he was to go and see Juliette. To this end, he decided to bring us together. Giering wanted only Berg to be present at our meeting, which was to take place without an interpreter. But Katz did not speak German, and Berg knew no French, so I suggested that we speak in Yiddish, which is a mixture of Hebrew and German. Giering agreed, not realizing that he was offering us an unhoped-for opportunity. In the course of the conversation, I would arrange to murmur to Hillel some words that were pure Hebrew, which would convey to him my advice and instruction.

Several days went by before we met. Giering was delaying our meeting. I realized he was using the time to allow my friend's wounds to become less conspicuous.

I will never forget the moment I saw Hillel walk in. They brought him into the office where I was waiting with Berg. To me, who had not seen him for a month, he was unrecognizable. In a month he had become another man. He walked over and threw his arms around my neck, sobbing. He was not wearing glasses and there were gashes all around his eyes.

"Look," he said to me, "look what they did to me. They drove glass into my eyes, and look at my hands!"

He lifted up his poor ravaged hands, the fingernails torn out, wrapped in bandages.

He bent closer and whispered in my ear, very proudly, "I didn't say a word!"

Berg, who had stayed a slight distance away but had observed every detail of the scene, broke in: "It wasn't us," he stammered. "It was that sadist Jung!"

What could I do to calm my friend, to comfort him and restore his courage when he was in such a state? I told him as gently as possible, quietly, but with determination, "Calm yourself, Hillel. Vengeance is at hand!"

We spent two hours together. Berg was called to the

telephone several times. I took advantage of these brief moments of respite to explain to Hillel what he was really supposed to do at Juliette's.

Toward the end of our meeting, his tormented face brightened. Once again we were able to act, and the desire to succeed increased our strength tenfold.

21

Four Meetings with Juliette

Madame Juliette Moussier faithfully stood her ground. Make no mistake: this was a mark of unusual courage. Not to give in when you are in the hands of the enemy constitutes one kind of valor; but not to waver, to confront the danger and stand your ground when you know that you are being watched, that the threat of arrest is hovering over you all the time, and that at any moment you may see "them" arrive is an exploit of another magnitude.

Madame Juliette knew that we still needed her, and she would hold out to the very end, like a real militant. I had arranged with her, as one of those precautionary measures that turned out to be indispensable, that anyone coming to her from me would give her a red button. Raichmann had reached an impasse because he had not known this detail. I had not glossed over the truth; I had warned her that the shop was certainly being watched but that it was indispensable that she remain there. I also added that it was necessary for her to sever all contact with her comrades of the resistance. Fernand Pauriol, whom I had informed of the situation, would continue to keep an eye on her.

Katz was to pretend to cooperate with the Germans, as I had instructed him at the time of our meeting in Berg's presence. When he returned from his mission he was to say that Juliette had been glad to see him, but that she had lost contact with the Communist Party. She would try to re-establish the liaison and would give her answer a week later. Hillel was to return from this second expedition with a positive reply: Juliette's contacts had agreed to the meeting, but they had not concealed their apprehensions, and they demanded that I be the one to deliver the message. The object of all this was to force Giering to allow me to go and see Madame Juliette. This way, I could finally send my report to the Center.

But why such a series of comings and goings? To reassure Giering and his superiors in Berlin.

Giering was hesitant to enlist Katz in the operation and confided his reasons to me.

"Katz was the ideal messenger before he fell into the hands of our men. For this same reason, he may try to trick us now. One cannot be sure that a man who has been so badly treated will not do the opposite of what is expected."

His logic was impeccable. I tried to set his mind at rest:

"Katz won't feel like a traitor. He is passionately committed to the idea of a separate peace. That alone will dictate his conduct."

But Giering still had reservations. He gave Hillel a statement to sign in which it was agreed that if he ran away or tried to warn Madame Juliette, his wife, his children, and I would all be shot.

He signed without flinching.

Several days before Katz went to the confectioner's shop, the Sonderkommando went into a fever of activity. Reiser mounted a large-scale operation. The whole neighborhood was surrounded; teams of Gestapo agents lurking in their black Citroens were put on the alert in the neighboring streets.

Everything went off like clockwork. Hillel, accompanied by Berg, walked into the store and came out with a little package of pastries—or at least what passed for pastries during the occupation. He told Giering what we had agreed on, that a second meeting had been arranged for the following Saturday. Giering was very pleased and decided that the next time Katz would send the Center a reassuring message. Everything was for the best in the best of all possible worlds, our group was intact, and we could continue along the same lines.

I persuaded Giering that I should suggest to the Director that we sever all contacts for a month, because this is what I would have done if I were still at liberty. This further delay offered the advantage of leaving the field free for Madame Juliette to disappear; I would give her instructions to this effect when I saw her. My contact with her seemed a strong possibility, since Katz would return from his second mission saying that it was necessary that I deliver the dispatch in person.

My report had to be ready. This job would normally have required only a few hours, but under the present circumstances I had to play hide and seek with my guards. This little system was worked out to the last detail. I had to refrain from my clandestine writing during the day, not so much because of the guards, who were used to seeing me work on my German, as to avoid arousing the curiosity of Berg, who was liable to appear at any moment. That left the night (the light was always on, for I suffered from insomnia and had obtained permission to read). The best time to work was between two and three o'clock in the morning, when the guards were asleep with their elbows on the table. Their orders were to get up and look at me through the grille to see what I was doing, but in fact they did not do this. Even so, I was prepared to hide my paper quickly under the blanket. I wrote my report on scraps of paper cut out of newspaper, in tiny letters, using a mixture of Yiddish, Hebrew, and Polish. If by ill fortune I should be discovered, the time necessary to decipher this puzzle would give me a little respite.

To convince the Center, I had to recapitulate everything that had happened in chronological order since December 13, 1941. I drew up a detailed list of the arrests, specifying dates, places, and circumstances. I told everything I knew about how the members of the network had behaved after their arrests. Next I listed all the transmitters that had fallen into the hands of the enemy, the dispatches that had been discovered, the codes that had been broken. I gave as complete as possible an explanation of the Great Game, its political and military goals, and the methods employed. Last came a list of all those who were in danger of being arrested.

In the second part of the report I suggested two alternatives for dealing with the situation.

In the event that the Center decided that it would be useful to continue the Great Game and to take the initiative, I suggested that on February 23, 1943, the Director send a dispatch offering his congratulations for the anniversary of the Red Army and my birthday.

In the event that the Center did not find it necessary to continue the Great Game, it should still keep on sending dispatches for a month or two, so as not to indicate that it was reacting suddenly to my report.

In addition, I wrote a personal letter to Jacques Duclos in which I explained the gravity of the situation. I asked him to make sure my report got into the hands of Dimitrov, who would deliver it to the leaders of the Soviet Communist Party. I also gave him a list of twenty people who should immediately be taken to safe places. At the head of the list were Fernand Pauriol and Madame Juliette.

Meanwhile, the Sonderkommando was preparing for the second meeting between Katz and Juliette. Giering did not know what language or code to use to draft the message to the Center. Kent had told him that in the case of dispatches sent through the Communist Party, we used a special code. I denied this categorically. In the end, Giering decided to use Kent's code and to write the dispatch in Russian.

This was an additional clue for the Center. My messages had always been written in German, in invisible ink, and translated into the code of the Communist Party.

The second meeting took place amid the usual decor: police cars surrounding the area, surveillance. Giering was convinced that Juliette would accept Katz' message, so he was very surprised to see Katz come back with a message and a box of candy in the bargain. With a smile that would have convinced a Franciscan he was an atheist, Katz told him, as we had arranged, that the comrades were very worried about what had become of me. Rumors were beginning to circulate that I had been arrested. Juliette had received instructions to accept only messages that I delivered to her in person. In any case, Katz had made a tentative date for a meeting between Juliette and me.

Giering was very upset and asked me my opinion.

"It doesn't surprise me at all," I explained calmly. "It's

been two months now since my arrest, and in that time no one has seen me, I haven't given a sign of life, and contact with the Communist Party has been broken. I have warned you several times that this might happen. Put yourself in the place of the militants of the French Communist Party. If you were in their position wouldn't you have serious doubts? Everything that's happening is your fault. You didn't want to have me collaborate in the Great Game; now the whole plan is in danger."

He replied quite sincerely that he had wanted to have me participate all along but his superiors in Berlin opposed the idea, although he had emphasized my good will in several reports. In Berlin, they were afraid that the Communist Party would try to release me from captivity by force.

"In any case," I replied, "if my meeting with Juliette does not take place within a week, you can say goodbye to the Great Game. As for me, I request to be sent to the prison at Fresnes."

After this conversation, Giering took a plane to Berlin. He returned a few days later with the consent of his superiors.

During his absence I had long friendly conversations every day with Berg, to whom Giering had given the job of feeling me out to learn my real intentions. During this period, I learned that Himmler himself was very much interested in the Great Game. For me this was further proof that the whole affair was distinctly malodorous.

Operation Juliette had to succeed. I realized that if it failed, if my night-time writings were intercepted, all the Red Orchestra prisoners would be executed.

All my life, I had done everything in my power to preserve human life, but in the present situation the stakes were so high that I did not doubt for a moment that I was right to risk my companions' lives. There are moments when all the responsibility rests on the shoulders of a single person. There was no one I could turn to for advice. I had to choose, and thirty years later, I am proud of my choice.

On Thursday evening—two days before the meeting with Juliette—I had a long conversation with Giering. This would be his last try, he told me. He admitted that he had had considerable difficulty in Berlin obtaining permission for this meeting and that all the responsibility rested on him.

"I am very anxious that this meeting be a success, because if we regain the confidence of the party, everything will go better with the Center," he told me.

He then began to consider various hypotheses to explain my behavior:

"I rule out the possibility of treachery on your part. However, if you are not absolutely convinced of the possibility of a separate peace, you may be using the meeting with Juliette to warn her in one way or another. I am warning you: if you try to escape or if you warn Juliette, I will have all the Red Orchestra prisoners in France and Belgium executed."

I flew into a rage. "Such a threat, toward a man with whom you are supposedly working to arrive at a separate peace, makes me think it would be better to proceed immediately to what I've been waiting for since my arrest. Take me before the firing squad!"

He never threatened me again. Actually, he saw things rather clearly, but having bluffed his superiors about the great successes he had had with me, he was obliged to take the risk of my meeting with Juliette. But he stayed on his guard.

On the night before the meeting I could not get to sleep. I pictured all the possibilities. I did not think Giering would have me searched; he knew that if he did, I would refuse to go. I was afraid, though, of what Giering's "friends" might do. Boemelburg and Reiser, the heads respectively of the Gestapo and the Sonderkommando in Paris, were hoping for Giering to fail. It was their job to assure the security of the meeting; it would be easy for them to simulate an escape attempt as an excuse to have Juliette arrested. Berg had warned me that several men in the Sonderkommando thought Juliette's arrest would clarify the situation.

In the end I decided to go to the rendezvous empty-handed. If everything went well, I would arrange another rendezvous with Juliette to deliver the two messages, Giering's and my own.

On that Saturday afternoon the courtyard of the Rue des

Saussaies was armed for battle. An enormous number of Gestapo agents surrounded the street where the confectioner's shop was. The plan was for Berg to go in with me; still, I suspected that other agents would be in the shop.

Juliette was very happy to see me. We embraced, and I took the opportunity to whisper in her ear that I would be back in a week and that I would give her a message which was to be passed on to another person as soon as I had left the shop. After this both of them were to disappear until the end of the war. Juliette took in everything, without losing her calm and natural expression, and handed me a box of chocolates.

On the way back to Rue des Saussaies, though Giering was very relaxed, he was surprised that I had not delivered the message.

"Juliette explained that she no longer handles liaisons, but that a militant—whom she doesn't know—was in the shop and was satisfied that everything went well. At the next rendezvous she will be able to accept the message," I explained.

This apparently logical version reassured Giering; he was completely satisfied with the three encounters with Juliette.

The final and decisive meeting with Juliette had been set for the last Saturday in January, 1943, just before the shop closed for the weekend. I had not picked this time at random; since the shop would be closed on Sunday and Monday, I knew that our friend would have more time in which to make her escape.

During the night before the rendezvous, I took the report out of my "strongbox" and simply put it in my pocket with a handkerchief on top. In the morning, Giering came to get me, and we chatted for a while. There within reach of my hand, and right under his nose, the bomb was ready to go off.

The expedition was less eventful this time: the surveillance had been reduced and was less conspicuous. I slipped the two reports into Juliette's hand at the same time and told her that a message in code was the work of the Germans and that the long report was of my own composition, and that both of them should be sent to the Center. I kissed her and advised her once again to disappear. I never saw her again. The difficult days that awaited me after the war deprived me of this pleasure.

I returned to my cell with a light heart. I was sure that the report would reach its destination, and that it would produce radical changes in the attitude of the Center. Whatever the Director's final decision with regard to the Great Game, one thing was certain: the enemy would no longer be able to exploit the transmitters of the Red Orchestra with impunity; the risk that the Center would be beguiled had been eliminated.

There was nothing left for me to do but wait for the answer.

Although he was not given to enthusiasm, Giering told me that once again he was happy with the results we had achieved. Juliette had taken the message, and he was convinced that the Soviet counterespionage agents who had been present in the shop had been convinced I was at liberty.

Giering was pleased, all well and good; but I knew I was going to have trouble explaining Juliette's disappearance. I strongly suspected that the Sonderkommando was keeping an eye on the confectioner's shop.

Yet Madame Juliette's disappearance was a necessity. I had no right to place her life in danger any longer, any more than I did Fernand Pauriol's.

Tuesday, when the shop reopened, Giering came into my cell in the afternoon, very worried. "You know," he said, "the woman didn't come to work today."

Obviously. I tried to reassure him:

"After all these arrests, it's a normal reaction. Juliette must have been afraid of having a run-in with your men."

This theory was difficult to defend; and Giering's suspicions grew. A week later he sent a member of the Sonderkommando who spoke French to the shop to ask for news of Juliette. The messenger returned with the answer of the woman who ran the shop: Juliette had received a telegram from a sick aunt and had had to leave to be with her.

Giering became more and more worried.

"You know," he told me, "the Communist Party must have suspected that you weren't free when you came to the rendezvous."

"I think Juliette acted on an impulse. With women, you never know. Let's wait for the Center's reaction. That is the only important thing; that alone will be decisive."

Giering shook his head; I had not relieved him of his doubts. We would see.

The state of mind of the head of the Sonderkommando was far from my greatest worry. When the time came I could always dream up another explanation. What worried me most was the reaction of the Center. Often in the night I too was overcome by doubts. I knew from my own experience that it often requires heroism to be able to admit one's own mistakes; and the Center had accumulated such an enormous number during the year 1942. Sometimes I wondered whether some evil spirit, or simply an enemy agent, had infiltrated the leadership. During the long sleepless nights, in the deep silence that encouraged all kinds of reflections, apprehensions and nostalgic thoughts, how I missed the presence of a Berzin at the head of the Red Army Intelligence Service.

February 23, 1943: one more day that I will never forget. Giering came into my cell, all smiles, to announce triumphantly that Kent's set had just picked up two dispatches from the Director. He showed them to me and I read the first:

"On the anniversary of the glorious Red Army, and of your birth"—I could have shouted for joy; it was done; the Center had been warned!—"we send you our best wishes. In appreciation of your great services, the directors have decided to ask the government to award you a military decoration."

And the second:

"Otto, we have received your dispatch, sent through the intermediary of our friends. Let us hope that the situation will improve. We feel it necessary, to insure your security, to discontinue the liaison until further orders. Make contact directly with us. Detailed directives follow regarding the work of your network in the future. Director."

I did not conceal my joy. All our efforts had been rewarded. The initiative for the Great Game was passing into the hands of the Soviet Army. The hour of revenge had come!

Giering was just as delighted as I was.

"Excellent," he told me, "excellent; we have proof of the Center's confidence!"

At the same time my wife, who had been evacuated with the children and all the families of the Soviet General Staff to Western Siberia to be safe from the invading German army, received the following message from the Center:

"Your husband is a hero. He is working for the victory of our country." And it was signed: Colonel Epstein, Major Polakova, and Major Leontiev.

Hell in Breendonk

ell cannot be described. You live in it, you may even survive it, but you never leave it. You endure it forever. A person who has not experienced the atrocities of the Gestapo cannot imagine them. Our understanding is insufficient, we have no way to think about what systematized horror is. The survivors of the Red Orchestra who have returned from hell carry the memory of ravaged flesh, which to this day jerks them awake in the night.

Blood dries as quickly as the ink on a front-page story. In the memory of the human race, the sound and fury of the war have grown dim; indeed, right now it is fashionable to glamorize it. Literature, television and the movies are giving evil the look of innocence and even of outraged virtue. War criminals are lounging around swimming pools drinking to the "good old days."

Those who defend atrocity, whether consciously or not, are numerous today, engaged in whitewashing the brown plague. Historians and film directors are removing the butcher's aprons from the Gestapo-Müllers, the Karl Gierings, the Pannwitzes, the Reisers, and their accomplices. White gloves hide paws that have beaten, mutilated, and disfigured. What do you expect, exclaim the artless innocents. These men—high-ranking civil servants and soldiers, specialists in counterespionage—were only obeying orders. These faithful servants of the Third Reich are now portrayed as peaceful citizens. Today they are being made respectable. Calmly, they go about all their everyday tasks—all, that is, except the one in which they excelled: bloody torture in the dungeons where martyrs died slow deaths! Interview the survivors of the Red Orchestra, ask them to tell you what they went through. It will not take you long to go back in time. The Middle Ages took place thirty years ago, and the "gentlemen" of the Gestapo were quite at home in them. Seven bloody letters were branded forever in the minds of their prisoners: GESTAPO.

On December 7, 1941, Hitler issued the famous *Nacht und Nebel* decree: "In the occupied territories, all measures are permissible in obtaining information from those responsible for crimes against the Third Reich. Such persons may be executed without appearing before a tribunal."

Toward the middle of 1942, Canaris and Himmler signed a directive, the so-called "Comintern line"; it specified that any and all methods were to be used to extract confessions from radio operators, coders, and informers who had been arrested. However, the heads of networks under no circumstances were to be tortured. On the contrary, no effort was to be spared in the attempt to enlist their support.

The members of the Sonderkommando derived considerable inspiration from these two directives. Throughout the period of the occupation the military fort of Breendonk, in Belgium, was one of the preferred sites of Nazi barbarity. There many of our comrades suffered and died.

Breendonk had been built in 1906 beside the road that leads from Brussels to Antwerp. During the 1940 campaign it served as general headquarters for King Leopold III. On May 28, 1940, Belgium surrendered; on August 29, Breendonk was transformed into an *Auffanglager,* a reception center, and the following September 20, Sturmbannführer SS Schmitt took his first prisoners there. The number of inmates increased regularly.

Starvation rations, slave labor, persecution, beatings, and torture constituted the prisoners' daily lot. After September, 1941, they were guarded by Belgian SS officers and traitors from the other occupied countries. One of them greeted new arrivals with these words: "This is hell, and I am the devil!" He was not exaggerating.

Most of the captives had never been tried. Some were passing through on their way to death camps, and the Gestapo wanted to keep their arrests secret. Others were being subjected to "examination," and for these the SS had made preparation. A torture chamber had been set up in a former arsenal, reached by way of a long, narrow corridor. Hanging by their hands from a pulley block, the prisoners endured the tortures of another century: thumb screws, head vises, electric needles, red-hot iron bars, wooden wedges. When SS Schmitt was not satisfied with the results of the interrogations, he would set his dogs on his victims.

When the camp was evacuated, the guards obliterated all traces of their crimes. They cleared the torture chamber of its most damning instruments, but they could not eradicate the memories of the survivors. Their testimony was taken, and the scene reconstructed faithfully. Schmitt was brought to the scene during the investigation that preceded his trial. He showed no emotion, of course; and he admitted that the original had been correctly restored—except for the scenes of horror, which the Nazis were pretending had never been there. He did point out, nonetheless, that the wooden wedge—which the prisoners had fallen back on after they had been suspended—was just a trifle too high!

Since Efremov's treason, we had lost track of several Red Orchestra combatants who had been arrested in Belgium. Dispatches continued to be sent in their names, and the Germans claimed that they had "turned" and were continuing their activities—for the other side. In reality, our radio operators, incarcerated in Breendonk, isolated and tortured, were totally unable to participate in the "game." On this subject, the research I subsequently undertook with the full collaboration of the Belgian authorities brought me a wealth of very instructive information.

To begin with, I would like to talk about the case of Anton Winterinck, the head of the Dutch group of the Red Orchestra. He was arrested on September 16, 1942, following one of Efremov's denunciations, and since then had apparently disappeared. After the war several "historians" of the Red Orchestra, particularly in Western Germany, wrote that our comrade had agreed to work with the Sonderkommando, and that he succeeded in escaping—in the enemy's trains, of course—in 1944. One added that Winterinck escaped with the complicity of the Gestapo. It sounded wrong to me—I did not credit this view. As I began my investigation, I discovered that the truth was altogether different. Winterinck, first incarcerated in Saint-Gilles Prison in Brussels, was transferred to Breendonk on November 18, 1942. Meanwhile his post started broadcasting again. If we are to believe our "specialists" on the Red Orchestra, he would have to have been writing his dispatches between torture sessions, for such, in fact, was the fate reserved for two years for this "collaborator." The real collaborators, those who had chosen the German side, like Efremov, enjoyed comfortable apartments that bore little resemblance to the cells of Breendonk. Winterinck's fellow-workers, Jacob Hilbolling and his wife, were also taken to Breendonk. Jacob was executed in January, 1943, but the fate of his companion is unknown.

Winterinck was brought back to Saint-Gilles Prison on July 6, 1944, and executed the same day at the Army Firing Range. In an effort to conceal his death, his executioners, according to their custom, wrote on his grave, "Unknown."

Auguste Sésée, a pianist also alleged to have been converted by the Germans to their side, was arrested on August 28, 1942, imprisoned in Breendonk until April, 1943, sentenced to death, transferred to Berlin, and executed in January, 1944.

In the case of Izbutski (Bob), dispatches were being sent to Moscow in his name. In reality, after his arrest in 1942, he was taken to Breendonk. In Breendonk he was brought face-to-face with Marcus Lustbader; Bob had been tortured so hideously that he was unrecognizable, Lustbader reported after his return from Auschwitz. Izbutski was executed on July 6, 1944, in Berlin, at the Charlottenburg Prison.

It was also in Breendonk that Alamo and David Kamy (Desmets) turned up in June, 1942. After being tortured, they were sentenced to death, February 18, 1943, by a military tribunal presided over by Roeder. Kamy was shot on April 30, but I succeeded in saving Alamo. Remembering that his sister worked in the same office as Molotov, I "revealed" to Giering during a conversation early in 1943 that he was actually the nephew of the People's Commissar for Foreign Affairs. The head of the Sonderkommando referred the matter to Goering, who decided to suspend the death sentence. Alamo was deported. He turned up again in the last days of the war, in a camp near the Italian border. After he was liberated by the Americans, he was turned over to the Soviet authorities.

Hersch and Mira Sokol, the doctors who had become radio operators, were also sent to the fort of torture a few months after their arrest, June 9, 1942. We know from a former prisoner the martyrdom they had to endure; Madame Betty Depelsenaire wrote in *La Symphonie fraternelle*:

> They tried every technique of police brutality to make Mira talk. After subjecting her to long days of waiting with her hands handcuffed behind her back, they play the scene of intimidation in the presence of several SS officers to urge Mira one last time to become "reasonable." After that several confrontations take place, accompanied by violent slaps. Then the torture begins.
>
> The examiner seizes Mira as if she were a wild animal, places his hand over her mouth, and drags her by the hair. A dark, narrow corridor, whose walls are like the walls of a cave, leads to the room. The room has no windows, and fresh air never reaches it. An odor of burned flesh and mildew rises to the nostrils and turns the stomach. A table, a footstool, a heavy rope attached to the ceiling by means of a pulley, and a telephone communicating directly with the Gestapo in Brussels. The examiner orders Mira to kneel and bend over the footstool. The whip falls, once, twice. The police realize they will have to be rougher on her. The commandant of the camp, two SS, and the police dogs are there to complete the scene. After they unfasten the handcuffs, Mira has to hold her arms out in front of her. Chains are applied, tightened a notch, and attached to the rope so that the body can be hoisted up in little jerks until the tips of the toes are just touching the floor. The blows from the whip rain onto the hanging body. But the whip is not stout enough. They use a club, and finally a heavy cudgel. Mira screams—it helps—but does not talk. The enraged examiner, the sweat running down his forehead, decided to raise the rope so that the body will swing in space. Its full weight falls on the wrists, and the edges of the steel handcuffs

cut into the flesh. Since the body does not remain motionless, the weapon has less purchase, and the major, at a sign from the examiner, seizes the body to keep the trunk in a vertical line; in this way the blows will be more effective. Mira can endure no more; she loses consciousness. When she comes to, she sees her hands all blue, completely deformed. She lifts her head and now Mira is ready to face her enemies again. Their anger is not long in coming. The whole process is repeated. Again, she loses consciousness. The torturer gives up for the day.

Hersch and Mira Sokol endured this treatment for many months. They knew the code used for the six hundred dispatches sent by their station, and they kept the secret to the very end. In an attempt to break them, the torturer made Mira witness Hersch's torture sessions, and made him witness hers. Hersch was ill and weighed only thirty-seven kilograms. Madame Depelsenaire reports that the camp doctor was amazed at his resistance: "My God, he's not dead yet! He's a tough one. It's amazing how long the human organism can hold out."

But the commandant of the camp wanted to get it over with, and he succeeded. He let his dogs loose, and they ate Hersch alive. His grave, along with that of three hundred other resisters, is at the Army Firing Range in Brussels.

Mira died, because she had no more strength to live, in a camp in Germany.

Grossvogel's wife Jeanne was imprisoned for four months in Breendonk, where she met the same fate as her comrades. Breendonk was also the end of the line for Maurice Pepper, liaison agent with Holland, shot February 28, 1944, and Jean Jeusseur, at whose home a transmitting set was found, and who met the same death. Maurice Beublet, legal adviser to Simex, spent several months in Breendonk during which he was frequently "invited" into the torture chamber before being shot in Berlin in 1943. William Kruyt, a member of the Dutch group, parachuted in at the age of sixty-three, was arrested immediately after he landed. He took cyanide, but recovered. The Gestapo tortured him to get him to confess the identity of the other parachutist who had jumped along with him. When he refused to talk, the Germans took him to the morgue and removed the cloth that covered the corpse of his companion. It was his own son, who had been killed when he landed. Kruyt was taken back to Breendonk and put to death.

Also in Breendonk, Nazarin Drailly, manager of Simexco in 1942, arrested January 6, 1943, was interrogated "with dogs." With his legs ripped to pieces he was taken to the hospital in Antwerp, where one leg had to be amputated. One of his fellow prisoners wrote to Germaine Drailly after the war: "He told me that after his arrival at the camp of Breendonk, he was hung from the ceiling and Major Schmitt turned his dog on him and the dog tore his legs to pieces." After Drailly's return to Breendonk, he was sentenced to death; he was transferred to Berlin by the train on which most of the Red Orchestra members arrested in France and Belgium were deported. His wife, Germaine, saw him go by, pale as death, between two Gestapo agents, but did not recognize him. Someone whispered in her ear,

"That's your husband!"

She managed to talk to him for five minutes in the corridor.

"Did you notice? One of my legs is shorter than the other," he told her.

She never saw him again. He was beheaded on July 28, 1943, in Berlin. Germaine, after a long internment in the prisons of Berlin, was sent to Ravensbruck, Schonfeld, and finally to Orianenburg, where she was to have been gassed on March 19, 1945.

On the 15th the camp was bombarded by English aircraft. She escaped by crossing a canal, although she couldn't swim. "I felt as if I were walking on the water," she said later. Recaptured by the Gestapo and sent to Sachsenhausen, she took part in the death march during the final days of the war. She survived, and she remembers.

On this same train to Berlin, the Corbins, Monsieur and Madame Jaspar, Robert Breyer, Suzanne Cointe, Vladimir Keller, Franz and Germaine Schneider, and the Griottos, all arrested in France, joined the members of the Belgian group: Charles Drailly, Nazarin's brother; Robert Christen; Louis Thevenet, the cigarette manufacturer; Bill Hoorickx, the painter friend of Alamo's who helped out by renting apartments; and Henri Rauch, a Czech relative of Margarete Barcza, but primarily associated with British Intelligence. To avoid confusion among the various networks, Rauch had withdrawn from Simex in 1942; but he was arrested in December and died in Mauthausen.

Of the 26 Red Orchestra combatants who passed through Breendonk, 16 were sentenced to death. The rest were sent to concentration camps under the *"Nacht und Nebel"* policy, which permitted them to be executed without trials. Thanks to the testimony of Betty Depelsenaire, we know that in April, 1943, in Moabit Prison in Berlin, in a cell filled with people sentenced to death, Jeanne Grossvogel, Kaethe Voelkner, Suzanne Cointe, Rita Arnould, and Flore Velaerts were reunited. These women waited for death with a courage that compelled admiration, even from their guards. In the evenings, Suzanne Cointe would sing while Flore danced.

When she was conducted to the site of her execution on the morning of July 3, 1943, Rita Arnould, who had given Springer's name after the Atrébates raid, begged the forgiveness of his wife, Flore, and received it.

Kaethe raised her fist when she had heard her death sentence and shouted to the court, "I am happy to have done my part for communism!" She, Suzanne, Flore, Rita, and their comrades died under the executioner's axe.

The man whose ferocity had earned him the nickname "Hitler's bloodhound," the prosecutor Manfred Roeder, who presided over all the trials of the members of the Red Orchestra, is today assistant mayor of a small German town. On September 16, 1948, during his preliminary investigation, which resulted in the charges being dropped, he stated,

"I know that the total number of prisoners of the Red Orchestra in France and Belgium did not exceed 20 to 25, of whom one-third were given capital punishment . . . In early April, 1943, I asked Marshal Goering to pardon the women who had been sentenced to death, and he gave his consent."

This same Roeder added that in Berlin, of the 74 who had been arrested, 47 were executed. I am obliged to observe that my own investigations have not produced the same results.

Of the 80 people arrested in France and Belgium, 32 were sentenced to death and 45 were sent to concentration camps, 13 of whom never returned. In Germany, of the 130 people arrested, 49 were executed, 5 died under torture, and 3 committed suicide. I should also mention the execution of 28 members of the Jewish youth group who were arrested at the time of the "Soviet Paradise" exhibit in Berlin.

This is the truth, and even today we do not know the whole of it. For instance, what became of Marguerite Marivet, secretary of Simex in Marseilles? Or Modeste Ehrlich, at whose home Hillel Katz was arrested? Or Schreiber, or Joseph Katz, Hillel's brother, or Harry Robinson, or the two sisters and the brother-in-law of Germaine Schneider?

How many innocent people were arrested for activities relating to the Red Orchestra! Entire families were struck: the Draillys, the Grossvogels, the Schneiders, the Corbins . . . In the archives of the German police, I discovered that after the Atrébates raid, the following people were arrested for belonging to the Red Orchestra: Marcel Vranckx, Louis Bourgain, Reginald Goldmaer, Emile Carlos, Boulangier. Not one of these men had the slightest connection with our network.

The German Sonderkommission's records on the Red Orchestra were burned at the Château de Gamburg in the spring of 1945 on orders from Berlin.

To save face after the war, the members of the Sonderkommando made up elaborate stories, each more extravagant than the last. By their account, the results they obtained were based only on spontaneous confessions and on the collaboration of agents of the Red Orchestra, the Big Chief included. Torture? What was that? They had never heard of it. They had only been soldiers, valiant knights who had fought only with honest weapons. Alas, they have found some unexpected allies and accomplices in violating the truth outrageously and in spreading a veil of silence over their crimes. But allies and accomplices notwithstanding, lies do not endure forever; the truth always comes out in the end.

In Berlin, Brussels, and Paris, death awaited dozens of Red Orchestra combatants at the bottom of a long staircase whose every step brought new suffering. Those who died to destroy the brown plague hoped from the depths of their distress that tomorrow a changed world would bear witness and remember. Tomorrow is today; but the world continues to turn on its axis imperturbably, and the silence thickens.

The leaders of the Sonderkommission in Berlin and the Sonderkommando in Paris have good reason to wish to erase the black record of these crimes. Take the case of Hauptsturmführer SS Reiser, who ran the Sonderkommando in France from November, 1942, to July, 1943. With his hand over his heart, he declared, "Torture was never used in my service." Reiser's conscience is immaculate. But how many times did that hand which never "touched" a prisoner sign an order turning his victims over to the professional torturers of the department of intensified interrogation? Who gave the order to torture Alfred Corbin three times in the month of December, 1942? Who gave the order to torment Hersch and Mira Sokol until they died? Torture was not used in Reiser's service—for lack of equipment, perhaps? Perhaps they did not possess those little kits of instruments which the professional torturers brought with them from Berlin, at Reiser's summons. Who indeed, if not Giering, Reiser, Piepe, or Pannwitz, gave the order to send 26 members of the Red Orchestra to Breendonk, where they were subjected to the most hideous atrocities?

Heinrich Reiser is only one example. I could list the names of all the members of the Sonderkommission in Berlin, or of the Sonderkommando in Paris. After the war, they lost no time in finding new masters who absolved them of all their crimes on the altar of the great reconciliation.

23

On February 23, 1943, the day that the "birthday" message arrived from the Center, I had a long conversation with Giering. He told me that his superiors in Berlin had been informed of its contents immediately. Like himself, they believed the hardest part was over, and that they could proceed with the Great Game. Giering knew his job too well to accept the information in the two dispatches at face value. The first one, particularly, warranted verification, and he asked Kent whether it was customary for the Center to send us its congratulations on the anniversary of the Red Army. Kent, who realized that somehow or other I had managed to get word to Moscow, and who was obviously looking for an opportunity to redeem himself, confirmed that this was indeed the custom. During this period, Kent showed other signs of good will. I noticed that he kept his distance from the Germans, and he persisted in this attitude until I disappeared.

Giering was very much impressed that I had been proposed for a decoration. He felt that this mark of confidence on the part of the Center was an excellent omen, and placed him in a favorable position in the eyes of Berlin, where they recognized that he had been right to insist on my role in the Great Game. He had been much less enthusiastic about the second dispatch: I had proposed that contact with the Communist Party be broken for a month, and the Director answered that contact should be broken permanently.

I knew that Giering's objective was to get to Jacques Duclos and the underground leaders of the French Communist Party by using Juliette as an intermediary—a good strategy for the policeman he continued to be in spite of everything. Therefore I fully understood his disappointment. This rabid anti-communist had seen a serious possibility of striking a major blow against Jacques Duclos' party and perhaps arresting him, and now the possibility was slipping away. He was having a hard time consoling himself, so I had to give him some arguments to calm him down.

"After all," I told him, "if you were the Director, you wouldn't have acted any differently; you would have given the same order. Contact with the Communist Party had been strictly forbidden in the beginning; we made an exception to this rule only because of our shortage of radio sets. Now that the liaisons are set up, and you are going to be able to communicate as much as you wish, why should we need the channel of the French Communist Party?"

A few days later a new dispatch arrived from the Director. It contained instructions for widening the base of radio transmitters to the maximum, and assigning each one new tasks, which would be strictly limited to military information. The Director also asked what had happened to Simex and Simexco. Giering decided to answer that the two commercial enterprises had fallen into the hands of the Gestapo, but that the Red Orchestra had not been affected by the arrests. In this way, the head of the Sonderkommando could do as he pleased with the staff of the two companies without losing the possibility of "playing" with Moscow. So we could expect the worst for our imprisoned Simex comrades. The blood-stained Manfred Roeder, president of the military tribunal, arrived in Paris in March, 1943, and organized a sham trial, in fact a premeditated massacre. The "judges" had gathered no decisive proof that the accused persons had belonged to our network, but they sentenced to death Alfred Corbin, Robert Breyer, Suzanne Cointe, Kaethe Voelkner, and her companion Podsialdo; many years after the war, we learned that they were beheaded July 28, 1943, in Plötzensee Prison, near Berlin. Keller was given a prison sentence. Particularly in the case of Robert Breyer, who was only an associate of Simex and had nothing to do with our group, it was murder pure and simple. Thanks to statements we made in the course of the preliminary investigation, Leo Grossvogel and I succeeded in saving Ludwig Kainz, the engineer from the Todt Organization in Paris.

Giering had exchanged his first dispatch with the Center since my warning to Moscow that the network had been dismantled. Now the Sonderkommando threw itself headlong into its campaign to dupe Moscow. Every effort was made to conceal the arrests of the agents of the Red Orchestra, particularly those of Grossvogel, Katz, Maximovich, Robinson, Efremov, and Kent. I myself was moved out of my quarters on the Rue des Saussaies, where my status as a "special prisoner" was beginning to be an open secret, to a residence in Neuilly. I was no exception to the rule that sooner or later every prisoner becomes accustomed to his cell. There, right in the heart of the Gestapo, I had succeeded in writing my report. Giering and his friends could go on saying whatever they liked, sending dispatches of their own choosing, pursuing their hazy objective of a separate peace by rummaging through their drawers for old formulas, straining their imaginations for ways to delude Moscow, but it did not matter. At the other end, in Moscow, they knew the truth.

In Neuilly, at the corner of the Boulevard Victor Hugo and the Rue de Rouvray, Boemelburg, head of the Paris Gestapo, had taken over a large private house for his more distinguished prisoners. With its ten bedrooms, its facade decorated with white columns, a lawn in front and a kitchen garden in the rear, the building was not without elegance. The iron grillwork fence surrounding the property and the abundant foliage concealed some famous inmates from the eyes of passersby. Boemelburg and his entourage, being good Nazis, had the proverbial conceit: they prided themselves on receiving "visitors" as well known as Albert Lebrun, the last president of the Third Republic; André François-Poncet, who had been French Ambassador to Berlin; Colonel de la Rocque, head of the Croix de Feu and the French Socialist Party; and Largo Caballero, former President of the Spanish Republican government. Boemelburg lived on the premises and spent his time in bouts of drinking. The concierge, Monsieur Prodhomme, did the cooking with his two daughters and took care of the garden. Although he did not dare address a word to them, he, too, was highly honored to be associated with such illustrious persons.

I was given a rustically furnished room on the second floor. The window had no bars, but the door was always locked. I was told that when I wanted to go out I should ring for the soldier on guard. I was allowed to walk in the garden for an hour or two every day, but I was strictly forbidden to talk to the other prisoners. The house had been placed under the surveillance of a small contingent of Slovak soldiers who, following the example of their boss, got drunk with monotonous regularity. They made an infernal racket. Hearing them snoring and singing, I got ideas about escaping, but I resisted the temptation for the present, since I had my part to play in the Great Game. During my sleepless nights I imagined myself forcing the lock, knocking out the guard at the main entrance, and making my escape.

A few days after my transfer to Neuilly, Berg announced to me that Hillel Katz, my "assistant," as he put it, would soon be joining me. I was very happy to hear this, but when I learned that they had put Katz in a room in the basement with the traitor Schumacher, I realized that the latter must have been placed with him to sound him out on my real intentions. Otto Schumacher was the man who had induced the poet Arlette Humbert-Laroche to trust him—after which Arlette was never seen again. Schumacher began telling Katz that I was only playing with the Germans, that he did not believe I was a traitor. I complained to Berg about this transparent attempt to cast doubt on my word. Schumacher was immediately removed from the premises.

Hillel's presence at Neuilly was a great comfort to me. He was permitted to come and see me and to accompany me on my walks. Since we were certain that a microphone was concealed somewhere in my room, we made a point of subtly reassuring Giering about my intentions. During our walks in the garden, however, we freely discussed our problems, speaking very quietly in Yiddish or Hebrew. Hillel was very upset about his family. They were under Gestapo surveillance, and we had been warned that the families of the Red Orchestra combatants were regarded as hostages, just as the prisoners were. In March, 1943, Kent arrived in Neuilly with Margarete Barcza. Kent worked all day on the coding of the dispatches that Giering was preparing for the Center. They were signed with my name, but they had been put into code by a Sonderkommando specialist. I had declared once and for all that there was no point asking me to do it, because I knew nothing about it. Giering consulted me about the messages he received from the Center, and how to answer them. From time to time Berg came and got me and took me to the Rue des Saussaies. There I frequently had occasion to meet my "host," Boemelburg, Giering's and Berg's colleague for many years. They hated each other openly, and this hatred turned to rage on the day Berlin advised Boemelburg to keep out of the Sonderkommando's business.

"Stay out of Boemelburg's way," Berg advised me, "especially when he's drunk." The advice was unneeded, and useless, too, since it was difficult to encounter him in any other state.

One afternoon, when I was with Berg, I heard shots. Seeing my look of amazement, Berg led me to the garden. Boemelburg was there, staggering drunk, with a pistol in his hand.

"But who is he firing at?" I asked.

"Look again!" answered Berg.

Boemelburg had made himself a shooting gallery. The targets were portraits of the leaders of the Soviet Union and the French Communist Party. Next to them were a series of caricatures representing Jews. So this was how the head of the Gestapo in Paris spent his time between drinking bouts and punitive expeditions!

Boemelburg went on with his target practice. Every time he fired, the dog at his side barked furiously. Suddenly Boemelburg struck the animal and shouted,

"Shut up, Stalin!"

Just then he noticed me and said, "You heard my dog's name?"

"Yes," I answered, "In Moscow there were dogs named Hitler."

Crazed with rage—and alcohol—Boemelburg rushed at me, aiming his gun.

"*Mein Gott*, Otto!" Berg had stepped between us, shielding me with his body.

Later he reproached me for my imprudence. "That was a close call, and almost the end of the Great Game."

24

The Sonderkommando Falls into the Trap

It was at this time that I began to be able to move around in Paris. I obtained permission to do this by inventing a story for Giering—which he swallowed whole. At the time of my first interrogations, I had given him to believe that for years, a special counterespionage group had been set up in the greatest secrecy to guard the security of the Red Orchestra. I told him that I was supposed to keep Moscow informed of the places I habitually frequented (cafés, barber, restaurants, tailor, shops) and the frequency of my visits. In this way the security group, whose agents were unknown to me, could follow me.

I told Giering that Moscow must be amazed at my not having appeared at these specified places for some time. In my report to the Director, I had gone to the trouble of writing that he should ask me to come to these routine encounters; a dispatch from the Center containing such instruction arrived, and Giering had no alternative but to give his consent. These outings became a habit. The first few times, two Gestapo cars flanked the vehicle I was in; later on, I was accompanied only by Berg and the driver, a simplified system which turned out to be very valuable, as we shall see. In this way I went to these imaginary meetings—with a barber on the Rue Fortuny, a tailor in Montparnasse, a haberdasher on the Boulevard Haussmann. Cafés and restaurants in the various arrondissements of Paris, and even its suburbs, were also on my itinerary. The agents of the Sonderkommando wasted precious time trying to locate the members of the counterespionage group, and this misplaced zeal filled me with joy. As long as Reiser's police machine was chasing imaginary enemies, it had to neglect those militants of the Red Orchestra who were still at liberty.

In the course of these "accompanied visits," I noticed that my guards were not using German identity papers, but false documents—Belgian, Dutch, or Scandinavian. I inquired discreetly why Giering had used this subterfuge, and I learned that he thought his men would be less conspicuous, better protected from any action on the part of the resistance. In case their papers were checked by the French police, the real nationality and profession of my guards would not be discovered.

I jumped at the opportunity to ask Giering to grant me the same privilege: "Suppose the French police were to check my papers. If you don't want my situation to seem unusual," I told him, "you should give me an identity card."

He thought my remark justified, and from then on, whenever we left Neuilly, Berg handed me an identity card and a sum of money which I gave back to him when we returned. It was a way of showing my good faith, and a very interesting point scored for the future.

Up until Operation Juliette, the Great Game could be summed up very simply. The Germans were riding high. The fact was that the Red Orchestra had changed color, and with the transmitters that were now being used by the Germans, the Brown Orchestra had completely outwitted Moscow. The Center was all the more color-blind and its suspicions more easily lulled because the material being sent had lost nothing in quality.

However, the Germans knew for a fact that even after the Director's answer of February 23, 1943, they would still have to keep on sending military information for several months. If the advocates of a separate peace were well informed on the diplomatic and political levels, they had to prove they were similarly well informed in the military domain.

It is well known today that Himmler's efforts to arrive at a separate peace with the west correspond chronologically with the Sonderkommando's attempt to launch the Great Game. I shall cite two examples to support this certainty: the first is that it was in December, 1942, that the lawyer Langbehn, with Himmler's approval, made contact with the allies in Zurich and Stockholm.

For a second example: it was in the month of August,

1943—the 23rd, to be precise—that Himmler met secretly with Popitz, a member of the Department of the Interior in Berlin, and also a member of the resistance. Popitz proposed that Hitler be sacrificed as the *sine qua non* for arriving at a separate peace. Heinrich Himmler—who was famed for his devotion to Hitler—gave a noncommittal answer, which Popitz took to signify that Himmler would accept such a solution. Langbehn left immediately for Switzerland to announce the good news to his colleagues among the allies. I do not believe it was a coincidence that during this same August, the new head of the Sonderkommando, Pannwitz, was trying to resume the Great Game.

Himmler, however, overestimated the disagreements among the allies. To be sure, the second front was slow in coming, and it was not out of the question to imagine that the English and American delay would cast a shadow on their relations with the Russians—but to interpret this as a rupture of the alliance was going too far. As the war advanced, and the chance for an armed victory for Germany diminished, a great number of the Wehrmacht heads—who had been particularly edified by the German defeat at Stalingrad in the beginning of 1943—believed the only solution for Nazi Germany lay in a separate peace. It was the action of the shipwrecked man who clings to a piece of drifting wreckage even though it cannot hold him up. Believing in a separate peace, up to the last minute, mistaking their desires for realities right to the end, Himmler and his entourage imagined that it was necessary to dupe Moscow accordingly.

What was the Center's strategy, after it received my report?

In the first place, to give the impression that it was totally unaware that the transmitters were now in German hands. The dispatches originating from the Center were still addressed to the various group leaders; I took advantage of this to convince Giering not to turn Katz, Grossvogel, and the others over to the authorities for trial. My reasoning had all the appearance of good logic. I said to Giering, "Look, at any moment Moscow may ask to contact them directly. If you put them on trial, and if you sentence them, you will be showing your hand."

He was convinced.

The Center made perfect use of the Great Game to ask, constantly, for more military information. After February, 1943, the Germans were forced to give Moscow information that a normally functioning network, however powerful, would have had trouble obtaining. Finally, the Center hit upon a way to prevent the Germans from infiltrating those networks that had not yet been discovered.

An interesting question: Moscow was soliciting military information, but who was deciding what would or would not be sent? The first priority was the approval of the leaders of the Great Game in Berlin, Gestapo-Müller and Martin Bormann. Next, the Sonderkommando had to go through the heads of the Abwehr in Paris, who transmitted the requests to the chiefs of staff of the Wehrmacht. It was Field Marshal von Rundstedt himself, each time, who gave the green light for the transmission of the material. Since he had no great affection for Himmler or the Gestapo—to put it mildly—and since, moreover, he was unfamiliar with the goals of the Great Game, as was the Abwehr, he had occasion to point out to Berlin the eminently secret character of the information requested.

Von Rundstedt was amazed, and this is easy to understand. As for the leaders in Berlin who were in on the Great Game, their only consolation was that the military information provided concerned only western Europe. Meanwhile, the Center was asking questions that were more and more important to the Red Army.

In the archives of the Abwehr in Berlin there are some documents relating to the messages sent by the Director which are very revealing of the Center's objectives. Here are a few examples:

February 20, 1943, dispatch sent to Otto:

Ask the manufacturer to send information regarding the transport of military units and armaments from France to our front.

And the next day, the sequel to this dispatch:

> Which German divisions are being kept in reserve, and where?
> This question is very important to us.

On March 9, the Center asked what troops were stationed in Paris and Lyon, the numbers of the divisions, and the types of weapons.

Questions of this sort threw the Sonderkommando into profound confusion. It was impossible for them not to answer, and to answer with false information was very dangerous; careful examination of the questions revealed that Moscow was trying not so much to obtain information as to verify information already in their possession.

> Which divisions are located at Châlons-sur-Marne and Angoulême? According to our information, the 9th infantry division should be at Châlons and the 10th armored at Angoulême. Verify.

The Sonderkommando had no choice but to give an accurate reply:

> The new SS division at Angoulême has no number, but the soldiers wear a grey uniform with black epaulettes and the insignia of the SS.

That dispatch went out on April 2; two days later, the sequel furnished details on the division's armaments.

Almost every day, very precise dispatches arrived from the Center, to which the Sonderkommando would reply in just as much detail. Such was the price that the architects of the "separate peace" had to pay. There were similar exchanges about the German troops stationed in Holland and Belgium. The messages asked the names of the officers in command and the results of the English bombardments.

Von Rundstedt increasingly distrusted and disapproved the release of such information. The dispatch that came May 30,

1943, was the last straw; it touched off conflict between the Wehrmacht chiefs of staff and the portion of the German secret service under Gestapo-Müller and Himmler.

"Otto," the Center asked,

> contact the manufacturer and find out whether the army of occupation is preparing to make use of gas. Is this type of material being transported at the present time? Are gas bombs being stored on the air fields: Where, and in what quantity? What is the caliber of these bombs? What is the gas used? What is its degree of toxicity? Are tests being made with it? Have you heard of a new poison gas for military use that goes by the name of 'Gay-Hellé'? Put all the agents working in France on this job.

This time it was too much. The leaders of the Wehrmacht grew very excited. They discussed the matter among themselves and informed Berlin that it was "completely impossible to answer these questions." Naturally, the Sonderkommando was not of this opinion. Giering was familiar with dispatches, deciphered in Berlin, which I had sent before my arrest; I had already given information on gases. Kaethe Voelkner and Vasily Maximovich, in particular, were very well informed by the management of the Sauckel Organization on the discoveries of the German chemical industry.

The head of the Sonderkommission in the German capital thought it necessary to answer this dispatch, even if only partially. But the Wehrmacht chiefs of staff meant to use this example to express their disapproval in no uncertain terms. Von Rundstedt said, "I do not see the necessity for continuing the Game." The Abwehr—not committed to the Great Game in the way Himmler was—informed Berlin on June 20, 1943, that "The High Command of the Army is of the opinion that for some time the Director in Moscow has been asking questions that are too specific. . . . The military High Command can no longer give accurate answers when, for example, Moscow asks the number of divisions or regiments, the names of the commanders, etc." And in conclusion: "The High Command of the Army feels that they can no longer furnish this type of information without posing formidable security problems." Then, on June 25th, they dropped a bomb, declaring, "The leaders of the Wehrmacht feel that they can no longer release material, for it is absolutely certain that the enemy in Moscow has seen through the Game. . . ."

This was the opinion of the head of the Abwehr, Admiral Wilhelm Canaris, who took a dim view of the ambitious maneuvers of the clique surrounding Gestapo-Müller and Himmler. In fact, neither the Abwehr, nor Schellenberg, head of German counterespionage, nor Von Rundstedt, had been informed of the true objectives of the Great Game. Laying the groundwork for the possibility of a separate peace was not the sort of thing to be discussed in Hitler's Germany. It had been necessary to give them an explanation—that the Great Game was making it possible to uncover Soviet spy networks in the occupied countries; but for the chiefs of staff of the Wehrmacht this was not sufficient reason to turn over important and specific military secrets. The Sonderkommando was not so amazed at the importance and precision of the information requested, because they knew that the Red Orchestra had all along been providing Moscow with material of considerable military value.

The Sonderkommando arguments won out in the end, and the military were forced to reply, as previously, to the precise questions that had been asked of them. On July 9, 1943, formal orders to this effect arrived from Berlin.

The Center also desired information about various problems outside the limited context of military organization. For example, some dispatches raised questions about the Vlasov Army.

Andrei Andreivich Vlasov was a brilliant young general in the Red Army who had been taken prisoner, along with his division. He was perfectly aware of the fate reserved for prisoners when they returned to Russia—Soviet soldiers were expected to reserve a final bullet for themselves, rather than allow themselves to be captured. This prospect had induced him to simply go over to the German side. The Wehrmacht heads suggested that he create a Russian army to fight at their sides. At the head of his units, they would place demoralized officers who wished to avoid the prison camps at any price.

A group of professional Nazi propagandists took charge of Vlasov and his army, but hunger turned out to be more persuasive than ideology. Soviet soldiers who had been taken prisoner—abandoned, often betrayed, in a weakened condition—agreed to wear the German uniform in order to survive. Thus the "Russian Army of Liberation" was born.

This army had very little military value; material compensations could not replace the conviction of fighting for a just cause, or the defense of national soil. Aware of its lack of combativeness, the heads of the Wehrmacht used the Vlasov Army chiefly on the western front, in actions of repression.

During the summer of 1943 it was, of course, very important for the heads of Soviet military intelligence to know the facts about the Vlasov Army: the number of units and the total number of troops, their geographical distribution, the names of the officers, the nature of the armaments and their use, and the nature of the political indoctrination to which the troops had been subjected. The Center asked for the most extensive information; and in order to have the maximum number of details at their disposal, asked for verification of those already in their possession. Berlin had no objection to satisfying their curiosity, and contrary to their habits, the chiefs of staff of the Wehrmacht offered no opposition either, for the good reason that they nourished no illusions about the military value of Vlasov's soldiers.

In April, 1943, the Sonderkommando received a long dispatch from the Center addressed to Otto, giving very precise details about the losses of the German army at Stalingrad, which Russia had recaptured on January 31. Giering was very surprised; he asked me why Moscow felt it necessary to inform me on this subject.

"From time to time," I told him, "the Center provides me with explanations which enable me to form an accurate picture of the military situation at a given point of the conflict."

"Sorry," Giering replied, "but I know through Kent that this is the first time that this type of dispatch has reached you."

I had to think fast. "There are inevitably a few things, above a certain level, which Kent knows nothing about."

Later I understood the meaning and purpose of this dispatch. The Center was trying to spread anxiety in Berlin by reporting casualty figures for Stalingrad much higher than those circulating in the capital of the Reich. In fact, the reports that had been sent by their own high command to German government circles underestimated the real losses. In this way, thanks to the Center, Himmler scored an impressive victory with Hitler by presenting him with an accurate picture of the enormous losses of the Wehrmacht.

The Sonderkommando, sure of the Center's confidence, began a propaganda campaign intended to spread anxiety in the anti-Nazi alliance. The techniques were a little obvious, but they give an accurate idea of the methods used by advocates of a separate peace in order to arrive at their ends. A series of dispatches were sent in my name that claimed to be based on a vast survey of the German population organized by Goebbels; the survey concerned the outcome of the war; it reported a strong anti-Soviet current in the public opinion of the Reich. The majority of Germans, these dispatches "revealed," believed in a final victory, but in case it became necessary to negotiate, all the people questioned stated that they were in favor of a separate peace with the west.

Other dispatches were sent to the Center on the subject of the state of mind of English and American soldiers. In my name, dispatches said that agents of the Red Orchestra made contact with English aviators shot down over the region of Paris, and heard them say they had no intention of dying for the USSR. Naturally, these aviators were wholehearted advocates of peace with Germany.

I had a hard time keeping a straight face when Giering handed me these dispatches. There would be general hysteria when the Center received these "top secret" documents.

You'd have to be pretty stupid to imagine for a moment that such obvious lies would have an effect on Soviet morale. They knew at the Center how to interpret a public opinion survey organized by Goebbels, that master of psychological manipulation; as if it were possible to express an opinion in Nazi Germany!

Since Giering did me the "honor" of consulting me, I informed him of my complete agreement with the content of the dispatches, and even added, with total seriousness, that such information would "give Moscow something to think about." He was pleased with himself. He continued to pursue this policy of sowing discord among the allies by drafting another dispatch designed to prove that the British were selling submachine guns to the Germans. The proof presented by Giering rested on the fact that in Calais, German policemen were carrying submachine guns of British origin. He stated that the Germans were buying these weapons in the neutral countries, and that the British had made only one condition: that they not be used on the Soviet front.

This information did not stand up under examination. There was no proof that the British had given their consent to such sales; and in any case these guns could very easily have fallen into the hands of the Germans during combat. This fiction was especially ridiculous since at the same time the allies were sending enormous quantities of armaments to the USSR.

During this same period, Giering tried to use the Red Orchestra to penetrate the Soviet intelligence network in Switzerland.

This network, which had been organized before the war broke out, was headed by Alexander Rado, who had been a communist militant since his youth and had played an active part in the Hungarian uprising of Bela Kun. Rado was a remarkably learned man; he was a well-known geographer; and he spoke several languages. All the efforts of Rado's network were directed against Nazi Germany. In principle, the Red Orchestra should not have had any contact with him, but in 1940 the Center sent Kent to Switzerland to teach Rado the technique of radio broadcasting and give him his code. The very idea of such a mission was a serious error, for in 1940 the Center had many alternatives, and had no need to send the working head of an occupied-zone network. When Kent was arrested two years later and went over to the German side, the information he turned over on the Rado group had very grave consequences. He knew Rado's address, his code, and the wave length of his broadcasts. Rado sent dispatches by three transmitters, the so-called "Three Reds"; they were all intercepted. In spite of Kent's collaboration, the Germans had considerable difficulty decoding them, and they decided to send some agents into the field.

Switzerland's neutrality posed a problem for German Intelligence. Giering had the idea of using Franz Schneider, a Swiss citizen who belonged to the Efremov group—which had been arrested in Belgium, and which was in contact with several very important agents of Rado's. Thanks to Schneider, Giering was very well informed about the composition of the Swiss group; but three successive attempts to infiltrate it failed.

The first time, he used an agent, Yves Rameau, who had once known Rado quite well. Rameau met with Rado and suggested that he work with him, pointing out that he had many connections in the French resistance and in Kent's group. Rado, sensing a trap, put an end to the conversation.

Giering's second plan was to send a German agent to Switzerland who would pose as Vera Ackermann, one of the coders of the French Red Orchestra group whom I had told to disappear after Hersch and Mira Sokol were arrested. I had sent her first to Kent's home in Marseilles and then, because of the threat of arrest, to a little village near Clermont-Gerrand. But through Kent, Giering knew that I knew Vera Ackermann's address. He planned to arrest her and isolate her until the end of the war, thinking that the German agent, by masquerading as her, could easily penetrate the Rado network; he need only inform the Center that she had been sent to Switzerland for reasons of security. As it was presented, this plan had a serious possibility of succeeding. So once again, I had to ward off the blow.

"Your agent will be discovered immediately," I told Giering. "Kent claims that I am the only one who knows Vera Ackermann's address. That is correct: she is in Geneva."

So Giering's second plan fell through, and Vera remained hidden in her village in the Massif Central until the end of the war.

The third plan—worked out by Kent—was to send a messenger to Alexander Foote, Rado's right arm. Giering questioned me to find out how a rendezvous of this sort used to be handled. I advised him in such a way that Foote realized at the first meeting whom he was dealing with. Moreover, as Foote related in his memoirs, *Handbook for Spies*, the Center had warned him of the danger and ordered him not to agree to another rendezvous and to make sure that the German messenger did not find out where he lived by following him.

Giering instructed his agent to hand the man he was supposed to meet a big book wrapped in orange paper, very conspicuous. Inside the book, stuck between two pages, some messages in code had been concealed. He was to ask that these messages be sent to the Center, and to arrange another meeting with the agent. This was what I had advised—and this procedure was enough to expose him by proving that he had never carried out any real missions. You would have to be out of your mind to send an agent across the border during the war carrying coded dispatches in a book so unusual-looking it would have aroused the suspicions of the sleepiest border guard. In those days, everything circulated in the form of microfilm, hidden inside clothing.

As a result, Foote gave the cold shoulder to this trumped-up emissary, who returned empty-handed. Two weeks later, the Center sent Kent a dispatch expressing amazement that the messenger was an agent of the Gestapo. Giering tried to save face by explaining that the real messenger had been arrested and that the Gestapo had sent one of their agents in his place.

One by one, attempts to infiltrate the Rado network by using captured members of the Red Orchestra had failed, but the work being done in Switzerland was too important for

Berlin to resign itself to giving up the game. Schellenberg himself was in charge of combating the Rado network. After long and patient efforts, he succeeded in infiltrating: one of his agents seduced Rose B., a young coder who worked for one of the Three Reds. Later a couple, the Massons, who had passed themselves off as old Soviet agents, overcame the vigilance of our Swiss friends and sent Berlin some precise information on the functioning of the network. Finally, Schellenberg exerted strong pressure on the head of Swiss Intelligence to liquidate the entire Rado organization. These maneuvers took time, and up until 1944, Rado continued to send Moscow important military material, which originated in fact from some high-ranking Wehrmacht officers.

Giering also came up against the problem of financing the Red Orchestra. Before the arrests, the commercial companies Simex and Simexco provided for the needs of the network, and Moscow did not have to concern itself with assuring them the means of survival. Since Giering had admitted in his messages to the Center that the two companies had fallen into the hands of the enemy, it was logical, to maintain the fiction, that he request funds.

In this area, as in so many others, I had occasion to discuss the matter with Giering, and I overwhelmed him with advice that made him completely ridiculous. I recommended he begin with Belgium and Holland and that he ask for a sum of money for Wenzel. A "gift" arrived for Wenzel from Bulgaria just after he had fled: at the bottom of a big can of beans, the ludicrous sum of ten pounds sterling. The men of the Sonderkommando, totally lacking in humor, tried to find a logical explanation for the modest size of the sum. I provided one that satisfied them completely:

"It's very simple," I told them. "The Center must have wanted to test the functioning of the liaison before sending more substantial amounts."

They waited a long time for the next payment.

For the Netherlands, the Sonderkommando requested a substantial payment in the name of Winterinck. The Center replied that they were perfectly agreeable, provided they be referred to a "mailbox" that was totally reliable. Delighted, the Sonderkommando hastened to send the address of a former member of the Dutch Communist Party. But a dispatch from the Director threw them into a state of consternation: how was it possible that they sent an address known to the Gestapo? The Sonderkommando fell all over themselves in embarrassed explanations. So the Center took the initiative and advised Winterinck to make contact with a certain Bohden Cervinka, a Brussels engineer, who would give him $5,000. Beside themselves with joy, the Sonderkommando sent an agent. The engineer was disconcerted and thought someone was playing a practical joke on him. Once again, the Sonderkommando were the victims of their fantasies.

The Center permitted itself the pleasure of another mystification by giving Efremov the address of a dealer in tombstones who supposedly owed the Soviet government fifty thousand francs. The truth was just the opposite, but the Center's sense of humor—for the address of the dealer in tombstones was meant to indicate symbolically that it was time to bury the whole business of money—was completely lost on the Sonderkommando.

25

In June, 1943, Giering's health grew worse: he had cancer of the throat, and the cancer was spreading. Even my own remedy—I had recommended cognac, though I am sure that even without my advice he would have chosen this treatment—was becoming ineffective. He was drinking more and more heavily. He felt that he was a doomed man and that soon he should pass his responsibilities on to someone else. In spite of the reports he sent to Berlin boasting of his constant victories, it is clear that he was not really confident. No doubt he was writing to reassure his superiors in Berlin that the Big Chief had gone over to the German side; but in the long conversations I had with him he harped constantly on a theme that revealed his anxiety: what were my underlying reasons for taking part in the Great Game? My answer was invariable: the prospect of a separate peace between the Soviet Union and Germany.

He was not really convinced. He knew—in spite of his attempts to convince himself otherwise—that I was Jewish, in addition to being a communist and violently anti-Nazi.

Giering was an intelligent cop, but as a good German he could not help reasoning in logical terms. If anyone had told him that down in my cell, where I was watched night and day, I had succeeded in writing up a report, and then in delivering it to Juliette, he would have replied: "Impossible." Similarly, the imaginary Soviet counterespionage groups terrified him, but he did not for a moment doubt their existence: it was "logical."

He had a fixed idea that only the head of the Sonderkommando should know everything about the progress of the operation. He frequently repeated in my presence, after taking a few swallows of cognac, the principles that guided his actions: "A man who is running a Great Game like mine," he would say, "must know how to mix truth and falsehood in dealing with his associates in the enterprise. As far as the leaders in Berlin are concerned, the main thing is to reassure them by convincing them that, no matter what happens, everything is going well. As for the military—who in any case would not understand very much about the subtleties of this business—and the Abwehr, it is best that they know as little about it as possible, and only what I feel it necessary to tell them. The only one in possession of the whole truth is myself." Subordinates had access only to information that was strictly necessary to their work.

When Pannwitz replaced Giering as the head of the Sonderkommando, he had nothing to go on but written reports that deviated widely from the reality of the situation. I had got used to Giering as an enemy—he was cruel and implacable, sly and cunning; nevertheless, I was afraid his successor might lead the Great Game toward a much bloodier conclusion. Reiser was dismissed at the same time and put in charge of the Gestapo at Karlsruhe. So the identity of my principal adversaries had changed.

I made the acquaintance of Pannwitz in early July, 1943. I remember very clearly the day he walked into my room in Neuilly. With the closest attention and with a understandable curiosity, I examined the new head of the Sonderkommando, the man who would be my chief adversary. Physically, he was very different from his predecessor: young, fat, with a round pink face and keen eyes hidden behind thick glasses, and elegantly dressed, with bourgeois mannerisms. He was calm and excited by turns. He gave the general impression of a slippery ball, difficult to grasp.

Pannwitz was born in 1911 in Berlin. As a small boy, he belonged to a Christian scouting organization. The very strict Christian upbringing in his family led him straight to the study of theology, to which he devoted three years. Instead of becoming a pastor, however, he ended up donning the mask of the executioner.

Pannwitz was twenty-two when Hitler came to power. An employee in the department of criminal police (Kripo), he had been assigned to major crimes, but the cases that fell within that jurisdiction were not really commensurate with his talents. All that was far too vulgar. What really appealed to him was political repression. In this field, he felt, he would really come into his own. To climb the rungs of the Nazi hierarchy, the surest and quickest route was by way of the Gestapo.

Fortune smiled on him. He was noticed and appreciated. The young wolf approached the king of the beasts; he became one of the assistants to Heydrich, who was gathering around him some young men who were talented, adventurous, and potential carnivores. Among them were two who would be heard from later; their names were Eichmann and Schellenberg.

On September 29, 1941, Hitler promoted Heydrich to Deputy Protector of Bohemia-Moravia, and Heydrich took up residence in Prague. Pannwitz was his right arm. This was the beginning of a period of terrible suffering for the Czech people. The concentration camps filled; those who resisted Nazism were tortured, deported, executed—by the hundreds. London and the Czech government in exile decided to send in partisans by parachute to assassinate Heydrich. On May 27, 1942, Heydrich's car was attacked, he was seriously wounded, and the butcher died on June 4th.

The reprisals were terrifying. Personally responsible for Heydrich's security and furious at himself for his failure, Pannwitz directed the manhunt. Goebbels had decreed that the Jews bore the primary responsibility, so several hundred Jews, gathered in the Theresienstadt camp in Bohemia, were murdered. In Czechoslovakia as a whole, three thousand people had been arrested, but after Heyrich's death, the terror heightened. It was a bloodbath. In Prague alone, 1,700 Czechs were executed; at Brno, 1,300. On June 10th all the men and children of the little village of Lidice were exterminated, and the women were deported to Ravensbrück.

Pannwitz personally conducted the search for those who instigated the attack on Heydrich, and Pannwitz is the one responsible for all those massacres. It was he, finally, who led the assault of a regiment of SS against the church of Saint

Charles-Borromée where a group of partisans responsible for
the attack had taken refuge.

After these events, Pannwitz had some difficulties with his
superiors in Berlin, and he preferred to disappear for a while.
He left for the Russian front. He remained only four months
with his unit, no doubt judging the climate too severe for his
health. In the beginning of 1943, he returned to Berlin as an
assistant to Gestapo-Müller. He was put in charge of examining the reports from the Sonderkommando in Paris, but his
new chief had assessed his qualities and knew that in addition
to his references as an accomplished butcher, he had the
qualifications for a role in high-level politics. Pannwitz had a
fertile imagination. No sooner had he returned from Prague
than he proposed a plan which, according to him, would put
an end to Czech resistance. For every patriot arrested, he
explained—and he spoke from experience—ten others rose
up. So there was only one solution: arrest the leaders and
make them turn traitor. By going over to the German side but
maintaining their role in the resistance, they would destroy
the underground movement.

Although very attractive on paper, Pannwitz' plan was
inadequate to the urgency of the situation. In Czechslovakia,
the Gestapo did not have a moment to lose. They had to
strike fast and hard. So they confined themselves to the good
old methods.

When he came upon the reports of the Sonderkommando
in Paris, Pannwitz was delighted. Here, at least, they were
applying his plan; here, at least, they had understood. And
Pannwitz was all the more convinced of the excellence of his
idea because Giering, in order to advance his own position,
had played up the treason of the Big Chief and the other
members of the Red Orchestra who had gone over to the
German side without a murmur. So his goal was obvious: to
get himself appointed to replace Giering, who was sick and
on the point of leaving his job. To achieve this end, he would
pull all the strings at his disposal.

When I saw Pannwitz for the first time, I did not suspect
that this little man, who looked like an accountant for some

modest firm, had hands red with the blood of Czech patriots. He played the part of a gentleman who dealt with politics at only the highest level. This was his chance, and he was arriving in the nick of time. His superiors in Berlin felt that the first phase of the Great Game was over. After doing everything they could—and sacrificing a great deal—to assure themselves of the confidence of the Center, it was now time to go further, to begin the second phase.

Events themselves dictated a new policy. The war had changed direction. After Stalingrad, the Russian steamroller had begun to move, and nothing could stop it. On July 10, 1943, the Americans landed in Sicily. On the 25th, Il Duce was overthrown. The probability of an English and American landing on the coast of Western Europe increased every day. In Berlin, everyone knew that a military victory was out of the question. Himmler, Schellenberg, and Canaris nourished no illusions about the final outcome—they placed all their hopes on a separate peace with the west. If we bear this hope and this line of reasoning in mind, we will understand that the Great Game took on primary importance in their eyes. Its pace had to accelerate. Heinz Pannwitz arrived in Paris with instructions to this end.

Yes, speed was essential. In the summer of 1943, even Martin Bormann—the Führer's right arm—became keenly interested in the project. Not only did he appoint a group of experts to prepare the material that would be used for the Great Game, but he wrote the dispatches with his own hand. Hitler knew about this, but he certainly was not aware of his lieutenant's real intentions. In the camp of those opposed to this strategy, Canaris and Von Ribbentrop held key positions. Ribbentrop's hostility was an obstacle—he was Foreign Minister, and the release of diplomatic material had to be cleared through him. After Bormann took matters into his own hands, however, the situation changed. He possessed the necessary authority to silence the reservations of Ribbentrop and Marshal Von Rundstedt combined. From this point on, the Great Game was referred to as "Operation Bear." All these strategies failed to reckon with the claws of the wild

animal they thought they had in a cage; the Nazis had
forgotten the proverb about not selling the bear's skin until
you've shot the bear.

Pannwitz began to talk. He started by criticizing his
predecessors at the head of the Sonderkommando. He stated
in my presence that Reiser's grasp of the situation had never
gone beyond that of a stupid cop. As for Giering, he had been
too timid, according to Pannwitz; he had run the Great Game
in slow motion. Pannwitz explained to me—and I listened
with all the feigned attention I could muster—that they
should long ago have proceeded to the political stage. But
Pannwitz' reasoning betrayed some serious gaps in his
knowledge of intelligence. His experience with the Gestapo
had opened his eyes to the thousand and one ways of
falsifying and padding reports—yet even so he was oblivious
of the untruths in the explanations Giering had sent to Berlin.

In Pannwitz' opinion, which he said was shared by his
superiors, radio contact with Moscow had become inadequate. It was necessary to enter a second phase now, to
establish direct contact. He had an ambitious plan to send the
Center an emissary who would inform Moscow that a
substantial group of German military personnel wanted to
discuss a separate peace with the Soviet Union. This special
envoy would take documents with him that gave evidence of
this attitude, but he would also carry proof to the contrary,
testifying that in other German circles the same solution was
being sought with the west.

All this elaborate strategy was designed to break up the
anti-Nazi alliance of nations. Pannwitz was very narrow-
minded, but above all he was a thoroughgoing Nazi, imbued
with faith in his racial superiority. Though he knew perfectly
well that I was Jewish, he was blinded by his stupid con-
tempt, and thus underestimated his enemy. He had to be
totally unconscious, overcome by his egotism, to imagine
that the Red Orchestra would consider for a moment going
along with the Nazis. Our struggle was a fight to the
death—but a Pannwitz was incapable of understanding this.

Himmler, when he heard about Pannwitz' plan, disapproved. Himmler felt it would be too risky to send an envoy to Moscow; Pannwitz told me Himmler was afraid of the attraction that communism might exert on a dyed-in-the-wool Nazi. The example of the Berlin group of the Red Orchestra was still present in Himmler's mind—the fact that people like Schulze-Boysen and Arvid Harnack could have become "Soviet agents"; that individuals who were perfectly at home in society and free of financial worries had committed themselves to the anti-Nazi struggle was beyond the comprehension of the men of the Gestapo.

Pannwitz did not become discouraged. Instead he made another proposal: we should suggest to the Center that they send a representative to Paris. Without hesitation, and even simulating the most enthusiastic approval, I answered that this idea seemed to me completely workable. Kent was also questioned, but he declared that the plan was Utopian. Like a pendulum swinging between two positions, Kent was returning to treason. He wanted to prove himself in the eyes of his new employer, and he was going over to the Nazi side again. Margarete Barcza was about to have a baby, and Kent was not a man to risk the peace and quiet of his family. I won out in the end by explaining to Pannwitz that if he continued to involve Kent in the Great Game, the whole thing would turn into a farce.

So a detailed dispatch was addressed to the Center explaining that a group of officers wished to make contact with Moscow. It proposed that the Russians delegate an emissary to the Germans. The plan was carried rather far, for the meeting was to take place in Hillel Katz's old apartment at 3 Rue Edmond-Roger. It was agreed that every ten days I would wait there for the envoy from Moscow.

The Sonderkommando feverishly prepared for the meeting. Pannwitz and his associates went over the scenario ad infinitum. Accompanied by Berg, I was to make the first contact, which would lay the groundwork for the main interview; then Pannwitz would play the role of delegate from the Berlin group. The enthusiasm he exhibited in building this particular sand castle was truly comical. The

wolf was donning the shepherd's cloak, the butcher of Prague
was playing peacemaker with Moscow.

While awaiting this historic encounter, the indefatigable
Pannwitz took it into his head to expand the circle of
transmitters working for the Germans in the neutral countries. Curiously enough, I observed, he omitted Rado's
network in Switzerland. This was because Walter Schellenberg was carrying on a veiled but bitter rivalry with Gestapo-
Müller, Pannwitz' immediate superior. (In his memoirs,
Schellenberg attempts to show that Müller had gradually
become an admirer of Stalin and his regime. He even
suspects him, as well as Bormann, of carrying on their own
game with Moscow, but gives no proof.) In Nazi Germany,
fighting among the clans took precedence over the interests
of the Third Reich. Evidence of this abounded—in one
instance, two emissaries from Schellenberg arrived in Paris
asking to question me and Kent about the Rado network.
Pannwitz made it quite clear to me that I was by no means
obligated to tell them what I knew.

Pannwitz' ambition was to infiltrate Soviet intelligence
networks in Sweden and Turkey with a view to expanding the
Great Game. Under cover of the commercial enterprise Au
Roi du Caoutchouc, Leo Grossvogel and I had lain the
foundations for intelligence activity in Denmark, Sweden,
and Finland. Renewing these liaisons depended solely on Leo
and myself—and we took pains to make sure Pannwitz' vague
schemes came to nothing.

During this period, the Center's requests for information
were concerned primarily with Italy after the fall of Mussolini, and it was also at this time that, in various Berlin circles,
the Germans were trying to make contact with the west.
Allen Dulles himself met with several German emissaries in
Switzerland. The Center was informed of this thanks to the
Great Game.

As for Pannwitz, he was waiting for the visitor from the
Center with increasing nervousness. This false trail brought
him bitter disappointment: the emissary from Moscow never
showed up. I knew I would gain nothing from the whole

business but a few excursions to 3 Rue Edmond-Roger, plus the satisfaction of keeping the Nazis busy with false hopes. So at the end of August I went to the apartment where I had spent so many hours of warm intimacy with the Katz family. It had now been transformed into a trap, with Raichmann serving as the bait; but the bait was getting moldy—the quarry was not coming.

When Raichmann saw me come into the apartment, he didn't have the courage to speak to me. He remained at a distance, keeping his eyes lowered. As I pretended to wait for the messenger from the Center, I kept thinking about the fatal proclivity that had led Raichmann, Efremov, or even Mathieu to treason. They had followed different paths, but each of them had let himself be tempted and the result was the same: they were betraying their comrades. Pannwitz, however, judged and treated them differently. Mathieu, in his eyes, was an "honorable" collaborator; Efremov had opted for the Ukrainian nation; but Raichmann, in the eyes of the "master," was at the very bottom of the heap. No matter what he did, for Pannwitz, he was and would always be a dirty kike.

Pannwitz did not forget these distinctions when he left Paris precipitously just before the liberation. In his hideout, the defeated butcher remembered that he had received from the Third Reich this first commandment: a visceral hatred of the Jews. Mathieu was paid off—oh, yes!—and discharged. He had served well, betrayed well, and he deserved the wages of his treason, and "freedom." Efremov the Ukrainian was also entitled to a special dispensation. He was given false papers and enough money to get safely to Latin America. But Raichmann was imprisoned in Belgium. He had not understood that even if he turned traitor, a Jew could never redeem himself in the eyes of the Nazis.

Ten days later, we returned to 3 Rue Edmond-Roger, according to Pannwitz' plan, still waiting for the emissary from Moscow. Katz came with us. At this time Raichmann made one last attempt to save himself in our eyes. He took Katz aside and instructed him to tell me that he knew that we were continuing the struggle and that he regretted his attitude. He offered as excuses the threats that had been made concerning his wife and children, but also the treason of his superior, Efremov, who had turned him in along with the others. Now he was ready to do something, to redeem himself. Katz pretended not to understand.

It was impossible to trust Raichmann. He had betrayed once, and he would betray again. Tomorrow, next week, at the first opportunity. He had sealed his fate with his own hands. When one has been abandoned to the mercies of the enemy, only two alternatives remain. And between collaboration and resistance, there is an unbridgeable abyss.

26

"The Big Chief Has Escaped!"

One day in early September, 1943, Willy Berg came to see me in the room where I was imprisoned in Neuilly. This was not unusual, but as soon as he came in I noticed something uncharacteristic about his attitude. He seemed very excited, as if he had just heard an extraordinary piece of news. I was intrigued, and even worried, although I was careful to conceal my apprehension. In fact, what he told me made my blood run cold.

"It's fantastic—Duval has been arrested!"

In my night-written January report, I had insisted particularly that Fernand Pauriol—Duval—disappear. He had been the object of a tireless manhunt, but at the beginning of the summer I had learned from a reliable source that the Germans had lost track of him. How had he fallen into the hands of the Gestapo? I was very upset. Berg soon provided the explanation.

Fernand had been arrested August 13 at Pierrefitte, north of Paris. A few days before, one of the communist radio stations had fallen into the hands of the Gestapo. One of the pianists had "managed" to escape, and he made contact with Pauriol. Pauriol agreed to meet him, although the whole affair smelled fishy, and thus fell into the trap that had been laid for him.

The Gestapo, meanwhile, did not really know whom they were dealing with. Since 1940, Fernand had been one of the most effective militants of the communist underground. He ran the radio service and was also connected with the Red Orchestra. It was he who trained the pianists. He had also built a number of transmitting sets and, in addition, he had been in charge of the liaison between Juliette and the party leaders. He had played a leading role in Operation Juliette in January. He had received the material addressed to the Center and had seen that the precious package got into the

270

hands of the party. Since the arrests at the Rue des Atrébates in Brussels on December 13, 1941, he and Leo Grossvogel had organized a special group in charge of verifying arrests within the groups of the Red Orchestra in Belgium as well as in France. Finally, before my arrest, he and I had worked out a system of making contacts that would by now have revealed to him the activities of the Sonderkommando against the Center. So he too was in on the Great Game. This should give an idea of the role played by Fernand Pauriol.

He insisted stubbornly that he was nothing but a mechanic, an unimportant agent. Alas, at the end of the month, the men of the Sonderkommando, going through a card file of persons suspected of belonging to the Communist Party, came across Fernand Pauriol's photograph, and realized that they had arrested the famous "Duval," whom they had temporarily given up seeking.

It was quite a blow. I knew Fernand well, and I was certain that he was capable of giving up his life, but despite his courage, how long would he be able to stand the martyrdom that awaited him? Who could guarantee that under torture not a single name would escape his lips? My confidence in him remained intact, yet I nevertheless prepared myself for the possibility that everything I had succeeded in putting together would fall apart, and that my own "game" would be completely exposed.

From Berg, who hardly needed coaxing, I learned what treatment Fernand was receiving, and unfortunately my apprehensions were confirmed. It was a calculated combination of unbearable torture and quiet conversation. The torturers asked him one question of capital importance to them, over and over: what had the leaders of the Communist Party told Moscow about my arrest and about the arrests of the other members of the Red Orchestra? He replied invariably that on a few occasions he had received small packages, which he had delivered—without ever opening them—to an agent who was unknown to him. He insisted that his activity was confined to playing intermediary between Juliette and the upper echelon.

Attempts at persuasion, torture, coercion, all failed to get him to change his answer. He held fast. The Sonderkommando threatened to arrest and execute his wife, Hélène, and his daughter, but it was wasted effort. This wonderful man, this extraordinary combatant, faced his tormenters without giving an inch, for an entire year. A year under the regime of the Gestapo, while Pannwitz and his henchmen, who were perfectly aware of the importance of their catch, never gave up hope of one day extracting his secret.

I lived in anguish through these early days of September, 1943. I spent my days and my nights—long nights without sleep—torn by conflicting feelings, a prey to the wildest fantasies, trying to figure out how to proceed, how to change the course of events, which from here on seemed inexorable. The days went by. Through Berg, I followed Fernand's calvary almost blow by blow. He still was not talking. For my own part, I was ready to suffer the worst. My fate, but above all the future of the Great Game, was being decided in a torture chamber where a man was learning the limits of human suffering. He did not reach them; he was a hero.

One disaster followed another. On the 10th of September, I learned through Berg that the Sonderkommando had scored another point—they had captured a radio broadcasting station of the Communist Party near Lyon. A large number of dispatches and files had been confiscated. The Germans were convinced that they had finally discovered the central underground station of the Communist Party leaders. Among the coded dispatches, they hoped to find messages sent to Moscow about the Red Orchestra.

The storm threatened to break any day. I learned that the Sonderkommando had decided to bring their special team of code experts, headed by the celebrated Dr. Vauck, to Paris. On September 11, on the Rue des Saussaies, I saw Dr. Vauck at work with his assistants; Berg, who was there too, told me the deciphering was going very well. The only problem would be to recognize among all these dispatches those that had to do with the Red Orchestra. But Berg added that this would be "the work of a day or two."

This was very instructive, and overwhelming—I knew that the Communist Party had a big broadcasting station somewhere in the south of France, and I assumed my report delivered to Juliette in January must have been sent by that channel. More serious still; since the report I had made on my scraps of paper had not been encoded by me, but according to the code of the party, if Vauck succeeded in breaking that code, the Sonderkommando would read my information in black and white.

The conclusion was blindingly obvious: the Great Game was on the point of being exposed. I had to act, and act at once before it was too late. The nights of the 10th, 11th, and 12th of September were one long nightmare for me. At any moment I might hear that they were in possession of the truth; at any moment I expected to see the sneering faces of Pannwitz and his accomplices appear before me. The idea of torture or death did not frighten me—it was the companion of my days. But I did fear—and I felt it in every fiber of my body—the supreme humiliation of having Giering's words at the time of my arrest come true: "Herr Otto, you have lost." To be defeated in the eyes of these thugs——

Impossible! I had to escape. Escape meant resistance. Escape meant the hope of going down fighting. During those days of inner turmoil, I was careful not to let my face betray the upheavals of my spirit. I spent hours on end chatting with Berg as if nothing had happened. I faced Pannwitz and the other members of the Sonderkommando; I spoke to them soothingly, assuring them with absolute poise, but at the price of constant tension, that I would be happy to see the decoded dispatches confirm my assumptions about the information sent by the Communist Party to Moscow.

On September 11th, during the walk we were permitted to take in the garden, I told Hillel what had happened. He came to the same conclusion as I, that we were in danger of being discovered at any moment. I suggested that he and I escape together on the night of the 12th. Getting out of my room and the basement where Katz was imprisoned would require no great skill, and reaching the main door, where a Slovak soldier was on guard duty, would not be much more difficult. With a little luck we could hope to knock out the guard, get through the door, and close it behind us. In our favor, we knew that the sentry was usually drunk—but we would probably have to reckon with the other guards. Nevertheless, we had a chance of succeeding.

Katz approved of the idea of escape but he told me that he felt he did not have the right, and that the prospect of dying in prison would not alter his decision. The reason he gave was that his wife, Cecile, and his two children were under the surveillance of the Gestapo at the Château de Billeron, and that the butchers would take it out on them if he were to disappear. I gave this argument its due weight, but I reminded him that he had already risked the lives of his family at the time of Operation Juliette.

"That was different," he replied. "Then I was acting for the common cause, to give the Center the key to the Sonderkommando's strategy. So it was my right and my duty to risk not only my own life, but the lives of my family. The stake was too high, and transcended considerations of personal morality. But today it's only a question of myself, and it's not worth subjecting my wife and children to such a risk."

What could I say to him? What objection could I make? Katz belonged to that rare breed of men whose whole lives are directed toward total self-denial and self-sacrifice. No, there was nothing I could answer. But we both knew very well that once I had left, the bestial violence of the Gestapo would be unleashed against him.

The next day I told Hillel about the new escape plan I had devised. He wished me luck and asked me, in the event that I succeeded, to do everything in my power to save his wife and children. That was his only wish. On the evening of the 12th of September, then, I said goodbye to my old traveling companion. It was all we could do to master our emotion.

Now I had to concentrate all my attention on my plan. The game would be a close one, and there would be no margin for improvisation. I reviewed the elements of the problem, and weighing my chances, I concluded that the circumstances had probably never been so favorable. Berg called for me every day at the prison in Neuilly and took me to the Rue des Saussaies. I had had occasion to observe that the surveillance had gradually been relaxed. The other cars, which had flanked us in the beginning, had been eliminated. Originally a guard had accompanied Berg in our own car, but lately there had been only the driver, a man from the Gestapo. With the driver concentrating on his driving, and with Berg's suspicions somewhat lulled by the relationship we had developed, the circumstances were, in fact, optimum. Owing to his various family problems, Berg was emotionally vulnerable. His health was poor, and he was seeking relief in the bottle. In his intervals of sobriety, he almost always complained of violent pains in the stomach.

Berg's vulnerability was a chink in the armor of the Sonderkommando that I had promised myself to exploit—a chink that, in fact, I had already made considerable use of in gaining his confidence. I had shown an interest in his health, I had advised him to see a doctor, and I had promised that one day I would take him to the Pharmacie Bailly at 15 Rue de Rome, where I told him he could find the ideal remedy for his pain. This suggestion was not made at random, since the pharmacy was one of a list of places I had had in mind for some time as lending themselves to my escape. It so happened that the Pharmacie Bailly had the interesting characteristic of having two doors, one on the Rue de Rome and the other on the Rue du Rocher.

When I arrived on the 12th at the Rue des Saussaies, Dr. Vauck informed me, with an assurance that was unmistakable, that he would be able to decode the dispatches the next day. So September 13th was the final deadline for my escape. After that the trap would close inexorably around me. I put the final touches to my plan. The next day Berg would call for me, as he did every day, to go to Rue des Saussaies, where we would arrive around noon. He was sure to suggest that we stop at the pharmacy, and he would come in with me. Instead of going upstairs, I planned to head directly for the cash register, and then escape through the opposite door. Berg would immediately be at a disadvantage. Shouting in German in the middle of a crowd of French people—it was always crowded in the Pharmacie Bailly—would not be very effective, and firing at me would involve the obvious risk of hitting customers. If he tried to chase me, I was counting on my own speed and his more or less perpetual state of intoxication. After I had left the pharmacy, I hoped to reach the Metro station in a few minutes, go to the end of the Neuilly line, and then take the bus to Saint Germain, where I had a preliminary stopping place. It was out of the question for me to take a train at the Gare Saint-Lazare, for once the alert had gone out, there was a strong possibility that the Gestapo would surround the area and block all the exits. I was not forgetting that I would have proper identification, since, as I have said, when we set out Berg always handed me an identity card and a sum of money.

I was ready. All night long, scenes flashed through my mind, and I saw in advance the film of what would be my successful escape.

September 13. I was a little feverish. I hoped that nothing would come along to upset my plan, that Berg, who was sicker than usual, would not cancel his visit and send someone else in his place. No, everything went smoothly. He arrived at 11:30 sharp. We got in the car and drove through the gate. I turned around: Hillel was there, and I waved goodbye to my comrade in arms. I knew that I would never see him again. We could not say a word, and this final farewell was silent.

The next thing I knew, we were in Paris. We were almost there. Berg handed me my identity card and five hundred francs. With all the sympathy in the world I asked him,

"How do you feel today?"

"Worse than ever." He seemed even more depressed than usual. "We've got to go to the pharmacy."

He was dozing when we stopped in front of the Pharmacie Bailly. I nudged him gently and asked,

"We're here. Are you coming in?"

Then he gave me this incredible answer:

"No. Go upstairs and buy the medicine, and come right back."

What was he up to? Was it a trick? Was he trying to test me? Very calmly, I looked him straight in the eyes and reminded him,

"But Berg, this pharmacy has another exit."

"I have complete confidence in you," he replied, laughing. "And besides, you know I'm too tired to climb the stairs."

I did not have to be told twice. I walked into the pharmacy, and almost immediately walked out the other side. In a few minutes I was in the Metro. I transferred to Pont de Neuilly. I had incredible luck: as soon as I got out of the Metro, the bus for Saint Germain was waiting for me. I was gradually recovering my calm. Nevertheless, with an automatic reflex, I looked around. No one was looking at me, so I started imagining Berg's reactions. For at least ten minutes he would not be surprised by my absence, for that was the minimum time necessary to make a purchase in a big store during the rush hour. After his curiosity had been aroused, he would walk up to the second floor of the pharmacy and look around for me; that would also take a good ten minutes. When he didn't find me, it would take him another ten minutes, if he was lucky, to get to Rue des Saussaies and give the alert. The Sonderkommando would not reach the scene of my escape until forty to fifty minutes after that. By that time I would be in a much quieter place.

I arrived at Saint Germain at half past noon. I was free; but only an escaped prisoner being hunted by the Gestapo could know how precarious that new freedom was.

Why had I chosen Saint Germain? In the first place, because I had decided to seek refuge among people I did not know personally rather than at the home of trusted friends. It seemed unnecessary and dangerous to expose members of the Red Orchestra who were still at liberty. Besides, the Gestapo could very well have infiltrated their agents among them. I knew that Georgie de Winter had rented a little house in Vésinet in 1942. I did not know whether she was still there, but even she was not that safe from complications. As an American citizen, she had been forced to go into hiding when the United States entered the war against the Axis. We had found her a Belgian identity card in the name of Thevenet, according to which she had been born in a village in the north. But Georgie's papers would not have stood up under a thorough examination.

I also knew that during the summer of 1942, Georgie's son had been in a boarding school in Saint Germain, run by two sisters. But this raised another question: would he still be there? Would he have been moved to another school in the meantime? In any case, I felt that by seeking refuge there I would be making the safest choice, the least risky. I could tell them I was a friend of Georgie's and ask for a place to stay and also, I hoped, find out where she was.

I found the boarding school without difficulty. A young girl with very Russian features came to the door. I decided to be completely open, and explain my situation to the two sisters. To my great astonishment, they showed no emotion at the story of my escape—and that I shall never forget.

They told me Patrick had left their school and was living with a family in Suresnes. As for Georgie, she had given up her lease, but she might still be living in Vésinet. My hostesses tried to telephone her all afternoon and offered to let me stay with them in case I could not find her. Finally, that evening, they succeeded in getting Georgie on the phone. She rushed over, very moved to see me again, not at all afraid to be associated with a man hunted by the Gestapo, determined to act. We left the two sisters, after thanking them warmly.

What a day! For Pannwitz and his henchmen, September 13, 1943, was a black day on the calendar.

I felt I had scored a very important point against the Sonderkommando, that I had regained control of the situation. The battle was beginning again. Still, how could I not be aware of all that lay in store for me?

It did not take long to realize that the house in Vésinet where Georgie gave me refuge was not the ideal hideout. In this rather isolated spot, the two of us would inevitably attract attention. We had to get out of there as quickly as possible. I was not—obviously—an ordinary escaped prisoner; I carried enormous responsibilities on my shoulders. Until that day, Georgie knew nothing about my work, but only that I had been engaged in the struggle against the Nazis. She never asked any questions, but she realized now that since she was directly involved in my activities, she was running enormous risks. I had involved not only her and her son, but all the people who had helped me.

The fight would go on, of that I was sure. I had no intention of crawling into a hole until the war was over. As soon as possible I had to renew contact with Michel, the Communist Party liaison, and inform Moscow of my escape. No matter what the risk, I had to find out whether the report I had made on scraps of paper back in January had gone through the Communist Party broadcasting station that had been taken by the Gestapo. The whole future of the Great Game depended on the answer to this question. Finally, protecting my friends in prison—who stood to suffer the consequences of my escape—was also a task of the utmost importance. I had only a few days to gain these objectives. After that, I had no reason to doubt that the pack that was after me would be closing in.

"Otto has escaped!"

When Berg, sicker than ever, returned to the Rue des Saussaies with this news, everyone went into a panic. Pannwitz realized at once that he would bear the brunt of the blame. As I had foreseen, he reacted like the great hunter, who tracks the game with every means at his disposal. The man who conducted the repression throughout Czechoslovakia, after Heydrich's assassination, knew what to do. The Pharmacie Bailly was surrounded and dozens of customers were arrested. Pannwitz had the entire building searched, thinking that I was hiding in it somewhere, waiting for the search to be over. Then the Gare Saint-Lazare was surrounded, as I had anticipated, and all departing trains were

thoroughly searched. The Gestapo checked all the places—
the stores, cafés, restaurants, barbershops—where I had
gone during my accompanied outings. Pannwitz used a
fishnet strategy. He imagined that if he arrested a hundred
people, he would find one who would give him some
interesting clues; but he was mistaken. So then he resorted
to the only method he had left: the use of terror against the
militants of the Red Orchestra.

To throw Pannwitz off the scent, I wrote him a letter. I told
him I had not escaped, but been forced to disappear. Two
strangers had approached me in the pharmacy and had given
me the password agreed upon with the Center for meetings
with the counterespionage group. The two men had assured
me that I was about to be arrested by the Gestapo, and that
they had orders to take me to a safe place. Then I explained
to Pannwitz that I had decided that it was necessary, "in
order not to jeopardize our common cause," not to argue with
the two men, but go with them. They took me to a car, and
we left Paris. A hundred kilometers outside the capital, we
took a train for the Swiss border. I added that I took
advantage of a moment of inattention on the part of my
guards to mail this letter at the railway station in Besançon,
and that I would keep him informed of the course of events.
In a postscript, I advised Pannwitz not to hold Berg responsible for what had happened since in any case his presence in
the pharmacy would not have changed anything. One of the
two sisters at the boarding school in Saint Germain agreed to
take a train to Besançon and mail my letter from there.

In taking this step, I was trying to make Pannwitz believe
that I was far from Paris, and in this way to put a curb on the
manhunt, but above all, in the event that the Gestapo did not
find my report in the files of the radio station, I wanted to
make it possible for the Center in Moscow to continue the
Great Game in spite of my escape.

Immediately, and with great courage, Georgie began trying to make contact with the Communist Party. The one way
I had of reaching the leaders of the party was calling a certain
telephone number and leaving the message: "Monsieur Jean

has just had surgery, and he needs medicine." On that signal, the party was supposed to send a liaison agent to each of four prearranged meeting places, north, south, east, and west of Paris. Two days after Georgie's phone call, I met a young girl in Vésinet and asked her for identity papers, poison, and news about that January report that had been transmitted through Juliette. She returned two days later with the papers I had requested and a capsule of cyanide for me to take if worse came to worst.

At the same time, I learned the disconcerting piece of news that the party radio station in the Lyon region was used only to broadcast propaganda material to other regions. The Gestapo had confiscated nothing but leaflets containing no secret information. Jacques Duclos—as I learned later—had decided that my report to the Center was too important to send over the radio, so it had been taken to London by a special courier and then forwarded to Moscow through diplomatic channels. It was obvious, therefore, that my escape had been unnecessary. If I had known these facts on the 13th instead of on the 17th, I would no doubt still be in Neuilly. There was not the slightest possibility that the Sonderkommando would discover the secret of the Great Game.

Now there was the serious risk that my escape might compromise the Great Game, to which the Center attached so much importance. I could not let the Gestapo capture me alive. Having the poison in my pocket restored my strength and confidence, but I came close to swallowing it the day after I had put it there.

That morning, Georgie had locked the door from the outside, as she did every time she left the villa. The shutters stayed closed all day long. We took this elementary precaution to make it seem that the place was uninhabited. Anyway, there was a long ring at the door, and then another. I was wide awake, ready to make my escape, but the visitor did not insist. It was a false alarm.

The same scene was repeated the next day. We were wrenched abruptly from sleep by a violent knocking at the

door. In a few seconds I had thrown on my clothes and
checked my cyanide capsule. I already had one leg over the
window sill and was ready to jump out, expecting the front
door to be broken in, but the noise stopped and I heard the
landlord explaining to Georgie that for several days he had
been trying to show the villa to the new tenants, and since he
had found the place all closed up, he had decided to try his
luck the first thing in the morning.

These two incidents persuaded us to act quickly. We had
just had proof that we were at the mercy of an indiscreet
word. We had to leave, that was obvious, but doing it was not
so easy with all the bloodhounds of the Gestapo on our heels.
Where could we go? After examining various possibilities, we
decided to ask the Queyries, the family little Patrick was
staying with, to take me in. They lived in a small house in
Suresnes. Their mother had a small flat in an apartment
house nearby; she was going to be away for a few days, and
they offered to let me stay there. I accepted immediately.

So I had a few days' headstart on the Sonderkommando—
yet prudence dictated that I not nourish too many illusions.
Pannwitz' men would certainly try to pick up my trail through
Georgie. Sooner or later they would work their way from
Saint Germain to Vésinet, and from Vésinet to Suresnes. A
week later, in fact, they had identified the boarding school in
Saint Germain, after having arrested and imprisoned (again,
Pannwitz left no stone unturned) numerous relatives of
Georgie's, both near and distant. In Brussels, her parents and
several of her friends were harassed by the Gestapo. Probably this was the way they learned that Georgie's son was in a
boarding school outside Paris. One piece of information was
enormously helpful to them: knowing Georgie had taken
dancing lessons in Place Clichy. They went to the dance
school and learned from a friend of hers, Denise, that Patrick
was in Saint Germain.

The Gestapo were getting warm, of this I had proof. I had
not been at Suresnes three days when I received a phone call
from the two sisters, informing me that a man had come to
the door claiming that he had something for Madame de

Winter. From the description they gave I recognized Kent, who had become the "brown eminence" of the Sonderkommando, and who kept turning up at all the hot points of the investigation. Three days later, another group of "visitors" showed up at the boarding school. Among them was Hillel Katz!

When I escaped, Pannwitz immediately focused all his efforts on Hillel. The head of the Sonderkommando had conceived the idea that through Hillel he could get to me. So before showing his claws, the monster tried his hand at trickery. First he asked Katz to telephone his wife, Cecile, and make an urgent appointment with her in Paris. Cecile knew very well that her husband had been in the hands of the Gestapo since December, 1942. She also knew that she herself was under constant surveillance, and that if she tried to escape she would expose herself to reprisals. She had no alternative but to respond to the call—she met Hillel in a café; he was accompanied by a stranger. Katz, who must have had no choice but to follow Pannwitz' instructions, nevertheless managed to reveal the truth about me: "My friends," he told her, "are very worried about Otto, and they are expecting his immediate return." She understood, this meant that I had escaped.

Only Pannwitz believed in the effectiveness of his method. In spite of his confidence he had not made an inch of progress, was ready to fall back on methods that were more familiar to him—arrests and torture—when he decided to try one last maneuver. He sent Katz to Saint Germain along with his henchmen. Here again Katz acquitted himself wonderfully; the bait eluded the hunter. After asking some innocuous questions about Georgie and Patrick, at the last minute he managed to whisper to one of the sisters: "Monsieur Gilbert's life is in danger; the Gestapo are after him." The heroic Hillel—who fought for our cause to the very end, and who, in order to save the lives of other people, risked his own.

Much later, on the day of the liberation of Paris, I went back to the house where we had been imprisoned at Neuilly, with a friend, Alex Lesovoy. Monsieur Prodhomme, the French concierge of the building, told us about the martyr-dom of Hillel Katz. About two weeks after my escape, the Sonderkommando started taking him to the Rue des Saus-saies during the night. They would bring him back every morning in a frightful condition. His calvary became more and more painful. The brutality he had to endure became worse; his wounds did not have time to heal from one torture session to the next. The concierge took advantage of the moments when he brought Hillel his food to exchange a few words with him and to learn what he was going through. The butchers of the Sonderkommando were accusing him of having planned my escape, of knowing where I was hiding, and refusing to tell them. They accused him of getting word to me at the time they planned the visit to Saint Germain.

Monsieur Prodhomme remembered vividly the day when Katz, his face and hands horribly ravaged, told him, "After the war Monsieur Gilbert will certainly come back here. Tell him that in spite of the torture and the suffering, I regret nothing, and that I am very happy to have done what I have done. My only request is that he look after my children." A few hours later, the men of the Gestapo took him away.

We never learned the circumstances of Hillel Katz' death, but Pannwitz the butcher knows—he who had him tortured, and then murdered, with or without the semblance of a trial. I can still see him, Hillel, that exemplary fighter. For him, heroism was no more than the natural behavior of someone who has dedicated his life to a better future.

In Saint Germain, the Sonderkommando arrested the two sisters. Very courageously, they did not talk. They revealed nothing about the trip to Besançon or the letter Pannwitz had received from me. The next day, however, the Gestapo knocked on the door of the villa at Vésinet. The pack was getting closer and in a few days, a few hours perhaps, their howls would be heard in Suresnes. So once again we had to act fast. I was able to persuade Madame Queyrie to leave—she and little Patrick would take refuge with her sister-in-law in Corrèze. Once again, Georgie and I had to move on.

Where would we go? We thought it over, and I decided on the
Spaaks, Suzanne and Claude, whom I had met for the first
time during the summer of 1942. I had gone to see them then
in their apartment on the Rue de Beaujolais, to warn them of
the arrest of their friends Mira and Hersch Sokol, and I had
been very much impressed by the composure with which
they had received this news. Not for a moment did they
doubt Mira and Hersch. They were convinced that the pair
would choose death before confession—and that was in fact
what happened. The Sokols, adding their names to the long
list of martyrs of the resistance against Nazism, carried what
they knew about the Spaaks, along with so many other
secrets, to the grave.

Georgie went to see the Spaaks and told them what was
happening, and they assured her that they would do everything in their power to help me. A spark of light in the
darkness.

Claude Spaak came to see me in my room in Suresnes.
What a consolation it was to know that we were no longer
alone! The most urgent necessity was to find me a hideout,
provided—and we were all agreed on this point—it had no
connection with the militants of the resistance. My next
priority was to re-establish regular contact with the French
Communist Party.

But first, a hiding place—since there was no question of
staying any longer at Suresnes—to serve as a way station
before we reached a safer refuge. Denise, Georgie's friend
from dancing class, had given her the keys to her attic
apartment on the Rue Chabanais, and we moved in on the
evening of November 24th. I agreed to this solution against
my better judgment. Something told me that Denise was not
very trustworthy, and that we might have just put our heads
into the lion's mouth. I spent a very restless night, unable to
sleep, listening to every noise, expecting the Gestapo to
appear at our door at any moment.

It was with a real sense of relief that we left this dubious
refuge the next day at dawn and went to the Spaaks'. My
forebodings proved correct and we could congratulate our-

selves on getting out of there in a hurry, for after Denise was arrested, she cooperated with enthusiasm. She divulged the address of the Queyries, which earned her an immediate release. Pannwitz was sure he had me. The pack descended on the villa, but they were too late. The prey had not yet been cornered—although Monsieur Queyrie, who had stayed behind, was given a difficult time of it.

Pannwitz then tried a different approach. He set a trap that he thought very clever, believing as he did that Patrick was my son. Since he had succeeded in finding out where Madame Queyrie was hiding with the child, he decided to use the boy to put pressure on me. He had a "neighbor" telephone her and say that her husband had broken his leg and that she must return to Paris immediately. But the trap was rather obvious, and Madame Queyrie sensed the danger and remained in Corrèze.

The head of the Sonderkommando was not discouraged. Very well, he decided, since Otto's "son" won't come to us, we will go to him. And he mounted an expedition to go and get little Patrick in Corrèze. Pannwitz put no faith in the demagogical and soothing speeches of Dr. Goebbels, who at the end of 1943 was shouting his confidence in the victory of the Third Reich. He knew very well that Corrèze was in the heart of territory that bristled with Maquis, the French guerrillas, and so he organized a regular military operation. Vehicles packed with Gestapo set off, their objective to arrest a dangerous agent of the Red Orchestra who was all of four years old.

The mission was accomplished. Pannwitz rubbed his hands. After hunting me down for two weeks, he now thought he had the key to my arrest. The son of the Big Chief is in our possession, he thought; we will soon have the father. He was even more certain now because he had made what he considered a decisive test: when he showed my photograph to Patrick and asked the boy to identify the "gentleman," the answer had been, "Papa Nanou." Now he was sure; but the head of the Sonderkommando did not know that Patrick used to call me by that name just as he used to call Madame Queyrie "Mamie Annie."

Although I was always pleased to see Pannwitz blunder, I could not, of course, help worrying about the child. I also suspected that Pannwitz would do everything he could to get his hands on Georgie. We learned later that the men of the Gestapo were divided about what to do with Patrick. Some wanted to send him to Germany; others preferred to keep him at their disposal. Since after all it would be difficult for them to put him in prison, they placed him with Madame Queyrie in Saint Germain, in a school that had been requisitioned by the Germans. They left him there until January, 1944, at which time they transferred the two of them to the house in Suresnes, which was under constant surveillance. They hoped I would be unable to bear being separated from my "son," and would start prowling around the neighborhood and fall into the trap.

Pannwitz had made a serious mistake; I was now hiding out with the Spaaks. But in spite of the great confidence I had in the Spaaks, the fact was that this was the least safe of all the places I had hidden since my escape. I knew that both the Spaaks belonged to the resistance, but at that time I did not suspect the degree to which Suzanne, in particular, was involved in a variety of underground activities. In 1942, she had devoted herself to rescuing Jewish children, and had been a militant in the national movement against racism; but I did not realize that by September, 1943, at the time she took me in, she was also working with several Gaullist and communist organizations. She took part in the most perilous actions, without regard for the danger. Consequently she was very much exposed. We decided it was wiser to part company, and we spent the next two nights at the Oratoire, a protestant church near the Louvre. We were received by the minister, who had been providing rooms for the Jewish children Suzanne Spaak saved from the clutches of the Germans.

After the Oratoire I ended up, thanks to the help of the Spaaks, in a home for the retired. It seemed to be one of the best possible places to elude the Gestapo, but the word "retired" sent chills down my spine.

27

A Close Duel with the Gestapo

At the age of thirty-nine, the head of the Red Orchestra was forced to masquerade as a somewhat senile retired gentleman in a quiet house, the Maison Blanche in Bourg-la-Reine. I had no choice. I decided to play the part of a sickly pensioner who required the care of a nurse. Since it was out of the question for Georgie to be there, we called on the services of Madame May, the widow of a rather well-known songwriter. Madame May hated the Nazis and was ready to take part in the underground struggle. We had Georgie to thank for the discovery of this rare bird; finding a woman who was completely trustworthy and determined enough to face risks of this sort was no easy task. In the eyes of the outside world, she would be a devoted old aunt. In fact, she acted as a liaison agent.

The first few days at the Maison Blanche were peaceful, but I noticed that several of the boarders seemed to be having as much trouble as I in playing the role of peaceful old men. Certain unmistakable signs betrayed both their real age and their real condition. I had the impression—and it worried me—that they too had been obliged to elude the curiosity of the Germans. The atmosphere was cordial, but everyone kept his distance, as if afraid of his neighbor's indiscretions, and we all took our meals in our rooms. Yes, it was a very peculiar retirement home.

The chances of thwarting Pannwitz' plans were not very good, but it was worth trying; so at the end of September I wrote him a second letter. In my first communication, I had told him I was leaving for Switzerland in the company of two Soviet counterespionage agents—but since then he had picked up my trail in Saint Germain, Vésinet, and Suresnes. Since I had to provide a plausible explanation, I told him that, with the consent of the counterespionage agents, I had returned to Paris.

I can hear the obvious objections: really, could I think of nothing better than to tell the Sonderkommando the name of the town I was in? For a man who had succeeded in escaping them and was still on the run, didn't that amount to putting the hunter back on the trail? Wasn't I taking an enormous risk?

I can understand the reaction, but the rather elementary psychology of the Gestapo agent must be borne in mind. If you told him you were in Paris, he would look for you in the four corners of Europe.

Besides, Paris is the ideal place for going underground; if the hunted man can succeed in cutting himself off from previous contacts, he will have a good chance of evading his pursuers.

I deliberately gave my letter a tone of calm certainty. I expressed my indignation at the attitude of the Sonderkommando, and accused them of knowingly creating panic by arresting innocent people who were strangers to my network. I added that in the future my behavior toward the Sonderkommando would depend on the release of the persons who had been arrested.

Pannwitz believed that the Sonderkommando had been in control of the Great Game from the beginning, so he was disconcerted by both the tone and the content of my letter. He puzzled over my intentions. He could not understand why, after my escape, I had not revealed the whole truth to the Center—of course, he did not know that Moscow had been aware of the true situation since Operation Juliette.

My primary objective was to re-establish stable communication with the Center through the intermediary of the leaders of the French Communist Party. I hoped to achieve this with the help of Suzanne Spaak. She was not a member of the party, but in her work rescuing Jewish children, she had collaborated with a young physician, Dr. Chertok, who was in contact with a communist militant, the lawyer Lederman. Lederman was one of the main leaders of Jewish resistance in France, and I had met him when I was a militant for the French Communist Party. On the national level, he was in touch with Comrade Kowalski, head of the groups of foreign resisters, who was assistant head of immigrant labor within the Communist Party.

I knew Kowalski well, and he was just the man I needed. He was in contact both with the party leaders and with Michel, the militant who had been the liaison between the French Communist Party and myself since 1941.

Getting to Kowalski was not an easy task; you had to go through the whole hierarchy. I started things moving in this direction, and in the meantime, on the 1st and the 15th of each month, I sent a messenger to the Buttes-Chaumont Church, which had been chosen a long time ago as a permanent point of contact with the Center. But was it still? Georgie had gone to the rendezvous on the 1st of October and had found no one.

The Spaaks had succeeded in getting Georgie away, with the help of two English friends, Ruth Peters and Antonia Lyon-Smith, who were living incognito in Paris. Antonia Lyon-Smith had offered to write to Dr. de Joncker, a relative of hers who lived in Saint-Pierre-de-Chartreuse, right on the Swiss border. A confirmed and committed anti-Nazi, the doctor took advantage of his privileged locale to help refugees escape into Switzerland. While we were waiting for his answer, we decided that Georgie would go and hide out in a little village in La Beauce, near Chartres. There she would wait for a signal to go to the Swiss border. But Georgie could not stand the wait. She arrived at Bourg-la-Reine on the 14th of October, a nervous wreck; I was able to persuade her to return to La Beauce. Before she left, on the morning of the 15th of October, without my knowledge, she gave Madame May a slip of paper on which she had written the new address where she could be reached. Madame May kept it with her.

It was agreed that Madame May would go to the Buttes-Chaumont Church, the possible point of contact with the Center, that same day. I went over the preparations for this rendezvous in detail with Madame May. She was to remain a discreet distance from the church and—I was very insistent on this point—she was not to go to her apartment, which was right around the corner, after making the contact.

You will recall that Denise had once done the *pas de deux* with Georgie in dancing class. Now, it was clear, she was doing the tango with the Sonderkommando. After the raid at Suresnes, we were convinced that she had dipped one toe into treason, and by now she was up to her ankles. Denise was well acquainted with Madame May, and with the address of her apartment.

I had got to know Madame May during my stay at the Maison Blanche. Although she was already an old lady, she was full of energy and enthusiasm. She was intelligent and, like all the people who had helped me since my escape, violently anti-Nazi; she was generous, courageous, but without the slightest notion of what underground and illegal activities involved. She belonged to that legion of wonderful amateurs whose lack of experience made the work of the professionals in the Gestapo that much easier. She had told me that her only son, to whom she had transferred all her affection since the death of her husband, was a prisoner of war. I could just imagine the hideous coercion those thugs would subject her to if, by ill fortune, she fell into their clutches. I asked her, in case she should run into trouble, to remain silent at any price for at least two or three hours.

The rendezvous at the Buttes-Chaumont was set for noon. I expected her to return in an hour or an hour and a half. Time passed, and still she was not back. At three o'clock, still no sign of her. It did not take great psychic powers to conclude that she had run into trouble, and I began constructing theories.

I found it inconceivable that Madame May would have been bothered at the scene of a rendezvous whose coordinates were known only to Georgie, the Center, and myself. My second hypothesis was that she had disobeyed my explicit instructions and gone to her apartment. Alas, I learned later, that was what had happened. First she waited for a quarter of an hour by the church, but no one appeared. Then, instead of returning to Bourg-la-Reine, she decided to go to her apartment. Try to imagine the emotions of a mother who has gone a long time without news of her dearly beloved son, a prisoner of war—— I had insisted she return directly to Bourg-la-Reine—but a few steps away, almost within arm's reach, some letters might be waiting for her. So, come what may, she would go and see, she would risk everything. Instead of letters, what she found in her apartment was the French auxiliary of the Gestapo, Lafont's men. In Madame May's pocket they discovered the little slip of paper with Georgie's address in La Beauce.

It was Pannwitz who had installed the murderous henchmen of the infamous Henri Chamberlin-Lafont in Madame May's apartment. He had confidence in them; they had already given him guarantees of their servility and their "competence." He knew that with them, any visitors who showed up at Madame May's apartment would be efficiently interrogated.

However, things did not proceed exactly as he had anticipated. Furious at having been trapped, Madame May began distributing blows right and left to Lafont's men, who were more in the habit of giving them than taking them. The killers were for once on the receiving end, and they had difficulty subduing her. They called Pannwitz, who rushed over—and he took some blows as well.

After this things got worse for Madame May. They took her to the Rue des Saussaies, where they gave her an ultimatum: her son's life, or the addresses. The poor woman had no choice, but she managed to remain silent for a few hours. At about six o'clock in the evening, unable to hold out any longer, she broke down and gave my address at the Maison Blanche, and the Spaaks' address, and confessed that she served as a liaison between them and me.

Poor Madame May, she was not cut out for the underground life. In a few hours, the Gestapo had brought off a very dangerous coup. The Spaaks, Georgie, and I were all threatened.

I had to act very quickly. At about three o'clock, when Madame May had not returned, I went to Madame Parrend, the directress of the retired-people's home. I warned her that the Gestapo might arrive at any moment, advising her to alert all her "special" boarders. Immediately, and with absolute calm, she warned everyone who was in danger to leave the premises.

I arranged with Madame Parrend that if anyone telephoned for me she would say I had gone for a walk and would be back between seven and eight o'clock. I did not think Pannwitz would send the pack to the Maison Blanche right away, but would try to reassure me about Madame May's lateness. If the Sonderkommando thought I would not be back from my walk until seven, they would have the impression that I was not worried. I imagined that Pannwitz would concentrate all his forces on Bourg-la-Reine first, for he was not capable of conducting more than one operation at a time. I had to keep him occupied as long as possible with the Maison Blanche.

At about three-thirty I left the Maison Blanche. I had papers, provided by the Communist Party, that showed I had German origins. The chief advantage of these papers was that they allowed me to be on the street after curfew. I was careful to leave all my things, and not to close my door, to make it look as if I did not plan to be gone very long. To underline this idea in the mind of a possible visitor, I arranged a little scene: an open book—something very innocuous—on the table, the bed unmade, bottles of medicine on the night table. All this to persuade the men of the Gestapo to wait for my return.

I remained very calm. This had become almost a reflex when I sensed the approach of danger. I walked straight to Plessis-Robinson without stopping. The sun was shining and the streets were full of strollers. The passersby seemed gay and carefree, no doubt an illusion produced by the contrast between the seething of my mind, filled with a thousand preoccupations, and the apparent serenity of the people in their Sunday clothes.

By an amazing coincidence, I caught sight of Michel, my link with the leaders of the Communist Party. He was not alone. The temptation was great to go up to him, describe the dramatic struggle in which we were engaged, and ask for his advice and help, but I abandoned the idea immediately. I did not have the right to endanger his life. Perhaps I was already being followed, watched. Since my escape, so many misfortunes had occurred: the sisters in Saint Germain, the Queyries, Madame May, the Maison Blanche, and now the Spaaks. From now on, I forbade myself to have any contact whatsoever with anyone who might have to suffer the consequences.

I reminded myself that escapees from Nazi prisons and camps had more than once had to depend on nothing but their own resources; but this thought, although it strengthened my determination and revived my courage, did not provide the answer to the question that obsessed me: what should I do? And also: where should I go?

Night was falling, A hunted man is lonely. I asked myself again, what should I do? Suddenly, with a half-unconscious gesture, I hailed a taxi and gave the driver the address on the Rue de Beaujolais where the Spaaks lived.

A strange idea, to be sure, and I can hear the objection, which one need not be an expert in underground warfare to make: the Spaaks?—but that was literally throwing myself into Pannwitz' arms! Granted, but what else could I do to save my friends? I was taking a big risk, but I could not do otherwise.

At least there was one thing I was sure of: the Gestapo had gone into action. At about six o'clock, I had telephoned the Maison Blanche, and a strange voice—strange to me, at any rate—had answered:

"Madame Parrend is not here."

I had answered very calmly, "Would you please go to my room and tell my aunt, Madame May, that I'll be back about eight, and that she should expect me for supper?"

These words, I found out later, had delighted the members of the Sonderkommando. Reassured, more and more confident of the outcome, they had settled down comfortably and continued to wait for me. I was expected at the Maison Blanche; still, though, I could not convince myself that there wouldn't be a welcoming committee waiting in the Spaaks' apartment as well.

If the torturers of the Sonderkommando had once succeeded in breaking down Madame May's resistance, using their
customary methods, there was no reason why they would not
exploit their advantage, and increase the pressure. With them
this was a common practice, which unfortunately had proved
effective. A man who has been broken down by torture first
tries to limit his confession to a single name, a single fact.
Once the word has been spoken, he again finds within
himself the strength to resist; but these specialists in human
suffering and its limits, these connoisseurs of the psychological state of the victim, increase the torture until they have
obtained a complete confession. They know that they have
every chance of succeeding, and I had no illusions. Madame
May, already elderly, more vulnerable, at least physically,
than a young person full of life, ill prepared for the hazards of
underground life, would not have the resources of a Hillel
Katz or a Hersch Sokol, who died under torture without
talking.

The taxi stopped in front of the Spaaks' residence. The
countdown was beginning. I felt like those Russian officers in
the time of the czars who, for fun, used to press a gun to their
temples after putting a bullet in the cylinder at random.
Russian roulette, it had come to be called. It was a gamble:
sometimes the hammer would encounter only empty space,
but sometimes——

I got out of the car slowly, gathering my strength. I
was—once again—on the threshold of destiny. Impossible to
turn back, of course. I climbed the stairs, clutching the
cyanide capsule that was always with me now, and rang the
bell. A few seconds later, the door opened. I glanced in—and
met the eyes of my friend. He was by all appearances safe
and sound. I was happy, but under too much pressure to
express my joy. My inquiring glance held only one question,
which he immediately understood: are you alone, are they
here? His attitude told me I could relax, and I felt as if my
blood, which had been about to freeze in my veins, began to
circulate again. I told him in one breath:

"You must get out of here immediately!"

Claude's reaction was astonishing: "I thought when you rang it might be the Germans. Sooner or later, every resister must find himself in that situation. But you're being hunted night and day by the Gestapo, and you come to warn me in an apartment that could have been turned into a police trap? I can't believe it!"

"I had no choice, after what happened in Saint Germain," I answered. "Not one more victim—that's all I can think about."

It was true, the idea had become an obsession.

It was a moment of intense emotion, but we had no time to listen to the beating of our hearts or to savor our feelings. We had to act, confront the situation. We turned without transition to practical questions: where was his family, how could we warn them, protect them from Pannwitz' reprisals? We decided that since Suzanne and the children were due back from Orléans that evening at about nine, Claude would meet them at the station and take them to the home of some friends. Madame Spaak and the children would leave for Belgium as soon as possible, while Claude would remain in hiding in Paris.

So much for the Spaak family. But even as we spoke, another danger, even more difficult to ward off, suddenly occurred to us, requiring immediate decisions and action. My meeting with Kowalski, the representative of the Communist Party, had been set for the 22nd of October at Bourg-la-Reine. The exact time had not been fixed—Dr. Chertok was to telephone it to Claude Spaak a few days ahead of time. But Madame May before her arrest had been the go-between who told me the date of the meeting—so the whole thing had to be cancelled.

There was only a week between now and the rendezvous. To get to Kowalski you had to go through the hierarchy, by way of Dr. Chertok and the lawyer, Maître Lederman. Finding them in the shadows of the underground was like finding an honest man in Pannwitz' den of thieves—almost impossible. The idea that Kowalski, national leader of the units of foreign combatants, in touch with the high command

of the Franc-Tireurs et Partisans, and confidential agent of
the French Communist Party, might fall into the clutches of
the Gestapo, put me in a cold sweat. Obviously, this had to be
prevented at any cost. Before we parted, I worked out a
number of procedures with Claude. We agreed to meet again
on the evening of October 21st at the Church of La Trinité.

Claude and I walked slowly down the steps of his building,
not saying a word. Would we even see each other again? We
shook hands, and we were standing in front of the door,
about to say goodbye, when he asked me: "Where are you
going? Do you at least have a place to stay?"

"Don't worry about me, I have a hiding place."

My only hiding place, in fact, was the streets of Paris. A
poignant spectacle, these two men disappearing into the
darkness.

I walked into a bar and had a few drinks. I needed a chance
to think about the situation, to relive—at my leisure, so to
speak—this dramatic October 15th: first Georgie's departure;
my joy at knowing she would soon be out of danger; then the
wait for Madame May to come back from the rendezvous at
the church; my hasty departure from Bourg-la-Reine; my
visit to Claude Spaak. My only consolation was that I had not
submitted passively but had tried to ward off the enemy's
blows. By keeping the Sonderkommando at the Maison
Blanche, I had succeeded in saving the Spaaks.

"For the moment, we have won!"—the proud victory cry of
anti-Nazis everywhere—I felt it applied to my situation.
Alone in this little café, sitting in front of my glass, sought by
all the Gestapo, I had the morale of the victor. However, the
war was not over. I was careful not to be overly optimistic. I
had outwitted them—but for how long? What should I do?
Where should I go? What about tomorrow, and the day after
tomorrow?

I had just left Spaak, and already I was obliged to evaluate
and re-evaluate. One point was obvious, a very important
one. No doubt the Sonderkommando and their auxiliaries,
the Lafonts and their accomplices, were even now deploying

all their means to catch me. However, the dogs that stalked me were obliged to muffle their barking: Pannwitz and his gang had to take precautions, because they did not know whether I had informed Moscow. They had to be careful not to give away my escape. Suppose the Center was unaware of these recent events? By touching off a general alarm, by setting all the police after me, Pannwitz would risk arousing their suspicions.

In the street, in the movie theaters or cafés, I felt relatively safe. Nowhere was I more at ease—all things considered—than lost, anonymous, in the ebb and flow of the Parisian crowd. This feeling was all the more reassuring because with my German identity papers I had some rather important privileges, more freedom than a French citizen. For example, they gave me the right to be on the street at night.

What does a lucky German do when he is in Paris for a few days? He leads the gay life; so I would be a *bon vivant*. I had not suspected, though, how difficult it is to enjoy yourself when death is dogging your footsteps. When I left the bar, I went into a movie house. No use asking what film was playing that evening. All I remember is that the seat was comfortable, the darkness reassuring and restful. It passed the time, and that was good enough for me.

When the film was over, I went to the Gare Montparnasse. It was already quite late. I walked up and down the streets, waiting for dawn. Soon the sky turned pale over the rooftops of Paris, and the city came alive with the first sounds of morning. A new day was beginning. After the events and anxieties of the day before, the time in front of me seemed to stretch like a great void. I would have to count the hours and the minutes, alone, on the lookout for the unexpected. Since I had no immediate occupation, I decided to keep the Sonderkommando busy. I called the Maison Blanche from a café:

"I'm sorry I didn't get back last night," I told the strange voice on the other end of the line, "but I was held up with some friends. I have to see my doctor this afternoon, but I'll be back this evening."

I would not be the only one waiting, impatiently, for the end of the day.

Empty hours, walking aimlessly, or stopping in cafés, a restaurant. Then back to the street, where I always ran aground again like a shell washed up on the sand. My stride was slow, but my brain was busy, my eyes watching, my tension high. When evening came, I knew I did not have the strength to spend another night in the open. I needed a bed for at least a few hours. A bicycle-taxi took me to the Gare Montparnasse, where I stopped for a moment, and then to the Gare d'Orléans. I dozed off during the ride. When we arrived at our destination, the driver woke me, surprised that I had not got out. What must I have looked like then? Certainly not very inspiring.

My driver, an older man with a sympathetic and intelligent face, leaned over and asked, "Do you need a place to stay? If you like, you can come home with me. But I still have to make one more fare."

Without my having to say a word, he had understood that I was in distress. I trusted him. I offered to reimburse him for the remaining fare.

The man lived alone in an attic room. If he had lived in a palace, I would not have been any happier. His presence comforted me; I no longer felt so alone. A spark of fellowship in my fugitive's night. To my great amazement, he did not ask a single indiscreet question. We chatted over a frugal meal, about the curfew, the shortages, rationing, the ordeal of the occupation. I went to bed, happy. When I woke up, at about four o'clock in the morning, I was a new man. My companion took me to the Gare du Nord, where I told him I was supposed to catch a train. I thanked him warmly, and we parted like old friends. What had I been in his eyes? No doubt some provincial adrift in Paris who was now going back home.

Dear fellow! I do not know who you are, and I probably never will; but if you are still alive, and if you should ever read these lines, I want you to know that I shall never forget what you did for me that night.

October 17. I had a faint hope of renewing some contacts. In addition to setting up the rendezvous with the representative of the Communist Party, Suzanne Spaak had arranged for me to meet with a friend of hers, Grou-Radenez, who belonged to a resistance group that was in touch with London. Through this intermediary I planned to make contact with the Soviet ambassador to England. We were to meet at noon in front of the Eglise d'Auteuil. So I went there at the appointed hour. Cautiously—as always, caution was a necessity—I approached the neighborhood of the church. As I came closer, I noticed that a black Citroen, the favorite car of the Gestapo, was parked in front of the porch. I turned on my heel without hesitation. I never found out what happened—whether the messenger I was supposed to meet had been apprehended.

Georgie was arrested on the evening of the 17th of October in her little village of la Beauce. I learned this later, of course. Lafont's men, on the 15th, had found her address on the slip of paper she had given to Madame May. The Sonderkommando had waited two days before going after her.

When I did not return to the Maison Blanche, Pannwitz concluded that I had gone to meet Georgie. The village was surrounded by Gestapo, who had rushed there in great numbers. The Sonderkommando stayed there, on the lookout, waiting for my arrival before closing in. At last, late in the evening, Pannwitz and Berg at the head of their troops charged in, pistols in hand. Pannwitz definitely had frustrated ambitions as a stage manager. Now he had both Georgie and her son; but it is strange that this professional in psychological and physical torture had not learned that in some cases such coercion is completely useless.

28

I did not know that Georgie had been arrested on the evening of October 17th, but the failed rendezvous at the Eglise d'Auteuil was alarming enough to put me doubly on my guard. The Gestapo were prowling; I should not be wandering the streets of Paris. It was too late in the day, however, to do anything else. Hence I resumed my aimless walking, keeping my eye out for an open bar, until I noticed a sign on the Rue Chabanais: *Nur für Deutschen.* This was one of the biggest brothels, reserved for the Wehrmacht. More than once, the members of the Sonderkommando had mentioned such places, which they frequented in the neighborhood of the Champs-Elysées.

It was midnight by then, and I needed a place to stay for four or five hours. Shouts and drinking songs rose from the building: drunken soldiers, forgetting the war in the arms of professional lovers. The soldiers were drunk enough that I would not attract their attention—and to the young ladies, there for the diversion of the victor, I would just be another Boche. So I pushed open the door and went in. I avoided the parlor, which was full of noise and confusion, and asked the mistress of the premises to take me right upstairs to one of the rooms. The decor was suited to its function. I sat down in a comfortable chair. After a moment, an "employee" of the house came in and asked me quite straightforwardly,

"For half an hour, or the whole night?"

I had not even thought of that detail. Half an hour would be too short to be worthwhile, so I told her I was in no hurry, and that a bottle of champagne would be a pleasant way of getting acquainted. My companion did the honors and returned with the wine. I began drinking, and we had a little conversation, but no sooner had I swallowed one glass than my head spun like crazy. I got to my feet with difficulty, staggered across the room, and collapsed on the bed fully clothed while the girl watched, dumbfounded. It was half an hour before I recovered consciousness and realized where I was. The girl was watching me, calmly, patiently. I sat up and we continued our conversation.

She understood perfectly that I was a special visitor who had not come to indulge in the usual activities of the establishment. She looked me straight in the eye and said, "Why did you come here? You could have gone to a hotel. Are you afraid of something? You have nothing to fear, you know, the German police never search here—you can stay as long as you like. You'll be safer here than anywhere else."

I replied that I had no reason to be afraid of anything, and I showed her my German papers, but to no avail. Nothing I said could convince her. Then she began telling me interminable stories about the German officers who frequented the house, and I thought in passing that the Pannwitzes and their ilk would have been well advised to request that their hostesses exercise more discretion. I learned a great deal about the morale of the non-commissioned officers of the Wehrmacht at the end of that year, 1943—as gloomy as the bottoms of the bottles they were draining in the parlor downstairs.

At five o'clock in the morning I left this hospitable place. I asked the girl what I owed her.

"No," she said, "I don't want anything. I did nothing to earn this money."

"Take it, just for friendship's sake!"

She finally agreed, and then advised me as we said goodbye, "Be careful. Don't hang around the streets! If you have no place else to go, come and see me. You'll be safe here."

I believed her, but I also suspected that in that house the proverbial warrior's repose would not be eternal.

October 18. For the fourth consecutive day, I resumed my wandering. I roamed here and there, without knowing exactly where I was going. One street led to another in a random pattern, and somehow I ended up in front of the building that was headquarters for Marcel Deat's pro-Nazi party. I remembered the famous article by Deat that had appeared in his newspaper *l'Oeuvre* under the title, "To Die for Danzig"; now this former socialist leader was urging his deluded flock to die for Hitler. It seemed to be just a question of choosing your death.

As I stood there it came to me in a flash that Madame Lucie, a nurse who had once given me some injections, lived in that building. I conceived the somewhat mad idea that I—the fugitive, the man hunted by the Gestapo—would seek refuge in the same building that housed the Rassemblement National Populaire, the most fanatical advocates of collaboration in France. What was more, it was only a stone's throw from the Rue des Saussaies, where Pannwitz was running the manhunt. Quite a disreputable neighborhood, in sum.

The idea smacked of mental derangement. But this was only appearance, I told myself, not reality: nobody in my circle knew Madame Lucie. Besides, the Sonderkommando would never think of looking for me so nearby, would never imagine I would hide two steps away from their lair. I noticed, however, that there were some guards on duty, and decided to wait for them to leave. So I cooled my heels for a while, to make the best of my chances, and at ten o'clock that evening walked with a confident step toward the part of the building that was not occupied by the collaborators.

I climbed up to the fourth floor and rang the bell. Madame Lucie came to the door, stared at me, and went as white as a sheet.

"What's the matter, Monsieur Gilbert?" the good woman exclaimed. "Are you sick?" I pushed her gently through the doorway so we could continue our conversation inside. She added, "You've changed terribly, you're scarcely the man I knew before." The man she'd known before had been a Belgian industrialist who spent a few days of the week in Paris.

"Madame Lucie," I told her in one breath, "I'm a Jew, I'm an escaped prisoner who's being hunted by the Gestapo, can you keep me in your apartment for a few days? Please just tell me yes or no. If it's impossible, I won't hold it against you, and I'll leave at once!"

Her eyes filled with tears, and she replied in a voice full of emotion, "How could you think for a moment that I would refuse you?"

She led me to a room. "You'll be safe here," she said. "You can stay as long as you like. I'll get you something to drink."

I had already pulled down the bedspread: white sheets and warm blankets awaited me. At this point my last strength deserted me and I passed out. I came to just as Madame Lucie came back into the room. I must have looked like a dying man, because she kept saying over and over, "What have they done to you! What have they done to you!"

I ate, and I was much more relaxed, but I kept thinking back over the past few hours, and I could not get to sleep. It must have been midnight when I heard someone ring the doorbell. Immediately I sat bolt upright and listened. Someone was at the door—suppose it was our neighbors from the Rue des Saussaies coming to pay us a visit? Hurriedly, I got out my cyanide.

A man's voice. There seemed to be whispering. There were steps outside my door, a knock, and then Madame Lucie came in, and stood in a shaft of light that came through the doorway.

"Who is it?" I asked.

She must have sensed my anxiety, for she came over to the bed and told me in a tone of great confidentiality, but with disarming naïveté, "Oh, don't worry, Monsieur Gilbert, it's only a friend of mine. He's an officer in the French army, he's in the resistance, and he came to spend the night here."

Two resisters under the same roof, right under Pannwitz' nose! It was too much. I explained this calmly to Madame Lucie, and offered to let her friend have my place. She refused, and walked out of the room. There was more whispering. She came back a minute later, and I heard the front door close again.

"It's all taken care of," she said. "He's gone to another address."

The next day, the 19th of October, I woke up with a high fever. I was too weak to get up, so I remained in bed, and for the first time in my life I sank into a sleep filled with hallucinations. From the depths of my unconscious, scenes from my life rose up in the form of nightmares. As in some mad kaleidoscope, the images crowded together, colliding and overlapping. Scenes from my youth in Poland, from the prison in Palestine, from Moscow, from Paris, succeeded each other chaotically. Everything seemed near and far, dark and light, confused and orderly, at the same time. I saw my father die. With surprising intensity and realism I relived my past emotions, my joys and sorrows, my renewed feelings of sadness and of love.

Finally, I escaped from this drifting delirium. Little by little, the present regained possession of my mind. But it was a dark, disturbing present. In two days I was supposed to meet Claude Spaak at the Church of la Trinité. On the 22nd of October there was the rendezvous with Kowalski in Bourg-la-Reine—in a house that had been taken over by the Gestapo! Were the Spaaks all in safe places? Had Claude been able to warn Kowalski? Exhausted, once again I slipped into sleep, and did not awaken until late on the morning of the 20th.

I was leafing through *Paris-Soir*, the collaboration's rag, when a brief notice, which appeared twice on the second page, caught my eye: "Edgar, why don't you call? Georgie." Georgie knew me as a man whose first name was Edgar.

Stunned, I reread the message several times.

The meaning was clear: Pannwitz had succeeded in getting his hands on Georgie. He was discreetly gloating, and at the same time warning me that soon I would be forced to "sing." I learned much later that this was the second time the head of the Sonderkommando had used the press to announce his victories. As soon as he was back from Corrèze, he had had this message published: "Georgie, why don't you come? Patrick is with his uncle."

I could not imagine how Georgie had got arrested. For a long time, until the liberation, I kept asking myself the same question: how was it possible, when all the people who had helped her get away were absolutely trustworthy, and when they were all—apparently—at liberty? Although I considered the question from every possible angle, I could not find the answer. The simple fact was, I had not known about that scrap of paper at the bottom of Madame May's pocket, and I did not find out about it until after the war.

Georgie's arrest was a blow as terrible as it was unexpected, and one that obliged me to take the initiative again. On the evening of the 20th of October, I left Madame Lucie's apartment and went downstairs to make two phone calls. First I called the Rue de Beaujolais to find out whether the Gestapo were occupying the Spaaks' apartment. There was no answer. It was inconceivable that my friends' home had not been spotted. More likely, the Sonderkommando had laid a trap there, which would have explained why there was no answer.

My second phone call was to the Maison Blanche in Bourg-la-Reine. I asked to speak to Madame Parrend. A voice with a foreign accent, and far from melodious, answered that she was not there at the moment. I asked the speaker to be so kind as to tell my aunt that I would not be coming back to Bourg-la-Reine, and that I would see her at her home in Paris. Nervously, the voice asked me to repeat the message, which I did, articulating very carefully. What was I trying to do? Insofar as possible, I wanted to draw the Gestapo's attention away from the Maison Blanche before Kowalski rushed into the trap. It was almost an act of desperation, but I repeated to myself the famous saying: "There are no desperate situations, only desperate men."

Meanwhile, on the 21st of October, I was supposed to meet Claude Spaak, as planned, at la Trinité. All day long, to kill time and to quiet my nerves, I looked out my window and watched the cars of the Sonderkommando drive up and down the Rue des Saussaies. They seemed caught up in a feverish whirl of activity. A little before nine o'clock I walked toward the church. The night was dark and I could see only a few yards. I struggled to remain calm—it was not easy, after the events of the past few days. At last there was Claude, waiting for me. We fell into each other's arms, unable, at first, to say a word.

When our moment of great emotions was over, we walked

toward the Rue de Clichy. Claude told me that his wife and children had left for Belgium on the 17th. He described how Suzanne, categorically refusing to believe in the danger, had not wanted to leave Paris, and how he had practically had to put her bodily on the train. He had worked out a code with her, as a precaution. If she signed her letters "Suzette," it meant that everything was going well, but if she signed "Suzanne," he was to put no faith in their contents.

Suzanne Spaak—with what emotion I write these lines— Suzanne Spaak was informed against three weeks later, on November 8, 1943. This marked the beginning of her calvary, which ended with her death in August, 1944.

But on this 21st of October, I was happy to learn that she and the children were far from Paris. After that, Claude and I talked about the rendezvous with Kowalski that was set for the next day. What he told me was not very encouraging. Dr. Chertok was to have phoned him on the 19th so they could set a time for the Kowalski meeting. Claude had gone back to his apartment to wait for Chertok's call. At the stroke of noon, the time they had agreed on, the telephone rang. Spaak picked up the receiver and shouted,

"Things are too hot, the meeting's off!"

The person at the other end hung up immediately.

But had Dr. Chertok understood? Would he succeed in warning Kowalski? These questions tormented us.

This was my last meeting with Claude Spaak during the war years; we did not see each other again until the liberation. In the meantime, much blood was to flow under the bridges of Paris.

I went back to Madame Lucie's, preoccupied, obsessed by the rendezvous at Bourg-la-Reine. The only way to divert the Sonderkommando from the Maison Blanche, since I was still at the top of Pannwitz' wanted list, was to draw attention to myself. After thinking it over, I worked out the following scenario:

Early on the morning of the next day, October 22nd, I called the Spaak residence. A woman's voice answered, and this short, unbelievable dialogue took place:

"To whom do I have the honor of speaking?"

"I am Monsieur Spaak's secretary."

Claude's secretary? He had never had one, at least not a private secretary. So the Gestapo was there. This person pretending to be my friend's associate was simply their accomplice.

I went on, trying to sound very serious. "Could you please tell him that his friend Henri will come to see him at two o'clock this afternoon? Thank you for your trouble. It's very important."

"Very well, I won't forget." And she hung up.

I realize that the trick was pretty obvious, but with the Gestapo it was not always necessary to be subtle. Although I would not want to call it a general rule, the least elaborate traps were often the most effective. That day, in any case, my diversionary tactic bore immediate fruit. At two o'clock, Pannwitz and his Kommando surrounded the building on the Rue de Beaujolais. Meanwhile, at Bourg-la-Reine, Lederman and Chertok took up positions near Maison Blanche and succeeded in heading off Kowalski. Luck was with us.

October 22nd was Claude Spaak's birthday. To celebrate the event, Claude had planned to go home and pick up a few bottles of wine. Before he did, he telephoned his cleaning woman, Madame Melandes, with whom he had worked out a system for his protection: If she called him "*cher monsieur*" over the telephone, it meant that the coast was clear, and he could come home without risk. But if, on the other hand, she simply said "*monsieur*," that meant that there was danger.

So Claude Spaak picked up the receiver and dialed his own number. Madame Melandes answered and said over and over, "*Monsieur, monsieur.*" Then she exclaimed, "Is that all I'm supposed to say to him?"

If after all this Claude had not understood, it would have been really hopeless. Just then, the connection was suddenly broken. The agents of the Gestapo had just fallen on poor Madame Melandes in a rage.

It was also on the 22nd of October that this little notice appeared in *Paris-Soir*: "Edgar, why don't you call?"

But Pannwitz was crying in the wilderness.

29

Forty days had passed since my escape, forty dramatic days of constant tension and anxiety. For the first time, thanks to the refuge Madame Lucie had offered me, I could examine my plans at leisure, and coolly, almost scientifically, take stock of my successes and my failures.

At the top of the list of my failures, although it had been beyond my control, was Denise's treason, which had enabled the Gestapo to pick up my trail in Saint-Germain, Vésinet, and Suresnes, and had brought about the arrest of the two sisters in Saint-Germain, and of the Queyries and little Patrick. I was responsible for two mistakes. The first was waiting so long to get Georgie out of the way, and the second, more serious, was using Madame May, who was too vulnerable and inexperienced, as a liaison agent. Through her, certainly, the Germans had found out about my presence in Bourg-la-Reine, my contact with the Spaaks, and the rendezvous with Kowalski. And somehow the Gestapo had found Georgie. My successes lay in the way I had, with the help of my friends, countered Pannwitz's moves: I had been able to hide Hillel Katz' family—Madame Cecile, the son and the daughter—from the Gestapo; and there was the Spaaks' timely getaway, Kowalski's narrow escape from the gentlemen of the Gestapo, and my own continuing freedom.

I concluded from these events that improvisation had cost us too much, and that I would have to create a new organization designed to avoid mishaps on such a large scale. I decided to put together a surveillance and action group made up of experienced militants.

Alex Lesovoy occurred to me as the ideal comrade for this new plan.

Lesovoy did not belong to the Red Orchestra. He was a Russian who had come to France as a child. After spending several years in the Foreign Legion, he had been naturalized as a French citizen. He was a dental technician, and before the war he had had a large laboratory on the Chaussée d'Antin.

Politically, he was a deeply committed man. A militant in the Communist Party, he had left for Spain during the civil war and acquired a formidable specialty: he manufactured little incendiary devices in the form of letters, books, or parcels which he sent to the tormenters of the Spanish people. He had scored a number of direct hits.

I had known Lesovoy's wife, Mira, since she was a schoolgirl in Tel Aviv. A native of Palestine, she had been a militant in the communist movement since her school days.

Alex had come to offer me his services in 1941. His military training and his temperament—he was a man of danger and action—suited him for the most arduous missions; but since the Center's approval was slow in coming, he had enlisted in another combat group.

Shortly after my arrest, the Sonderkommando had become interested in him, because his name appeared in dispatches that had been decoded. I had managed to drag things out so that Alex Lesovoy was temporarily protected from the Gestapo investigation, but Spanish counterespionage had provided Pannwitz and his cohorts with a photograph, and singled him out as a "very dangerous individual." If arrested, Alex would immediately have been turned over to the Spanish authorities.

For a while I had succeeded in directing the Sonderkommando's investigations toward the south of France, whereas I knew that he was hiding in Paris. But the net was growing tighter and tighter around him at the time that I escaped. The first thing I did was warn him. I advised him to join a group of partisans and leave Paris. He in turn asked me to join the Maquis with him, but when I told him this was out of the question, he made the following offer:

"I'll stay with you. I'll sever all my previous connections"—this was an elementary precaution—"and I'll help you in your work."

Done. During my days at the Maison Blanche in Bourg-la-Reine, we had sketched out a plan of action whose most important element was the formation of a special surveillance group.

To begin with, Alex would set up a little group of six to eight people. Each would be responsible for a specific job, and no one of them would know the others. Their mission would be to follow the activities of the Sonderkommando very closely; to anticipate their moves and ward them off; to warn people who were in danger and help them get away; and to establish the necessary contacts.

When I saw Alex again at Madame Lucie's at the end of October, 1943, he had not wasted any time. The liaisons with the Communist Party were all set up, and five experienced militants were ready to go into action. I asked Alex, who had many connections, to procure me an identity card—one belonging to a businessman from some village in the north of France that had been wiped out by bombs, its town hall razed, and all the official birth records lost in the rubble. To complete the picture, our unfortunate industrialist would also have lost his family, his friends, and his home.

We decided, Alex Lesovoy and I, to meet again in the new hideout Madame Lucie was trying to find for me.

Since my escape, my major preoccupation had been to make it possible for Moscow to continue the Great Game, which is what I had in mind when I sent my two letters to Pannwitz. His interrogation of Georgie de Winter confirmed the head of the Sonderkommando in his illusions about my intent: Georgie followed my instructions to the letter. I had told her that if she were arrested, she should pretend that she understood nothing about this complicated business. She confirmed everything that I had written in my letters to Pannwitz, and added that I often talked about a separate peace, and was constantly quoting Bismarck.

But Pannwitz, who by this time understood—or at any rate believed, which amounted to the same thing—that the Great Game depended solely on my good will, became very nervous. Wishing to exploit this advantage, after the arrest of Suzanne Spaak, I sent him a third letter. I reminded him that he had not released a single one of the people who had been arrested, and I threatened him: "If you do not free the hostages, I will ruin your Great Game." To leave no doubt about my determination, I telephoned him directly and repeated my ultimatum. In this respect, I was to obtain satisfaction. But at the same time, the head of the Sonderkommando lost his head.

Shortly after I renewed contact with Alex Lesovoy he showed me a surprising document. "Look," he said, "here's a present from your friend."

The present was a copy of a notice that had been sent to all the police: "Wanted: Jean Gilbert. Infiltrated police organizations on behalf of the resistance. Fled with documents. Must be apprehended by any means. Report to Lafont." A photograph, taken by the Gestapo after my arrest, was included, along with a detailed description of my person. A substantial reward was promised for any information. At the same time, all sections of the Gestapo and the Abwehr, all German administrative, economic, and military organizations in France, Belgium, and the Netherlands, received posters with my photograph—and later, Claude Spaak's as well—topped off by the inscription "Escaped spy—very dangerous."

This was not something to be ignored. Undoubtedly, Pannwitz' action marked a turning point in his strategy against me.

Alex and I discussed what Pannwitz' motivation could have been and what he could hope to accomplish by this move. Up until then, he and his men had reserved for themselves the exclusive right to hunt for me, alerting neither the French police nor the army. Convinced that I had not been able to reach the Center since my escape, he was trying to discredit me in the Center's eyes. We had proof of this intention when we learned that Kent had been instructed to send a telegram to the Director telling him of my flight. In this way, according to Pannwitz' reasoning, the Director would discover that I had been arrested and would lose confidence in me. Furthermore, by making me look like a provocateur who had infiltrated the police, Pannwitz hoped to get the resistance to lose interest in my case, and Lafont's name—Lafont, who commanded the French auxiliary of the Gestapo—was calculated to further complicate this mysterious business.

From now on every German in uniform, plus the police, plus the gangs of collaborators, paid and unpaid, and mercenaries of every stripe and even ordinary people lured by tempting rewards, all were invited to hunt me down and turn me in. Pannwitz' chief ambition was to get his hands on me; and so I was now at the mercy of an attentive eye or an accurate memory. Fortunately for me, my appearance had changed considerably from the photograph published by the Gestapo. My face had lost its former fullness, I had grown a thick moustache, and I wore glasses. Finally, Madame Lucie had managed to find me a hideout that answered all the traditional requirements of security. In November, 1943, I moved to the Avenue du Maine, to an apartment owned by an employee of the Crédit Lyonnais.

The story that was told about me suited my situation: I was a man alone in the world, I was sick, and I had been mistreated by fate. I had lost my whole family in an air raid. The neighbors I passed on the stairs, who had heard about my misfortunes through neighborhood gossip, treated me with great sympathy. My landlord, Monsieur Jean, a bachelor whose family name I have unfortunately forgotten, was a calm and intelligent man with whom I got along very well. He had no idea whom he had under his roof, but my new refuge turned out to be so safe and so hospitable that I stayed there until I left for Moscow in January, 1945.

Pannwitz meanwhile heeded the ultimatum in my last letter. Fearing, in spite of everything, that I would reveal the Great Game to the Center, he had freed the prisoners in rapid succession, even as he was setting the whole pack on my heels. On January 8, 1944, he put another notice in the paper stating: "Patrick is fine, he is back at the house." Shortly afterward, the whole Queyrie family were released; and Madame May, who had been sentenced to death, also regained her freedom, by the personal decision of Marshal Goering, it seems.

The head of the Sonderkommando was certainly keeping busy. At the same time, he was preparing a new strategy, which was no less dangerous for being classic. He made an index of all the persons I was believed to know or have known, and threatened to arrest them if they failed to notify him of my visits. As soon as Alex and I found out about this attempt at coercion, we drew up our own list of those who were in danger and had them warned.

A survey of my old contacts indicated that Pannwitz' threat was real and that he had started carrying it out. We paid a visit to a woman I had known for years, who ran a lingerie shop on the Boulevard Haussmann, across from the Simex building. She informed us that several men, including Kent—the description she gave us left no room for doubt—had come to her shop and threatened to arrest her unless she cooperated. Terrified, she had promised to alert them as soon as she saw me and to keep me with her until they arrived.

The same coercion and the same threats were used on an old schoolteacher who had rented me a room near Place Pigalle in the days when I was posing as a Belgian industrialist. The poor woman almost fainted when she saw me. She told us that two men, one of them the inevitable Kent, had come to her. Identifying themselves as police officers, they had read her a letter from Marshal Pétain encouraging "all good French citizens" to turn over to the authorities a "fierce enemy of their country" by the name of Monsieur Gilbert. My former landlady declared that the reference to Pétain (whose nonsense she swallowed eagerly) had impressed her very much, but she suspected that the letter was a forgery. Kent and his accomplice had forced her to sign a statement testifying that she had read the letter, and had ordered her to proceed in the same manner as the shopkeeper. She was to go downstairs and telephone them, after asking me to stay with her for a while. The terror that this visit had inspired in the unfortunate woman was painful to behold. "What if they come back? What if they come back?" she kept saying over and over. "What if they find out that I didn't warn them?"

I realized that this elderly woman was running a great risk

on my account, and it was possible that she was physically incapable of withstanding another investigation.

"Listen," I told her, "as soon as we've left, you can rush to the telephone and tell them we were here. Explain that you called as soon as you could, and you'll be off the hook."

She looked at me in bewilderment. Had I gone mad? she seemed to be asking herself—but deep down, I felt, she was very much relieved.

I picked up my suitcase—a suitcase I had left with her long before, which was my reason for this visit. Just as we were leaving, she went to the telephone. Alex looked at me incredulously—it seemed he shared the woman's astonishment. He said nothing. I walked without hurrying.

It was I who broke the silence. "I know them," I told him. "It's Sunday, the middle of a Sunday afternoon. There's hardly anyone at the Rue des Saussaies. Most of them are in the bars and cafés."

I had not been wrong. After the liberation, I found out that the men of the Sonderkommando, interrupted in the midst of their *dolce vita*, had arrived three hours later.

After that I sent Pannwitz my fourth and final letter, informing him that I was sick and that I was retiring from the field. I went on, "You can continue the Great Game. I won't stand in your way, provided you stop arresting innocent people."

In 1940, the Germans had requisitioned a townhouse belonging to a Monsieur Weil-Picard on the Rue de Courcelles. The sole reason for this requisition was that Monsieur Weil-Picard was Jewish. His belongings, and those of all his fellow Jews, were turned over to looters and transferred by the railroad carload to Germany, where they went to enrich the private collections of those dignitaries of the regime who appreciated art. Goering, in particular, kept a close watch over these operations of organized robbery and deducted from the booty all that appealed to his aesthetic sensibilities. The Weil-Picard painting collection, which was one of the finest in France, had aroused the cupidity of the thieves, but the house itself had been left uninhabited.

It was here that Pannwitz, who sensed that this spring would be his last in Paris, took up residence in April, 1944. The torturers knew that the hour of their defeat was fast approaching. All over Europe the oppressed peoples were lifting up their heads; in France, the resistance was harassing the enemy. Barbed wire was replacing the "hand outstretched" to the French people, machine guns were posted in front of the buildings of the Wehrmacht, and those grotesque parades of Franco-German friendship groups, conducted under the aegis of the Führer, were a thing of the past.

Pannwitz' new quarters reflected the style of the day. Monsieur Weil-Picard's townhouse was transformed into a fortress, courtesy of the head of the Sonderkommando. The main entrance was blocked up; a single small door, which was opened electrically from the inside, now gave access to the interior courtyard. In front of the interior facade a machine gun was set up, and security measures were in effect on all sides of the building. The Wehrmacht used the area to the left of the townhouse as a garage for automobiles which, as a precautionary measure, were never brought into the courtyard; visitors left their cars in this parking area and walked through an opening in the adjoining wall, unseen from the outside. Meanwhile the cellar had been turned into cells, and—macabre effect—the former picture gallery into a torture chamber. So beauty made way for horror. And it was in this house, in April, 1944, that the son of Margarete Barcza and Kent was born.

All Pannwitz' precautions proclaimed the imminence of the denouncement, that Paris was going to rise up again and her streets bristle with barricades. Alex Lesovoy planned an operation with the support of a group of Franc-Tireurs et Partisans (FTP) designed to cut off the Sonderkommando's escape route when the time came. Lesovoy's group kept a close watch on the building, taking hundreds of photographs of everyone who came and went. The outings of Kent and Margarete, the transfer of prisoners, the comings and goings of the black Citroens, were all observed and noted. An old Jewish prisoner, Levy, whom the Germans used as a gardener, gave us precious information. Our initial idea was to block the Sonderkommando when Paris was liberated, to prevent them from getting away, with the help of an armed group of some thirty FTP. We told the Center of our plan, with the Communist Party serving as intermediary, but since we received no answer we dropped the project.

Pannwitz' criminal adventure was almost over, but the butcher of Prague did not want to go down with the ship. He wanted first to try to redeem, if not to exonerate, himself— for he was well aware that he would have to answer to the justice of men—and next to obliterate, insofar as possible, the traces of the atrocities for which he was responsible.

It was clear that in the allied camp nobody still seriously considered the possibility of a separate peace with a Germany that was falling apart. A few members of Hitler's entourage, who had not renounced their false hopes, were still trying to make contact with the English and Americans; but these were isolated attempts. Pannwitz knew the game was up. After the unsuccessful attempt on his life on July 20, 1944, the Führer himself gave orders to discontinue Operation Bear— otherwise known as the Great Game.

That was one thing. The personal ambitions of Pannwitz

were another. The Nazi regime—of which he had been one of the most zealous servants, foremost of the butchers of Prague—was crumbling. But what did that matter? It was every man for himself, and Pannwitz, whose hands were stained with the blood of so many victims, had to save his skin! He could either run away, like the others, and hide out in Latin America; or he could be trapped like a rat and treated as a war criminal by the English—obviously, that was out of the question. Or, another possibility, he could maintain contact with the Center in the hope that the Soviet Union would make allowances for services rendered.

Pannwitz opted for the third course. Today we have proof that until May, 1945, with the collaboration of the faithful Kent, he carried on a private game, continuing to send military information until the final moments of the war. Kent had told the Center he was in touch with a group of Germans who occupied very important positions, and that he would consequently be able to send information of the highest quality. In July, 1944, when the allied armies were approaching the gates of Paris, Kent asked the Center whether he should remain in the capital or leave with his German friends. The Director answered that he should go with the Nazis but stay in contact with the Center.

Pannwitz was obviously very pleased with these directives. For him, collaboration with the Russians looked like an opportunity to pull his chestnuts out of the fire—so through Pannwitz, the Great Game took on a new dimension. Himmler's initial plan had been to destroy the anti-Hitler coalition by simultaneously duping Moscow, on the one hand, and the English and the Americans on the other. Through the transmitters of the Red Orchestra, the Sonderkommando had tried to make the Russians believe that the Allies were ready to negotiate with the Third Reich, while, at the same time, they were trying an identical strategy on the allied side. However, this phase of the Great Game could not be carried far enough. From mid-1943 on, the outcome of the war was no longer in doubt. At that point, the Nazi leaders oriented the Great Game toward a real quest for a separate peace—

with the west, for Himmler, though in the case of Bormann, who supervised the whole affair, this is less certain.

In any event, it was too late. The attempt had no chance of succeeding, for neither Roosevelt nor Churchill, and certainly not Stalin—all of whom believed in a total military victory— was willing to negotiate. It was at this stage, during 1944, that Pannwitz tried to use the Great Game for his own personal ends.

Before leaving for Moscow, Pannwitz wanted to cover his tracks—in other words, silence the witnesses to his activities as head of the Sonderkommando. The butcher of Prague was still there beneath the mask of the secret agent. Suppression and murder were his stock in trade: one by one the heads rolled; one after the other, our imprisoned and tortured comrades were executed. Leo Grossvogel was the first. He was sentenced to death in May, 1944, by the German military tribunal, although he had been a prisoner in Fresnes since December, 1942, without any decision on his fate. Fernand Pauriol and Suzanne Spaak, also prisoners in Fresnes, were struck down by the same sentence.

When we heard that Grossvogel had been sentenced to death, it was our alarm signal. We were sure that other death sentences would follow, that the Sonderkommando had decided to murder the prisoners before making their get-away. Maximovich and Robinson shortly suffered the same fate.

All the executions took place in the last few weeks before the liberation of Paris. On July 6, 1944, Izbutski was behead-ed in Berlin and Winterinck was shot in Brussels on the Army Firing Range. Jeanne Pesant, Grossvogel's wife, was execut-ed in the German capital on August 6, 1944. Fernand Pauriol and Suzanne Spaak were shot on August 12, 1944, in Fresnes—thirteen days before De Gaulle entered Paris. After the war, Pannwitz explained his actions on several occasions—make no mistake, he tried to justify himself: "The Red Orchestra agents executed under my command had been sentenced to death before I appeared on the scene." This is untrue, and in any case the head of the Sonderkommando had the power to suspend these executions. He did not do so because he wanted to "clean up the place" before he left.

I would like to clarify the circumstances surrounding the deaths of Fernand Pauriol and Suzanne Spaak on the eve of that liberation of Paris they had so longed for. I can almost see them, adding their joy and and their cheers to those of the multitudes who went down into the streets to celebrate the great event——

For many long months, Pannwitz had been hoping to make Fernand and Suzanne talk. In the panic that preceded his departure, he decided to silence them. Our two comrades were murdered in a cowardly manner in their cells and buried secretly. Pannwitz carried cynicism so far as to write Paul-Henri Spaak, Suzanne's brother-in-law and then Secretary of Foreign Affairs of the Belgian government in exile, assuring him that he had done everything possible to protect her life. Paul-Henri Spaak could rest assured: she would await the end of the hostilities in complete safety. Knowing Pannwitz, I would not put it past him to have sent this letter the same day he turned Suzanne over to the executioners.

On August 27, 1944, after the liberation, I went with Alex Lesovoy to the prison at Fresnes to try to find out what had become of our friends. No one was able to give us exact information, but after we insisted, we finally learned that the Germans had not taken them with them. Since we were familiar with the habits of the Gestapo, we resigned ourselves to the worst. If Suzanne and Fernand had not gone with the men of the Sonderkommando, they must have been killed and were probably buried somewhere in the vicinity. So we started going to the cemeteries around Fresnes, one after the other, and consulting the burial records. Since the Germans were in the habit of recording the name, date of birth and date of execution of their victims, we thought this would facilitate our investigation. But we were underestimating Pannwitz' cool dissimulation, and his desire to obliterate all traces of a double crime for which he would be blamed more than for any other.

After a thorough search of the cemeteries in the suburbs south of Paris, we discovered the remains of Suzanne Spaak and Fernand Pauriol in Bagneux. At the bottom of the page in the register, bearing a date that corresponded to their presumed time of death, appeared the entry, "A Belgian woman and a Frenchman." There was no doubt that this referred to Suzanne and Fernand. We besieged the guards with questions. At first they pretended not to know anything about it, but in the end we wore down their resistance and they told us the truth. Still in the state of terror caused by the visit from the Gestapo, who had threatened them with reprisals if they talked, they told us that on the evening of August 12th the Germans had come with two coffins and had asked to be taken to a damp part of the cemetery. They requisitioned two gravediggers, had them dig two holes, put the bodies in, and sprinkled them with a chemical product that accelerated decomposition.

Pannwitz hoped that, with all these precautions, his crimes would remain undiscovered.

In Copenhagen, in March, 1974, Helene Pauriol told me about the last time she saw Fernand and how she found out about his death, and discovered his remains in the cemetery at Bagneux, just as Alex Lesovoy and I had done:

In early January, 1944, I think it was either the 15th or the 16th, I received a letter with the address in my husband's handwriting. The letter was addressed to Madame Hélène Pauriol, in care of Madame Prunier, 19 Avenue de la Grande-Pelouse, Le Vésinet. Inside were a few lines asking me to go to the Rue des Saussaies on the 19th—perhaps I would be able to see him—and to bring him a suit. So on the 19th of January I went to the Rue des Saussaies, taking the letter with me. I brought my little girl along. It wasn't until I was inside the building that I said to myself, "I'm crazy, I shouldn't have brought the child with me." I hadn't realized at first . . . how much I longed . . . to see whether he was alive, to see if it was really him, to see—— I didn't realize that it was madness to bring a child, because they could just as easily have taken the girl, and besides, you know how it is, you never know how you're going to react at certain times, you can't know ahead of time. If you haven't been there before, you never know how you'll react, what you will do——

I was taken upstairs to the fourth floor, I think. I waited in a room, on a sofa, with the girl, and after about five minutes two Germans came in, and behind them was my husband. He sat down beside me. He had on the same suit he had been wearing the day he was arrested. There were bloodstains on it. He took the suitcase. They stayed about fifteen or twenty minutes, and then they made me leave. After that I waited outside, and I saw him leave in a Gestapo car. And that was all.

After that, I heard nothing, so I thought perhaps he had taken part, you know—there had been a rebellion in Fresnes, an armed uprising, and I told myself, "They didn't kill him between August, 1943, when he was arrested, and January, 1944." It wasn't possible that he was dead. You know, you always . . . believe that some things are impossible, that they can happen to other people, but not to you. Especially since he was so young. I said, "It's not possible, he must be somewhere, either he's been deported or else he was on that train." And after the liberation of Paris, I went to the newspaper *L'Humanité* because they had lists there. They told me, "No, there's nothing, we have no information, but you mustn't give up hope."

The first Sunday in October, 1944, my doorbell rang. It was a young girl. She asked if I was Madame Pauriol, and I told her I was. She asked whether she could come in, so I showed her in. After she had sat down she said, "Your husband was arrested?" I said, "Yes, I'm sure he'll be coming home any day now, I'll be hearing news of him." She hesitated for a moment, and then she said, "You know, I have sad news to tell you. Your husband is . . ." At that point, I asked her to leave. It wasn't possible, a thing like that. But she came back two hours later. I apologized to her. She simply handed me a letter from my husband, and she explained what it was. There was my husband's last letter, his wedding rings, and inside the letter was the certificate, which the pastor had saved. You know, that German pastor who was at Fresnes saw condemned prisoners in their cells, he must have been with them to the end. He even went to the cemetery in Bagneux to recover this blue slip, on which someone had written: "Unknown Frenchman, executed August 12." When I saw that, I had to understand; at a certain point, one is forced to face the truth. But I still didn't think it was possible. I said to myself, "Perhaps there's been some mistake," and I couldn't rest until I had identified the body. I was able to do this on November 14, 1944. At Bagneux, when we went there, there were only two unknown persons who had been executed that day, a Belgian woman and a Frenchman. And when they opened the coffin, he had on the suit I had brought the day—it was a grey flannel suit. It was him.

All the prisoners of the Red Orchestra whose interrogations had been conducted by Pannwitz, with the exception of Suzanne Spaak and Fernand Pauriol, were sent to Germany. Georgie de Winter was transferred from the prison at Neuilly to Fresnes, where she was able to make contact with Suzanne Spaak. Then, on August 10, 1944, she was taken to the Gare de l'Est. On the platform, she recognized Margarete Barcza and her two children. Pannwitz himself presided over her departure, and reminded her that if she escaped, her son, little Patrick, would pay for it. Pannwitz, the master manipulator right up to the last second.

The train that took Georgie away stopped first at Karlsruhe. Reiser, who, as I have said, had been appointed head of the Gestapo for that town after being transferred from Paris, had been alerted to Georgie's arrival. Impelled by a delicate intention—I expected no less of him—he came to see her and by way of greeting repeated Pannwitz' threats. Georgie de Winter was dragged from prison to concentration camp. After Karlsruhe, Leipzig, Ravensbrück, Frankfurt, and Saxenhausen were the stages of her calvary.

As for Kent, his back was to the wall. No matter which way he turned, he knew he was lost. If I escaped the Gestapo, he knew, I would reveal his treachery to the Center. And he could expect no better from the Sonderkommando, whose faithful decoy and spineless tool he had become since my arrest; ruthless elimination, with no appeal, would be his fate if such was Pannwitz' pleasure. The scythe that rusts is thrown on the rubbish heap—even after it has served so well.

His only means of earning the supreme indulgence was to outdo himself in zealousness toward his masters, to furnish them with one final proof of his expertise in treachery. His last work was by far the most destructive.

At the end of 1940, the Director had asked me to investigate a certain Waldemar Ozols, alias Solja, who had once worked for Soviet Intelligence. The Center suspected this Latvian former general, who had fought in Spain on the Republican side, of having made a deal with certain Vichy circles; the Center wanted to know if Ozols was to be relied on or not. I replied that, upon investigation, Ozols appeared to be far from trustworthy, and I recommended avoiding him. Kent was well aware of this exchange with the Center, since he had personally decoded the dispatches containing the question and the answer.

Giering had been interested in Ozols. Suspecting a maneuver on his part, I had thrown him off the scent, but a few days before my escape, Pannwitz succeeded in tracking Ozols down. Kent managed to make contact with him, and the results were disastrous. He got Ozols to introduce him to Captain Legendre, former head of the Mithridates resistance network. Legendre, foolishly assuming that he was dealing with a Soviet agent, furnished a list of French resisters. Then at Kent's insistence—this was Kent's master stroke—Legendre agreed to furnish him, with the assistance of his own groups, military information on the territories liberated by the Allies. Pannwitz was in seventh heaven, and congratulated Kent, or at least I assume so, for obtaining such results. When Legendre asked Kent why the Soviets were "curious," Kent told him that the English and American chiefs of staff were avoiding cooperation with the Red Army in the area of intelligence, and that this lack of coordination threatened to have most unfortunate consequences. So Kent was counting on Captain Legendre's network to make up for this deficiency.

Yes, Kent had really earned his stripes as a full-fledged member of the Sonderkommando and had acquired an extraordinary claim to Pannwitz' gratitude. He would not be liquidated. The chief would remember this final *tour de force* as he was packing his bags.

Paris was in arms, it was time to abandon the townhouse on the Rue de Courcelles. The members of the Sonderkommando disappeared into cars crammed with baggage. Just before they left, one of them shouted at the concierge of the townhouse,

"You'd better watch out, if you talk!"

It was Kent.

The great day arrived at last. Early on the morning of August 25, 1944, Alex Lesovoy called for me on the Avenue du Maine. We were in a hurry to get to the Rue de Courcelles and the large house occupied by the Sonderkommando.

The trip across a Paris waking to freedom was full of excitement. Arriving at the Rue de Rivoli, where the battle was raging, we were forced to stop. Immediately we found ourselves shoulder-to-shoulder with the partisans, who were doing battle with the Germans—the soldiers of the Wehrmacht were offering a last resistance. Shots were ringing out everywhere. These young Frenchmen wearing armbands, their shirts wide open at the neck, their faces deeply lined, were shouting their demand to be free of oppression; these boys, who had come rushing from all over Paris to sweep away the last vestiges of the occupation, had a large supply of grenades—which they did not know how to use! It was up to us, who had fought in the shadows and who had returned to the light, to lend them a hand. Alex Lesovoy, delighted to be confronting the enemy face to face after hunting him down in the dark, became an impromptu military instructor. The demonstration was conclusive: the barrier erected by the Germans was blown up.

Further on, we took part in the fighting around the Hotel Majestic, which had been the general headquarters of the Wehrmacht. In the Place de la Concorde there was another confrontation near the Hotel Crillon. It wasn't until afternoon that we finally arrived at the Rue de Courcelles. The Sonderkommando had left the premises two hours before.

We were in the den of Pannwitz and his sadists. Here, our tortured comrades had suffered hideously. My throat was constricted with emotion. We advanced cautiously, not from fear, but because we sensed that we were about to look upon the very face of horror. They had left, and everything indicated that their flight had been precipitous. The offices were littered with documents they had not had time to burn. In the cellar, on the floors of cells where the prisoners had been thrown, there were little piles of filthy straw. We walked into a bathroom: there were bloodstains in the tub, on the floor, on the walls. They had been tortured here. On the second floor, in the art gallery, there were large dark stains. We walked up to the third floor. On a table in one room were papers covered with numbers. Without doubt, Efremov the engineer had been staying there. The concierge confirmed our assumptions: Efremov had left Paris with the Sonderkommando.

We gathered all the documents we could salvage and took numerous photographs of the house of crime. This damning evidence, this irrefutable proof of the enemy's barbarity, we would send to Moscow.

PART THREE

THE RETURN

1

A Remarkable Journey

A few days after the liberation of Paris, in an apartment on the Boulevard de Strasbourg, the home of an old lady who had acted as a liaison between Alex Lesovoy and myself, I received a dispatch from the Center congratulating me on my work and asking me to await the arrival of the first Soviet military mission.

Everywhere people were breathing the air of regained freedom, but in this atmosphere of gaiety, this exalting sense of release, I was not allowed to forget that it was still too early to disarm. Sometimes it is when you least expect it, when you think the enemy has been defeated, that he seizes the opportunity to knife you in the back. It was possible that Herr Pannwitz, who had run away to escape justice, had left behind some time bombs and hired some thugs to liquidate me.

My apprehensions turned out to be well founded. Alex's group, always on the alert, picked up traces of some suspicious individuals who seemed to be looking for me. They had turned up at Katz' former apartment on the Rue Edmond-Roger, and at other apartments that appeared in the files of the Gestapo. These crooks, survivors of Lafont's gang, had clearly received orders from Pannwitz—Alex was convinced of it—to track me down and take care of me. So I had to be careful not to expose myself, not to get carried away by the general intoxication and offer myself as a target to these eleventh-hour assassins. I continued to live a semi-clandestine existence in the apartment on the Avenue du Maine.

On November 23, 1944, the first airplane from the Soviet Union landed near Paris. On board were Maurice Thorez and Colonel Novikov, head of the military delegation in charge of repatriating Russians who were expected in Moscow. Novikov received me very warmly and informed me that I could leave very soon in the same plane, which would be making the return trip.

The wait turned out to be longer than anticipated. On January 5, 1945, I finally boarded the plane, equipped with a Soviet passport and using an assumed name. There were twelve of us, including Alexander Rado, the head of the Swiss network, whom I had met for the first time a few days before at Novikov's home, and his second-in-command, Alexander Foote.

The war was still raging in the heart of Europe. To get to Moscow, we thus had to make a long detour. The plane headed south. After stopping in Marseilles and Italy it landed in North Africa, at an airport occupied by the Americans, then took off again, headed for Cairo. Rado sat next to me, and gave me the benefit of his considerable knowledge as a geographer by telling me all about the regions we were flying over. The other passengers weren't very talkative. One of them, however, a man of about sixty with white hair, a stocky build, and the strong hands of a man accustomed to manual labor, introduced himself.

"Comrade Chliapnikov."

Chliapnikov! What a surprise! "Chliapnikov, the leader of the Worker Opposition?"

"The same."

A metalworker and an old Bolshevik, Chliapnikov had been the guiding spirit, along with Alexandra Kollontai, of a movement within the party in 1920–1921 that advocated the independence of labor unions and defended the right to strike. His legitimate pride at being a real proletarian with "calloused hands" had earned him the sarcasm of Lenin, who had remarked in the middle of an argument, "As usual, the comrade makes the most of his authentic proletarian background."

Yet it was Lenin who, in spite of his disagreement with Chliapnikov's ideas, had come to his defense before the Central Committee at the time they were discussing excluding the Worker Opposition. I had been sure Chliapnikov had been carried away by the wave of purges, like all the old Bolsheviks.

"After the defeat of the Worker Opposition," he explained, "I left the USSR with the help of Lenin and moved to Paris, where I worked as a carpenter. The victory of the Red Army and my attachment to my homeland made me decide to go back. I wrote my friend Molotov and asked him to help me. He sent me a very warm letter encouraging me to come. I'm sure he'll meet me at the airport in his car. I am very impatient to serve the party and the country once again."

I was touched by the naïve enthusiasm of this old Bolshevik, who still had faith despite everything he had been through. I hoped he would not be too disillusioned.

In Cairo we were taken to a hotel in the Old City. The day after our arrival, I visited the Soviet Embassy along with the other passengers. We were all there except Rado. Why hadn't he joined us? I paid no particular attention at the time. I went with the others to spend the little money we had been provided with on souvenirs; this time Rado went along. But I noticed another curious thing—he was keeping his money, not spending it.

The next day, early in the morning, we gathered in front of the hotel to wait for the bus that was to take us to the airport. Rado was not among us. Everyone was astonished. They went to his room: the bed was still made, he must not have slept at the hotel. Had he been attacked in the Old City?

In fact I knew what had happened to him, but I was careful not to breathe a word. The night before, he had come to my room and asked me some questions that left no doubt about his intentions:

"What do you know about living conditions in Egypt? Do you think it would be hard to get established in this country?"

Rado was not found. At around noon, the plane took off in the direction of Iran. Now there were only eleven passengers on board.

I thought my life would end in the plane that took me back to Moscow: we had been in the air only a few minutes when the weather changed—rain was coming down in gusts, but the plane kept climbing anyway. Visibility was zero. Anxiety showed clearly on the faces of the crew. The wings were starting to freeze. The air grew thin. We had no oxygen masks, and little by little our arms and legs grew numb. The pilots shouted constantly in order to keep awake. The aircraft continued to climb. Catastrophe seemed imminent. How absurd, I thought. It was too idiotic: to fight as I had, only to find myself trapped in this flying coffin!

At last we stopped climbing and the plane started earthward. Gradually we returned to a reasonable altitude. When we arrived in Teheran, the pilots told us we had gone off course because of the bad weather. Navigating without visibility, they had feared the worst. But it was written that my last hour had not yet come.

Atmospheric conditions delayed our takeoff from Teheran. Alexander Foote and I were invited to the home of the Soviet military attaché, who told us that Rado's disappearance was already known in Moscow. He thought we might be able to throw some light on the incident.

Foote was understandably anxious. That he might have been Rado's accomplice was a logical assumption that some people would not hesitate to make. "How am I supposed to go to Moscow and make a report on our activities in Switzerland, after this?" he said to the Soviet military attaché. "I'll be suspect. They won't believe a word I say!"

While we were flying toward Moscow, Rado's disappearance obsessed me. I knew he had performed his mission beyond all expectations, that he had nothing to reproach himself for. During his many years as a militant, from the time he had taken part in Bela Kun's revolutionary movement in Hungary as a very young man, he had accumulated a rich fund of political experience. In Switzerland, he had contributed substantially to the victory. But precisely because of his profound understanding of the facts, his realism as a man of learning, he felt that in spite of the victory, nothing had changed in the kingdom of the OGPU. He foresaw the fate that awaited him in Moscow. He did not care for the prospect of ending his life in one of Stalin's jails; hence he disappeared in Cairo after making sure that his wife and children were safe in Paris.

Rado's freedom was of short duration, though. After taking refuge in an English camp, he was immediately and energetically reclaimed by Moscow. Rado's destiny was insignificant in comparison with relations between Great Britain and Russia. In a few months the officers of the NKVD came for him.

The truth Rado perceived did not strike me with its blinding light until later. I was too naïve. I believed that now that the fighting was over, the terror would cease, and the regime would evolve. Such credulity on the part of a man who had lived through the prewar purges may be surprising, but there was a decisive argument that would have caused me to return to the Soviet Union in any case: my family was there. Unlike Rado, I did not have the calm assurance of knowing they were safe in Paris; and I knew that if I were to stray from the path, they would risk suffering the consequences.

Moscow was getting closer. Of all the contradictory feelings I was experiencing, I remember above all my overwhelming joy at the thought of seeing my loved ones again after so many years of separation. When our wheels touched the landing strip, I felt like a man who is satisfied with a job well done. I was proud of what I had accomplished and looked forward only to a well earned rest. My thoughts went out to my comrades, the dead and the tortured.

As I walked down the steps, I tried to make out my people in the darkness that had fallen. In vain; no one was waiting for me, or for any of the other passengers either. A group of officers formed our welcoming committee: soldiers to greet fighters—that could be explained, I supposed.

Some high-ranking officers—colonels—walked over and greeted me warmly. They invited me to get into a car. The light shifted, suddenly, and I recognized one of them. In 1937, he had been a captain—he had not wasted his time. I asked the question that had been on the tip of my tongue since my arrival: "Where are my wife and children?"

"Don't worry," replied one of my chaperones. "They're very well; your wife's taking a cure in a rest home. We didn't have time to inform her, because we didn't know the exact date of your arrival. Anyway, the chiefs at the Center think you ought to spend two or three weeks in an apartment, so you can prepare your report without being disturbed. That's where we're taking you."

Two rooms had been prepared for me in the apartment of a colonel away on assignment. His wife and daughter greeted us. Before they left, the two colonels who had escorted me presented a young captain:

"This is your orderly. He'll see that you have everything you need."

Isolation—to permit me to write my report. An orderly—as if I needed one. The peculiar attitude of the two colonels; above all, the absence of my wife—all these elements combined to give me a sense of strangeness and mistrust.

I settled into my new quarters. At least they were more comfortable than the damp streets of Montparnasse I had haunted like a soul in torment after my departure from the Maison Blanche.

The very next evening I had visitors. There were three of them, two men in uniform, and a third in civilian clothes whom I recognized as having been in charge of political work for the Center in 1938. This function concealed another: he was a general in the NKVD.

They had brought a sumptuous dinner, but I broke this gastronomic truce to ask one of the questions that was bothering me:

"Did you receive my January, 1943, report promptly, the one I sent through the leaders of the party?"

"Yes, yes, we received it and we took it into account." There was a silence. Then the general changed the subject.

"Well," he said, "what are your plans for the future?"

I thought: that will be up to you. But I answered, "I'm through with intelligence; that chapter of my life is closed. But before going back to Poland, I would like to go over with the Center everything that happened during the war." And then I added, enunciating very clearly, "I expect an explanation of the grave mistakes of those in charge!"

The investigating general scowled. "Really, is that all that interests you?"

"Doesn't it interest you? Above all, I would like to submit a proposal for a final operation involving the Red Orchestra——"

The general cut me short. "Very well, we will study your suggestion tomorrow."

The next day I received a visit from two colonels. I realized immediately that they were well acquainted with the dossier of the Red Orchestra.

"I am convinced," I began, "that Grossvogel, Makarov, Robinson, Sukulov, and Maximovich are still alive. They can and must be saved, but the most important question is whether you are still in contact with Pannwitz."

"We have it from a reliable source that he has taken refuge in the Austrian Alps."

I then proposed that Pannwitz be sent two officers who were familiar with the history of the Red Orchestra. They would tell him that since February, 1943, thanks to my report, the Center had been aware of the Great Game. He would agree to do whatever was necessary to save the members of the Red Orchestra who were in prison; in return, the officers would promise to take these efforts into consideration after the war. If he refused to cooperate, Himmler and Bormann would immediately be informed. If they learned that the leaders in Moscow had been pulling the strings for such a long time, Pannwitz would be held responsible and would risk paying very dearly for it, for they still had ways of making him pay.

This proposition seemed to me perfectly fair and reasonable. (As head of the Sonderkommando, Pannwitz had full authority to suspend executions, inasmuch as the presence of the prisoners he was holding was necessary to his "work." Naturally, at this time, I was not aware that they had already been executed.) My two visitors promised they would submit it to our superiors.

I spent my first week in Moscow drafting my report, with the help of a typist. But as the days went by, I became increasingly aware that clouds were gathering over my head. I would have had to be unconscious and blind to believe that my troubles were over. No, I was not a fighter being welcomed home with gratitude.

I had been in this apartment three days when two NKVD officers brought me my suitcase. I had left the airport with Chliapnikov's suitcase, which was exactly the same as mine. Chliapnikov had also noticed the mistake; the two officers of the NKVD had been instructed to make the exchange.

The affiliation of these two ambassadors was instructive. It was clear that Chliapnikov was in their hands, and I understood then how Molotov, who had written him such a warm letter inviting him to come back, had welcomed his "dear comrade." It was the height of cynicism. My heart constricted. I felt a deep pain and profound disgust as I imagined the enormous disappointment of this old Bolshevik, so happy to be returning to the homeland of socialism, ready to devote his last energies to it, and discovering the trap he had walked into. He had been expecting Molotov's car; instead, he was met by a police car, which drove him straight to Lubianka.

The sole function of my "orderly" was to spy on me with his little ferret's eyes. The time he did not spend with me he devoted to the daughter of the house. One afternoon when he had gone out I went into his room, and what I found there was illuminating. The idiot had left a report on his table—he was recording my every act and gesture in complete detail. He had taken down every last word I had uttered, and some words I had not. An informer and a liar—the ideal companion. I decided to correct the homework of this perfect spy by underlining all the inaccuracies in red ink and writing the word "false" in the margin.

My guardian angel came in very late that night. The next day he had disappeared. No doubt he decided to speak to his superiors before I spoke to them.

My situation since my return could be described very simply. Despite some transparent formalities, I was for all intents and purposes a prisoner.

They sent me a new "orderly," younger than the first, who

used the technique of charm. He invited me to go to the movies, and I accepted. The images passed before my eyes but held my attention for only a few seconds. I was obsessed with one thought: what were they going to do with me?

Ten days later, the three men who had been my first visitors came to dinner again. As before, I had no need to play host, because they provided large quantities of food.

In spite of the abundance of dishes and the generous supply of vodka, the atmosphere lacked warmth. I did not doubt that they had instructions to pump me, and that they were hoping to find me in a better frame of mind than I had displayed at our first banquet. The general from the NKVD broke the ice.

"Well," he asked, "what do you intend doing in the future?"

"I've already told you: return to Poland, to my native land; but first I want to talk with the directors."

He shook his head. Decidedly, I was incurably obstinate. He shot back crisply, "If you're so interested in the past, Otto, we're not the ones you'll be talking to." He laid great stress on the next four words: "That will happen elsewhere. Do you understand?"

"I understand perfectly, and I'll tell you frankly I don't give a damn!"

I had gone too far. The general and his companions got up and left without another word. I would bet a small fortune that he made his report at once. My behavior was damning. To demand explanations from the Center and to dream only of returning to my native land, Poland—these were absurd ambitions, immoderate, unpardonable.

I noticed that we had scarcely touched the food, although it was very appetizing.

I spent another quiet night. The next day, I was prepared for the worst. Let it come! A colonel, a new one, appeared, and I almost said, "Come in, I've been expecting you."

He said, "You have to move to another apartment."

I had to bite my tongue to keep from asking him whether it was heated, and how thick the bars were. I got my things

together and went with him. We got into a car. Not a word
was said. Night had fallen, but I knew Moscow well enough
to have some idea what direction we had taken. When we
arrived at Dzerjinski Square, my last doubts, if I still had any,
vanished; for this was the site of the infamous Lubianka.

The massive swinging doors of the first gate had closed
behind us. We arrived in front of a second closed door. The
colonel, who had not said a word, rang a bell and spoke with
someone through a spyhole. The door opened. We were in
the reception room of that noble institution. The colonel took
a receipt out of his pocket, handed it to the officer on duty,
who signed it, and then turned to me. To my great astonishment, he shook my hand for a long time, with feeling. Then
he stood there for a few seconds. There were tears in his
eyes—I can testify to that. At last, he walked away.

I looked around. I was in the heart of a fog, and yet the
reality was blinding: I was a prisoner—a prisoner in Lubianka.

2

The name has since become famous. All over the world, Lubianka is the symbol of police terror. Right in the heart of Moscow, this group of buildings houses the Ministry of Internal Security. In the middle is a little prison reserved for a few hundred "distinguished guests." Long corridors connect the ministerial offices with the cells, so that it is possible to go back and forth without leaving the building. All very cozy and convenient.

I was in the waiting room. All around me were doors leading to a dozen little cubicles. I was taken to one of them. The only furniture was one table and a chair. The door slammed behind me.

I felt very tired and I dropped into the chair. I was inert, drained, incapable of any reaction. I felt as if my brain were emptying, ceasing to function, ceasing to register. I touched my head, my arms. "Yes, it's me, it's really me. I'm here, a prisoner in Lubianka."

The sound of the door opening wrenched me from this state of semi-consciousness. I heard a voice: "Why aren't you getting undressed?"

I realized this noncommissioned officer in the white coat was speaking to me. I answered,

"Why should I get undressed? I don't see a bed."

"Get undressed and don't ask questions."

I obeyed and waited, stark naked. The door opened again, and two men, also dressed in white coats, came in. They searched my clothing thoroughly and put the contents of my pockets in a pile. When they had finished, one of them ordered:

"Stand up!"

He began examining me from head to foot. All that was missing was a stethoscope to make me think I was in a doctor's office. He examined my hair, my ears, asked me to open my mouth, stick out my tongue. He felt me all over, made me raise my arms.

"Raise your penis. Higher!"

"Turn around!" (I did as he asked.)

"Hold your buttocks in your hands, spread them apart— wider, wider!"

He leaned over and inspected my rear end. At the end of my patience, I remarked, "Did you lose something in there?"

"Don't provoke me, or you'll pay for that too. Get dressed."

He rummaged through my suitcase and took out a kilo of unroasted coffee beans, which I had bought when we stopped at Teheran.

"What's this?"

"Barley."

I observed with satisfaction that he put the coffee with the things they generally let you have in prison. He made a list of the objects he was keeping: necktie, shoelaces, suspenders, etc. I signed endless papers. A lieutenant came in, and signed a receipt stating that the objects had been delivered to him. Then he told me to come along. We walked through some long deserted hallways. He opened a door. I walked into a cell containing two beds. In one of them a man was asleep with his face turned toward the door and his hands resting on the blanket.

"There's your bed. Get undressed and go to bed!"

I obeyed, but sleep did not come. All night long I kept my eyes open. My open eyes worried the guard. Every three minutes the peephole opened and an eye appeared and looked at me. That night I learned my first lesson: if you can't sleep, close your eyes anyway; you'll get more privacy.

Morning. A hand passed "breakfast" through the grating: a bowl of a dark liquid that resembled coffee until you tasted it, a small lump of sugar, and a slice of bread. A voice beyond the door advised:

"That's your bread for the day."

I took a mouthful of coffee, but it wouldn't go down. I took a bite of the bread, which was the consistency of modeling clay. All this was immaterial to me; I felt disembodied, detached from material things. My cellmate woke up, said good morning, and did not utter another word. He was an officer.

Four days went by. I saw no one.

On the morning of the fifth day, at the changing of the guard, the noncommissioned officer asked,

"Do you have any requests?"

"Yes," I told him in a voice I tried to make energetic. "I would like to see one of the directors of the prison."

An hour later a captain came into the cell: "What's the matter?"

"I want to see the head of the Ministry at once, about a matter of great importance that does not concern me directly."

Two days went by. An officer came into the cell and asked me to come with him. We walked down the long hallways until we came to a little room where a woman handed the officer a receipt. Another noncommissioned officer appeared, signed a paper—ah, bureaucracy!—and conducted me through another interminable hallway, this one carpeted. We took an elevator. He pushed open a door and led me into an enormous room. On the floor was a huge red rug; on the wall, a portrait of the "little father of the people," the eyes grave, the moustache heavy: "he" was watching. Behind a long desk sat a man who was still young, dressed in civilian clothes. He was wearing a magnificent tie which immediately attracted one's attention. He got up, walked over, and said with a southern accent:

"So it's you! You're the one who belonged to the big intelligence network controlled by Berzin and his counterrevolutionary gang."

His mouth twisted with hatred as he said the last words. I made no reply.

"Do you know where you are?"

"If it weren't so luxurious, I'd say we were in a den of fascists."

My answer irritated him. He motioned me to walk over to

the large bay windows and, pointing to the prison, he asked me:

"Do you know where you are down there?"

"I guess so."

"Why did you let that gang of traitors talk you into working in a foreign country?"

"Excuse me, how should I address you?"

"General." This was General Abakumov, who ran SMERSH, a special section of the Ministry of Security created in 1943; the name meant, literally, "death to spies."

"Comrade General," I went on, "I did not work for a gang. During the war I ran a military intelligence network for the Red Army high command, and I am proud of what I've done."

Changing the subject, he asked, "Why did you ask to see someone in the ministry?"

"When I arrived in Moscow, I made some suggestions to two colonels in the Intelligence Service; I have received no reply. The matter does not concern myself; it is a question of saving the lives of fighters in the network. I ask that I be permitted to meet with someone high up at the Center to prepare this operation."

"It will be taken care of. That will be all."

We retraced our steps until we reached the border room that separated the ministry's offices from the prison. There were more receipts to be signed, and then I returned to my cell.

Two days later they came and got me; they took me to a room where two men in civilian clothes were waiting. Did they belong to the Intelligence Service or to SMERSH? Whatever the answer, they knew all about my case.

"Let's talk about your plan. There is no question of saving the persons of whom you speak. For the most part, they are not members of the military personnel of the Intelligence Service."

I clenched my fists to keep from shouting. "But the fighters of the Red Orchestra were military personnel, weren't they?

Don't their lives mean anything to you, after what they've done for victory?"

"We are interested in only one thing: bringing Pannwitz and Sukulov"—Kent—"to Moscow. If you have concrete suggestions to make, we will carry them out."

"Good," I said. "In two or three days, I will have a plan of action."

Several days went by, and then we met again. I asked,

"Are you in radio contact with Pannwitz, and if not, can you establish it quickly?"

"We are in intermittent contact. We can communicate with him."

Back in the thick of it, I almost forgot where I was. Suddenly I no longer felt like a prisoner, and I presented my plan to my two listeners:

"Until my escape in September, 1943, Pannwitz and his superiors were convinced that the Center had not seen through the Great Game. They were afraid that after I ran away I would warn Moscow. It was for this reason that Pannwitz had "Wanted" posters about the spy Jean Gilbert put everywhere. This way, I would be washed up in the eyes of the Center."

"Yes," said one of the two officers, "at that time Kent sent the Center a dispatch drawing their attention to these notices, which proved both your arrest and your escape. But here at the Center, in order to go on with the Great Game, we answered Kent that Otto had probably turned traitor."

"Precisely," I went on. "You must reinforce that impression. At regular intervals, send dispatches to Pannwitz always asking the same questions: Where is Otto? After a few weeks, you will warn him that you have succeeded in finding out that Otto has fled to South America. When they hear this news, Pannwitz and Kent will seriously start to consider coming to Moscow. But by carrying out this plan, you will condemn all the fighters of the Red Orchestra still in the hands of the Germans to death. Before he leaves, Pannwitz will get rid of all the witnesses to his crimes."

And I added forcefully, "You must take steps at the same time to save the survivors."

They got up and left without answering.

I was transferred to a small cell, where I was to spend many long weeks alone. The regimen became much more severe. Little by little, you become accustomed to the immutable rhythm of the days. At six o'clock in the morning, the guard's head appeared in the spy hole and a shout wrenched you from sleep:

"On your feet!"

You got up, picked up the pail, and headed for the toilet. Three minutes' stop, maximum. You left again for the lavatory. Two minutes to wash, then back to the cell. Seven o'clock: breakfast. A bowl of coffee—often no more than boiled water—a piece of sugar, and the day's ration of bread. In the cell, during the day, everything is forbidden. It is strictly prohibited to lie down on the bed, or to sit with your back to the door. All you can do is walk up and down, from one wall to the other, resting for a few moments on a little footstool. Then back to walking, up and down, up and down. At this rate you covered several kilometers a day.

Lunch was a bowl of soup, that is, a bit of greasy water with a few grains of barley floating in it. Same menu in the evening. In these postwar years, when the whole country was suffering from shortages, the rations in the prisons were more and more reduced. Often the soup was made from the heads of herring. You had to be starving in order to swallow this potion, which stank horribly, but habit took over and you ate it anyway, in order to stay alive.

At ten o'clock in the evening, the peephole opened and the same sinister voice shouted,

"Lie down!"

Even in bed you could not lie the way you wanted. You had to lie on your back with both hands outside the blanket and your face turned toward the door. The light burned all night. It was impossible to turn over, or to escape that blinding glare that ate into your eyelids. Later I learned some prisoner's tricks for getting to sleep: putting a sock over your eyes, for example.

The farce started all over again. They came and got me and took me to the examining officer. In one corner of the room was a little table and a stool for the prisoner. At the other end was a desk with a captain behind it. I sat down.

"Keep your hands on the table!"

The officer picked up a piece of paper; this was an interrogation.

"Last name, first name?"

"Trepper, Leopold."

"Nationality?"

"Jewish."

"If you're Jewish, why is your name Leopold? That's not a Jewish name."

"Too bad you can't ask my father; he's dead."

"Citizenship?"

"Polish."

"Social background?"

"What do you mean?"

"Was your father a laborer?"

"No."

He said aloud as he wrote, "Background: *petite bourgeoisie.* Profession?"

"Journalist."

"Political party?"

"Member of the Communist Party since 1925."

He wrote, still talking out loud, "He says that he has been a member of the Communist Party since 1925."

The interrogation was over. I walked out with a taste of ashes in my mouth. Polish citizen, Jewish, *petit-bourgeois* "background": so that was the total record of my twenty years of militant activities. I felt like weeping, but I held back my tears. I would not give them the satisfaction.

Every night at ten o'clock they came and got me for interrogation, which lasted, after that first one, until 5:30 in the morning. After a week without sleep, I wondered how long I could hold out. Remembering my hunger strike in Palestine, I observed that a "sleep strike" was even more difficult, and this time I was striking against my will. For the moment I was standing up under the interrogations. Interrogations? They were more like sessions designed to wear me out. Every night the same game started all over again:

"Tell me about your crimes against the Soviet Union," the examining officer would repeat, and I would answer like an automaton,

"I have committed no crimes against the Soviet Union."

During the next stage, the captain would pay no attention to me. He would read the papers and every so often he would repeat the question without raising his eyes. I would repeat mechanically,

"I have committed no . . ."

The intervals between questions would grow longer. The time would pass, and I would remain silent. I got used to sitting on my little stool without moving for seven hours at a time.

At dawn I would be taken back to my cell. A few moments later, the voice of the guard going from door to door would thunder:

"On your feet!"

No sooner had I lain down than another day began. They were trying to break me. Keep walking, hold on, hold on, hold on——

The second and third weeks following the start of my "investigation," they let me sleep one night out of seven. I would collapse, and in the morning the treadmill would start all over again.

One night during the fourth week a little man with an unhealthy yellowish face came into the interrogation room. He was intensely excited. This was the colonel in charge of the section on interrogation, notorious throughout Lubianka for his cruelty and sadism, a man who took real pleasure in hitting with his own hands. Without pausing for a breath he asked the captain,

"What results have you obtained?"

"None. He persists in denying his crimes; he hasn't started to talk yet."

The colonel turned to me and launched into a long tirade that lasted at least half an hour. It was a flood of oaths, insults, threats and abuse, interspersed with terms from the vernacular. Generally speaking, when you insult someone in Russian, you start with his mother; this experienced professional went back three or four generations! His imaginativeness—his "erudition"—impressed me at the time, but later I found out that he was only reciting a litany, prepared in advance and carefully studied as part of the elementary education of an examining colonel.

I did not react. Noticing that he was up against a blank wall, he broke off and threatened,

"The holiday in Lubianka is over! I will find the way to make you talk! You will confess your crimes!"

He opened the door and screamed hysterically, "Get this scum out of here!"

The guards rushed in. It was only one o'clock in the morning. Putting up with this clown was the price I had to pay to get a few hours of sleep.

For the next few nights they left me alone.

3

had been in Lubianka over a month on the evening a guard came into my cell and repeated the ritual phrase: "Come with me!"

As I started to fall in step with him, he added, "Bring your things!"

So I was changing domicile again? A few gestures sufficed to gather up all my possessions. Heavily guarded, I left the prison. A vehicle well known to the Muscovites—the *czorni woron*, or "black crow"—was parked in front of the gate. It was a small truck that looked no different on the outside from an ordinary delivery van; in big letters painted on the side were the words "Meat, Bread, Fish." But the interior had been arranged to transport another kind of merchandise. The space was divided into small cubicles, placed in such a way that the passengers could not communicate with one another. I was pushed into the truck; the ride lasted about half an hour.

We arrived at Lefortovo Prison, well known throughout the Soviet Union. The building reminded me of the medieval fortress Saint Jean d'Acre, where I had been imprisoned in Palestine. A military prison constructed under the Czarist regime, Lefortovo imposed such severe hardships on the prisoners that they came out of it disabled. It was closed after the October Revolution, but Stalin had it reopened in 1937 to accommodate Tukhachevski and his friends. The interior resembled a stadium: three stories of circular galleries onto which the cells opened, with a big empty space in the center from which every level could be observed.

Once again I was subjected to a search. It was absurd, since I was being transferred from one prison to another, but this obvious fact was beyond the comprehension of the penal administration. All my clothes were dipped in a disinfectant bath, from which they returned limp and shapeless. I was

348

conducted to a private cell. The walls were sweating and porous, and the dampness soon penetrated all my possessions. The cell had one luxurious feature: a pipe connecting the spiggot on the washbasin with the toilet; unfortunately, it was plugged up, and I was obliged to use the mess tin in which my meals were served in order to flush the toilet with water from the sink.

The day after I arrived, the barber appeared. He shaved me and got out a pair of scissors.

"And now," he announced, "I'm going to cut your hair."

"But I'm not going to be executed!"

"That makes no difference. Everyone has to have it, and if you refuse, I'll shave a cross on your head."

The guards at Lefortovo were much tougher than those at Lubianka. The prisoners never had a moment's respite. The guards were constantly slamming the doors of the spy holes and coming into your cell ten times an hour for every conceivable reason—"You're walking too much." "You've been sitting down too long." "You don't move around enough." The food, though I thought I had experienced the ultimate, was even worse than Lubianka's.

Every night around ten o'clock the prison awoke to an active nocturnal life: doors slamming incessantly, the footsteps of people being taken to interrogation. A few days after my arrival, it was my turn.

The captain who interrogated me asked some strange questions:

"Will you tell me how you, a Polish citizen, were able to enter the Soviet Union? Who helped you?"

He greeted my answers, which he did not write down, with a thick, cynical laugh. The session lasted all night. A few days passed, and once again I was brought up for examination. The captain, the same one, returned to the attack:

"Do you know what has become of the gang who ran the so-called communist university where you studied for three years?"

I mentioned the names of a few old Bolsheviks: Marchlevski, Budzinski, Frumkina. Frumkina was the principal leader of the Bund; she joined the Bolshevik party after the revolution, and was rector of the communist university for national minorities.

"All that rabble have been exposed as counterrevolutionary, haven't you heard?"

"Well, I'll tell you frankly that I'm proud to belong to that rabble!"

He froze up like an iceberg. "It's too bad you left the USSR. If you'd stayed, you would have been taken care of long since, and I wouldn't be wasting my time with you today." Then the refrain: "Tell me about your crimes against the Soviet Union."

All through this series of interrogations, not a single question was asked about my work during the war, or about the Red Orchestra. I had the impression that I was in prison solely because I belonged to that "gang" of old communists who had been eliminated before the war. My survival was an anomaly that my examiners wanted to correct.

One night at about four A.M., I had just returned from interrogation when the door of my cell opened and two guards came in, carrying a stretcher on which a man lay inanimate. They threw him on the unoccupied bed and left without saying a word. I walked over, and with a damp rag I bathed his swollen face, which had been badly beaten. The man lay on his stomach breathing in gasps; an officer of the Red Army had just been subjected to intensified interrogation. In the morning, the guards took him to another cell.

They called for me that night; a colonel sat in on the examination with the usual captain. When I sat down, the colonel asked me, with a little self-satisfied smile: "Well, you saw him this morning; what do you have to say?"

"Are you referring to the man who was brought into my cell in such pitiful condition?"

The colonel: "Of course. We wanted to show you what could happen to you."

"See here, colonel, I warn you solemnly that if any of you lays so much as one finger on me, you will never hear the sound of my voice again. If you subject me to that shameful treatment, I will regard you as enemies of the Soviet Union, and strong in that belief, I will fight back, even if it costs me my life!"

The colonel looked at me for a moment, surprised by this language, then exploded. I was treated to another tirade, which enriched my vocabulary. At last he left, slamming the door.

My usual examiner, the captain, asked me to be reasonable and not provoke him. I had no use for his solicitude.

"I do not regard you as representatives of the Soviet regime," I told him. "I have the hope and the will to survive you, be it only for one day. As for the members of the 'gang' you mentioned the other day, whom you have murdered here or elsewhere, don't deceive yourselves: you will meet the same fate as they did."

"Why do you insult me?" protested the captain. "I am only doing my duty."

"Your duty? Do you think I'm naive enough not to know what has happened since the death of Kirov? This may be the so-called 'Devil's Mill,' but don't forget—many men like you have ended up like the victims they falsely accused."

He did not reply. My outburst made me feel better. As I left, I repeated:

"You can go on asking me for years to confess my crimes against the Soviet Union, but you'll always get the same answer: 'I have committed no crimes against the Soviet Union!'"

This was my last encounter with the examining captain.

For several weeks, I remained alone in my cell. Then one night, the door opened and the familiar scene was enacted again:

"Take your things and come with me."

Moving again? Where to? To my great surprise, I found myself back in Lubianka, and I returned to my old cell with a certain pleasure: I felt almost at home there. I was left in peace for two weeks, and then one night at ten o'clock the interrogations started all over again. A new examiner—a colonel—had taken over my dossier.

About forty years old, with a sympathetic face, he invited me to sit down. The atmosphere was unusual. He picked up a box of fancy Kazbek cigarettes from his desk and offered me one. During the war I had become a great smoker, and for over three months I had not touched a cigarette. I looked at him, then at the little white tube I was craving, and told him, "No, thank you, I don't smoke."

To take a cigarette was already to enter into their game, it was the beginning of capitulation.

His first question rang strangely in my ears: "How do you feel? Aren't you exhausted after all these interrogations?"

Was I in Lubianka or in a café? It had been a long time since anyone had been concerned about my health. The heads of the interrogation section had obviously changed their tactics. My examiner released me at about two o'clock, and this would be the pattern of the days that followed. It was a considerable improvement.

For two months this new regimen continued. The man sitting opposite me did not write an official report, but he did take notes. He often talked interminably about Paris, Brussels, Rome, and Berlin, and I realized that he knew all of Europe and that I was dealing with a former counterespionage officer who had traveled a great deal. Gradually, he became interested in my work during the war, made inquiries about how I got established in Brussels, wanted to know why I sent for my family, and recorded my memories on the first day of the war in the west. His curiosity was insatiable, and in the course of our "interviews" I became convinced that he was perfectly familiar with the history of the Red Orchestra, but that he had trouble understanding how the network functioned and imagining how it had been possible to operate on such a vast scale with so few professional intelligence people. This question obsessed him; the Red Orchestra met none of his requirements for organizing a network as he conceived it.

He allowed me a few nights to myself. I was able to sleep, and I took heart again. This thing would eventually be resolved; they could not stop me from dreaming, even inside the four walls of Lubianka.

The fate of my family, however, tormented me. I knew only too well what usually happened to the families of prisoners; belonging to the family of a prisoner was a terrible disgrace. But somehow I could not imagine my wife and children being deported to Siberia. One night, unable to stand it any longer, I told my examiner that I feared my family might suffer a worse fate than my own. He made no reply, but a few days later he informed me that he had seen my family. He had taken them the gifts I bought in Cairo, which he had picked up at the prison office. He had told my wife that he himself had just returned to Russia, and he had given her my many messages.

"So they haven't been sent to Siberia?"

"Don't worry, nothing will happen to them."

Even if I did not completely believe it, I was reassured; it made it easier for me to bear my life as a prisoner. Then one night in June, they came and got me around two o'clock in the morning. My examiner was smiling. He asked me,

"Guess who I just met at the airport?"

"Pannwitz and Kent!" I was sure of it.

He laughed: "That's not all. Pannwitz brought his secretary, his radio operator and fifteen suitcases! He's become very zealous: he brought a list of German agents operating on Soviet territory and a code with which we can decipher the correspondence between Roosevelt and Churchill."

That very night, Pannwitz and his accomplices slept in Lubianka. History was playing a big joke: the head of the Red Orchestra and the head of the Sonderkommando, a few yards away from each other, in the same prison.

That night my interrogation concerned Pannwitz and his long list of crimes. I told the examiner about the murders of Suzanne Spaak and Fernand Pauriol, Pannwitz' attempts to "clean up" before he left.

For the past four months, we had been discussing every detail of the Red Orchestra: the Great Game, the meeting with Juliette, relations with Berlin, etc. During the fifth month, I was not interrogated; my examiner was writing up an official report based on his notes.

One night he sent for me, and handed me the document:

"Here's the report. Read it, and if you find it accurate, sign it."

I read it once, and then a second time. I was speechless with astonishment. He had written exactly the opposite of what I had told him.

"Look here, colonel, one of us has lost his mind. This report is false from beginning to end."

"So you won't sign it?"

"Surely you don't think I'm going to sign four pages of lies."

He remained imperturbable. "You're not signing it?"

"Of course not!"

He took the document and placed it on his desk. As if nothing had happened, he started making conversation about neutral subjects. This comedy went on for two weeks. "Will you sign it?" "No." "So you won't sign it?" "No!" "Why won't you sign it?"

One night the head of the section, his face just as bilious and contorted with nervous tics as ever, came in and asked the colonel, "Well, how long is this going to go on?"

I answered, "Until the last day of my life!"

There was a volley of insults. Then the colonel threatened, "Don't forget that you have a family. Your obstinacy may cost them dearly."

Two or three days later I was summoned in the middle of the night. The hallway outside the interrogation rooms was quiet. Instead of taking me to the usual room, they led me to the last room, at the end of the hall. The colonel was there. I headed for the little table, like the table I sat at in the usual room, but he invited me to sit by his desk. I did not see the report on his desk.

"I have decided to discontinue the investigation. I am turning your file over to my superiors," he informed me.

This statement of intent left me skeptical.

"That changes nothing for me. You were able to write a report that was nothing but lies. So will the examiner who replaces you, you're all the same."

He laughed. "So you think we are all the servants of the devil?"

"Yes, I do. The forms change but the goal remains the same. From the Minister of Security down to the most insignificant employee of this 'house,' you are all pursuing the same goal: to wipe out the best people in the party."

"I would like to talk to you confidentially. If I didn't trust you, I wouldn't say anything. If you were to tell my superiors what I am about to say, I would be sharing your cell this evening."

He paused for a moment. "The first thing I want to say to you is to hold onto your will and your determination during the long years of prison that await you. Above all, don't do anything foolish."

"Oh, so you think I'm going to commit suicide? Oh, no! I shall fight to the end. My whole being is bent toward a single objective: to survive you."

He looked at me, smiling sadly. "I was hoping you would talk that way," he went on. "I have decided to give up your case because my conscience as a man and a communist won't let me go on with it. I know this is going to get me in serious trouble, but I'm ready. Before we say goodbye, I would like to explain something which many prisoners like you do not understand. You think that the responsibility for the tragedy we are going through rests here, in the Ministry of Security. Not so! We are merely carrying out the policies of Stalin and the heads of the party."

"You carry them out faithfully."

"Of course, but the NKVD is not an institution above the party. It obeys the party. Naturally, in carrying out Stalin's plan, the leaders of the NKVD may be overzealous and go beyond the limits. Stalin says that the class struggle constantly deepens during the construction of socialism, and the NKVD is always liquidating more enemies to prove the correctness of this policy."

"Why are most of the examining officers so ferocious toward prisoners they know are innocent?"

"You mustn't put everyone who works here in the same category. The young ones are inexperienced; they perform their work, convinced that they are destroying the enemies of the party, Stalin, and the Soviet Union. Others continue to go through the motions without conviction; they don't believe in what they are doing, but if they refuse, they know that tomorrow they will be accused themselves. Terror is the driving force of the system. Finally, there are the 'careerists' and the sadists."

"One question bothers me constantly," I said. "When I was still in Paris, Marshal Golikov made a tour of the prison camps in the liberated territories and solemnly declared, in the name of Stalin and the party, that all Russians who had fallen into the hands of the enemy would be welcomed in their homeland. When these hundreds of thousands of prisoners of war returned to the Soviet Union, they were immediately arrested and deported. Why?"

"Stalin, you see, does not rule out the possibility of a war in the near future with our allies of yesterday; so he is undertaking on a vast scale the purification of all the circles he regards as dangerous to the security of the state. He is starting with all those who fought in Europe during the war: soldiers, officers, agents on assignment. Stalin has also declared that in the long chain of nationalities within the Soviet Union, there were 'weak links.' After the victory, he proposed a toast to the Russian people. At the same time he pointed out those who were suspect to the NKVD: Ukrainians, Belorussians, Asiatics, Ouzbeks, Jews—all the national minorities. All this will end some day, we will have a change of direction at the head of the party; but personally, I no longer want to be an accomplice in these crimes. Your fate, like that of all the old members of the Berzin team, was decided even before your first interrogation."

He repeated again, with force, "But my conscience as a communist won't let me go on."

While he was speaking, I drew toward me the pack of cigarettes that was lying on the table, took one, and lit it. He broke off, surprised.

"You smoke?"

"I'm a chain smoker."

"And you haven't accepted a cigarette for five months, because I was on the other side? I don't regret speaking frankly to you; you have given me another proof of your determination to hold out. I am convinced you won't end up like those who lose all hope and choose a slow death!"

It was seven o'clock in the morning, and day was beginning to break. We shook hands for a long time. As I was walking out of the room, the colonel added,

"I hope we will see each other outside this prison!"

In 1955 I met him in front of a public bath in Moscow. Transferred and stripped of his rank after my case, he had managed to leave the NKVD two years later.

This conversation between the prisoner and the NKVD colonel who was supposed to outwit him occupied my thoughts for weeks. It consoled me and brought me a measure of hope. I had just been given certain proof that truth could win out even in the kingdom of lies and falsehood—a temporary victory, to be sure, but one that shed a ray of light in the dark corners of my cell.

Meanwhile, the NKVD was attempting to erase all evidence of my presence in Lubianka. I was not the only one who was subjected to the rule of secrecy and silence. Luba, my wife, received an official letter from the Military Intelligence Service informing her that I had disappeared during the war. The "missing person" was, in fact, twenty minutes by foot from her. Since my fate was still unknown—the term "missing" covered a multitude of possibilities—my family did not collect a pension; but this solution did save them from being deported to Siberia. My wife subsequently bought a little shack on the outskirts of Moscow and moved in with our children. If some friend from France or elsewhere should come and make inquiries about me, it could be proved that my family was living in freedom and good health. After my return to Poland in 1957, I learned through one of my former contacts that when she had been in Moscow, she had been instructed to arrange "accidental" meetings with persons who were worried about me and to reassure them.

"Trepper?" my former contact would say, "Why, he's on assignment outside the country—highly confidential! But if you'd like to see his wife and children . . ."

The Jewish writer Isaac Pfeffer had been arrested in 1948

with all the members of the Jewish anti-Fascist committee. Some time later, the American Negro singer Paul Robeson had passed through Moscow and asked to see his old friend Pfeffer.

"Of course, but you'll have to wait a week; he's taking a cure on the Black Sea."

For a week, the NKVD stuffed Pfeffer with food and medicine to cure his prison pallor. Then they dressed him in new clothes and took him to Robeson's hotel. When the visit was over, they took him back to his cell. He was executed in August, 1952.

In the beginning of 1946, I was sent to Lefortovo again. I stayed there almost a year. A new examining officer, a major, started my dossier over from the very beginning, and knowing that my fate had already been decided, he did not try to obtain spectacular results with me. But he did introduce the new tactic of watching with a jealous eye to make sure the conditions of my confinement were as painful as possible. The imagination of torturers is unlimited.

At first I had shared my cell with a Russian officer, who was accused of being a spy for the United States because the camp in which he had been imprisoned by the Germans throughout the war had been liberated by American troops. The fact that this poor man's entire family had been murdered by the Nazis in his native village in Belorussia had entitled him to neither leniency nor compassion.

We were offered another companion. When he introduced himself to us, we found his service record edifying. He was—by an amazing coincidence!—one of the top men of the Gestapo in Belorussia, one of those who had exterminated the population in the region around Minsk.

"Don't you ever feel any remorse?" I asked, after listening to this criminal's memories.

"Remorse?" he answered. "Not at all—I was only carrying out orders from my superiors. But sometimes I do have nightmares, in which I relive the terrible scenes I witnessed. Don't be surprised if I scream in my sleep."

The Soviet officer, who had heard everything without

saying a word, was deathly pale, and I saw from the trembling of his body and the fixity of his expression that he was controlling himself with difficulty.

In a low, almost inaudible voice, he kept saying over and over, "He could have been the one who murdered my family!"

The Nazi left for interrogation. We sent for the officer on duty and requested that he relieve us of the presence of this individual. He looked us up and down contemptuously and answered,

"You're forgetting that you belong to the same rabble. There is no question of taking him away."

And he left, slamming the door.

About one o'clock that morning, the Gestapo man returned from interrogation. He lay down and fell asleep immediately. I couldn't get to sleep, and I observed that my companion's eyes were wide open too. Suddenly the Nazi began shouting. It was terrifying and unbearable.

Then I saw the officer get up, grab him around the throat, and knock his head against the wall. The Gestapo man woke up, of course, dazed, his head in his hands, wondering what had happened to him.

"You warned us that you screamed in your sleep," I told him, "but we didn't realize that you thrashed around too. While you were dreaming, you knocked your head against the wall."

The scene created a big uproar, and the guards rushed into our cell. Nothing was said—the condition of our cellmate spoke for itself. They understood. They left without asking any questions.

That same night, when I arrived for my interrogation, my examiner greeted me with a laugh. "So you don't feel like a prisoner any more—you've already taken the place of the judges."

"What are you referring to?"

"Come now, don't act so innocent. The Gestapo officer— was that your work, or your pal's?"

I looked him squarely in the eyes. "Both of us. And I'm

warning you, if we're not relieved of the presence of that individual, I won't be responsible for the consequences. They could be even more serious."

When I was returned to my cell, the Nazi had disappeared.

He was replaced a little later by a former captain in the Red Army. During the war he had been hit by a shell, and had lost part of his forehead. He was still suffering from the after-effects of this wound, and had just spent several months in a psychiatric clinic.

The day after his arrival, at noon, they brought us some cabbage soup, or what passed for it, actually just a few stagnant remains in an unappetizing broth. My new cellmate stared despondently at this meager fare and then, after a moment of silence, he said,

"Oh! The Jews, the Jews, the dirty Jews—they're the ones who are responsible for all our misfortunes!"

I grabbed him by the shoulders and shook him, saying,

"Listen, my friend, you'd better calm down and shut up, because you're talking to a Jew!"

He calmed down immediately and excused himself: he was sick, and he sometimes lost control. This I had occasion to observe, and I had to adjust as well as I could to the presence of this half-crazed fellow who ate the Jews at every meal.

After that it was Colonel Pronin. I recognized him immediately when he came into the cell, although he had changed a great deal physically. At the Center, Pronin had been responsible for all problems concerning the Red Orchestra in its beginning phases.

He had aged, and his face bore the marks of the suffering he had endured. We embraced, surprised to find each other in this place.

"What? You're here, too?"

"And you, what are you doing here?"

This rather stupid dialogue went on for a few seconds.

Then the door opened again, and an officer came in, grabbed Pronin by the arms, and dragged him away, saying,

"There's been a mistake, you're not supposed to be in this cell!"

A mistake? Come, now! This meeting had been deliberately arranged to show us that the purge of former members of
the Intelligence Service was still going on. The same operation was repeated later with Klausen, Richard Sorge's radio
operator. He arrived from Vladivostok, where he had spent a
long time in the hospital. Emaciated, his face contorted and
sickly, his tall frame bent by illness, he had trouble walking
erect. Psychologically defeated and disoriented, he did not
understand why, after many long years spent in Japanese
prisons, he had been arrested as soon as he returned to the
Soviet Union. To tell the truth, for any sane person who did
not follow the logic of the NKVD, it was truly incomprehen-
sible. It was Klausen who told me that Richard Sorge had
been arrested in 1941, and executed by the Japanese on
November 7, 1944—not until then.

Later I shared my cell with a man of about sixty, still
vigorous and impressively calm and assured. The last of
Soviet Intelligence in China, he had been arrested on his
return. He talked about his work with detachment, as something that belonged irremediably to the past.

During these conversations, I always remained discreet
about my previous activities. How could I be sure that the
prison administration had not introduced a spy among my
fellow "tenants," or that a microphone was not picking up
what we said? The walls of the prison were thick, but they did
not prevent secrets from making the rounds. A long time
after the fact, for example, I learned snatches of Wenzel's
story. An officer who had been imprisoned since 1945 told me
that he had had a German officer as a cellmate. This officer
had previously been imprisoned with Wenzel. I learned that
Wenzel had been horribly mistreated after his arrest. Exhausted, almost at the end of his strength, he continued to
hope that his nightmare would someday end. Until the end of
the war, the "professor" had been in hiding in Holland. As
soon as the war was over, he went to the Soviet Union—
voluntarily; and there the fate of all who had worked with
Berzin awaited him. The attitude toward Wenzel was worse,
though, than toward some others, because until 1936 Wenzel

had been a close collaborator of the German communist leader Ernst Thaelmann; after 1936 he worked for Berzin. To humiliate him, they put him in the same cells where former Gestapo officers were kept.

On the other hand, I saw neither Kent nor Pannwitz.

The House of the Living Dead

arewell, Lefortovo.

This time the police van left Moscow and took a road that plunged into a forest. After traveling for several hours we arrived in front of a building, lost among the trees, whose external appearance in no way suggested a prison. I had heard about this very special establishment, which the prisoners called the *dacha*, but even today I do not know its real name. A guard walked over and murmured in my ear,

"Here, we speak in whispers."

Every last detail had been thought out in order to avoid noise. The doors did not creak, the keys turned soundlessly in the locks, and the corridors were silent. Without having to be searched, I was conducted directly to a cell. It was an amazing cell: three feet long and two feet wide. The walls were covered with soundproofing material. Up above, a small window let in a little air. The silence! It was audible: absolute, dense, oppressive to the point of madness. I arrived in the middle of the night. In other prisons, from evening to morning the racket is incessant. Here, I was in a world of silence. Blinded by the light that shone all night, I tried to fall asleep, waiting in vain for some sound to come and trouble this sea of tranquility.

I awoke with a start. Someone was talking in my ear. It was the guard, telling me to get up. I had not heard him come in, and for good reason. He was wearing big felt slippers on his feet. The door had opened without a squeak.

Morning already. The hours, which were not punctuated by the noises characteristic of other prisons, went by without your realizing it.

Days or weeks passed in this deathly silence. I lost all sense of day and night, of time flowing. No one asked for me, no one talked to me. I was given food, without a word, without a sound, through the spy hole. My cell was a tomb, and I began to think I had been buried alive. Now and then a terrible, inhuman scream would pierce the silence, penetrate the insulated partitions, and make me jump with fright. Down the corridor, a few yards away, a prisoner was in the process of losing his mind. He was screaming his head off because he felt death prowling in his "tomb," he was screaming just to hear the sound of a human voice.

How could we withstand the anguish that gripped us? There was nothing to do from morning to night but pace back and forth the three feet between one wall and the other. You had to have a terrible will to survive to fight off the grip of the sense of death. And yet, curiously, after the year I had spent in Lefortovo this total calm was like a respite. I could sleep as much as I liked, sleep without fear of sudden awakenings or surprise interrogations. I had got used to living with my thoughts, with only my questions, my fears, and my reason for company. These constant companions reassured me that I could hold out. And then, contrary to all expectation, they came and got me and took me to a room in which there were an examining officer and two other individuals in civilian clothes: specialists in charge of checking the condition of the living dead.

The officer addressed me. "Well, how do you feel?"

"Very well, thank you; I'm quite content."

My answer seemed to surprise him. "Quite content? But what do you do all day, alone, without company or books?"

"Books? I'm writing one!"

They looked at each other knowingly. The "treatment" seemed to be working after all.

"A book? But how can you write a book?"

"I'm writing it in my head."

"And may we inquire the subject?"

"Certainly: *you*; you and everyone like you. That is the subject of my book."

"So you don't want us to take you back to a regular prison?"

"It's all the same to me; I can just as well stay here!"

They took me back to my burial vault. Once again I plunged into a silence that was occasionally rent by the animal cries of prisoners seized by madness. At these times I had the impression that it would take very little for these howls to become contagious, as among wolves. I, too, felt an overwhelming need to open my mouth and scream. Time passed, and I was unable to keep track of it. I was summoned a second time and I recognized the same people.

"Well, how do you feel, now that you've been here for two months?"

Two months since I had come here—two months in which they had tried to make me crack. They hoped I was going to get down on my knees to them and beg them, implore them to let me out. They expected me to surrender. Confident, mocking, they thought that time was on their side, that an endless series of days and nights all jumbled up in my mind would have reduced me to a spineless creature who would lick their boots. This was the logical result of the treatment, the inevitable outcome of the isolation. Well, not for me! I had to disappoint their optimism. They didn't have me yet. I shouted,

"If you want to make me die here, it will take a long time, a very long time. I feel just as well as ever."

They said nothing, but looked at this troublemaker who had come to disturb their order. In the brain of a bureaucrat of the NKVD, a prisoner in a special prison designed to drive people crazy, must go crazy. Logical, irrefutable! But you can break only people who no longer have the strength or the will to fight. As long as I felt that will in myself, I would fight. Did they understand that rage to survive that kept me going, which neither threats, nor pressure, nor walls of silence could extinguish?

A few days later, I was sent back to Lubianka, and I sensed that my worst moments were over. The interrogations ceased and I was left in peace. Only once did I have the honor of being called to the Ministry again. In the long hallway, my attention was attracted by a poster which in this setting was not lacking in humor. It announced a gala evening at the officers' club, starring Reikin, an actor from Leningrad. The theme of this event: "Come for a friendly conversation."

As I walked into the office of General Abakumov, who

since our last encounter had become Minister of Security—
previously, he had been running SMERSH—I was still
laughing at that invitation.

Abakumov, again wearing a magnificent necktie, asked
me,

"Why are you so cheerful?"

"It makes a strange impression on a prisoner to see a
poster inviting him to a 'friendly conversation!' You have
accustomed the prisoners to discussions of another sort . . ."

He ignored this remark, but said, "Tell me, in your
network, why did you have so many Jews?"

"In my network, Comrade General, we had fighters from
thirteen nationalities. The Jews didn't need any special
authorization, and no *numerus clausus*, no quota, was used.
The only criterion for selection was the desire to fight Nazism
to the end. Belgians, Frenchmen, Russians, Ukrainians,
Germans, Jews, Spaniards, Dutchmen, Swiss, and Scandina-
vians worked together like brothers. I had absolute confidence in my Jewish friends, whom I had known for many
years, because I knew that they would never turn traitor. The
Jews, Comrade General, were waging a double war: against
Nazism, but also against the extermination of their race. For
them, even treason was not a solution, which was not the
case for an Efremov or a Sukulov"—Kent, that is—"who tried
to save their skins by selling themselves."

Abakumov did not react, but returned to a subject he had
brought up before, at the time of our first conversation:

"You see, there are only two ways to thank an agent in the
Intelligence Service: either cover his chest with medals, or
cut off his head."

And he went on with a note of regret in his voice:

"If you hadn't worked with that gang of counterrevolutionaries—Tukhachevski, Berzin, and so on—you
would be a man laden with honors today; but you went
about it in such a way that you're good for nothing but a
prison cell. Did you know that at this very moment you're
being hunted by the American and Canadian secret services?
One of our networks has been broken in Canada. In several

North American newspapers, the experts have recognized the style of the Big Chief."

Amused and cynical, very pleased with his joke, Abakumov added,

"Do you realize the danger you'd be exposed to if you were at liberty? Here you are completely safe and undisturbed."

I put on the austere and serious expression of an employee of the NKVD and replied, "Thank you, Mr. Secretary, for being concerned about my safety."

"Don't mention it. Oh, I realize that the life you lead here may not be ideal. Alas, we don't have the means of the king of England, who receives secret agents, raises them to the rank of lords, and confers magnificent estates on them. We are poor, you know, and we give only what we have. Well, what we have are prisons—and prison is not so bad, don't you agree?"

He dismissed me with a gesture.

I returned to my cell. Now I was convinced: my activities in the Red Orchestra were not in question. No, what they could not forgive me for was having been chosen by General Berzin. The examining officer who had the guts to give up my case had spoken the truth: I had been suspect since 1938.

5

Some Lessons in History

The preparation of my dossier was over, but I knew very well I had been declared guilty before I had been heard. On June 19, 1947, the Council of Three, a representative of the Ministry of Security, a prosecutor, and a judge, sentenced me to the heavy penalty of fifteen years of confinement. Like so many others, I was found guilty by agents carrying out Stalin's orders. I filed an appeal against this arbitrary decision, and a little later I was called in by an assistant to the prosecutor.

"This verdict is totally unjust," I told him, "and it will come as no surprise to you when I say that I contest it."

"You know that in the USSR traitors and spies are liable to the death penalty; but in your case, reasons of state have dictated isolation."

"But anyone would think you weren't aware of what I did during the war!"

"Well, write to the prosecutor."

Under this obscurantist regime, those who had been sentenced still had one remote chance. Twice a month they had the option of making their observations in writing. I had to take advantage of this possibility, and in very small handwriting, I wrote a history of the Red Orchestra, which I sent in installments. In the desert wastes of Siberia or in the half-light of dungeons, captives were disappearing by the millions, but I had unlimited confidence in the Stalinist bureaucracy's love of paperwork. Individuals pass away, but writings remain and files accumulate. I knew the Stalinist bureaucracy still had a passion for documentation, and that it was not useless to leave evidence in their archives.

On January 9, 1952, the "troika" reduced my sentence from fifteen years to ten, but I greeted this news with indifference. Unless the regime changed, I nourished no illusions about my fate: at the end of my prison term I would be relegated to some lost corner of Siberia.

I learned, much later, that my report had not been useless. In 1964, when I had been living in Poland for several years, I got a telephone call from a journalist on the staff of *Novosty*, a press service that put out books and articles intended for foreign distribution.

"You must remember me," he said. "We worked together on *Der Emes* in 1935. I have been assigned, with two other writers, to write a history of the Red Orchestra, and we need information on the Unity group you ran in Palestine."

"And all the rest you know?" I asked, surprised.

"Yes, and I hope we'll have a chance to talk about it soon."

Several months went by. Then in April, 1965, the journalist came to Warsaw with a delegation that took part in a ceremony commemorating the twenty-second anniversary of the uprising in the Warsaw Ghetto. He told me the circumstances under which he had learned the history of the Red Orchestra:

"In 1964, I went to see the Vice Attorney General of the Soviet Union in connection with an article I was writing for *Novosty* on Richard Sorge, whom everyone was talking about at the time. He listened as I explained the purpose of my visit, then got up and walked over to a safe. He said, 'Everyone knows all about Richard Sorge, but we have an account of the life of a network that rendered just as great service.' He opened the safe and took out a file folder containing a large bundle of papers. 'Here are the notes,' he said, 'but I warn you they can't be published without authorization by the Central Committee.' I asked him who the head of this network had been. Imagine my surprise when I heard him say 'Trepper.' Very much interested, I addressed myself to the Central Committee, which appointed a team of three writers, myself included, to prepare a report on the Red Orchestra. Unfortunately, it has not been published, because the leaders of the Communist Party in East Germany have felt that it was too soon to talk about the Berlin group."

So the little papers I had sent to the prosecutor had not been lost. In the Soviet Union, files last forever, and the day they are opened——

But I had not reached the time of my liberation. My life in

Stalinist jails was only beginning. I was to know several of them but of all the ones I knew, the prison in Butirki—a renovated former barracks from the time of Catherine II—left me with the least unpleasant memory, with its huge, light, well-ventilated rooms. We were transferred there when it got too crowded in Lubianka, and this was a very revealing indication that the repression was being redoubled. Stalin had given his own meaning to the old Russian proverb that says "a holy place never remains empty." The security services were working according to the principles of Stakhanov—they over-fulfilled their quotas. The elite of the country were confined behind high walls and barbed wire. The successive waves of repression filled the cells with engineers, officers, writers, and professionals.

From the outset of the cold war in 1947, Stalin set about eliminating those whom he judged too lukewarm in the event of another world conflict. National minorities, those who made up the famous "weak link" in the view of the despot, were severely affected.

Once again, the army was purged. To tell the truth, Generalissimo Stalin—"the most inspired strategist since Alexander the Great"—was growing more and more intolerant of the brilliant success of Marshal Zhukov, the "victor of Berlin." Eisenhower had extended an invitation to the marshal to visit the United States, at the time of Eisenhower's visit to Moscow, and Stalin took that as an unbearable affront. Zhukov was becoming a rival, a competitor—a threat. Showered with honors and praise, he was given command of an army—the minuscule, out-of-the-way army of Odessa. All the officers in his entourage were sent to prison. The Jews, the most suspicious elements of the "weak link," were affected by the repression in 1948. The tide of the purged was next swelled with "hardened offenders," engineers and scientists who had been taken out of the camps at the beginning of the world war so they could be put to work in war industries. And then? And then all the others, who were guilty of being innocent!

Of course, there was also a very small minority of prisoners who were guilty: Vlasov and his staff, who had gone over to the German side to create a so-called army of liberation; Gestapo members who had committed their crimes on the territory of the Soviet Union; White Russians who had taken up arms against the Red Army. All of them were notorious for collaboration with the enemy, their subordinates having already been tried on the actual sites of their crimes.

With these exceptions, the prisoners I met were absolutely innocent. Each one of them could have been the subject of a whole book describing years of sacrifice and devotion to the party and to the Soviet Union; instead they were rewarded with sentences of ten, fifteen, or twenty-five years in prison. Each life may seem unique for the person who lives it, but in the great whirlwind of the purge, how similar their destinies seemed!

I am grateful to the "little father of the people" for introducing me to the intellectual elite of the Soviet Union. In Lubianka, Lefortovo, and Butirki, most of the men I met had led exemplary and fascinating lives which taught me a great deal about the history of our century.

I would like to describe a few of these exceptional encounters in the prisons of Stalin.

onversations with high-ranking officers who had been imprisoned taught me many details of the defeat of the Red Army at the beginning of the war. The Soviet soldier took an oath never to be captured alive, and was expected to save his last bullet for himself. But you don't fight wars with oaths; from the very beginning of their offensive, the Wehrmacht succeeded in surrounding entire divisions. Many soldiers managed to run away, many were taken prisoner. The second group were guilty of not committing suicide. The others, those who succeeded in getting through enemy lines and rejoining the Red Army, were accused of espionage. In both cases, the prison sentences were heavy.

I spent several months sharing a cell with three generals. They are still alive, so it will be understood if I do not give their names. One of them had been fighting in the Red Army since the civil war, in which he had taken part as a very young man. At the beginning of the Second World War, he commanded a division of Cossacks that was cut off and surrounded by the enemy. Seriously wounded, he still succeeded in escaping and taking refuge at the home of peasants, who took care of him secretly for several months. When he recovered, he rejoined friendly lines—after a long series of adventures. He was immediately asked, "Why did you come back? What intelligence mission did the Germans give you?" He was dumbfounded, and before he had a chance to reply, he was arrested, and sent to Lubianka.

My second co-prisoner had been a communist since the civil war, and at the outbreak of hostilities he was general of a division. Battered by the German attack, his troops held out well and fought courageously, but suffered considerable losses. The division was soon decimated. The general, with a small group of soldiers, plunged into the woods, where he organized a group of partisans who continued to fight for

372

several months. This guerrilla force was discovered and attacked. The general narrowly escaped, with two companions, and while the partisans covered his retreat, he rejoined the Red Army. He was suspected of espionage and arrested. He had committed the unpardonable offense of surviving. He was sent to Lubianka.

The last general of this *troika* had been incarcerated for no reason. His crime was having worked on Zhukov's staff during the war. He too was sent to Lubianka.

These three generals did not give way to discouragement. They said that they were still communists; and they paid little attention to the abuse from our guards. They still had their fur caps with the red star. I remember that they passed the time playing endless games of dominoes, which they had fashioned from breadcrumbs.

One day, a new guard—a sergeant, at the most—came into the cell and demanded that the prisoners stand up and greet him. Imperturbable, the three officers went on with their game. One of them remarked, without bothering to turn around,

"Since when does a general in the Red Army have to rise in the presence of a subordinate?"

The subordinate in question did not insist. In the future this was understood.

Between games of dominoes, we had lengthy discussions. The most politically aware of my three companions knew very well that what had happened to him was no accident resulting from the zeal of some hireling of OGPU, and he told me, with great conviction,

"Everything the butchers of the Ministry of Security do is accepted, desired, encouraged, and directed by Stalin himself."

Too many separate pieces of evidence lent confirmation, making up a picture of frighteningly methodical repression on a mass scale. For example, there was the experience of the two Jewish doctors—two brothers—which the general told me of. They were serving in a military hospital in Belorussia, and wondered what attitude to adopt in the face of the

German advance. In the end one of the two, who was the head doctor, could not bring himself to abandon his patients, and decided to stay and take care of them under the enemy occupation. In this way he saved many lives. The other brother, who wanted to avoid falling into the hands of the Nazis at any price, fled—along with all the hospital's doctors except for his brother—and joined the partisans. After the war, both brothers were arrested. The head doctor was accused of collaborating with the enemy, the other one of having fled and abandoned his patients.

Long live the dialectic!

Then there was that incredible party in the Kremlin, which a member of the Rumanian Communist Party told me about. Before being arrested, he had served as an interpreter—he spoke Russian perfectly—when a delegation from his country came to Moscow. Giorgiu Dej himself, secretary general of the Rumanian party, made the trip to meet with the Soviet leaders. At the end of a day of discussions, Stalin invited the Rumanian delegation to an intimate dinner, which the interpreter attended. After dinner, the atmosphere was very gay and relaxed. Stalin, in a jovial mood, came over to Giorgiu Dej and took him cordially by the shoulders.

"You know, Giorgiu," he said, "you're a good boy, but you're still uneducated. You don't know enough to be running a country. You're like a second lieutenant in command of an army—in short, you still have a lot to learn!"

The guests, suddenly sobered by the brutality of the attack, did not dare open their mouths. They put Stalin's remark down to the well-known dry humor of this great wit—who was just as good at telling jokes as he was at expounding the theories of Marx and Lenin. Ah, there was nothing like friendly relations between brother parties!

Another of my cellmates, an old militant of the Polish Party who had miraculously escaped the purge of 1938, told me about another of Stalin's parties. In 1945 the leader of the international communist movement received in the Kremlin a delegation of Polish communists who were going to form the new party leadership. Stalin shook hands with them, chatted about one thing and another, and asked,

"Before the war, one of the leaders of the Polish party was a woman, Kostrzewa, who was very devoted and very intelligent. What ever became of her?"

The militants present looked at each other, and then at their feet, confounded. Comrade Kostrzewa, like the rest of the Polish leadership, had been liquidated in 1938 by Stalin's orders. The great liquidator of communists frequently feigned ignorance, the better to cover up his overwhelming responsibilities in the purges. He delegated his powers of execution, as in the case of Bela Kun, which I have already related; at that time Manuilski had been assigned to do his dirty work.

Then there was Stalin's son's psychiatrist.

In 1949, or perhaps in 1950, I shared a cell with one of the greatest psychiatrists in the Soviet Union. He was a Jew who had been born into a very religious family in Vilna; his father assisted the rabbi at the synagogue. He left home as a very young man, and over the years he became completely assimilated. In language, manners, and culture, he felt Russian. Called up during the war, he ran the health service for the army that subsequently liberated the Baltic countries. By the time of the liberation, he was a well-known psychiatrist, and he became personal physician to Vasily, Stalin's younger son. (The other son was taken prisoner by the Germans and abandoned to his fate by his father.) Vasily, appointed a general at the age of twenty-three, was a mediocre aviator whose chronic alcoholism made him an object of ridicule throughout the Soviet Union. The psychiatrist had been assigned the ambitious task of curing him; after which, deciding that he knew too much, the gentlemen of the NKVD decided to arrest him. During the interrogations, Stalin's son was never mentioned; on the contrary, the doctor was accused of "Jewish chauvinism." The evidence?

When the Red Army entered Riga, which was in ruins, hundreds of orphans, starving and destitute, had formed gangs of juvenile delinquents. The general responsible for the area suggested that the psychiatrist set up a center for the lost children. He did this, and took in a majority of Jews. The men of the NKVD seized on this fact and accused him of Jewish chauvinism:

"It is obvious," they said, "that you gave these children priority over the others."

"Not at all. If the Jews were more numerous, it was because more Jewish families suffered!"

The interrogations took on a more and more pronounced tone of anti-Semitism. As the examiner was filling out his personal questionnaire, he asked him:

"Nationality?"

"Russian."

"You're not Russian, you're nothing but a dirty Jew! Why do you conceal your nationality?"

A new examining officer came in, and the interrogation began all over again: "Nationality?"

This time my friend answered, "Jewish!"

The examiner reeled off the traditional string of insults. "Aren't you ashamed to call yourself Jewish, when you're Russian!"

"It was here, in your prison, that I realized that I am a Jew," retorted the psychiatrist. "I am not ashamed to belong to a race that has given the world Jesus, Spinoza, and Marx. If in a socialist country you do not permit the Jews to be integrated into the population, so much the worse for you! On the day when humanity eliminates distinctions between peoples, races, and nations, we Jews will be the first to prove our internationalism."

When he came back into the cell after that interrogation and told me what he had said, my friend was very proud. The scene reminded him of the day he had sent a copy of his first scientific book to his father. His father had responded, "I am very happy for your success. I hope it will last—and that one day you won't be made to feel you are an intruder because you are a Jew."

But finally the psychiatrist, who was so good at helping other people, could no longer help himself. For the crime of taking care of Stalin's son, he had been condemned without appeal. He lost his courage. His health deteriorated. He became depressed and stopped fighting, gradually abandoning himself to his fate. He was taken away in serious condition and I learned later, from the woman doctor of Lubianka, that he had died of heart disease.

One morning at about five o'clock the door opened and the guards brought in a well-dressed soldier. In the half-light it was difficult to tell whether he was Chinese or Japanese. He introduced himself as General Tominaga. Chief of staff of the Japanese army in Manchuria, he had been taken prisoner toward the end of the war. He had been brought from a camp to testify in a trial of Japanese war criminals that was to have taken place in Tokyo. The first day, he looked at the meals we were given, and demanded to see the director of the prison.

"I have a serious stomach ailment," he explained, "and I can't eat this food." As a prisoner of war, the Japanese general got the same menu as the officers' mess, which was much better than the meager rations his cellmates received. But Tominaga complained, "I don't need all this, I don't need very much—just a few bananas a day!" He did not understand what we found so amusing: bananas in Moscow, after the war, and especially in prison—you might as well look for oranges at the North Pole!

Tominaga had to give up the diet of bananas, but he was given special food. We did not know Japanese, and the directors of the prison thought we did not know English; since they were afraid Tominaga would talk about his interrogations, they had him put in our cell. But our jailers were wrong: my cellmate and I did understand the language of Shakespeare, even if we spoke it badly. After several days, I was surprised to hear Tominaga speaking French, and to learn that he had been military attaché in Paris. After that, we no longer had any communication problem.

"Do you know anything about Richard Sorge?" I asked him.

"Naturally. When the Sorge affair broke out, I was Vice-Minister of Defense."

"In that case, why was Sorge sentenced to death at the end of 1941, and not executed until November 7, 1944? Why didn't you propose that he be exchanged? Japan and the USSR were not at war." (The USSR officially declared war on Japan August 8, 1945.)

He cut me off energetically. "Three times we proposed to the Soviet Embassy in Tokyo that Sorge be exchanged for a Japanese prisoner. Three times we got the same answer: 'The man called Richard Sorge is unknown to us.'"

Unknown, Richard Sorge? When the Japanese papers were full of stories about his contacts with the Soviet military attaché? Unknown, the man who had warned Russia of the German attack, and who had announced in the middle of the battle of Moscow that Japan would not attack the Soviet Union, thus enabling the Soviet chiefs of staff to bring fresh divisions from Siberia? They preferred to let Richard Sorge be executed rather than have another troublesome witness on their hands after the war.

The decision had not come from the Soviet Embassy in Tokyo, but directly from Moscow. Richard Sorge paid for his intimacy with General Berzin. After Berzin was eliminated, Sorge, in the eyes of Moscow, was nothing but a double agent, and a Trotskyite in the bargain! For months his dispatches were not decoded, until the Center finally realized the inestimable military value of the information he had provided. After his arrest in Japan, the directors at the Center abandoned him like a cumbersome piece of luggage; such was the policy of the new team.

Moscow allowed the "unknown" Richard Sorge to be executed on November 7, 1944. Since then, Moscow has proclaimed, proudly, the history of Sorge's work. I am particularly happy to expose this imposture today, and to make this accusation before the world: *Richard was one of us.* Those who allowed him to be murdered have no right to claim him as theirs.

Another witness to history: the man who joined us was short, and the leanness of his face brought out the energy of his features. He stated his name, which today escapes me. Even at the moment it made no impression on me. And then, suddenly, as soon as he started telling the story of his life, I realized who he was with a start: he was Vlasov's number two man! His was a strange destiny.

When the October Revolution broke out, he had been a young officer in the Czarist army. A fanatical anti-Bolshevik, he choked down his hatred for the triumphant revolution, and joined the Red Army. The years did not erase his dislike of the regime; patiently he awaited his hour. The German attack delighted him. From the very beginning of the war, he looked for a way to go over to the other side. He was one of the first to join Vlasov when the latter created the famous Army of Russian Liberation under the authority of the Germans.

Disillusionment! The admirer of the old Czarist regime, who allied himself with the Nazis out of ideological sympathy, discovered the bluff of the Vlasov Army, which primarily served German propaganda. Now political commissar of Vlasov's units, our man tried in vain to inculcate some National Socialist ideology into men who had been driven by hunger to enlist under the enemy flag. Between dying of starvation in a prison camp and putting on the uniform of Vlasov's Army, many Red Army soldiers chose survival.

Vlasov's aide told us how, at the first serious engagement, the men deserted *en masse* and rejoined the Russian lines. A unit of aviators, which had been organized with great difficulty, flew away to Soviet airfields.

Even the officers on Vlasov's staff lacked real conviction; they had more appreciation for the bottle than for *Mein Kampf.* As the months went by, the leaders of the Army of

Russian Liberation turned into a gang of hardened ruffians. Their force had no military value, and the German High Command used it to do the dirty work of repression in the occupied countries.

Vlasov's aide shared our cell throughout the trial of his superior and his staff. Every evening our man, now as cynical as he had been fanatical, gave us an account of his day in court. He reported the sessions with an amused detachment, as if he were attending as an observer and not as an accused man.

On the first day, as soon as the trial opened, he told us, Vlasov had wanted to make a solemn statement. Posing as a hero, he told his judges in a loud voice: "Whatever your decision may be, I will enter history!"

In the silence that followed his peroration, the court heard another voice coming from the box of the accused: "Yes indeed—you will enter history through the asshole!"

It was our man, Vlasov's former aide, who had chosen to amuse himself to the end.

After the reading of the verdict, which sentenced them to hanging, the presiding judge asked the accused whether they had anything to say. Our cellmate rose and addressed his judges with deep solemnity. "I have a request to make. I earnestly ask the court that I not be hanged next to Vlasov."

"Why not?" the judge asked, astonished.

"It will be a comical sight. Vlasov is very tall and I am very short. It might detract from the gravity of the ceremony."

When they came to get him to take him to the cell of the condemned, he shook hands with each of us and said,

"I was and I have remained an irreconcilable enemy of the Soviet regime. I have only one regret: that I ever got involved in that bullshit Vlasov Army."

After Vlasov's aide and so many others, the world of captivity still had more surprises in store for me. The manner in which I made the acquaintance of the new boarders seldom varied. The door would open, revealing the face and form of the newcomer; I would study his face—his first steps and gestures, too—for a few seconds, to try to give him a name, to gather together a few memories. Where did he come from? Had he been one of us?

Here was a new one, now. Age had not yet bowed his tall frame, or altered the intelligence of his face. His costume contrasted with the elegance of his manner: the too-short trousers that bared the calves, the too-big jacket thrown over his shoulders. As if he were entering a drawing room in "good society," he came over to each of us and introduced himself in an obsequious tone, bowing his head slightly.

He was standing in front of me, and I heard, "Vitali Szulgin."

I stared at him in astonishment.

"Vitali Szulgin, head of the Black Hundred?"

"In person; I see that you have read the leaflet about me published in Moscow; but believe me, it is far from accurate——"

"I must tell you immediately," I interrupted, "that I am Jewish." The Black Hundred was a group of armed gangs who had made a specialty of pogroms, before 1917.

"In prison we have nothing to hide from each other, but I would like to point out that many years ago I stopped being an anti-Semite. In 1935, in Paris, I gave a lecture before a Masonic lodge on the subject, 'Why I am no longer an anti-Semite.'"

Szulgin lay down on the bed next to mine and for many long hours he told me the story of his life.

At the beginning of the war, the Nazis had invited him to Berlin and proposed that he take part in the anti-Bolshevik crusade. But Szulgin—a reactionary with fascist sympathies and an anti-communist to the tips of his toes—had refused. He felt that these Germans cared very little whether Russia was red or white, that their only ambition was the conquest of vast territories. Szulgin spent the whole war living anonymously in a small village in Yugoslavia. After the defeat of Hitler's hordes, he decided to return to the Soviet Union. The victory had gratified his "great Russia" chauvinism. He was attached to his native land, and wanted to end his life there, even in prison.

He presented himself at the Soviet military mission in

Belgrade. The young NKVD officer on duty stared in amazement at this man who was volunteering to become a prisoner. He consulted the list of wanted persons. Szulgin was not on it. "You may go; we do not know you," he said.

But Szulgin did not give up; he came back the next day. This time a colonel was sitting behind the desk. As soon as Szulgin gave his name, the colonel got up, rushed at him, and shouted, losing all control,

"You mean you are Szulgin, the organizer of the pogroms in Russia?"

"At last, someone who recognizes me," the former head of the Black Hundred said, without losing his composure.

They put him on a plane for Moscow, and he who had dreamed all his life of being a pilot had his first airplane ride, from Belgrade to Lubianka.

Then came his hearing. "What's the use of wasting your time with me?" he asked the examining officer. "Put me in a private cell, and I'll write the story of my life and my crimes against the Soviet Union."

He filled several hundred pages. Every time he went for interrogation, the room was full of officers who came to listen to the "lecture." Szulgin made an original contribution to the pre-October history of Russia. As the head of the Black Hundred, he had been part of the delegation that went to ask the czar to abdicate. Nicholas II was deep in a game of chess and did not want to be distracted. When he learned the object of their visit, the czar did not try to conceal his joy: "At last, it's over!"

"What do you expect?" Szulgin added. "He was the biggest idiot in the whole dynasty."

Szulgin's political ideas were really extraordinary. He frequently held forth on his favorite subject, the greatness of Russia: "Under the leadership of Stalin, our country has become a world empire. It has achieved the goal to which generations of Russians have aspired. Communism will fall away like a wart, but the empire will remain. It's too bad that Stalin isn't a real czar; he has all the qualifications. Ah, if only Stalin weren't a Bolshevik. You communists don't understand the Russian soul: the people have a quasi-religious need to be guided by a father they can trust."

Szulgin rested all his hopes on the greatness of Stalin's empire.

"I do not want to be released," he said, "because everywhere I went I would be received as you have received me. I hope they will give me a cell where I can continue to write books on the history of our country."

Szulgin, the fanatical anti-Semite, the promoter of pogroms, was released well before the communist militants. He was assigned a *dacha* in a village where, even today, he continues to work, the tireless eulogist of the Stalin regime.

In my long voyage in the shadows, these encounters were exceptional highlights, brief moments of respite from the monotony of the days. I have taken only a few pages to cover wasted years of my life. Of time spent in a prison, one remembers only the unusual event. The rest, the thousands of identical days, melt in the memory: the hours when hope runs out, the daily gestures repeated a hundred times, the anguish of time irrevocably lost, the habits that take over. What is there to tell? We did not live during those years that marked us forever; we only survived.

7

Freedom!

In early March, 1953, the regime at Lubianka suddenly
became more severe. The air vents in the cells were covered
over and for ten days walks were discontinued. The guards
wore sinister expressions. We asked each other whether a
new war had broken out.

One morning, rounds of gunfire were heard. The officers
in our cell recognized the pattern of shots fired during an
official ceremony. Was it a day of celebration, or a day of
mourning? From the looks on the faces of the guards, we
leaned toward the second hypothesis. Then everything went
back to normal.

Weeks went by. Then one day a new prisoner informed us
that Stalin was dead. The prisoners reacted in various ways.
No one regretted Stalin's passing, but some were afraid that
the regime would become even more severe. This anxiety
intensified when we were transferred to Lefortovo. In May, I
was called before the director of the prison.

"You can write to a higher court," he told me, "and ask for
a review of the decision of the Council of Three."

I addressed my request, which I wrote out immediately,
right there in the director's office, to the secretary of the
Central Committee, Comrade Beria, the head of the Ministry
of Internal Security.

Two months went by. In July I sent a letter to the director
to find out why I had not had an answer. The next day he
called me into his office. He was holding my request in his
hand. "I accept your request; but why did you address it to
Beria?"

I looked at him uncomprehendingly. "But isn't that how
it's done? Whom should I write to?"

"The Minister of Security, or the Secretariat of the Central
Committee."

I returned to my cell with this news: Beria was in disgrace, **384**

no longer at the head of the Ministry! The prisoners constructed hypotheses and wondered about the future. In
August, we were taken back to Lubianka. Another two
months went by.

At the end of 1953, I was summoned to the Ministry. Again
I walked the now-familiar route that led to Abakumov's
office. To my surprise, an old general, bald and moustachioed, was sitting behind the desk; he rose when I entered
the room and greeted me very warmly:

"Sit down, Lev Zacharevich."

I jumped: it had been years since anyone had addressed me
by my patronymic.

He asked me in a friendly tone, "Have you read the newspapers in the last few years?"

"The newspapers? Certainly not."

"First, let me introduce myself. For several weeks I have
been Vice-Minister. I was a close collaborator of Dzerzhinski,
but I left that job, as it wasn't right for me. I have gathered
several newspapers for you. Read them, and tell me what you
think, forgetting the fact that you're a prisoner."

The general ordered tea and sandwiches, and handed me a
newspaper dated January 13, 1953. On the first page was an
editorial headed "Despicable Spies and Murderers Pose as
Professors of Medicine," and on the last page a communiqué
from the Tass Agency summarized the "Conspiracy of the
White Coats":

> Some time ago, state security agencies discovered a terrorist
> group of doctors whose aim was to shorten the lives of leading
> personalities of the Soviet Union through harmful medical
> treatment.

Nine names followed, including those of six Jewish professors well known in the Soviet Union. "Most of the members
of this terrorist group were associated with the bourgeois
nationalist Jewish international organization," the communiqué stated.

The general watched my face, and when I had finished

reading he asked, "What is your frank opinion of this matter?"

"It's grotesque. If someone wanted to do away with the leaders, he would hire assassins, not doctors."

"Precisely. We have succeeded in learning the truth in the case—none too soon, alas."

He handed me *Pravda* for April 4, 1953. On the second page, a comuniqué from the Ministry of the Interior announced:

> It has been established that the depositions of the accused persons confirming the charges made against them were obtained by members of the investigation service of the former Ministry of Security through the use of methods of investigation that are inadmissable and strictly prohibited by Soviet law.

The general took back the newspaper and showed me the issue edged with black, announcing the death of Stalin. I pushed it away without reading it; we already knew that news.

Then he took out his last issue of *Pravda*, dated July, 1953. It contained the news that Beria, that "enemy of the people," had been excluded from the Central Committee and driven from the ranks of the Communist Party, and that all his responsibilities at the Ministry of Security had been withdrawn.

"You are on the first list of prisoners whose hearings the head of the ministry has decided to review," he told me, "because we know you are innocent."

Excitement filled the cell when I reported these words. Everyone began to hope again, and with reason. A few days later, one of my co-prisoners, a general, was summoned before the investigating committee and informed that his dossier was going to be reviewed.

At this time, the purge was in full swing, conducted by the new Minister of Security, Serov, a close associate of Khrushchev's. After the elimination of Beria on June 26, Abakumov, the man with the flamboyant neckties, was arrested, as was Rumin, the inventor of the conspiracy of the white coats.

A new examiner took over my dossier in December, 1953. The interrogations no longer took place at night, but in broad daylight—more than a symbol—and their vocabulary had completely changed. The officer, who was thoroughly familiar with the history of the Red Orchestra, did not talk about the "agents of the network," but about the "heroes of the struggle against Nazism."

In January, the counter-inquiry was over. My examiner informed me that he was sending his conclusions to the supreme military tribunal of the Soviet Union, and that in a short time I would be released.

In February I was transferred to the hospital of Butirki Prison along with some other prisoners whose dossiers had also been re-examined. For several weeks the doctors tried to restore our health, which had been ruined by years of imprisonment and privation. When we returned to prison, our cells resembled hotel rooms: abundant food, books, newspapers, the guards as obliging as the best waiters in a restaurant. Times had changed!

On February 23, 1954, I was called to the Ministry of Security, where a general congratulated me on my fiftieth birthday and on the anniversary of the Red Army. Three months later, on May 23, 1954, I was again summoned. I was received with great solemnity, and a general read me the decision of the supreme military tribunal. All the charges brought against me in the past had been declared unfounded.

Slowly, my brain registered these words and translated them: I was going to leave, recover my freedom, see my family again. An unbearable pain gripped my heart, and somehow I got out the words:

"And what about my family—what has become of them?"

"Don't worry. One of our officers will take you to your home. Tomorrow the heads of the Intelligence Service will see you and take care of all material problems, in gratitude for the enormous services you have rendered to the Soviet Union, so that you and your family will be able to live in a suitable manner."

He handed me the official documentation of my release. I signed it, looked at the old general, and asked, "Isn't there anything else to sign?" I knew that usually a released prisoner was required to sign a pledge of silence about everything that happened during his imprisonment.

The general's face reddened. "No, absolutely nothing! You have the right, and even the duty, to talk about everything you have lived through during these tragic years. We no longer fear the truth. We need it, it is as necessary to us as oxygen."

Alas, this campaign of the "hundred flowers"—as Mao called a similar period in China—did not last, and once again silence was demanded of prisoners who were released. But I was happy that May, in 1954, to hear these words, which had governed the conduct of my whole life. These magnificent speeches came very late, but when one has built a kingdom on lies and falsification, one does not easily discover the path of truth.

It was over. Accompanied by a colonel, I walked out of Lubianka, which I had entered nine years and seven months before.

My first contact with the light of day was strange. I was a little like a drunken man. I had trouble walking. My eyes were veiled and I felt disoriented by so much open space, unlimited by the bars of a prison.

We got into a car and drove off. I was obsessed by one thought, which constricted my throat: In what state would I find my family? We had had no communication since the war. Would my sons recognize me? What about Luba? Had they been notified of my release? We drove for a while, until we came to the little village of Babuchkin, a dozen kilometers from Moscow. We stopped in front of No. 22 Naprudnaia Street.

"Here we are," the colonel said simply.

I got out and the car drove away. I stood there for a moment, trying to catch my breath, for my emotions were very powerful. I glanced down at my costume. With this bundle I was carrying, and wearing the pants and pullover sweater some of my fellow prisoners had given me, I looked exactly like a vagabond. The suit I had been wearing at the time of my arrest had worn out over the years, and all I had left from those days was an old overcoat that had stood me in good stead on winter nights. At No. 22, I asked a tenant where the Trepper-Brojde family lived.

The man looked me up and down, and in a tone that was half-intrigued and half-hostile, he said,

"Behind the house, in the shack."

The shack: so that was the best they could do for them! I walked around the building, looking at a wooden hut that was the very image of poverty. I walked toward it slowly and knocked. A young man opened the door: it was Edgar, my second son. He did not recognize me; he gave me a suspicious look. I realized then that my return was not going to be easy. I was free, but I would never have imagined that freedom would be so difficult. Controlling my emotion, I said,

"I'm a friend of your father's, and I have news of him."

He looked at me intently and shook his head. "You're mistaken, we have no father. He died during the war."

I felt my legs give way, and I had to make a super-human effort to control myself. "What about your older brother—is he home?"

"No, he's in Moscow, he'll be back this evening."

"And your mother?"

"She's in the country."

I felt weary, very weary. My son was greeting me like a stranger who was annoying him.

"I'm very tired," I told him. "Do you think I could rest in the next room?"

"If you like: you can lie down on the bed."

Edgar brought me a cup of coffee and disappeared. And then I sank into a vast, bottomless despair. Through all my ordeals I had never given up hope, but now I broke down. My feelings overwhelmed me and I felt the tears running down my cheeks. I was a stranger to those I loved: this horrible thought tore me apart, and I felt a deep and vivid pain pierce my breast. For hours on end I sobbed like a child. From time to time I tried to calm myself, to reason with myself, to recover some hope, but it was useless. I had no hope, I had lost everything.

I was lying this way when I heard the front door bang. People were whispering in the next room. I got up and opened the door a crack. Michel, my eldest son, had just come in. I walked over to him and found the strength to murmur,

"Hello. Do you recognize me?"

He looked me over, reflected, and replied, "I'm sorry, sir, but I don't remember meeting you."

He, too.

"Come on," I said, with all the insistence I was capable of, "try to remember your childhood."

"Now that you mention it, I do have the feeling I've seen you somewhere."

Michel told me later that the man who was there reminded him vaguely of his father, but that this old gentleman with the grey hair and the sickly look bore only a very remote resemblance to the image he had in his mind. Anyway, my family had been officially notified that I had disappeared during the war.

I struggled to remain calm as I told Michel,

"I am your father. Ten years ago I returned to Russia, and for ten years I have been in prison. I have just been released and brought here to you—— Do you have any questions to ask me?"

"Only one," he answered. "Why were you sentenced? In this country, innocent people don't spend ten years in prison."

I dropped into a chair. I'm told that I was very pale. I took a document out of my pocket and handed it to my son. It was a statement from the supreme court of the USSR to the effect that all the charges that had been brought against me were without foundation, and that I had been rehabilitated.

Michel read it and said nothing, but his expression changed.

"And now," I said, "perhaps we can embrace."

He came toward me. I held him in my arms, at last. I was filled with a joy that was very sweet and very strong.

I was impatient to find out: "Where is Mama?"

"She left for Georgia two days ago. She's a traveling photographer. She frequently takes three-week trips and brings back money for us to live on. I'll send her a telegram and let her know."

"Papa is back; come home immediately!" When she received the telegram Luba thought it was a ruse on the part of the security services. She could not believe that I was back. However, she could not totally rule out the possibility, and so she borrowed some money to make the trip. The trains were filled to capacity, so she showed the telegram to a conductor, who understood the situation and let her ride in the compartment reserved for railway employees.

Luba arrived at last. In our first look, after those fifteen years of separation, there was more than in a thousand words. Tears of joy and of infinite sadness combined. No "rehabilitation" could erase those lost years, and this knowledge heightened our sorrow.

This newly regained happiness—how fragile it seemed to me, like a dream which a merciless reality could shatter at any moment.

And then, in no time, the whole street was repeating the news: "Luba's husband is back!" Neighbors, bystanders, and the inevitable complement of gossips hurried over. Many hands stretched toward me; I had to explain, tell my story.

A few days later, a magnificent limousine stopped in front of the house. A colonel introduced himself and informed me that, at the request of the Director of Military Intelligence, he had come to take me to the Center. So I found myself again in the office where General Berzin had received me in 1937. A general, an older man, came over and greeted me effusively.

"At last," he said, "at last!"

Surprised by this beginning, I asked him—not without heat—"Why, during all these years, didn't the Director come to my defense?"

My question made him laugh. "But who could defend you? We were all in the same place you were. It was only after the death of Stalin that we could eliminate the gang responsible for arresting intelligence men who were residents of foreign countries when they returned to the Soviet Union. You must regard these years in prison as so many years spent fighting the enemy. Forget the past. At fifty, you are still young. We will do whatever is necessary to restore your health, and we will find you an apartment in the center of Moscow. We have already submitted a request to the government for you to be paid a pension for services rendered. And now, what do you intend to do?"

"What I wanted to do in 1945: return to my country, Poland. My work in the Intelligence Service came to an end the day of the liberation of Paris. What happened after that was beyond my control."

The general hesitated for a moment, then said, "But your children were raised in the Soviet Union. Wouldn't it be more reasonable to remain in the USSR, where you can enjoy all the honors due a man like yourself? You will easily find work."

"No, I am still a Polish citizen. In my country, three million Jews were exterminated during the last war. My place is with the little community that survived the holocaust."

He wished me good luck and I bade him goodbye. This was my last contact with the Intelligence Service. After that day, I buried my past in Soviet Intelligence at the bottom of my memory. For me, oddly enough, that period of my life became ancient history.

The Director kept his word. They kept me in a sanitorium for several weeks; a few months later, an apartment was assigned to us; and in 1955, I was granted a pension for "services rendered to the Soviet Union." On my employment record, my years in prison were listed as years spent working for the Intelligence Service.

A very special assignment!

Return to Warsaw

To return to Poland, to tread once again the soil of my native land, to revisit Novy-Targ, the cradle of my ancestors: during the years of my captivity I had lived in this hope. From the first day of my liberation, I had expressed my desire, but I was told that I should wait. The good news was given to me in April, 1957: I was authorized to return to Polish territory. I was at last a happy man.

My contacts with the leaders of the Polish party were very encouraging. Poland was feeling the effects of the liberalization of the regime under the leadership of Gomulka in the fall of 1956—this was the "Polish October." The leaders I met assured me of their desire to preserve the Jewish community. On April 7, during my visit, the Secretariat of the Central Committee sent all party organizations a circular stating that anti-Semites were counterrevolutionary and would be compulsorily excluded. The leaders promised to help the Jewish community to preserve their life as a national minority, and at the same time assured assimilated Jews that they would not be subjected to any discrimination. This policy suited me perfectly.

The presence of the party leaders at services commemorating the insurrection in the Warsaw Ghetto seemed to me to be a sign of this new desire. When the chorus of the Polish army sang the hymn of the Jewish partisans in Yiddish along with the choir of the Jewish community, I was moved by a communion that seemed more than symbolic.

I went back to Moscow to get my family. In the fall of 1957, we were all in Warsaw. One of the first places I visited was my birthplace. You can guess my feelings as I left for Novy-Targ.

The town had changed. A shoe factory had been built there—the largest in the country, employing thousands of workers. But the little streets of my old neighborhood had been preserved, and in them I met a few old people who remembered the Treppers. I went to the cemetery, where an old gravedigger told me about the extermination of the Jews of Novy-Targ.

It was during the summer of 1942. A freight train had pulled into the station, releasing a pack of Gestapo killers. Apparently there were several hundred of them. All the male Jews of the village were rounded up and herded into the train, which left for Auschwitz. About fifty young people were sent to a sawmill, where manpower was needed. The women and children were taken to the cemetery.

"You see," the old man told me, "in this spot the Nazis forced their victims to dig their own graves. Then they slaughtered them with machine guns. I remember that some who were still alive when they fell into the ditches were crushed by the bodies that were piled on top of them."

He told me exactly which members of my family had been sent to Auschwitz, and which had died in the ditch.

At the end of the war, a few dozen Jews who had survived the massacre returned to Novy-Targ. They were murdered by gangs who had taken up arms against the new regime and were using the opportunity to organize pogroms.

The old gravedigger's story haunted me, but I returned to Warsaw determined to devote my time and energy to the small Jewish community of Poland. I became the director of the Yiddish Buch, the only Jewish publishing house in all the "socialist" countries. Later I was elected president of the social and cultural association of the Jews of Poland. Our activities took various forms: we published a daily paper and a literary weekly, we started a state theater and a historical society, and in thirty-five towns, popular clubs for young people and buying cooperatives. Of the 25,000 to 30,000 Jews who were living in Poland at the time, some of them completely assimilated, 9,000 were members of our organization. The government and the party gave us political, psychological, and financial support.

However, all traces of anti-Semitism had not disappeared

overnight—and a certain Piasetski, who before the war had led one of the most reactionary parties, and who was now said to be a Soviet agent, had taken up the standard of the old fanatics. On the whole, though, developments had been clearly favorable, the young people were impervious to the old slogans, and the official church was fighting resurgences of anti-Semitism in Catholic circles.

Those years, spent in the bosom of my family, at last reunited, were among the happiest of my life. My responsibilities in the Jewish community kept me very busy; but I saw an unfavorable sign in the growing influence on party leaders of a general named Moczar, and I was beginning to run into difficulties carrying out my work. We Polish Jews realized that our situation would continue to be precarious until some radical change occurred in the Kremlin.

Sometimes during those peaceful days—a peace that was quite temporary, alas—I found myself wishing there were a book telling the story of the Red Orchestra. Oh, there were books on our network, but they were worthless because they had been written by enemies who falsified reality. In 1964 I had read a book about Richard Sorge by a Japanese writer who had completely captured the rich and complex personality of his subject, a book that seemed to me a model of the genre. I was very much tempted to write a book of my own, and I mentioned my project to the appropriate Polish authorities, but they indicated that the enterprise was premature and that in any case I would be subject to censorship. When I thought it over, I realized that while I was living in Warsaw with my family I would not really be free as a writer. How, for example, could I write about the elimination of Berzin, or the German-Soviet pact?

It was then that I met Gilles Perrault. In October, 1964, a young Frenchman with a sympathetic face and an open and straightforward manner, a little shy, came to see me. "Monsieur Trepper," he said, "I am writing a book on the Red Orchestra."

I looked at him, amused. "Don't you have anything better to do?"

In fact, I was skeptical that such a young man would be able to assimilate such a complex story. He handed me a book with his name on it; the book had a remark of Churchill's as an epigraph—"In wartime truth is so precious that she should always be attended by a bodyguard of lies"—and related the activities of British Intelligence in preparation for the landing at Normandy. I read it in one sitting. I no longer doubted that the author was capable of writing a full-scale history of the Red Orchestra—and subsequently he did. *The Red Orchestra* met with considerable success, and, despite minor inaccuracies, through its pages I relived the drama of our brotherhood.

I shall not dwell on the success the book had in the west; but less is known about the repercussions it had in Eastern Europe, where it was never published. (It was to have been published in Czechoslovakia, but the Russian tanks got there first.) Even in Poland, I saw the French edition being passed from hand to hand; the copies had been read so many times the pages were falling out.

The great merit of Gilles Perrault's book is that it has enabled specialists and the general public alike to know and understand the truth about the Red Orchestra in spite of the lies of the Nazis, the shadow of the cold war, and the omission of our adventure from the great chronicles of the resistance.

In the German Democratic Republic, survivors of the Schulze-Boysen group, such as Professor Heinrich Scheel, Vice President of the Academy of Sciences, and Greta Kuckhoff, published eye-witness accounts. In August, 1969, the weekly *Die Weltbuhne* published a very laudatory article on Perrault's book titled, "The Pianists of the Red Orchestra." On November 18, 1970, the educational radio station of the German Democratic Republic devoted a broadcast to the network, titled "The Big Chief Outwits the Gestapo." In the USSR, meanwhile, the story of the Red Orchestra was told in various forms. In December, 1968, in Moscow, I met a very well known writer who hoped to write a book about it. My wife read his manuscript at the end of 1969, but the book never appeared. A few other books, the work of party hacks, sold several thousand copies; among them were *Forget Your Name* and *Locked Houses*. The weekly *Ogoniok*, with a circulation of three million, published a series of articles on the subject over a period of months.

Even in Poland, the Red Orchestra eventually emerged from oblivion. At the end of 1969, an exhibition was organized in honor of Adam Kuckhoff, one of the leaders of the Berlin group.

I was vacationing at the seaside with my wife in September, 1970, when a newspaper headline caught my eye: "Jean Gilbert Warns the Director." There were some excerpts from Perrault's book, followed by the questions: "What has become of Jean Gilbert? Where is he today?" I learned later that this article, prepared by a press service, appeared in various newspapers. The Polish authorities had consented to dispel a few of the clouds surrounding Jean Gilbert, but continued to sling mud at a certain Leopold Trepper, whom Gilles Perrault's book had made world-famous.

Trepper was Jewish, whereas Jean Gilbert——

The Last Battle

On June 17, 1967, Gomulka, first secretary of the Polish Communist Party, took the floor at a meeting of labor unions, and launched into a frenzied diatribe against the Jews. The Six Days War had just ended in the Mideast, and Gomulka took advantage of the opportunity to introduce the slogan, "The Jewish community is the Fifth Column." An anti-Semitic campaign of unprecedented violence was organized by the Minister of the Interior, General Moczar, in the newspapers, on television, and in the workers' meetings. Student demonstrations in Warsaw in the spring of 1968 provided a new pretext for those in power to revive the tired campaign—it was claimed that Jewish students had provoked clashes between the police and the Polish students. The attacks were concentrated on the Cultural Association of Polish Jews, which I directed. Jewish students were expelled from the university, and old militants were driven out of the party by the hundreds. Moczar organized "spontaneous" demonstrations with cries of "Send the kikes to Dayan!" In this epidemic of hysteria, all that was missing was a little pogrom.

Yes, more than twenty-five years after the end of the war, in the country of the Warsaw Ghetto, where the Jews had suffered more than anywhere else from Nazi barbarity, and under a regime that called itself socialist, the monster of anti-Semitism was rising from its ashes. Indeed, it was not long before hostility toward Israel and Zionism turned into open hostility toward Polish Jews. It was becoming increasingly clear that the government wanted to put an end to our community.

The only solution was to leave, and we knew that it corresponded to the deepest desires of the authorities. Later, to my cost, I learned that I was to be an exception. If I had asked for a visa then, General Moczar would undoubtedly have been only too happy to authorize the president of the Jewish community to leave the country. My eldest son, Michel, who was out of work, was the first to go.

Pierre, my youngest son, who was an electronics engineer, had been accused of being a "student agitator." He turned in his party membership card, applied for a visa, and left with his wife, Anna. Anna's paralyzed father, who had been a devoted communist militant since his youth, had been following the events on television. When he felt his end approaching, he called his wife to him, and said: "I am convinced that in the Near East the Jews and Arabs will work out their differences eventually. In our country, true socialism will prevail, but it will take many years. For the present, the situation is hopeless. Draw up a list of our Polish friends who are in a position to hide you, and then get out as soon as you can."

Edgar, my second son, a professor of Russian literature, saw all the doors of the universities close in his face. After many difficulties, he, too, took the path of exile.

For me, the choice was clear: I had to rejoin the struggle. I wrote Gomulka, the party secretary, a memorandum on the anti-Semitic campaign. Naturally, it went unanswered, and I suppose it provided an occasion to label me a Zionist before consigning me to oblivion.

Deprived of my children, no longer able to devote myself to a Jewish community threatened with extinction, I became a mistrusted stranger in my native land. In the spring of 1968 I handed in my resignation from the presidency of the Cultural Association of Polish Jews. With two exceptions, all the members of the board followed suit. In August, 1970, I asked the Polish authorities for permission to emigrate to Israel. Their refusal reached me ten months later. I repeated my request seven times in two years, and each time it was denied. Beginning in March, 1971, I wrote six times to the Minister of the Interior, five times to the First Secretary of the party, and six times to the secretary of the Central Committee.

My persistence exasperated the Polish leaders, who seized the first opportunity to make trouble for me.

In June, 1971, a team of Belgian filmmakers under the direction of Roland Perrault came to Poland to make a documentary on the Red Orchestra. My wife and I accompanied the filmmakers to Zacopane. On the afternoon of June 8, we were in the middle of shooting when dozens of policemen in civilian clothes surrounded us. Two colonels from Security, who no doubt imagined that they were on a battlefield, directed the operations. They took us all to the police station in Zacopane, where we were subjected to several hours of tedious interrogation. The Belgian filmmakers' equipment was confiscated, and they were forced to leave the country, but before they left they saw Luba and me taken away in a car to an unknown destination. Convinced that we had been arrested, they alerted the international community as soon as they got to Brussels. A few hours later the police released us, though they kept us under surveillance.

Our troubles were only beginning. We became a favorite target for police investigations.

While we were off being questioned, our apartment in Zacopane was visited by some individuals who made no effort to remove the traces of their presence. In the apartment next to ours, on the floor above us, on the floor below, and all through the house, in the building opposite us, on both sides of the street—everywhere, agents from the Security Department, about as transparent as granite, spied on us day and night. In our neighborhood, the streetlights burned constantly, and when we went out, an impressive team walked at our heels. Did we want to go to the cemetery in Novy-Targ?* The Security agents would be there ahead of us. After ten days of this program, we returned to Warsaw, certain that we would be arrested on our arrival. Before we left, Luba managed to evade the vigilance of our guards long enough to mail a letter to friends outside the country, telling them of our situation. On the train, both ends of our car were

---

*On the site of the monument erected to the memory of the Jewish martyrs, only a gaping hole remains.

guarded. In the station at Warsaw, I immediately spotted the new shift. As we were walking toward the row of taxis, one of the gentlemen came over and asked obligingly, "Would you like a ride home?"

"No, thank you, we can manage."

But the moment we got into a taxi, a man appeared, got into the front seat with an air of authority, and gave the driver our address. In another minute he would be helping us carry our baggage upstairs. Naturally, the apartment had been gone over with a fine tooth comb during our absence. Agitated by these events, and shocked to observe that the surveillance around the house had been reinforced, I became ill on the night of our return. I telephoned my doctor, who ordered me to stay in bed; no sooner had I hung up the receiver than a police ambulance appeared, with all its sirens wailing.

This state of affairs continued for a week. I went to the Central Committee to protest, and was received by the man in charge of security. He tried to calm me down, pretending to be sympathetic:

"You're wrong to be upset," he told me. "It's not you they're interested in, but the Belgian filmmakers, who didn't ask for authorization."

A bureaucrat's bad joke; he had increased the surveillance and harassment, and now he was advising us not to take offense. In the meantime, my friends had received our letter, and were worried about us. Gilles Perrault rushed to Warsaw, but could verify only the fact that I was at liberty. The Polish authorities were preserving appearances for a little while longer, but I was not taken in. In the eyes of Moczar's gang I was suspect, an enemy, a counterrevolutionary—you can add to the list. In December, 1971, once again the Ministry of the Interior refused to grant me a visa. I informed my friends of this decision, and they decided to go into action. Gilles Perrault, the lawyer Soulez-Larivière, Vercors, Vladimir Pozner, Jacques Madaule, and the Fanfanis met at the home of Matarasso, a lawyer in Paris, and decided to form a committee to get me out of Poland. On January 12, 1972, the Trepper

Committee held their first press conference, which was given wide coverage the following day. Soon, committees were formed in Switzerland, Belgium, Great Britain, and Denmark; and in Holland a petition signed by all the deputies (except the communists), and by numerous prominent people, was delivered to the Polish Embassy. I was profoundly moved by the size of the movement of solidarity and protest. In Geneva, an appeal to the Polish government was sent by the League of the Rights of Man and the International Committee of Jurists and Socialist Deputies. In Brussels the committee, under the leadership of the president of the League of the Rights of Man, included deputies, ministers, and resistance organizations. In Paris, people of every persuasion came forward. André Malraux and Monsignor Marty, Archbishop of Paris, sent letters of support to the committee. A wide political spectrum was included, from the extreme left to organizations involved in the Zionist movement. François Mitterand, speaking for the Socialist Party, expressed their concern. In London, Michael Stewart, former Secretary for Foreign Affairs, Patrick Gordon Walker, and former Attorney General Frederick Elwyn-Jones wrote to Edward Gierek, First Secretary of the Polish Communist Party:

"Leopold Trepper has fought many long and dangerous battles against the forces of fascism. He made a unique contribution to the overthrow of Nazi power, and consequently, helped to drive Nazi tyranny out of the occupied countries, including Poland."

This letter was signed by twenty-one Laborites, seven Conservatives, and five Liberals. Some American senators also wrote to the government in Warsaw, and a petition was signed by labor leaders in Brazil, Australia, Colombia, Great Britain, Costa Rica, and Israel.

Impressed by the movement that was developing in my support, and harassed by the questions of reporters, the Polish authorities eventually made a statement. On February 29, 1972, the Minister of Information, Janiurek, gave the following statement to a representative of the Agence

France-Presse: "The reasons for the decision of the Polish authorities regarding Mr. Trepper are not of an ideological or national nature. It is for reasons of state that Mr. Leopold Trepper may not leave Poland. As for Mrs. Trepper, she is free to join her children."

The Polish government was taking refuge behind alleged "reasons of state" in order to keep me where I was. Luba took advantage of the permission that had been granted her, and left in April, 1972. My son Michel went on a hunger strike in Copenhagen and Edgar did the same in Jerusalem. In Europe and America, the campaign of solidarity was growing steadily.

In Paris, however, a Monsieur Rochet, director of the DST (Défense et Surveillance du Territoire), took umbrage at all this support. He revealed his position when he telephoned the lawyer, Soulez-Larivière, on January 13, 1972, the day after the support committee's press conference.

"There are other Jews to be defended," he said, to put Soulez on guard.

As if by chance, the French Minister of the Interior refused to give my wife a visa of entry. In defense of this decision, Monsieur Rochet wrote a letter to the newspaper Le Monde, titled "The Trepper Case," in which he made some very serious accusations against me. The director of the DST called into question my "extremely suspicious behavior" after my "arrest by the Abwehr at the end of November, 1942," and accused me of betraying several members of my network. "No one can deny," Monsieur Rochet went on, "that Monsieur Trepper consented to at least some degree of collaboration with the enemy in order to save his life."

I could not allow charges of this nature to go unanswered, and on the advice of my friends, I initiated legal proceedings. Monsieur Rochet's position at the head of French counterespionage lent a certain undeserved credibility to his assertions, and it was dangerous to allow the public to accept them as truths. Moreover, the Polish authorities immediately exploited the letter to try to undermine the campaign of solidarity. In Denmark the press attaché at the Polish Embassy sent

Rochet's accusing letter to newspapers there. He was made
to regret it: the editorial staffs replied that they did not want
to participate in another Dreyfus case. But the incidents
continued.

Soulez-Larivière, who took up my defense along with
another lawyer, Matarasso, came to see me in Warsaw on
June 23, 1972, to prepare my case. There was no question of
talking in the apartment, so we took long walks in the parks,
far from prying ears. Whenever a passerby approached, we
discontinued conversation on our true topic and launched
into a weighty discussion of the weather.

On June 26, I took Soulez back to the airport. The taxi that
appeared "spontaneously" had no meter. In the rear-view
mirror I caught the attentive eye of Warsaw looking at me
more than once. As soon as I had said goodbye to my friend
and turned away, he was seized by seven muscular "customs
inspectors" who dragged him into a room, where he was
undressed and searched from head to foot. His luggage was
thoroughly examined, tubes of toothpaste and shaving cream
conscientiously emptied, rolls of film confiscated. Soulez held
on to his briefcase as if it were a life preserver and stubbornly
refused to open it. But they threatened to resort to "vulgar
methods," and he had to give in to their greater numbers.
The Polish police seized the papers in the dossier. At last,
after several hours, my lawyer was permitted to get on the
plane.

As soon as I was informed of this incident, I sent a protest
to the Central Committee, who were perfectly aware of
Soulez's trip to Warsaw. They feigned ignorance, of course,
and all I got out of the bureaucrat on duty was the disingenu-
ous reply:

"A routine customs inspection, no doubt."

At the end of July, 1972, Soulez, persistent but
mistrustful—a lawyer forewarned is worth two—returned to
Warsaw. We immediately became aware that we were being
watched even more closely than before, and we decided to
communicate with each other by writing on little pieces of
paper which we immediately threw into the toilet. Exasperated, he asked, "How can one live like this?" At one point, my

lawyer wrote on a piece of paper a magnificent four-letter word—which I promised myself I would leave in plain sight when we finished. This time Soulez-Larivière left Poland without incident.

My friends in Paris continued to assure me of their active support. On October 2, 1972, when the First Secretary of the Polish Communist Party arrived in Paris on an official visit, he was greeted by posters prepared by the committee of support asking, "What about Trepper, Mr. Gierek?" And the leaders of the Socialist Party referred in a communiqué to the "painful Trepper affair."

Since the case against Monsieur Rochet was scheduled to be heard at the end of the month, my lawyers asked the French Minister of the Interior to grant me a safe-conduct, and to support my request Gilles Perrault and Bernard Guetta, Ruth Valentini, and Christian Jelen—journalists on the *Nouvel Observateur*—went on a hunger strike. The Minister of the Interior granted my request, but the Polish government refused to let me leave.

So it was in my absence that the director of the DST appeared before the Seventeenth Correctional Court of Paris on October 26, 1972. Friends I knew—Hélène Pauriol, Cecile Katz, Lederman, Claude Spaak, and Jacques Sokol—and also friends I had not met came before the bar to testify in my behalf. Vercors, the famous writer and member of the resistance, wrote the court:

"I regard Leopold Trepper as one of the great heroes of the resistance to Nazi Germany during the Second World War. As leader of the Red Orchestra, he contributed to the final victory to an extent infinitely greater than was possible in the case of a man like myself . . ."

Colonel Rémy, who had been decorated for his role in the liberation, also endorsed me:

"If I had had an occasion to serve in the ranks of the Red Orchestra," he wrote in a letter read before the court, "I would be proud; I would have made a real contribution to the victory of the Allies and consequently to the liberation of France."

In his deposition, Gilles Perrault traced the history of the

Red Orchestra and answered all questions with precision and clarity. The lawyer Matarasso delivered a solid, cohesive, and convincing summation. But it was Soulez, at the end of his eloquent summation, who created the real sensation of the trial:

"I've been wondering what became of all the members of the Gestapo. I thought about it, and I did some research.

"Roeder, Hitler's bloodhound, who boasted that he had sent forty resisters of the Red Orchestra to the scaffold, is today assistant mayor of Glasshuten in the Taunus. He runs a flourishing law office.

"Piepe, the man who recovered the by-products of the interrogations conducted with dogs, died two years ago; he was president of the Rotary Club of Hamburg.

"Reiser is today retired in Stuttgart.

"Pannwitz, the butcher of Prague, has a government pension and is managing director of a bank.

"For all these men, actually, the war is no longer very important—a bit of ash on their hands, which they blow away. I thought about these men, and then I thought about Trepper."

Before the trial was over, Rochet resigned from the DST and was named a departmental prefect. The Minister of the Interior, by way of explanation, wrote to the court: "Of course there is no connection of any sort between this reassignment and the Trepper case." Of course——

But so it was that the court found against a mere prefect instead of the boss of the French secret service.

Meanwhile, the campaign of solidarity had been marking time. In March, 1973, the Trepper committees of France, England, the Netherlands, Denmark, and Switzerland met in London under the chairmanship of M. Schor, a member of the French Socialist Party.

Absent from discussions in which my honor was involved, I remained in Warsaw in total seclusion. Since January 23, 1973, I had been "under surveillance," in the singular position of a prisoner at liberty in his own apartment. Through official channels I was given to understand that I was in no sense under police supervision, that the measures taken had no other object than to "ensure my security." But who was threatening me, and to whom was I a threat?

What did they want from me? What charges did they have against me? As the days went by, I turned these questions over in my mind again and again, but I found no answer. I realized, however, that if I did not take action, the situation would undoubtedly persist until the day the Polish government gave me a fine funeral with wreaths and flowers. Then in September, 1973, I became seriously ill. After a telephone conversation with Gilles Perrault, I realized that I would have to resort to extreme measures, and I wrote a letter to the Central Committee, with copies for the news agencies:

> Knowing perfectly well that everything I say over the telephone is recorded by the Polish police, I have decided to reveal for the first time the whole truth about the life I am forced to lead here in Warsaw.
>
> I am watched night and day. They are everywhere: on the floor above me, on the floor below me, in the street. I have just come back from the hospital, where I had been taken, apparently on the edge of death. They were in the hospital too, watching me and allowing no one to see me. No one can imagine my solitude. This is not a life, it is a vegetative existence. The nervous tension has become unbearable, my patience is at an end. They have my back to the wall, and I know that all that remains for me is to die. But I will die on my feet, as befits the man who was head of the Red Orchestra.
>
> If nothing happens to change the situation within the next two weeks, I will go on a hunger strike which will either end with my leaving Poland or with my death.
>
> In killing myself, I will be performing an act of humanity toward my family, whom my present situation has plunged into misery. My wife and children have a right to a normal life, and not to this hell. My existence is that of a prisoner. One way or another, I am going to leave this prison.

A few days later, two officials from the Ministry of the Interior and the Ministry of Health came to inform me that the Polish authorities were authorizing me to go to London for treatment.

The door of freedom had been opened. On November 2, 1973, I arrived in the English capital, where with intense emotion I was reunited with my family. Mrs. Wendy Mantle, president of the English committee, welcomed me. Thanks to them and to the magnificent movement of international solidarity, I won the last and most painful battle of my life, the battle against those who had once been my own.

A final word: I belong to a generation that has been sacrificed by history. The men and women who came to communism in the glow of October, carried along by the great momentum of the rising revolution, certainly did not imagine that fifty years later nothing would be left of Lenin but the body embalmed in Red Square. The revolution has degenerated and we have gone down with it.

What? Half a century after the storming of the Winter Palace, with "deviations" being treated by electric shock, the Jews persecuted, Eastern Europe "normalized"—with a system of coercion of this kind, people dare to talk about socialism!

Is this what we wanted, was it for this perversion that we fought, sacrificing our lives in the search for a new world? We lived in the future, and the future, like the paradise of believers, justified the uncertainties of the present.

We wanted to change man, and we have failed. This century has brought forth two monsters, fascism and Stalinism, and our ideal has been engulfed in this apocalypse. The absolute idea that gave meaning to our lives has acquired a face whose features we no longer recognize. Our failure forbids us to give advice, but because history has too much imagination to repeat itself, it remains possible to hope.

I do not regret the commitment of my youth, I do not regret the paths I have taken. In Denmark, in the fall of 1973, a young man asked me in a public meeting, "Haven't you sacrificed your life for nothing?" I replied, "No."

No, on one condition: that people understand the lesson of my life as a communist and a revolutionary, and do not turn themselves over to a deified party. I know that youth will succeed where we have failed, that socialism will triumph, and that it will not have the color of the Russian tanks that crushed Prague.

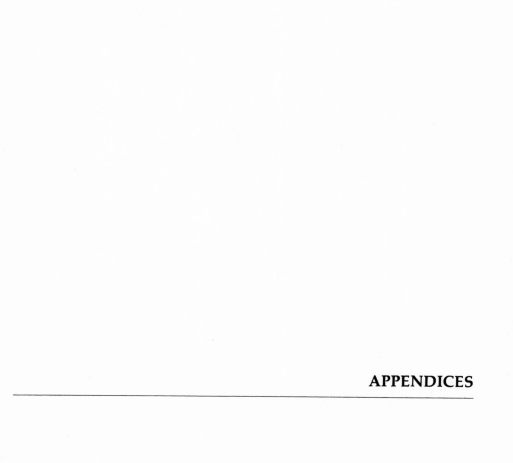

APPENDICES

Appendix I: Farewells

The letter Fernand Pauriol wrote to his wife just before he was shot.

My dearest love,

This letter that goes to break your heart, I write it to you with feelings you can imagine. I told you one day that if I were to die, my last thought would be for you, because to leave life will be to leave you; that day is come for me.

You know so well what I am thinking, what I would say to you if I were able to talk to you, to hold you again in my arms, there is nothing else I can add to this, which is, I know only too well, like a dagger that I am plunging into your heart.

I was sentenced to death last January 20, the day after the day I saw you (you and Mireille, whom I can never think of apart from you, my dearest love). You can imagine what my thoughts and my life have been like since then and how I felt when I saw you, looking exactly as you had in my happiest dreams.

I want to tell you again that it is my most sincere desire that you take everything that life can give you, without exception, with the thought that in this way you are being faithful to my wish, which is that you be happy. Don't let yourself be overcome or dominated by grief, for your own sake and for Mireille. You must tell Mireille that she has been the image of the future for me, and that I wish her a love like ours.

You will tell our friends that I died as I have lived until today, and that I am applying the words of our dear Gabriel to myself . . . You will kiss my family and tell them that my thoughts have never left them during these past months. I have been reliving my childhood and feeling how great my love has been for them, my beloved parents, and my beautiful country.

Perhaps some day I will be able to lie by your side. That is my last wish.

Live, my darling, with the feeling that I am living through you and each time you are happy, think that I would have been glad.

Goodbye, my dearest love.

413 Your Fernand

Mon si bel amour

Cette lettre qui va te déchirer le cœur, je te l'écris avec les sentiments que tu devines. Je t'ai dit un jour que si je mourais ma dernière pensée serait pour toi, car quitter la vie serait te quitter : ce jour est venu pour moi.

Tu sais tellement ce que je pense, ce que je t'aurais dit si j'avais pu te parler, tu serais encore dans mes bras, que si ne me reste rien d'autre à ajouter à ceci qui est, je ne sais plus écrire un poignard que j'enfonce dans ton cœur.

J'ai été condamné à mort le 20 ... dernier, ...

Ten o'clock
August 12, 1944

After you receive this letter, you must turn to our friends so that they can provide you with all the material help that you and Mireille will be needing. Tell them that I did everything I could to remain myself to the very end and that I am proud to have done so and to feel a part of our great family, for whom I can perceive at this moment a wonderful future.

A few pages from the journal Alfred Corbin kept in his Berlin prison in Lehrter Strasse, after being sentenced to death. On pages 6 and 7 he describes the events of November 19, 1942, the day of his arrest, and the tortures he endured. The journal breaks off abruptly on July 28, the day Corbin was beheaded.

The instructions for the tortures were given by Reiser, the head of the Sonderkommando.

. . . of what happened to me since the day of my arrest, November 19. First I was subjected to two short interrogations by the ordinary policemen who arrested me. They hit me a few times, but nothing really serious. On the 30th they brought me together with you and Denise and this marked the beginning of an odious psychological blackmail—"Your wife and daughter will be shot as hostages, unless . . ." On December 3 they came for me at 6:30 in the evening and took me to the Ministry of the Interior, to what they called the Tribunal, and there I was tortured by a specialist!! and left half dead. I was hit with a club on the soles of the feet, the thighs, and the buttocks, and kicked—in short, a thorough job!! This went on for three hours.

On the 7th and the 8th, more interrogations; on the 17th, Michel's visit; on the 4th of January, a visit from the administrator appointed at Giverny, another form of fraud, for this appointment was not necessary; on the 27th another interrogation, and on the 27th of February a final interrogation about you. This time I got angry because they tried to make me say that you were aware of the activities of people you had never heard of, nor I either, for that matter.

Finally on the 8th of March this farce of a trial and a death sentence for almost everyone!! This, without any possibility of appeal.

Moreover, throughout our stay in Fresnes I was kept in solitary confinement and handcuffed night and day; I still have the scars!

I have no fear about writing all this here, for if we are to be "tried" again, as they call it, I will tell the examining judge everything I have endured! And I will protest energetically again, even if it does no good.

Well, my dear love, that is a brief account of the last five months. I cannot forgive myself for being the cause of your arrest and Denise's, for in the course of the interrogations I said that I loved you more than anything in the world, and that nothing else mattered to me, but since then I have realized . . .

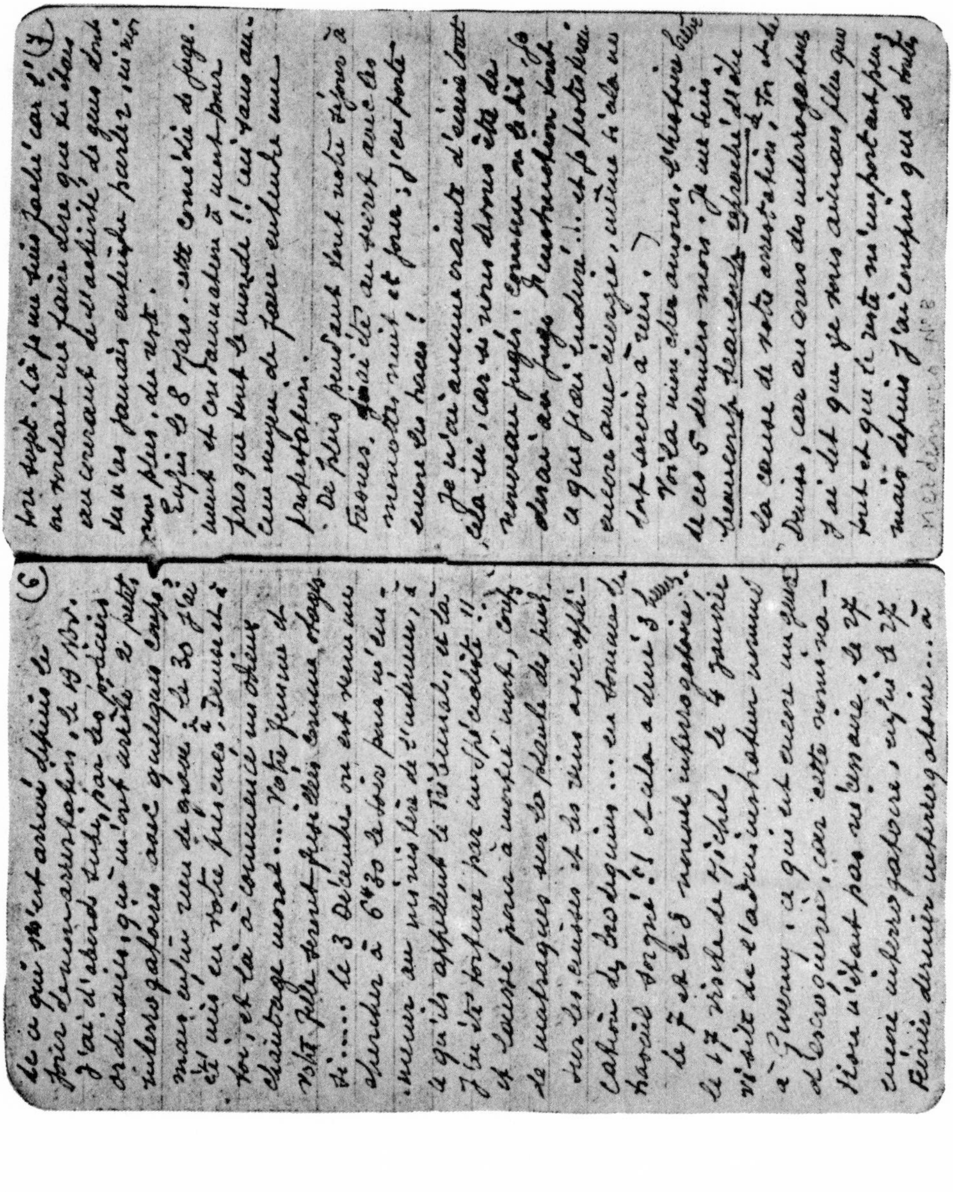

*These words were written by Suzanne Spaak on the walls of
her cell in Fresnes:*

> *To understand everything is to forgive everything.*
>
> > *Oh! let my bars burst open,*
> > *Oh! let me go to the sea!*
> > —RIMBAUD
>
> *You might have found a better wife than me,*
> *But I have given you our son.*
>
> *Ah, that I might be sitting in the forests' shade.*
> —RACINE
>
> *My enemies can kill me, but they cannot harm me.*
> —SOCRATES
>
> *To be alone with my thoughts is still to be free*
>
> *Hail and courage, comrades.*
>
> *Where the children are there should the mothers
> be, to watch over them.*
> —KIPLING
>
> > *Nightingale of melodies,*
> > *Sing a song and close my eyes.*
> > —Dream of a Summer's Night
>
> *I regret nothing.*

Hillel Katz's last letter to his daughter (Katz's nom de guerre was André Dubois).

June 19, 1943

My dear little Annette,

You are seven months old today. When you were seven days old I was just getting used to your presence. I saw you every day. I was beginning to accept the reality of the miracle of your appearance, although it had long been awaited. When I saw you for the last time, you were twelve days old. I had time for only one quick, tender glance, for I was pressed. I had many cares. I had to arrange for your departure for the country. I had brought news of your brother; your mama was very unhappy about being separated from him. I was, too, for the look of silent reproach he gave me as I left him stayed in front of my eyes no matter what I did, and weighed on my heart. I had other serious worries. Your mama encouraged me with a luminous smile, which did me so much good and which I still see very often these days, and it cheers me up in very sad moments. That day you were sleeping, as usual, it was the most helpful thing you knew how to do at that moment, and glancing one last time at your rosebud mouth, which was moving in a dream of milk, sweet and warm, which you must have been having, I said goodbye. Since then, I think of you often. Your desire to appear in our lives was fierce. Nothing counted with you, neither the dangers of wartime, nor our desire that you wait until after the war. Obviously, you could not share our earthly point of view, you who were still in eternity. It was with love, joy, and courage that we submitted to your imperious will. Your birth gave us such life as we have now. If you had not appeared, would our fate be any better? Perhaps worse. What do we know about it? We welcomed you with our hearts open, smiling, loving, and brave, and, as with your brother, with all our paternal and maternal love, instinctive and reasoned. We are determined to do whatever is necessary to make both of you capable of happiness. For happiness is not an external thing, which one obtains, but an internal capacity determined by one's wealth of soul and heart. And this wealth, I am convinced, we are capable of providing for you. I only hope that circumstances will make this possible. I must confess, not from weakness but by way of the truth, that I suffer at being deprived of the pure joy, the profound felicity I would have experienced in the contemplation of

19 Juin 1943

Ma douce petite Annette,

Tu as 7 mois aujourd'hui. Quand tu avais 7 jours j'ai commencé à m'habituer à ta présence. Je te voyais tous les jours. J'ai commencé à me faire à la réalité du miracle de ton apparition, quoique longtemps attendue. Quand je t'ai vue, la dernière fois, tu avais douze jours. Je t'ai regardée d'un coup d'œil attendri et rapide, car j'étais pressé. J'avais beaucoup de soucis. Je devais préparer ton départ à la campagne. J'avais apporté des nouvelles de ton frère, ta maman avait le cœur gros d'être séparée de lui. Moi aussi, car son regard, plein de reproches muets, qu'il m'a lancés au moment de le quitter, restait fixé devant mes yeux, sans que je ne puisse m'y échapper et me chagrinait. J'avais encore d'autres ennuis très graves. Ta maman m'encourageait d'un sourire lumineux qui me faisait

your being, conquering life, of your gradual discovery of your body and the world around you; of your brave and amazing struggle to acquire your capacity for movement in the universe. And then your smile, your charm, your prattling, and all the rest, which I can only guess at with the help of your mama, whom I had the great good fortune of choosing for you. On the other hand, I am happy to know that you are in surroundings that are excellent for your physical development and your health, and this consoles me. I know that it will be a long time before my words reach your consciousness, but I feel the need to talk to you now. In the meantime, mama will try to explain them to you as best she can. I hope that you will become an intelligent, modest, brave, and beautiful girl.

I kiss you tenderly,
André

Harro Schulze-Boysen.

December 22, 1942

My dear parents,

Everything I have done has proceeded from my intelligence, my heart, and my conviction, and therefore as my parents, you must regard it as the best thing that could happen. I beg you to do so!

This death suits me. In any case, I have always known what it would be like. It is "my own death," as Rilke put it!

. . . If you were here, watching me unseen, you would see me laugh in the face of death. I conquered it a long time since . . .

Your Harro

Arvid Harnack.

December 22, 1942

My dear ones,

In the hours to come, I will be leaving this world. I wanted to thank you one more time for the love you have shown me, especially in these last days. This thought has made it easy for me to bear everything that was painful. Today I am calm and happy. I am also thinking of the power of nature, to which I feel so connected. This morning I recited aloud to myself, *"Die Sonne tönt in alter Weise . . ."* (The sun is coloring the world as usual.)

I would like to have seen you all again, but unfortunately that is impossible. My thoughts are with you all, and I'm not forgetting anyone; each of you must feel it, especially Mama.

Once again, I hold you in my arms and kiss you.

Your devoted Arvid

It is important that you really celebrate Christmas. It is my last wish. And you must sing *"Ich bete an die Macht der Liebe"* (I Adore the Power of Love).

Erika Von Brockdorff.

May 13, 1943

My only love,

. . . No one will be able to say of me, without lying, that I wept, that I clung to life or trembled because of it. It is in laughter that I shall end my life, just as it is in laughter that I have loved life and that I love it still . . .

Your Erika

Name des Briefschreibers:

Schulze-Boysen, Harro
Berlin-Plötzensee, den 22. Dez. 1942.
Königsdamm 7
Haus

Gelesen:

> Geliebte Eltern!
>
> Es ist nun soweit! In wenigen Stunden werde ich aus diesem Ich aussteigen. Ich bin vollkommen ruhig und ich bitte Euch, es auch gefasst aufzunehmen. Es geht heute auf d. ganzen Welt um so wichtige Dinge, da ist ein Leben, das erlischt, nicht sehr viel. Was gewesen ist, was ich getan, — davon will ich nicht mehr schreiben. Alles was ich tat, tat ich aus meinem Kopf, meinem Herzen u. meiner Überzeugung heraus, und in diesem Rahmen müsst Ihr als meine Eltern das Beste annehmen. Darum bitte ich Euch!
>
> Dieser Tod passt zu mir. Irgendwie habe ich immer um ihn gewusst, Es ist mein eigener Tod, — wie es einmal bei Rilke heisst!
>
> Das Herz wird mir nur schwer, wenn ich an Euch Lieben
> ... nah und teilt mein Schick=

Horst Heilmann.

My dear parents,

. . . My life has been so beautiful that even in my death I hear the echoes of a divine harmony. I have asked that my body be sent to you; I would like to be buried with my friends.

I am so grateful to you for all your love and kindness. Remember me with love, with as much love as I have always had for you.

I die strong and sure of myself.

Walter Husemann.

My dear father,

Be strong! I die just as I have lived: a first class fighter! It is easy to call yourself a communist as long as you don't have to pay for it with your life. You don't prove that you are one until the hour of truth. I am a communist, father!

It is easy for me to die, because I know why I must. Those who are killing me will soon confront a difficult death, I am convinced of it.

Be tough, father! Tough! Don't give in! In each of your hours of weakness, remember this last request of your son,
Walter

Adam Kuckhoff.

Plötzensee, August 5, 1943

My Greta,

I know that this is more painful for you than if you had gone with me, but I must be glad that you are staying—at least I hope so: for your son, for everything that is so alive in you, I feel so clearly in advance—yes, I know it—"how you will live" when you are free once again . . .

. . . How many human beings can say that they have been as happy as we? What else? "Nothing remains of the way we walked together . . ." It was that way when we saw each other for the last time, and nothing has changed . . .

. . . It is three o'clock, not much time left before I must go, I write my last farewell.

Since 1973, my main concern in connection with these memoirs has been to find out what has become of my Red Orchestra comrades. In my research, I have gone over the ground covered by my friend Gilles Perrault, who succeeded in learning the fates of a great many of my friends. He was the first to bring to light the sinister role of Breendonk, where Hersch and Mira Sokol were imprisoned. Thanks to the Belgian authorities, I was able to continue that investigation, with the help of my friends Jacques and Sarah Goldberg. The Research Department of the Belgian Ministry of Public Health and the administration of the monument to the dead at Breendonk made their files available to me.

In this way, and with other important aid from survivors, scholars, and records, I have been able to compile these partial lists, and to draw up a preliminary report—which is undoubtedly not definitive.

Here I must add some statistics: between May, 1940, and November, 1942, over 1,500 radio messages were sent to Moscow by the various Red Orchestra groups. The Nazi code-breaking team, headed by Dr. Wilhelm Vauck, decoded between 200 and 250 of these. Between May, 1940, and June, 1941, not a single radio message was decoded. Of the several hundred sent by the Laffitte transmitting station in Paris (Hersch and Mira Sokol's station), not a single message was decoded. Not one of the numerous—and crucial—messages sent through the French Communist Party to the Moscow Center was deciphered.

According to Gestapo records, 76 persons were sentenced in Germany (death, prison, deportation, or disciplinary battalion) in connection with the Red Orchestra; according to Dr. Manfred Roeder's testimony, 28 persons were sentenced in France, Belgium, and Holland—one-third of them to death. But the Gestapo "records" were those in existence after the Nazis lost, and Dr. Roeder's testimony suffers from the same transforming circumstance.

According to the thorough investigation I have been making—which is not yet complete—217 persons were arrested in connection with the Red Orchestra in France, Belgium, Holland, and Germany, of whom 143 were executed or murdered during interrogation, or died in concentration camps, or committed suicide.

Sixty-five persons escaped arrest by the Gestapo—twenty in Germany, thirty-one in France, nine in Holland, and five in Belgium.

The dead for whom I have found fairly thorough or complete documentation follow:

Arnould, Rita: Arrested December 13, 1941, at the Rue des Atrébates; imprisoned in Saint-Gilles and then in Moabit in Berlin; sentenced to death April, 1943; executed August 20, 1943 in Plötzensee.

Behrens, Karl: Arrested September 16, 1942 in his unit on the eastern front; beheaded May 13, 1943, in Plötzensee.

Berkowitz, Liane: Arrested in September, 1942, in Berlin; beheaded August 5, 1943.

Beublet, Maurice: Arrested December 4, 1942 in Brussels; imprisoned in Saint-Gilles until February 12, 1943, then in Breendonk (Number 1165) and Moabit until July, 1943; executed July 28, 1943 in Plötzensee. Recognized posthumously as a political prisoner, March 27, 1950.

Bohme, Karl: Arrested September 16, 1942; horribly tortured; executed October 29, 1943 in the house of detention of Halle.

Bontzes van Beek, Cato: Arrested September 20, 1942, in Berlin; executed August 3, 1943 in Plötzensee.

Breyer, Robert: Arrested November 25, 1942, in Paris; imprisoned in Fresnes; sentenced to death in March, 1943; beheaded July 28, 1943, in Plötzensee.

Brockdorff, von, Erika: Arrested September 16, 1943, in Berlin; beheaded May 13, 1943, in Plötzensee.

Buch, Eva Maria: Arrested October 10, 1942; beheaded August 5, 1943, in Plötzensee.

Clais, Josephine: Imprisoned in Breendonk (Number 1160, PA 169) April 16, 1943, to February 12, 1944; deported to Ravensbrück March 3, 1944; died at the beginning of 1945. Posthumously recognized as a political prisoner August 3, 1960.

Clais, Renée: Imprisoned in Breendonk, then Moabit, until October 1, 1943; sentenced to five years at hard labor; deported to Ravensbrück January 24, 1945; died March 10, 1945, in Mauthausen. Posthumously recognized as a political prisoner August 3, 1960.

Cointe, Suzanne: Arrested November 19, 1942; sentenced to death in March, 1943; beheaded in July, 1943, in Plötzensee.

Coppi, Hans: Arrested September 12, 1942, in Berlin; hanged December 22, 1942, in Plötzensee.

Coppi, Hilde: Arrested September 12, 1942, in Berlin; beheaded August 5, 1943, in Plötzensee.

Corbin, Alfred: Arrested November 19, 1942; sentenced to death March 8, 1943; beheaded July 28, 1943, in Plötzensee.

Corbin, Marie: Arrested November 26, 1942; died in Ravensbrück.

Drailly, Charles: Arrested November 25, 1942; deported to Mauthausen, Buchenwald, "*Nacht und Nebel*"; died January 4, 1945, in Vaihingen. Posthumously recognized as a political prisoner March 31, 1949.

Drailly, Nazarin: Arrested January 6, 1943, in Brussels; imprisoned in Breendonk (Number 977) until April 18, 1943; sentenced to death March 16, 1943, in Breendonk; beheaded July 28, 1943, in Plötzensee. Posthumously recognized as a political prisoner on February 6, 1951.

Ehrlich, Modeste: Arrested during the night of September 1, 1942; died during deportation, date and place unknown.

Eifler, Erna: Arrested around the middle of October, 1942; murdered by the Gestapo at the end of 1942 or beginning of 1943.

Fellendorf, Wilhelm: Arrested October 28, 1942; tortured; murdered by the Gestapo at the end of 1942 or beginning of 1943.

Fellendorf, Katharina: Arrested around the middle of October, 1942; executed in March, 1944, in Plötzensee.

Gehrts, Erwin: Arrested October 10, 1942, in Berlin; executed February 10, 1943, in Plötzensee.

Giraud, Pierre: Arrested in December, 1942, in Paris; committed suicide at the beginning of 1943 in Fresnes.

Goetze, Ursula: Arrested in September, 1942, in Berlin; beheaded August 5, 1943, in Plötzensee.

Goldenberg, Joseph: Arrested at the beginning of 1942; imprisoned in Breendonk September, 1942, to March, 1943 (PA Number 14, Number 557); died in Breendonk following interrogation. Never belonged to the Red Orchestra, but Gestapo were convinced that he did.

Gollnow, Herbert: Arrested in autumn, 1942; shot in February, 1943, in Berlin-Tegel.

Grasse, Herbert: Arrested October 23, 1942; committed suicide October 24 as he was being taken to police headquarters in Berlin to be interrogated.

Graudenz, Johann: Arrested September 12, 1942; hanged December 22, 1942, in Plötzensee.

Griotto, Medaro: Arrested in December, 1942; sentenced to death in March, 1943; beheaded July 28, 1943, in Plötzensee.

Grossvogel, Jeanne Pesant: Arrested November 25, 1942, in Brussels; imprisoned January 26 to April, 1943, in Breendonk (Number 1133), then in Moabit; beheaded July 6, 1944, in Berlin-Charlottenburg. Posthumously recognized as a political prisoner October 26, 1949.

Grossvogel, Leo: Arrested December 16, 1942, in Brussels; sentenced to death in May, 1944. Posthumously recognized as a political prisoner December 21, 1951 (File No. 9465).

Guddorf, Wilhelm: Arrested October 10, 1942; beheaded May 13, 1943, in Plötzensee.

Harnack, Arvid: Arrested September 7, 1942, in Preil, Eastern Prussia; hanged December 22, 1942, in Plötzensee.

Harnack, Mildred Fish: Arrested September 7, 1942, in Preil, Eastern Prussia; beheaded February 16, 1943, in Plötzensee.

Heilmann, Horst: Arrested at the beginning of September, 1942, in Berlin; hanged December 22, 1942, in Plötzensee.

Hilbolling, Henrika Voogt: Arrested August 19, 1942, in Amsterdam; fate unknown.

Hilbolling, Jacob: Arrested in August, 1942, in Amsterdam; imprisoned in Breendonk (Number 408, PA 214); died under torture or was shot in 1943.

Himpel, Helmut: Arrested September 17, 1942, in Berlin; executed May 13, 1943, in Plötzensee.

Hossler, Albert: Arrested at the end of September, 1942, in Berlin; murdered by the Gestapo at the end of 1942.

Hubner, Emil: Arrested October 18, 1942; executed August 5, 1943, in Plötzensee.

Humbert-Laroche, Arlette: Arrested in December, 1942; deported to Ravensbrück; died shortly before the liberation.

Husemann, Walter: Arrested September 19, 1942, in Berlin; executed May 13, 1943, in Plötzensee.

Imme, Else: Arrested in October, 1942; beheaded August 5, 1943, in Plötzensee.

Izbutski, Hermann "Bob": Arrested August 13, 1942, in Brussels; imprisoned in Breendonk until April, 1943, and cruelly tortured; sentenced to death in 1943; beheaded July 6, 1944, in Berlin-Charlottenburg.

Jaspar, Claire Legrand: Arrested November 30, 1942, in Marseilles; deported to Ravensbrück, to Auschwitz in January, 1944; gassed in November, 1944. Posthumously recognized as a political prisoner March 23, 1949.

Jeusseur, Jean: Arrested in October, 1942; imprisoned and shot in Breendonk.

Kamy, David: Arrested December 13, 1941, at the Rue des Atrébates in Brussels; imprisoned in Breendonk; sentenced to death February 18, 1943; shot April 30, 1943, in Breendonk (Number 803).

Katz, Hillel: Arrested December 2, 1942; tortured; disappeared in November, 1943. It is still not known when and where he was murdered.

Katz, Joseph: Arrested in December, 1942, in Lyon; died during deportation, date and place unknown.

Krauss, Anna: Arrested September 14, 1942, in Berlin; beheaded August 5, 1943, in Plötzensee.

Kruyt, William: Arrested in July, 1942; imprisoned in Breendonk (Number 368), and shot immediately in Breendonk.

Kuchenmeister, Walter: Arrested September 16, 1942; executed May 13, 1943, in Plötzensee.

Kuckhoff, Adam: Arrested in September, 1942, in Berlin; executed August 5, 1943, in Plötzensee.

Kummerow, Hansheinrich: Arrested in November, 1942; executed February 4, 1944, in the house of detention of Halle.

Kummerow, Ingeborg: Arrested in November, 1942; executed August 5, 1943, in Plötzensee.

Marivet, Marguerite: Arrested in November, 1942, in Marseilles; died during deportation, date and place unknown.

Maximovich, Anna: Arrested in December, 1942. The date and place of her death are unknown.

Maximovich, Vasily: Arrested December 16, 1942. The date and place of his death are unknown.

Neutert, Eugen: Arrested October 23, 1942; hanged September 9, 1943, in Plötzensee.

Pauriol, Fernand: Arrested in August, 1943, in Paris; imprisoned in Fresnes; tortured; sentenced to death in January, 1944; killed in his cell August 12, 1944.

Pepper, Maurice: Arrested in August, 1942, in Brussels; imprisoned in Breendonk; shot February 24, 1944.

Pheter, Simone: Arrested in December, 1942. The date and place of execution are still unknown.

Podsialdo, Johann: Arrested in January, 1943; sentenced to death March 15, 1943; beheaded July 28, 1943, in Plötzensee.

Poznanska, Sophie: Arrested December 13, 1941, at the Rue des Atrébates in Brussels; committed suicide September 29, 1942, in Saint Gilles Prison.

Rauch, Henri: Arrested December 28, 1942, in Belgium; died

January 8, 1944 in Mathausen, *"Nacht und Nebel."* Recognized as a political prisoner September 11, 1950.

Rehmer, Friedrich: Arrested November 29, 1942; beheaded May 13, 1943, in Plötzensee.

Rittmeister, John: Arrested September 26, 1943, in Berlin; beheaded May 13, 1943, in Plötzensee.

Robinson, Harry: According to my investigations, he had not appeared before a military tribunal by the end of 1942, and was still alive, in a German prison, at that time. According to publications based on Gestapo sources, Robinson was executed in 1943 or 1944. Only Pannwitz knows.

Ryck, Henri de: Arrested November 25, 1942, in Brussels; died in Mauthausen.

Schabbel, Klara: Arrested October 18, 1942; executed May 13, 1943, in Plötzensee.

Schaeffer, Philipp: Arrested October 2, 1942, in Berlin; executed May 13, 1943, in Plötzensee.

Schlosinger, Rose: Arrested in October, 1942; beheaded August 5, 1943, in Plötzensee.

Schneider, Germaine: Arrested January 31, 1943, in Paris; sentenced to death in March, 1943; reprieved following an agreement between the Swiss and German authorities concerning Swiss nationals sentenced to death; imprisoned in Fresnes until April 19, 1943, and in Moabit until November 30, 1944; died in November, 1945, in a hospital in Zürich. Posthumously recognized as a political prisoner May 8, 1955.

Schottmüller, Oda: Arrested in September, 1942, in Berlin; executed August 5, 1943, in Plötzensee.

Schreiber, Jeschekel: Arrested in December, 1942; died during deportation, date and place unknown.

Schulze, Kurt: Arrested September 16, 1942; tortured; hanged December 22, 1942, in Plötzensee.

Schulze-Boysen, Harro: Arrested August 31, 1942, in Berlin; hanged December 22, 1942, in Plötzensee.

Schulze-Boysen, Libertas Haas-Heye: Arrested September 3, 1942, in Berlin; beheaded December 22, 1942, in Plötzensee.

Schumacher, Elisabeth: Arrested in September, 1942; executed December 22, 1942, in Plötzensee.

Schumacher, Kurt: Arrested in September, 1942; hanged December 22, 1942, in Plötzensee.

Schurmann-Horster, Wilhelm: Arrested October 29, 1942, in Constance; hanged September 9, 1943, in Plötzensee.

Sésée, Auguste: Arrested August 28, 1942 in Brussels; imprisoned in Breendonk until sentenced to death in April, 1943; shot in January, 1944, in Berlin. Posthumously recognized as a political prisoner September 16, 1949.

Sieg, John: Arrested October 11, 1942, in Berlin; tortured; committed suicide October 15, 1942, in the Gestapo building in Prinz Albert Strasse in Berlin.

Sokol, Hersch: Arrested June 9, 1942, in Maisons-Laffitte; imprisoned in Breendonk (Number 546); murdered during a torture session in January, 1943. To cover up this death, the Germans buried him at the National Firing Range in Brussels and listed him as having been shot.

Sokol, Mira: Arrested June 9, 1942, in Maisons-Laffitte; imprisoned in Breendonk; transferred to Germany in April, 1943; died of the after-effects of torture.

Spaak, Suzanne: Arrested November 9, 1943, in Brussels; imprisoned in Fresnes; sentenced to death in January, 1944; killed in her cell August 12, 1944, in Fresnes.

Springer, Flore Velagst: Arrested December 19, 1942, in Lyon; beheaded in July, 1943, in Berlin.

Springer, Isidore: Arrested December 19, 1942, in Lyon; committed suicide December 24, 1942, in Fresnes.

Stobe, Ilse: Arrested September 12, 1942; cruelly tortured; beheaded December 22, 1942, in Plötzensee.

Strelow, Heinz: Arrested in September, 1942; executed May 13, 1943, in Plötzensee.

Terwiel, Marie: Arrested September 17, 1942; beheaded August 5, 1943, in Plötzensee.

Thevenet, Louis: Arrested November 25, 1942, in Brussels; imprisoned in Breendonk; deported to Sachsenhausen, *"Nacht und Nebel"*; died a few days after his release, in a hospital in Bremen.

Thiele, Fritz: Arrested September 16, 1942; executed May 13, 1943, in Plötzensee.

Thiess, Wolfgang: Arrested October 21, 1942; hanged September 9, 1943, in Plötzensee.

Tohmfor, Erhard: Arrested at the end of November, 1942; tortured; hanged May 13, 1943, in Plötzensee.

Voelkner, Kathe: Arrested January 31, 1943, in Paris; sentenced to death March 15, 1943; beheaded in July, 1943, in Plötzensee.

Weise, Martin: Arrested December 1, 1942; executed November 15, 1943, in the house of detention at Brandenburg.

Weissensteiner, Richard: Arrested at the beginning of October, 1942; executed May 13, 1943, in Plötzensee.

Wesolek, Frieda: Arrested October 18, 1942; executed August 5, 1943, in Plötzensee.

Wesolek, Stanislaus: Arrested October 18, 1942; executed August 5, 1943, in Plötzensee.

Winterinck, Anton: Arrested September 16, 1942, in Amsterdam; imprisoned November 18, 1942, in Breendonk (Number 409-806); tortured; shot July 6, 1944, at the National Firing Range in Brussels.

The following members of the Herbert Baum group were executed during 1942 and 1943:

Hans Adler, age thirty; *Marianne Baum*, age thirty; *Kurt Bernhard*, age forty; *Heinz Birnbaum*, age twenty-three; *Herbert Budzislawsky*, age twenty-two; *Editz Fraenkel*, age twenty-one; *Felix Heymann*, age twenty-six; *Hardel Heymann*, age thirty-one; *Alice Hirsch*, age nineteen; *Hilde Jadamowitz*, age twenty-six; *Hans Joachim*, age twenty-one; *Marianne Joachim*, age twenty-one; *Martin Kochmann*, age thirty; *Sala Kochmann*, age thirty; *Hilde Lowy*, age twenty; *Gerd Meyer*, age twenty-two; *Hanni Meyer*, age twenty-two; *Herbert Meyer*, age thirty-two; *Helmut Neumann*, age twenty-one; *Heinz Rotholz*, age twenty-one; *Lotte Rotholz*, age twenty; *Sigi Rotholz*, age twenty-one; *Lothar Salinger*, age twenty-three; *Werner Steinbrink*, age twenty-six; *Irene Walter*, age twenty-two; *Susanne Wesse*, age twenty-nine.

These names are engraved on the commemorative plaque at Herbert Baum's grave in the Widensee Jewish cemetery in Berlin.

Appendix III. The Later Circumstances of Some Nazis

What became of the principal leaders of the Sonderkommando after the war?

Horst Kopnow: Kriminalrat, one of the leaders of the Sonderkommando Rote Kapelle in Berlin. He was arrested by the English and released in 1947. Under the name of Cordez, he lives in excellent health in the town of Gelsenkirchen.

Heinz Pannwitz: Hauptsturmführer SS and Kriminalrat, and, after the summer of 1943, leader of the Sonderkommando Rote Kapelle in France, Belgium, and Holland. From 1945 to 1955, he was imprisoned in the USSR in Lubianka and in a work camp. Now living in Ludwigsburg in West Germany, where he is managing director of a bank and where, as a war criminal, he also collects his pension.

Friedrich Panzinger: administrative director and principal head of the Sonderkommando Rote Kapelle. He fell into the hands of the Russians and was not released until 1955; committed suicide in 1959.

Captain Piepe: Abwehr, conducted the investigation against the Red Orchestra in Belgium after the summer of 1941. He was arrested in 1946 by the Belgian military authorities, interrogated, and acquitted. He died a few years ago in Hamburg, where he was a member of the administrative board of the Rotary Club.

Heinrich Reiser: Hauptsturmführer SS and commissioner of police, head of the Sonderkommando in Paris from the end of November, 1942 to June, 1943. He was not bothered after the war. In fact, the French Secret Service made him several job offers. Today he is living comfortably in Stuttgart.

Dr. Manfred Roeder: principal representative for the prosecution in the trials against the Red Orchestra in Berlin, Brussels, and Paris; "Hitler's bloodhound." He fell into the hands of the Americans and was cleared of all charges in 1947. Today he is assistant mayor of the little town of Glashütten.

The original French edition contains the following appendices in addition to those printed here:

Lists of the surviving Red Orchestra members.

Certificate of change of name to Leopold Domb.

Complete translation of Leopold Trepper's certificate of graduation from the Communist University (one page of this document appears in the photo section of this edition).

Notification that Leopold Trepper is a "missing person," sent to his wife while he was in Lubianka.

Record of Leopold Trepper's employment by the Soviet Union.

Henri Piepe's 1946 deposition.

Trepper's corrections of Piepe's deposition.

Some of the court record of Reiser's interrogation, 1949.

Trepper's corrections of Reiser's testimony.

Description of the deaths for which Pannwitz was responsible (Suzanne Spaak, Fernand Pauriol, Hillel Katz, Anton Winterinck, Jacob Hilboling, Leo Grossvogel, Jeanne Pesant-Grossvogel, Harry Robinson, Hermann Izbutski, Auguste Sésée).

Report by Gestapo-Müller to Himmler on the Red Orchestra, 1942.

General report by Gestapo-Müller, 1942.

Letter from employee of Maximovich family about their worried attitude in 1942.

Letter from Dr. Albert Maleplate about the arrest of Leopold Trepper.

Abwehr documents about the radio game, 1943.

Documentation of Anton Winterinck's execution (after which the Gestapo claimed he "turned" and later escaped).

Abwehr report on Juliette Moussier.

Record of interrogation of Juliette Moussier, 1954.

Interrogation in 1954 of the French policeman whom the Sonderkommando had sent after Juliette Moussier.

The first two telegrams congratulating Trepper after his escape from Poland.

Index